SOCIAL SUSTAINABILITY IN DEVELOPMENT

MEETING THE CHALLENGES OF THE 21ST CENTURY

New Frontiers of Social Policy Series

This series is designed to address issues of importance for social sustainability covering themes of inclusion, resilience, social cohesion, and process legitimacy. Titles in this series undergo internal and external review under the management of the Social Sustainability and Inclusion Global Practice.

Titles in This Series

Opening the Black Box: The Contextual Drivers of Social Accountability

Institutions Taking Root: Building State Capacity in Challenging Contexts

Inclusion Matters: The Foundation for Shared Prosperity

Societal Dynamics and Fragility: Engaging Societies in Responding to Fragile Situations

Living through Crises: How the Food, Fuel, and Financial Shocks Affect the Poor

Local and Community Driven Development: Moving to Scale in Theory and Practice

Social Dimensions of Climate Change: Equity and Vulnerability in a Warming World

Delivering Services in Multicultural Societies

Building Equality and Opportunity through Social Guarantees: New Approaches to Public Policy and the Realization of Rights

Assets, Livelihoods, and Social Policy

Inclusive States: Social Policy and Structural Inequalities

Institutional Pathways to Equity: Addressing Inequality Traps

NEW FRONTIERS OF SOCIAL POLICY

SOCIAL SUSTAINABILITY IN DEVELOPMENT

MEETING THE CHALLENGES OF THE 21ST CENTURY

Patrick Barron

Louise Cord

José Cuesta

Sabina A. Espinoza

Greg Larson

Michael Woolcock

 **WORLD BANK GROUP**

Table of Contents

Foreword   ix
Acknowledgments   xi
About the Authors   xiii
Main Messages   xvii
Executive Summary   xix
Abbreviations   xxxv

1   From Aspiration to Action   1
   Introduction   1
   Context   3
   Notes   16
   References   18

2   What Is Social Sustainability?   25
   Overview and Literature Review   25
   Definitions and Conceptual Framework   29
   Strengthening the Empirical Foundations of Social Sustainability   51
   Annex 2A Empirical Annex   54
   Annex 2B Social Sustainability and Developmental Outcome
      Correlations, Controlling for Income   56
   Notes   61
   References   63

3 Closing the Implementation Gap   73
Introduction   73
Challenges in Operationalizing Social Sustainability   73
What Has Worked to Promote Cohesion, Inclusion, and Resilience?   76
Leveraging Process Legitimacy: *How* Things Are Done Matters   83
Notes   95
References   96

4 Conclusion   101
A Perfect Storm   101
References   102

Boxes

1.1   The Conceptual Foundations of Social Sustainability
       at the World Bank   7
1.2   Global Estimates of the Population at Risk of Exclusion   12
1.3   Social Media's Effects on Social Cohesion   16
2.1   Vignettes to Illustrate Social Sustainability   26
2.2   Social Sustainability Global Database   32
2.3   Four Vignettes on the Importance of Process Legitimacy
       in Development   49
3.1   Social Inclusion in Uruguay   75
3.2   Strengthening Community Bonds: Insights from Indonesia   77
3.3   Strengthening Cohesion and Resilience in Nigeria   77
3.4   Strengthening the Integration of Migrants in Colombia   80
3.5   Social Inclusion of Persons with Disabilities in Nigeria   81
3.6   Stopping Female Genital Cutting and Other Harmful Practices
       by Building on Community Values and Leaders   82
3.7   Resilience—Kenya's Financing Locally Led Climate
       Action Program   84
3.8   Social Sustainability and Inclusion Country Diagnostic   86
3.9   Typology for Social Sustainability   87
3.10   Fostering Process Legitimacy through the Environmental and
       Social Framework   90
3.11   Strengthening the Links between Communities and
       Elected Officials   92
3.12   Working with Civil Society for Third-Party Monitoring in Tajikistan 92
3.13   The Panama Indigenous Peoples Plan   94

Figures

ES.1	The Triad of Sustainability	xxi
ES.2	Conceptual Framework of Social Sustainability	xxiii
ES.3	Drivers of Process Legitimacy	xxv
ES.4	Correlations between the Four Components of Social Sustainability and Development Outcomes	xxvii
1.1.	The Triad of Sustainability	8
B1.2.1	Global Rate of Poverty and Estimated Share and Number of the Population at Risk of Exclusion, 2017	13
1.2	Share of Countries with Social Unrest Events, 12-Month Moving Average, by Region, 1985–2020	15
2.1	Appearance of Key Types of "Sustainability" in Published English Books, 1985–2019	28
2.2	Conceptual Framework of Social Sustainability	31
B2.2.1	Indicators of Social Cohesion and Inclusion	33
B2.2.2	Understanding Countries' Income Levels and Process Legitimacy	34
2.3	Association between Social Cohesion and Poverty, Income, Inequality, Human Capital, and Human Development	37
2.4	Association between Social Inclusion and Poverty, Income, Inequality, Human Capital, and Human Development	39
2.5	Association between Resilience and Poverty, Income, Inequality, Human Capital, and Human Development	42
2.6	Drivers of Process Legitimacy	45
2.7	Process Legitimacy—Illustrative Scenarios	46
2.8	Association between Process Legitimacy and Poverty, Income, Inequality, Human Capital, and Human Development	49
2.9	Sustainability Triad: Potential Scenarios	53
2A.1	Pairwise Correlations between Social Sustainability Components	56
B3.8.1	What Is an SSI Country Diagnostic?	86
B3.9.1	A Typology for Social Sustainability	88

Tables

2A.1	Variables Used in Social Sustainability Indexes	54
2A.2	Correlations among the Components of Social Sustainability	56
2B.1	Unconditional and Conditional Regressions of Social Sustainability and Developmental Outcomes	57

Foreword

Today's global community enjoys greater access to education, health care, gainful employment, financial services, infrastructure, and basic services than its forebears. Yet, the gains remain fragile and incomplete. The recent COVID-19 pandemic dealt the biggest setback to global poverty in decades, showing how fragile progress is. Climate shocks and conflict among the world's biggest food producers have hindered a swift recovery. To achieve the ambitions laid out in the Sustainable Development Goals (SDGs), much more needs to be done to ensure that the gains achieved to date become sustainable—particularly for those at greatest risk of marginalization and exclusion.

For this to happen, however, progress must be consolidated and today's most pressing global challenges—including climate change, pandemics, threats to biodiversity, displacement and migration, and conflict—must be urgently addressed. Far too many countries and far too many poor people all over the world have already experienced severe "reversals of fortune" in recent years. Moreover, achieving sustainable development for all societies involves tackling complex challenges over many years in ways that are often highly contentious and ultimately disruptive. In poor and rich countries alike, the development journey always brings about difficult transitions: urbanization can erode rural communities and upend traditional ways of life; technology can render workers' hard-won skills obsolete; changing norms and values can alter socioeconomic interactions, unsettling communities; and social media can widen divides across and within societies, undermining their ability to tackle challenges collectively.

These dynamics—and many more in the story of development—illustrate the vital importance of social sustainability to meet the SDGs and build the coalitions and programs to tackle global challenges. Over the last quarter century, the concept of "sustainability" has been frequently invoked, studied, and debated in the context of economic and environmental matters—to make inclusive economic growth *sustainable*, for example, or to ensure that natural resources are used *sustainably*. While there have also been many calls for development to be *socially* sustainable, there is much less consensus over what social sustainability means in theory or practice, much less how it can or should be achieved.

What is uniquely important about the social components of sustainability? How can all societies—and development, in particular—promote social sustainability? Grounded in empirical findings, this book articulates a framework to begin answering these questions—and offers key principles and practical examples to guide policy makers, implementers, and community leaders seeking constructive ways to navigate development in ways that are socially sustainable.

A key message of the book is that the people, policies, and processes driving development need to be inclusive and legitimate, enabling communities to advance while remaining (or becoming more) cohesive and resilient in the face of development's challenges. Social sustainability is undermined when development strategies and country conditions exclude large shares of the population, leave them vulnerable to exogenous shocks, and limit the voice and mechanisms people need to influence policies and programs.

Managing these and the many other difficult trade-offs that development entails requires a collective effort to better understand and promote social sustainability. Meeting the challenges of the 21st century may involve more than this effort, but it will be impossible without it.

Juergen Voegele
Vice President, Sustainable Development
The World Bank

Acknowledgments

The authors are grateful for insightful discussions, guidance, and substantive inputs provided by Margaret Arnold, Senait Assefa, Trichur K. Balakrishnan, Sara Batmanglich, Elena Bonometti, Hana Brixi, Helle Buchhave, Helene Carlsson Rex, Robert Chase, Alexandru Cojocaru, Clifton Cortez, Richard Damania, Simeon Ehui, Vivien Foster, Jonathan Fox, German N. Freire, Verena Fritz, Gannon Gillespie, Maria González de Asis, Scott Guggenheim, Asli Gurkan, Anirban Hati, Jesko Hentschel, Arturo Herrera Gutiérrez, Ann-Sofie Jespersen, Soukeyna Kane, Aart Kraay, Saroj Kumar Jha, Elisa Liberatori-Prati, Luis-Felipe López-Calva, Lucia Madrigal, Charlotte McClain-Nhlapo, Robin Mearns, Anas Mohammad, Nikolas Myint, Hoveida Nobakht, Anna O'Donnell, Natalia Pecorari, Pia Peeters, Nicolas Perrin, Jean Pesme, Dianna Pizarro, Aly Zulficar Rahim, Nigel Roberts, Paula Rossiasco, Michal Rutkowski, Audrey Sacks, Gustavo Saltiel, Deepti Samant Raja, Carolina Sánchez-Páramo, Jennifer Sara, Renaud Seligman, Vivek Sharma, Janmejay Singh, Margot Skarpeteig, Sonya Sultan, Jeff Thindwa, Kevin Tomlinson, Hasan Tuluy, Varalakshmi Vemuru, Juergen Voegele, David Warren, Deborah Wetzel, and Ingo Wiederhofer.

About the Authors

Patrick Barron is the Global Lead for Social Cohesion and Resilience within the Social Sustainability and Inclusion Global Practice at the World Bank. He was previously Lead Regional Adviser on Fragility, Conflict, and Violence for Asia. After working for local nongovernmental organizations in Cambodia and China, he joined the World Bank, where he ran the Bank's conflict and peace-building programs in Indonesia. From 2005 to 2009, he led the Bank's support for the Aceh peace process and worked across the region with a particular focus on Afghanistan, Myanmar, the Philippines, and southern Thailand. Before returning to the World Bank, Barron served for four years as the Asia Foundation's Regional Director for Conflict and Development. He has published two books: *Contested Development* (Yale University Press), which was awarded International Development Book of the Year by the American Sociology Association, and, most recently, *When Violence Works: Postconflict Violence and Peace in Indonesia* (Cornell University Press). He has master's degrees from the University of Edinburgh and Harvard University and a doctorate from Oxford University.

Louise Cord is the Global Director for the Social Sustainability and Inclusion Global Practice at the World Bank. Previously, she was the Country Director for Cabo Verde, The Gambia, Guinea-Bissau, Mauritania, and Senegal, based in Dakar, Senegal. Prior to her appointment as country director, she was Practice Manager in the Poverty Global Practice responsible for Latin America and the Caribbean, where she also covered gender equality. A US national, Cord joined the World Bank in 1991 as a Young Professional. She has since held various positions in the World Bank's poverty reduction and sustainable development departments, working specifically on inclusive growth, poverty reduction, and rural development. She has worked in Africa, Eastern and Central Europe, and Latin America. Cord holds a PhD in development economics from the Fletcher School of Law and Diplomacy at Tufts University.

José Cuesta is a Lead Economist in the World Bank's Social Sustainability and Inclusion Global Practice and an adjunct professor at the Georgetown University School of Foreign Service. He was previously Social Policy and Economic Analysis Unit Chief at the United Nations Children's Fund (UNICEF) Office of Research, Florence. Before that, he was an assistant professor in development economics at the Institute of Social Studies in The Hague. He also worked as a research economist and social sector specialist for the Inter-American Development Bank and as an economist for the United Nations Development Programme in Honduras. Cuesta's research interests revolve around poverty, exclusion, and conflict economics, specifically the distributive analysis of social policies, intrahousehold allocation, social protection, and labor distortions. He has experience in countries in Africa, Asia, and Latin America. He codirected the *Poverty and Shared Prosperity 2016* report (World Bank) and the *UNICEF Report Card 2018* (UNICEF). A Spanish national, Cuesta holds a PhD in economics from Oxford University.

Sabina A. Espinoza is a Social Development Specialist in the Social Sustainability and Inclusion Global Unit at the World Bank. She leads research and provides project support to foster the inclusion of groups at risk of exclusion or discrimination. She cowrote the World Bank's flagship report on social inclusion (*Inclusion Matters*) and is coauthor of *Inclusion Matters in Africa* (World Bank) and "Economic and Social Inclusion in Development" in *Untapped Power* (Oxford University Press). Espinoza has worked for the United Nations Global Compact and the European Parliament. In Brussels, she worked for a network of nongovernmental organizations supporting migrants' rights across Europe. Previously, she was a postgraduate teaching assistant at the School of Public Policy at University College London. Espinoza holds a bachelor's degree in philosophy, politics, and economics from the University of Oxford and a master's degree and PhD in political science from University College London.

Greg Larson is a consultant with the World Bank's Social Sustainability and Inclusion Global Practice. He is a writer and consultant who supports organizations, leaders, and academics in the spheres of public policy, economic development, and social impact. He has worked with the World Bank, United Nations Development Programme, Brookings Institution, Harvard's Center for International Development, Yale's Economic Growth Center, and other organizations and helped to write Pinelopi Goldberg's *The Unequal Effects of Globalization* (MIT Press). Previously, Larson served as an international economist and senior adviser at the US Treasury Department for six years. He started his career in publishing before helping to establish the VAD Foundation, a nonprofit that supports community education in South Sudan founded by former refugee Valentino Achak Deng and author Dave Eggers. Larson has a bachelor's degree from Stanford University and a master's degree from the Harvard Kennedy School.

Michael Woolcock is Lead Social Scientist in the World Bank's Development Research Group, where he has worked since 1998; for 17 of these years, he has also taught part time at the Harvard Kennedy School. His current research focuses on strategies for enhancing state capability for implementation, on transformations in local social institutions during the development process, and on the use of mixed methods to assess the effectiveness of "complex" interventions.

In addition to more than 100 journal articles and book chapters, Woolcock is the author or coeditor of 13 books, including *Contesting Development: Participatory Projects and Local Conflict Dynamics in Indonesia*, with Patrick Barron and Rachael Diprose (Yale University Press), which was a corecipient of the 2012 best book prize by the American Sociological Association's section on international development; *Building State Capability: Evidence, Analysis, Action*, with Matt Andrews and Lant Pritchett (Oxford University Press); and was colead, with Samuel Freije-Rodríguez, of the biennial *Poverty and Shared Prosperity Report 2020: Reversals of Fortune* (World Bank). Most recently, he coedited three scholarly volumes on case studies, popular culture, and the future of multilateralism and a book for broader audiences on the role of development in both intensifying and (potentially) resolving humanity's greatest challenges. An Australian national, Woolcock has a PhD in comparative historical sociology from Brown University.

Main Messages

1. Current crises—COVID-19, climate change, rising levels of conflict, and a global slowdown—are exacerbating deep-rooted inequities, with intense social repercussions ranging from polarization and declining levels of trust to social unrest.

2. Ensuring sustainable development and poverty reduction will require greater attention to *social sustainability* in addition to economic and environmental sustainability.

3. Social sustainability increases when more people feel part of the development process and believe that they and their descendants will benefit from it.

4. Communities and societies that are more socially sustainable are more willing and able to work together to overcome challenges, deliver public goods, and allocate scarce resources in ways perceived to be legitimate and fair so that all people may thrive over time.

5. Social sustainability has four key components: social cohesion, inclusion, resilience, and *process legitimacy*—the extent to which a community or society accepts who has authority, what goals they pursue, and how policies and programs get implemented.

6. Key priorities to foster social sustainability include
   - understanding the policy arena by identifying the key stakeholders, their objectives, and prevailing norms and values;
   - fostering space in the policy arena for all to provide input and voice concerns, especially those at risk of exclusion; and
   - engaging for the long haul: change can be slow, but staying engaged, deepening relationships, and building trust typically pays off.

7. *How* development occurs matters greatly: How governments and development organizations manage social change has important implications for achieving and sustaining poverty reduction and inclusive growth.

Executive Summary

Development is a dynamic, transformative process that fundamentally changes how people live. People are the means and ends of development—the goal of which is to equip, link, and enable groups of people to create something new and different for the benefit of society. This process is often slow and nonlinear as well as inherently complex and challenging; by changing how people live, development affects social systems in often unpredictable and destabilizing ways. When sustained over time, however, it can promote cohesive, inclusive, and resilient societies in which all people can participate and thrive. However, the change process, particularly its social aspects, can be complex, challenging, and even contentious.

There is growing recognition that *how* development occurs matters greatly. How governments and development organizations navigate and manage the social dynamics of change has important implications for achieving and sustaining poverty reduction and inclusive growth.

Yet continued progress toward sustainable development is not guaranteed. More than two decades into the 21st century, a perfect storm has gathered force: the overlapping crises of COVID-19, climate change, rising levels of conflict, and a global economic slowdown are inflaming long-standing challenges and exacerbating inequality, persistent structural barriers, and deep-rooted systemic inequities. These challenges have intense social repercussions, including polarization, declining levels of trust, social tensions, and unrest, and addressing them will require social sustainability in addition to economic and environmental sustainability.

For much of the last 75 years, social sustainability has taken a backseat to growth and, more recently, the environment. Despite growing recognition of its importance, however, there is less clarity over what social sustainability is and how it can best be pursued. This book aims to advance the concept of social sustainability and sharpen the analytical foundations on which it rests. Specifically, it offers a clear definition of, a coherent conceptual framework for, and initial operational guidelines regarding social sustainability for the global development community to engage with, respond to, and use. In particular, the book explores three critical questions: What is social sustainability? Why does it matter? And how can it be operationalized?

From Aspiration to Action

Chapter 1 starts by putting social sustainability in historic context. Current efforts to articulate and enact a social development agenda began in the middle of the 20th century, when today's global institutions were established and important proclamations like the Universal Declaration of Human Rights were signed. However, that era's prevailing model of economic development often saw social dynamics (for example, countries' traditional practices and cultural beliefs) primarily as obstacles to accelerating "progress" toward modernization. While attitudes eventually evolved, the social dimension of development remained largely peripheral for many years.

Development theorists in the 1960s began to underscore that local context and social factors influenced the success of development efforts, with particular focus on infrastructure projects. Social concerns took on a more explicit and operational focus in the 1970s and 1980s, as more targeted programs reflected growing recognition that excluded and vulnerable groups often did not benefit from development or were even undermined by the process. At the World Bank, this recognition coincided with an increased focus on women in development and efforts to manage social risks better (that is, "do no harm"), particularly in projects involving resettlement issues and indigenous peoples.

The social agenda broadened in the late 1980s and 1990s, as concerns about the impact of structural adjustment on the poor and vulnerable amplified demands to link development more explicitly with poverty reduction. A consensus emerged around putting people at the center of development. Early World Bank efforts to operationalize these principles included social funds, a growing focus on gender equality, and community-driven development, which emphasized participatory approaches and local decision making. In practice, however, these efforts remained relatively circumscribed, with the primary focus during this period still being to ensure that development projects "do no harm."

The new millennium was a turning point for social development. In 2000 the United Nations Millennium Development Goals reflected major shifts in mainstream thinking about development, moving beyond narrow monetary definitions of poverty and promoting social concepts like inclusion, voice, empowerment, equity, and gender equality. At the World Bank, years of path-breaking social development research culminated in a 2013 corporate strategy emphasizing all three pillars of sustainability—environmental, economic, and social—as being critical for the twin goals of ending extreme poverty and promoting shared prosperity (figure ES.1).[1]

In the past decade, important strides have also been made to elevate and operationalize social sustainability. In 2015 the Sustainable Development Goals (SDGs) further enshrined social issues as central to development. Throughout the 2010s, the World Bank took concrete steps to embed social factors in its operations—including the Global Partnership for Social Accountability, the Strategic Framework on Citizen Engagement, and the Environmental and Social Framework (ESF), which applied a comprehensive package of social standards to all investment projects. More recently, responding to the COVID-19 crisis in 2021, the Green, Resilient, and Inclusive Development framework acknowledged the importance of inclusion as a strategic priority alongside resilience and growth.

While important progress has been made, much work remains to be done, and social sustainability is now at a crucial point. The world is becoming more divided, polarized, and unequal, with exclusion and vulnerability compounded by persistent shocks, discrimination, conflict, and climate change. After slowing in recent years, the pace of poverty reduction reversed in 2020 and remains threatened by economic slowdown, the lingering effects of COVID-19, and the war in Ukraine

Figure ES.1 The Triad of Sustainability

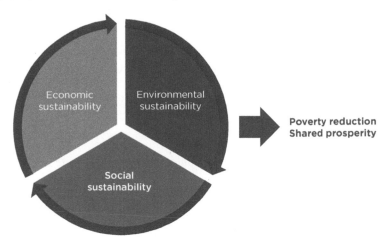

Source: World Bank.

(World Bank 2022a). Progress on global inequality also has deteriorated, and the gaps between the ultra-rich, the middle class, and the poor continue to widen—all increasingly exacerbated by climate change (Alvaredo et al. 2018; Islam and Winkel 2017; Lakner and Milanovic 2016). In the decades ahead, climate effects are expected to push hundreds of millions of people into poverty and forced migration (World Bank 2020).

Efforts to respond to these issues are increasingly challenged by rising tensions, social frag-mentation, and a weakening social contract. Conflicts are becoming more common, complex, and long-lasting (World Bank 2021), and nearly half of the global poor now live in economies affected by fragility, conflict, and violence (United Nations and World Bank 2018). Evidence suggests that social unrest is rising (Barrett et al. 2020), trust in public institutions is declining globally (European Union 2021; Perry 2021; Pew Research Center 2021), and social media as well as unequal access to the digital economy are driving a wedge between communities and eroding the social fabric (Adriano 2020; World Bank 2020). More broadly, an estimated 2.3 billion people—approximately one-third of humanity—is at risk of social exclusion due to economic status, gender and gender identity, race, religion, ethnicity, nationality, age, sexual orientation, or disability (Cuesta, López-Noval, and Niño-Zarazúa 2022).

Addressing these challenges requires socially sustainable solutions. Growth, while necessary, is not sufficient; the *social* sustainability of policies, programs, and outcomes must also be central. Although many known policies are effective at promoting these goals (for example, fiscal redistribution, low-car-bon growth strategies, and human capital investments), they are unlikely to emerge on their own in sufficient scope. This book seeks to move the agenda forward, proposing new approaches and initial operational guidelines to accelerate momentum and inspire action in support of social sustainability.

What Is Social Sustainability?

Social sustainability is a more elusive concept than environmental or economic sustainability. While the latter can be measured with objective indicators like greenhouse gas emissions or debt dynamics, measuring social sustainability is more complex. An emerging and diverse literature offers some initial principles—focused on community connections, well-being, resilience, and engagement (Dempsey et al. 2011)—but the analytical foundations of social sustainability remain underdeveloped.

Chapter 2 seeks to fill that gap. It proposes a definition of social sustainability that is grounded in the literature but aligned with global development priorities and World Bank institutional objectives:

> *Social sustainability increases when more people feel part of the development process and believe that they and their descendants will benefit from it.*

> *Communities and societies that are more socially sustainable are more willing and able to work together to overcome challenges, deliver public goods, and allocate scarce resources in ways perceived to be legitimate and fair so that all people may thrive over time.*

This definition highlights four critical components of social sustainability: social cohesion, inclusion, resilience, and "process legitimacy." A cohesive society has high levels of trust, enabling it to work together to overcome challenges. An inclusive society is one where *all* people can thrive. A resilient society can withstand shocks without significant losses to the well-being of current and future generations. Process legitimacy—a relatively new concept—is about *how* policies and programs are designed and implemented, ensuring that they are accepted as fair and credible by all key stakeholders. The four components are in line with the Universal Declaration of Human Rights and, more specifically, with the human rights principles of nondiscrimination, inclusion, rule of law, dignity, participation, accountability, transparency, and empowerment.

Figure ES.2 presents a conceptual framework for these four components. It illustrates that the baseline levels of inclusion, cohesion, and resilience in a given community or society are affected by *how* programs and policies are designed and implemented and how, over time, efforts to strengthen these components can enhance social sustainability.

In spite of the framework's simplicity, the interactions it portrays are, in practice, highly complex, nonlinear, and context-dependent, reflecting the rich dynamics at play in all communities and societies. The framework functions within a conceptual space known as the "policy arena": the institutions and forums where public resources are allocated and decisions are made among individuals, government, and stakeholder groups through debate, negotiation, and compromise, with ample potential for disagreement, tensions, or even conflict (World Bank 2017). Expanding access to the policy arena, especially for marginal and vulnerable groups as well as sharing information and building in feedback loops and other social accountability measures are important for resolving tensions. A key contention of this book is that where process legitimacy exists, the policies and programs designed and implemented in the policy arena will promote greater inclusion, cohesion, and resilience.

Social sustainability and its components are important objectives in and of themselves, but they are also important drivers of development. Chapter 2 considers each component in turn.

Social Cohesion

> *Social cohesion is a sense of shared purpose, trust, and willingness to cooperate among members of a given group, between members of different groups, and between people and the state for a common good.*

Figure ES.2 Conceptual Framework of Social Sustainability

Source: World Bank.

Social cohesion allows people to work together and respond to challenges, while avoiding conflict, crafting solutions, and forging sustainable compromises (Chatterjee, Gassier, and Myint 2022). Different forms of cohesion matter at different levels. Cohesion between individuals in a community is *bonding* cohesion,[2] while cohesion across groups is *bridging* cohesion—the "horizontal" forms of cohesion. "Vertical" relations between citizens and people or institutions in power, which help to establish and protect the social compact, are *linking* cohesion.

Cohesion is increasingly seen as both a means and an end for development and as important for a range of outcomes, including peace, trust, and prosperity (OECD 2011). While particularly vital for addressing fragility, conflict, and violence, cohesion offers broad development benefits; it facilitates beneficial change processes and enhances resilience for many types of crises (Aldrich 2012; Gates 2002; Migdal 2001; Staniland 2014; Townshend et al. 2015). Weak cohesion, by contrast, is linked with social discontent, political instability, and social tensions (Alesina and Perotti 1996; Esteban and Ray 2011).

Inclusion

Inclusive societies are those where everyone has access to basic services and markets as well as to political, social, and cultural spaces in order to participate in society with agency and live with dignity.

Many individuals and groups face constraints to socioeconomic participation beyond poverty and inequality. Exclusion and discrimination can be due to gender, age, location, occupation, race, ethnicity, religion, citizenship status, disability, sexual orientation and gender identity (SOGI), or other drivers and are sustained through formal and informal norms, behaviors, laws, and institutions. The costs are often significant both for individuals, including less education, lower lifetime earnings, and worse health outcomes (Buehren, Gonzalez, and Copley 2019; Lamichhane and Sawada 2013; Male and Wodon 2017; Turner 2013; Wodon and de la Brière 2018; World Bank 2014), and for societies overall, including lost human capital and economic output.

By enabling all members of society to thrive, inclusion has large development benefits, ranging from reducing conflict to bolstering productivity. Inclusive socioeconomic participation promotes more efficient human capital accumulation (Rauch 1991) and more equitable financial access, which often leads to better outcomes in terms of income growth, poverty reduction, and entrepreneurship (Freire et al. 2020; World Bank 2013b, 2020). Addressing SOGI exclusion alone would increase global output by an estimated 1 percent (Badgett 2020), while achieving gender parity in labor markets would generate global economic benefits of an estimated US$28 trillion over a decade (Madgavkar, Ellingrud, and Krishnan 2016).

Resilience

Resilient societies are those where everyone, including poor and marginalized groups, are safe and can withstand shocks and protect the integrity of their culture.

Resilience is the ability, capacity, and flexibility to prepare for, cope with, recover from, and adapt to shocks over time. Risk reduction and mitigation are preparation measures that aim to lower the probability that shocks will occur or to mitigate their negative impacts if they do (Obrist 2010; World Bank 2001, 2013a). Coping measures, by contrast, aim to relieve the impact of shocks after they occur without resorting to unsustainable strategies like reducing consumption, taking children out of school, resorting to illegal activities, or exhausting finite resources (Garschagen, Renaud, and Birkmann 2011; Tawodzera 2012; World Bank 2001, 2013a). *Transformative* resilience—less common and more challenging—is society's broader ability to strengthen, transform, or create new institutions that better prepare citizens to weather major shocks in the future (Béné et al. 2012; Keck and Sakdapolrak 2013; Lorenz 2013; Smith and Frankenberger 2018; Voss 2008), as has been attempted amid the COVID-19 epidemic and the climate crisis (Moshy, Bryceson, and Mwaipopo 2015; Mozumder et al. 2018; Solórzano 2016).

Resilience is particularly important for poor and marginalized groups, who are more frequently exposed to shocks, lose a greater share of their wealth when hit, and typically have less external support (Hallegatte et al. 2017). Resilience has strong links to cohesion and inclusion: building and maintaining social relations and network structures enhance resilience, while exclusion and discrimination leave people more vulnerable. Resilience also matters for economic and environmental sustainability; when shocks occur, resilience can determine the difference between swift recovery and prolonged crisis.

Process Legitimacy

Cohesion, inclusion, and resilience are the core components of social sustainability, but a fourth component—which this book calls process legitimacy—is a critical driver for achieving social sustainability in practice.

Process legitimacy is the extent to which a community or society accepts who has authority, what goals are formulated, and how policies and programs get implemented. It also encompasses the approaches for reconciling disagreements or tensions, especially among those who stand to bear the greatest cost.

Process legitimacy concerns the "how" of policy making, program design, and implementation and the extent to which these components are consistent with a given context. When successful, process legitimacy ensures that who has *authority*, what policy and program *goals* are pursued, and how those policies and programs get *implemented* are broadly accepted by all and that disagreements or tensions are accommodated, especially among those who may "lose out" as a result. Process legitimacy concerns what happens in the "policy arena"—the space for collective public decision making where groups interact and bargain, resulting in agreements that lead to change.[3]

Process legitimacy has five key sources or drivers (figure ES.3). First, public decision-making authority often derives from *explicit mandates* (for example, elections, designations, or technical expertise). Second, all communities and societies have *agreed-upon rules* and approaches (for example, legal precedents, professional standards, or traditions and customs) that lend legitimacy to policies, programs, and authority figures. Third, *shared principles* or beliefs about what and how things should be done (for example, religious and ideological convictions or widely accepted conventions like international law) serve a similar function. Fourth, when key stakeholders believe that they are better off (for example, due to rising incomes or greater security), *perceived benefits* can imbue legitimacy in ways that some may regard as dubious or morally fraught. Fifth, legitimacy is often derived via *participation and transparency* (for example, dialogue, engagement, and feedback between authorities and key stakeholders, coupled with open and transparent decision making).

In the best-case scenario, the authority is deemed legitimate, its goals are accepted, and implementation is seen as fair, beneficial, and culturally resonant, with high levels of participation and transparency. In the worst-case scenario, illegitimate authority seeks goals that few accept

Figure ES.3 Drivers of Process Legitimacy

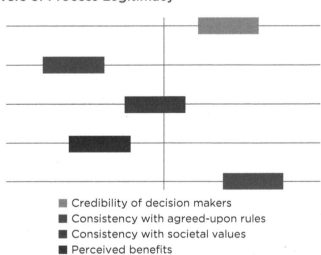

■ Credibility of decision makers
■ Consistency with agreed-upon rules
■ Consistency with societal values
■ Perceived benefits
■ Participation and transparency

Source: World Bank.
Note: The five drivers of process legitimacy are related and can reinforce one another; they also can function independently of one another. They are dynamic and change over time.

through strategies regarded as unfair and nontransparent, with little to no engagement with affected populations. The more "typical" scenarios, however, are mixed and highly dynamic, where some members and groups disagree (to varying extents that change over time).

Process legitimacy shapes how stakeholders experience the development process and the extent to which they accept its outcomes. Often, development itself alters the types and sources of process legitimacy, influencing who has authority, what goals they pursue, how policies and programs get implemented, and the rules, norms, values, and principles on which their legitimacy rests. In practice, such changes can be complex, contentious, and challenging to navigate. The development process can often help to resolve disagreements over these issues, but it can also intensify them. Enhancing participation and transparency, particularly by bringing new groups (especially vulnerable and marginal groups) into the policy arena, often plays a crucial role in forging broad acceptance, especially around policies and programs that are not fully consistent with agreed-upon rules or shared principles. Moreover, such efforts are typically most effective when the process is seen as endogenously driven. Several types of interventions offer evidence on the positive effects of process legitimacy. Efforts to strengthen social accountability, for instance, have various benefits for socially sustainable development (for example, see Mubarak et al. 2020).

Links to Poverty, Inequality, and Human Capital

Social sustainability and its key components have both intrinsic and instrumental value: while they have unique innate value in much the same way as peace, freedom, or sovereignty have inherent value, they also have instrumental value for supporting poverty reduction and inclusive growth. To this end, the book documents recent progress toward an empirical understanding of social sustainability. This understanding includes a small but growing body of micro-level evidence as well as the World Bank's new Social Sustainability Global Database (SSGD), which finds that inclusion, cohesion, resilience, and process legitimacy are all correlated with poverty reduction, human capital, human development, and inequality at the macro level.

The SSGD constructs indexes for each component, using 71 indicators for 236 countries and territories from 2016 to 2020. The inclusion index focuses on access to basic services and markets and political participation; the cohesion index includes measures of trust; the resilience index compiles sources of income, savings, and financial access indicators; and the process legitimacy index combines measures for rule of law, access to justice, and government effectiveness.[4]

Cross-country SSGD analysis finds that inclusion, cohesion, resilience, and process legitimacy are all correlated with poverty reduction, human capital, human development, and inequality (figure ES.4). Several of these correlations are strong—namely, inclusion and process legitimacy with poverty reduction and human capital as well as process legitimacy with inequality—but some are weaker. This variation likely reflects data shortcomings and measurement challenges (including the need to refine SSGD indicators) as well as the inherent difficulty of unpacking complex social relationships that are often affected by long-standing structural factors. A key finding of this book is that more efforts are needed to measure, analyze, and understand the role and impact of social sustainability and its components. Beyond data considerations, a weak correlation also implies that progress

Figure ES.4 Correlations between the Four Components of Social Sustainability and Development Outcomes

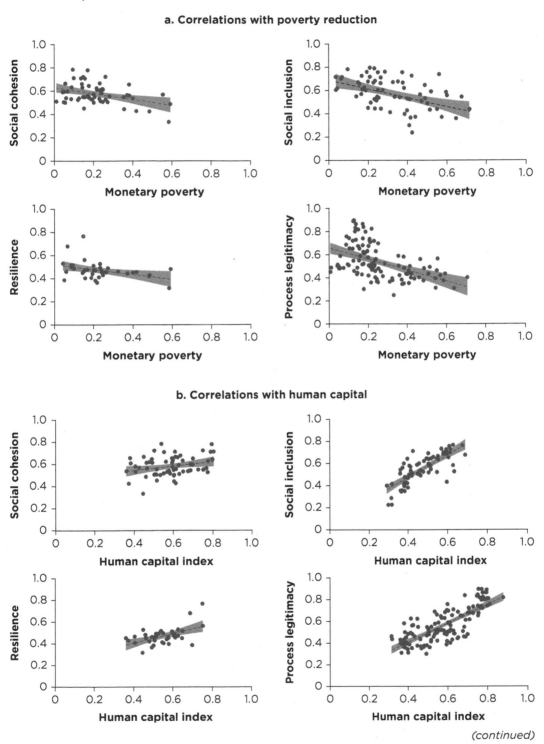

a. Correlations with poverty reduction

b. Correlations with human capital

(continued)

Figure ES.4 Continued

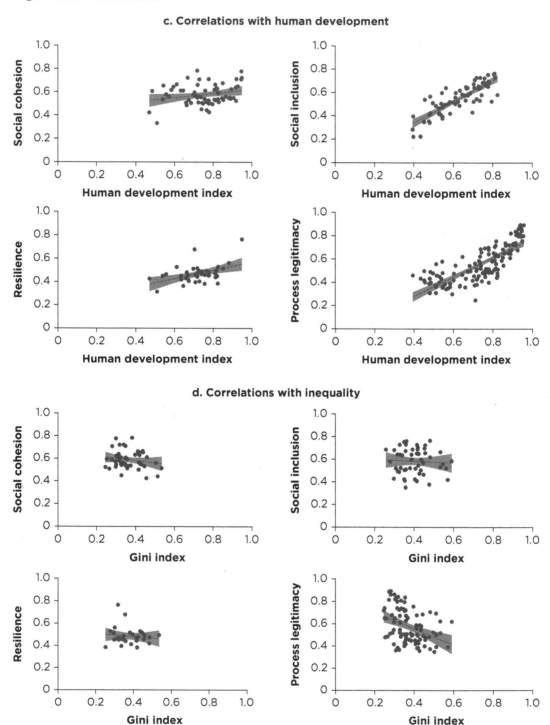

c. Correlations with human development

d. Correlations with inequality

Source: World Bank 2022b.
Note: The figure shows the following: all components of social sustainability are correlated with poverty reduction (panel a); all components are correlated with human capital (panel b); all components are correlated with human development, but some more so than others (panel c); and most components are slightly correlated with inequality, except process legitimacy (panel d).

on the twin goals of ending extreme poverty and promoting shared prosperity can be achieved in a way that is not socially sustainable (even though that progress might well be short-lived). Ultimately, social sustainability matters by itself, intrinsically, for its ability to deliver development and not exclusively for its instrumental value in contributing to poverty reduction or economic growth.

Interlinkages

While they function independently of one another, the core components of social sustainability can be mutually reinforcing: the presence of all four components offers a virtuous circle, which, in turn, helps to drive poverty reduction and shared prosperity. In reality, however, the components often work at cross purposes. Some of the least inclusive societies, for example, are also the most resilient, and they may appear to be cohesive only because minority groups are suppressed or marginalized. Likewise, resilience often entails significant trade-offs: highly resilient communities can be too tolerant of adversity, for instance, and efforts to enhance inclusion can generate resentment from groups who fear losing out. Such instances can undermine social sustainability, leading to heightened tensions or conflict.

Moreover, there may be consequential trade-offs between social sustainability and the other two pillars of sustainability. Lack of economic or environmental sustainability can stoke social tensions and exacerbate other social challenges, while the presence of economic or environmental sustainability can enable and support social sustainability—and vice versa. Without cohesion, for example, societies may find it difficult to agree on policies to promote economic or environmental sustainability, and those policies will be less effective when certain groups are excluded or vulnerable. Often, the trade-offs can move in both directions. For instance, failure to address climate change may undermine resilience and worsen exclusion by affecting certain groups more than others, but policies to address climate change (such as higher taxes, subsidy removals, and coal exits) can often trigger social unrest.

Communities and societies would ideally pursue social sustainability while managing these trade-offs. Indeed, process legitimacy helps to ensure that such tensions are meaningfully accommodated, especially among those who stand to bear the greatest costs from a given policy or program. In practice, however, stakeholders and policy makers may choose or prioritize one component or dimension over the others. Likewise, development actors hoping to support social sustainability often face competing priorities, budget constraints, and limited time frames, complicating efforts to translate aspirations into action. Figure 2.9 in chapter 2 presents three stylized scenarios of how societies experience such trade-offs. The book contends that efforts to achieve poverty reduction and shared prosperity or the SDGs are best enhanced when all three dimensions of sustainability are present.

Closing the Implementation Gap

Chapter 3 discusses key insights from development practice on what works to foster and support social sustainability, including examples of interventions that have proven effective at supporting cohesion, inclusion, and resilience and key priorities for promoting process legitimacy.

The chapter begins by acknowledging five common operational challenges around social sustainability. First, *progress is often nonlinear and time-consuming*, particularly regarding efforts to promote deep social change, where achievements are often followed by setbacks. Moreover, *the factors that drive or impede social sustainability are nonuniform and context-dependent*, varying across countries and communities. Likewise, the *obstacles are often complex, multidimensional, and entrenched*, involving deep-rooted social norms, structural barriers, or elite resistance, so solutions must work across sectors to address constraints where they exist. Similarly, *progress may involve normative changes, which can be difficult to generate* and occasionally are contentious or even destabilizing, aggravating deep-rooted social tensions. Finally, *the context is always evolving*, as new challenges arise and norms, values, behaviors, and practices change. Social sustainability will thus always remain aspirational and continue to inspire progress.

Despite these challenges, many approaches have proven to be effective, and recent decades have generated a wealth of experience on which policies and programs can enhance social sustainability:

- *Cohesion.* Local and community platforms, cash transfers and livelihood support programs, social accountability mechanisms, and other interventions can improve trust, bolster group dynamics, and help to resolve or reduce conflict in contexts both with and without fragility, conflict, and violence.
- *Inclusion.* Legal reforms, targeted benefit programs, efforts to bring groups at risk of exclusion into the policy arena, and affirmative action or quotas for groups that historically faced discrimination have all shown promise at expanding access to markets and services and fostering voice and agency for excluded groups.
- *Resilience.* Efforts to improve peoples' livelihoods, reduce their risk exposure, strengthen access to information and services, invest in climate change adaptation, and promote agency and self-organizing capacity building can be particularly effective at strengthening resilience.

Cutting across these examples, enhancing process legitimacy is also critical. A useful starting point is recognizing that development efforts have the potential to be socially disruptive and that supporting process legitimacy involves proactively addressing stakeholder concerns or grievances.[5] More broadly, process legitimacy (and socially sustainable development in general) is supported when development actors embrace three high-level and overarching priorities:

1. *Understand the policy arena.* Promoting social sustainability starts by identifying key stakeholders, their objectives, the prevailing norms and values, and other political or policy realities—for example, existing power structures, incentive systems, or vested interests (Fritz, Levy, and Ort 2014). In some cases, shortcomings can be addressed; in others, it may be better to avoid direct investment and find alternative ways to engage.

2. *Work with all key stakeholders.* Socially sustainable development fosters space in the policy arena for all key stakeholders to provide input and voice concerns, especially vulnerable groups, those at risk of exclusion, and those who may lose out from a given policy or program. Engagement also creates opportunities for real-time feedback loops, emergent learning, and efforts to promote positive norms and behaviors through iterative and participatory efforts (Appiah 2010).

3. *Engage for the long haul.* Social change tends to happen slowly, and windows of opportunity are often difficult to anticipate. But staying engaged, investing in relationships, and building trust typically pay off (Green 2016, especially ch. 1). This slow process can pose challenges for development actors, who often face pressures to deliver results in shorter time frames amid incentives for growth, efficiency, and measured effectiveness, but it enhances the social sustainability of their efforts.

This book is not meant to be the final word on social sustainability. Rather, it seeks to promote discussion and research, to refocus the development agenda on this critical concept, and to highlight the ambitious agenda ahead. By articulating the key components of social sustainability, identifying interventions that work to promote them, and highlighting the evidence of their links to key development outcomes, it provides a foundation for understanding the concept and identifies opportunities to strengthen the analytical framing and evidence base for it. There is much work to be done, particularly regarding efforts to measure social sustainability and its core components, to capture trends over time, and to understand their links to key development outcomes. Such efforts could help to motivate policy makers, development institutions, and other stakeholders to adopt and implement policies to foster and support social sustainability.

To address the challenges of the 21st century, including climate change, conflict, the need for sustainable growth, inequality, and erosion of the social fabric, it is critical to elevate social sustainability as a key pillar of development and an equal partner with economic and environmental sustainability. In practice, this effort means drawing greater attention to the concept and deepening the collective commitment to cohesion, inclusion, resilience, and process legitimacy. Above all, it means elevating social sustainability as a local, national, corporate, and global priority and committing time, resources, and collective energy to pursuing it.

Notes

1. Economic sustainability refers to fiscal and debt sustainability.
2. The terms bonding, bridging, and linking social cohesion are drawn from Woolcock and Narayan's work on social capital (Woolcock and Narayan 2000).
3. The concept of the policy arena was first developed by the *World Development Report 2017: Governance and the Law* (World Bank 2017).
4. Annex 2A includes a full list of each index's indicators and details on their construction.
5. In this sense, the World Bank's ESF, and instruments like it, is a key tool for process legitimacy.

References

Adriano, A. 2020. "Friend or Foe? Technology Can Boost Either Resilience or Inequality, Depending on How Much You Have of It." Finance and Development, International Monetary Fund, Washington, DC.

Aldrich, D. 2012. *Building Resilience: Social Capital in Post-Disaster Recovery.* Chicago, IL: University of Chicago Press.

Alesina, A., and R. Perotti. 1996. "Income Distribution, Political Instability, and Investment." *European Economic Review* 40 (6): 1203–28.

Alvaredo, F., L. Chancel, T. Piketty, E. Saez, and G. Zucman. 2018. "The Elephant Curve of Global Inequality and Growth." *AEA Papers and Proceedings* 108 (May): 103–08.

Appiah, K. A. 2010. *The Honor Code: How Moral Revolutions Happen.* New York: W. W. Norton.

Badgett, L. 2020. *The Economic Case for LGBT Equality: Why Fair and Equal Treatment Benefits Us All.* New York: Beacon Press.

Barrett, P., M. Appendino, K. Nguyen, and J. L. Miranda. 2020. "Measuring Social Unrest Using Media Reports." IMF Working Paper 2020/129, International Monetary Fund, Washington, DC.

Béné, C., R. Godfrey-Wood, A. Newsham, and M. Davies. 2012. "Resilience: New Utopia or New Tyranny? Reflection about the Potentials and Limits of the Concept of Resilience in Relation to Vulnerability Reduction Programmes." IDS Working Paper 405, Institute for Development Studies, Brighton.

Buehren, N., P. Gonzalez, and A. Copley. 2019. "What Are the Economic Costs of Gender Gaps in Ethiopia?" Gender Innovation Policy Initiative, World Bank, Washington, DC.

Chatterjee, S., M. Gassier, and N. Myint. 2022. "Leveraging Social Cohesion for Development Impacts: Framing Paper." World Bank, Washington, DC.

Cottyn, I. 2018. "Livelihood Trajectories in a Context of Repeated Displacement: Empirical Evidence from Rwanda." *Sustainability* 10 (10): 3521.

Cuesta, J., B. López-Noval, and M. Niño-Zarazúa. 2022. "Social Exclusion: Concepts, Measurement, and a Global Estimate." Policy Research Working Paper 10097, World Bank, Washington, DC.

Dempsey, N., G. Bramley, S. Power, and C. Brown. 2011. "The Social Dimension of Sustainable Development: Defining Urban Social Sustainability." *Sustainable Development* 19 (5): 289–300.

Esteban, J., and D. Ray. 2011. "Linking Conflict to Inequality and Polarization." *American Economic Review* 101 (4): 1345–74.

European Union. 2021. "Public Opinion in the European Union." *Eurobarometer* 96 (April). https://europa.eu/eurobarometer/surveys/detail/2553.

Freire, G., M. E. García Mora, G. Lara Ibarra, and S. Schwartz Orellana. 2020. *Social Inclusion in Uruguay.* Washington, DC: World Bank.

Fritz, V., B. Levy, and R. Ort. 2014. *Problem-Driven Political Economy Analysis: The World Bank's Experience.* Directions in Development. Washington, DC: World Bank.

Garschagen, M., F. G. Renaud, and J. Birkmann. 2011. "Dynamic Resilience of Peri-Urban Agriculturalists in the Mekong Delta under Pressures of Socio-Economic Transformation and Climate Change." In *Environmental Change and Agricultural Sustainability in the Mekong Delta,* edited by M. Stewart and P. Coclanis. Advances in Global Change Research 45. Dordrecht: Springer.

Gates, S. 2002. "Recruitment and Allegiance: The Microfoundations of Rebellion." *Journal of Conflict Resolution* 46 (1): 111–30.

Green, D. 2016. *How Change Happens.* Oxford: Oxford University Press.

Hallegatte, S., A. Vogt-Schilb, M. Bangalore, and J. Rozenberg. 2017. *Unbreakable: Building the Resilience of the Poor in the Face of Natural Disasters.* Climate Change and Development. Washington, DC: World Bank.

Islam, S. N., and J. Winkel. 2017. "Climate Change and Social Inequality." UNDESA Working Paper 152, United Nations Department of Economic and Social Affairs, New York.

Keck, M., and P. Sakdapolrak. 2013. "What Is Social Resilience? Lessons Learned and Ways Forward." *Erdkunde* 67 (1): 5–19.

Lakner, C., and B. Milanovic. 2016. "Global Income Distribution: From the Fall of the Berlin Wall to the Great Recession." *World Bank Economic Review* 30 (2): 203–32.

Lamichhane, K., and Y. Sawada. 2013. "Disability and Returns to Education in a Developing Country." *Economics of Education Review* 37 (December): 85–94.

Lorenz, D. 2013. "The Diversity of Resilience: Contributions from a Social Science Perspective." *Natural Hazards* 67 (1): 7–24.

Madgavkar, A., K. Ellingrud, and M. Krishnan. 2016. "The Economic Benefits of Gender Parity." *Stanford Social Innovation Review,* March 8, 2016.

Male, C., and Q. Wodon. 2017. "Disability Gaps in Educational Attainment and Literacy. The Price of Exclusion." Disability and Education Series, World Bank and Global Partnership for Education, Washington, DC.

Migdal, J. S. 2001. *State in Society: Studying How States and Societies Transform and Constitute One Another.* Cambridge, UK: Cambridge University Press.

Moshy, V. H., I. Bryceson, and R. Mwaipopo. 2015. "Social-Ecological Changes, Livelihoods, and Resilience among Fishing Communities in Mafia Island Marine Park, Tanzania." *Forum for Development Studies* 42 (3): 529–53.

Mozumder, M. M. H., M. A. Wahab, S. Sarkki, P. Schneider, and M. M. Islam. 2018. "Enhancing Social Resilience of the Coastal Fishing Communities: A Case Study of Hilsa (Tenualosa Ilisha H.) Fishery in Bangladesh." *Sustainability* 10 (10): 3501.

Mubarak, K., E. Johnson, A. Beath, M. Latif, and X. Luo. 2020. "Impact Evaluation of Cambodia's Implementation of the Social Accountability Framework." World Bank, Washington, DC.

Obrist, B. 2010. "Multi-Layered Social Resilience: A New Approach to Migration Research." *Progress in Development Studies* 10 (4): 283–93.

OECD (Organisation for Economic Co-operation and Development). 2011. *Perspectives on Global Development 2012: Social Cohesion in a Shifting World.* Paris: OECD.

Perry, J. 2021. "Trust in Public Institutions: Trends and Implications for Economic Security." Policy Brief 108, United Nations Department of Economic and Social Affairs, New York, June.

Pew Research Center. 2021. "Public Trust in Government: 1958–2021." Pew Research Center, Washington, DC, May 17, 2021. https://www.pewresearch.org/politics/2021/05/17/public-trust-in-government-1958-2021/.

Rauch, J. E. 1991. "Productivity Gains from Geographic Concentration of Human Capital: Evidence from the Cities." NBER Working Paper 3905, National Bureau of Economic Research, Cambridge, MA.

Smith, L. C., and T. R. Frankenberger. 2018. "Does Resilience Capacity Reduce the Negative Impact of Shocks on Household Food Security? Evidence from the 2014 Floods in Northern Bangladesh." *World Development* 102 (C): 358–76.

Solórzano, A. 2016. "Can Social Protection Increase Resilience to Climate Change? A Case Study of Oportunidades in Rural Yucatan, Mexico." IDS Working Paper 465, Institute of Development Studies, Brighton.

Staniland, P. 2014. *Networks of Rebellion: Explaining Insurgent Cohesion and Collapse.* Ithaca, NY: Cornell University Press.

Tawodzera, G. 2012. "Urban Household Survival and Resilience to Food Insecurity in Crisis Conditions: The Case of Epworth in Harare, Zimbabwe." *Journal of Hunger and Environmental Nutrition* 7 (2-3): 293–320.

Townshend, I., O. Awosoga, J. Kulig, and H. Fan. 2015. "Social Cohesion and Resilience across Communities That Have Experienced a Disaster." *Journal of the International Society for the Prevention and Mitigation of Natural Hazards* 76 (2): 913–38.

Turner, A. 2013. "The Business Case for Racial Equity." W. K. Kellogg Foundation and Altarum Institute, Battle Creek, MI.

United Nations and World Bank. 2018. *Pathways for Peace: Inclusive Approaches to Preventing Violent Conflict.* Washington, DC: World Bank.

Voss, M. 2008. "The Vulnerable Can't Speak: An Integrative Vulnerability Approach to Disaster and Climate Change Research." *Behemoth: A Journal on Civilisation* 1 (3): 39–56.

Wodon, Q., and B. de la Brière. 2018. *Unrealized Potential: The High Cost of Gender Inequality in Earnings.* Washington, DC: World Bank.

Woolcock, M., and D. Narayan. 2000. "Social Capital: Implications for Development Theory, Research, and Policy." *World Bank Research Observer* 15 (2): 225–49.

World Bank. 2001. *World Development Report 2000/2001: Attacking Poverty.* Washington, DC: World Bank.

World Bank. 2013a. *Building Resilience: Integrating Climate and Disaster Risk into Development—The World Bank Group Experience.* Washington, DC: World Bank.

World Bank. 2013b. *Inclusion Matters: The Foundation of Shared Prosperity.* Washington, DC: World Bank.

World Bank. 2014. *Strategic Framework for Mainstreaming Citizen Engagement in World Bank Group Operations.* Washington, DC: World Bank.

World Bank. 2017. *The World Bank Environmental and Social Framework.* Washington, DC: World Bank.

World Bank. 2020. *Poverty and Shared Prosperity 2020: Reversals of Fortune.* Washington, DC: World Bank.

World Bank. 2021. "Social Cohesion and Resilience." World Bank, Washington, DC. https://www.worldbank.org/en/topic/social-cohesion-and-resilience#1.

World Bank. 2022a. *Poverty and Shared Prosperity 2022: Correcting Course.* Washington, DC: World Bank.

World Bank. 2022b. Social Sustainability Global Database 2022. World Bank, Washington, DC.

Abbreviations

CDF	Comprehensive Development Framework
CLD	community and local development
CMC	community management committee
COVID-19	coronavirus disease 2019
CSO	civil society organization
ESF	Environmental and Social Framework
FLLoCA	Financing Locally Led Climate Action
GDP	gross domestic product
GRID	Green, Resilient, and Inclusive Development
ID	identification
KDP	Kecamatan Development Program
LGBTI	lesbian, gay, bisexual, transgender, intersex
NGO	nongovernmental organization
PRSP	Poverty Reduction Strategy Paper
SDCE	Strengthening Democracy and Civic Engagement
SDG	Sustainable Development Goal
SOGI	sexual orientation and gender identity
SSGD	Social Sustainability Global Database
SSI	Social Sustainability and Inclusion (World Bank Global Practice)
TPS	temporary protection status
UN	United Nations
UNDESA	United Nations Department of Economic and Social Affairs
UNRISD	United Nations Research Institute for Social Development

CHAPTER 1

From Aspiration to Action

Introduction

Development—by definition and by design—changes how people live. It is a dynamic, transformative process in which people are both the means and the ends, key agents, and principal actors. From infrastructure, education, and public health to markets, governance, and justice reform, the goal of all development is to equip, link, and enable groups of people to build on their strengths while creating something new and "better" from what came before. The development process is complex, challenging, nonuniform, and nonlinear, often moving two steps forward and then three steps back, before resuming forward motion again. When sustained over periods of time, however, it can promote societies that are more inclusive, cohesive, and resilient, in which all people are able to participate with dignity, fulfill their potential, and voice their needs to responsive and accountable governments. The efforts, goals, and aspirations of the World Bank and other development organizations are to support low- and middle-income countries along their journey to achieve these ends.

Compared to the long history of human civilization, this "development process"—and the priorities it represents—is a relatively new phenomenon. Through most of human history, change happened slowly, and most people relied on long-standing social systems built around family, community, clan, tribe, religion, traditions, and norms to survive, prosper, deal with challenges, allocate resources, and make sense of the world.[1] By changing how people live, development interacts with and affects these social institutions in often unpredictable and destabilizing ways. The process is inherently disruptive, encompassing both "creation" and "destruction," as has long been recognized.[2] Just as the benefits of development accrue to people through improved capabilities, material well-being, and expanded choices, the changes wrought can also displace old ideas, incumbent institutions, and existing power dynamics. Even when achieving "progress" or "results," such change can aggravate deep-rooted social tensions, create or exacerbate inequities, and heighten the risks of unrest or conflict, ultimately threatening (often suddenly) to undermine whatever development gains have been achieved.

As the world grapples with high inequality and an economic slowdown alongside the "three Cs" of conflict, climate change, and COVID-19—and as the social fabric is eroding in many countries amid fragmentation and polarization as well as persistent exclusion and vulnerability—continued progress toward sustainable development is not guaranteed. The social dimensions to these challenges are significant, and social systems must be understood and used to address them. How governments and development institutions navigate these social dynamics—how change is managed and how it interacts with existing social systems to produce better outcomes—has important implications for the sustainability of development and for the achievement of poverty reduction and inclusive growth (see, for instance, Acemoglu and Robinson 2019; Rajan 2019). Despite the emerging consensus that social sustainability is vital for achieving development and addressing global challenges, there is less clarity over what it is and how it can best be advanced.

The challenges of the 21st century present a crucial opportunity to elevate social sustainability as a key pillar of development, on par with economic and environmental sustainability. This book endeavors to establish greater clarity, affirming the centrality of social factors within the development puzzle. In particular, it has three key aims:

1. *Articulate a clear definition of social sustainability and a coherent conceptual framework.* For the purpose of this book, "social" refers broadly to the relationships between individuals and groups and the diverse characteristics that shape those relationships (norms, values, shared identity, culture, institutions),[3] rather than narrower programmatic applications like "social sectors" or "social policies." The book adopts the United Nations (UN) Brundtland Commission definition of "sustainability" as "meeting the needs of the present without compromising the ability of future generations to meet their own needs" (World Commission on Environment and Development 1987). To clarify a principle as broad, complex, and highly context-dependent as "social sustainability," the book offers a framework for understanding the concept (see chapter 2) as well as an intuitive two-part definition:

   Social sustainability increases when more people feel part of the development process and believe that they and their descendants will benefit from it.

   Communities and societies that are more socially sustainable are more willing and able to work together to overcome challenges, deliver public goods, and allocate scarce resources in ways perceived to be legitimate and fair so that all people may thrive over time.

2. *Demonstrate why social sustainability matters.* The book contends that social sustainability and its key components—inclusion, resilience, social cohesion, and "process legitimacy"—have both intrinsic and instrumental value. Their value is unique and innate in much the same way as peace, freedom, or sovereignty have inherent value. Likewise, they have important instrumental value for supporting poverty reduction and inclusive growth as well as for complementing one another. A key message is that social sustainability can be measured. The book highlights recent progress toward an empirical understanding of social sustainability, including the World Bank's new Social Sustainability Global Database (World Bank 2022e), while underscoring the need to address data, measurement, and methodological issues. It emphasizes that social sustainability is not binary; it exists on a spectrum, and

process legitimacy—the extent to which a community or society accepts who has authority, what goals are pursued, and *how* policies and programs get implemented—is a vital ingredient for socially sustainable development.

3. *Highlight key insights from development practice on what works to foster and support social sustainability.* Building on previous experience and ongoing efforts from the World Bank and across the development sector, the book illustrates core principles and practical guidelines for how development actors can operationalize social sustainability. Specifically, the book offers suggestions for how the World Bank and the broader development community can deepen efforts to integrate social sustainability into analytics, dialogue, and financing.

The book is organized as follows. The rest of this chapter provides historical context and highlights why now is a unique moment in time to promote and pursue social sustainability. Chapter 2 proposes a definition for social sustainability, drawing on relevant academic and policy literature, and presents a conceptual framework for understanding its four components, including a summary of evidence for why they matter and their broader links to key development outcomes. Chapter 3 illustrates key principles for operationalizing social sustainability, takes stock of progress to date, and briefly lays out some entry points to strengthen social sustainability. Chapter 4 concludes.

Context

For much of the last 75 years, social sustainability has taken a backseat to a focus on economic sustainability (that is, sustainable growth) and, more recently, environmental sustainability. While social development has made important conceptual and operational strides in recent decades to elevate its profile in development discourse, in everyday practice it is still largely on the fringes. However, the world is reaching a critical point, as overlapping crises are making it harder to meet key development goals and threatening the gains already achieved. Development's current tools and approaches, while necessary and important, are insufficient for today's vexing challenges because the broad social consensus needed to respond to them effectively and legitimately is so often lacking. This moment presents a critical window of opportunity to advance the concept and cause of social sustainability.

A Brief History of Social Sustainability

Current efforts to articulate an agenda for socially sustainable development build on a long, if not always venerable, history. The architects of the post–World War II era sought to build a new world order to maintain international peace and security, provide humanitarian assistance to those in need, protect human rights, and uphold international law. The establishment of the United Nations and the World Bank in 1945 marked a new era of multilateral efforts to promote peace and prosperity—followed in 1948 by the Universal Declaration of Human Rights, with 29 articles focused on many of the principles that would later be fundamental to social sustainability, such as inclusion, participation, accountability, and nondiscrimination. Article 22, for instance, guarantees every person's right to take part in government, directly or through freely chosen representatives; guarantees the right of equal access to public services; and establishes the will of the people as the basis of government authority. Of course, it would take several decades for many countries to realize these principles, while others have yet to embrace them.

Even as this important declaration was signed, however, social institutions were often seen as impediments to the development process. During the initial postwar period, the actions of today's multilateral and bilateral organizations were guided in large part by that era's prevailing model of economic development: modernization theory (Latham 2011). Among its many assumptions, modernization theory posited that history largely unfolds along a single path, that human reason and resources can and should be deployed to accelerate "progress" along this path, and that a country's social dynamics are often one of the primary obstacles to attaining this acceleration. Replacing traditional practices and cultural beliefs with technological progress and focusing on democracy and the individual were seen as desirable. Indeed, in 1951, a major UN report could openly declare,

> *Rapid economic progress is impossible without painful adjustments. Ancient philosophies have to be scrapped; old social institutions have to disintegrate; bonds of caste, creed, and race have to burst; and large numbers of people who cannot keep up with progress have to have their expectations of a comfortable life frustrated. Very few communities are willing to pay the full price of economic progress* (United Nations 1951, 15).[4]

Fortunately, this view did not prevail. In the 1960s, experts began to recognize that local context and social factors played some role in the success of development projects, and academics and development practitioners increasingly paid attention to these dynamics. Hirschman's *Development Projects Observed*, for example, highlighted that "people matter," documenting how local culture, context, and social and economic structures affected the performance of World Bank projects, while highlighting the need for emergent learning so that projects adapt to, interact with, and even shape their context in "co-evolutionary" collaboration (Hirschman 1967). In 1963 the creation of the United Nations Research Institute for Social Development (UNRISD), dedicated to cutting-edge research on social development, marked the growing global importance of social dimensions.

During the 1970s and 1980s, increased global attention on exclusion and poverty elevated the role of social issues in development. The concept of vulnerable or excluded populations entered into political discourse, particularly in Europe, amid growing evidence that the processes of economic growth, urbanization, and development often excluded, displaced, or negatively affected certain groups and that these groups required targeted assistance.[5] At the same time, concerns about the link between poverty and the environment also emerged, giving rise to the concept of sustainability. The UN Stockholm Conference on the Human Environment in 1972 was the first to note the link between human development and environmental sustainability. By the late 1980s, the concept of sustainable development was further defined by the UN Brundtland Commission as development that meets the needs of the present without compromising the ability of future generations to meet their own needs. This definition put an explicit emphasis on the social dimensions of development and underscored that economic, environmental, and social factors are interlinked and mutually reinforcing (World Commission on Environment and Development 1987).

At the World Bank, concerns over exclusion and poverty also grew during this period.[6] Starting in the 1970s under President Robert McNamara, there was an important shift toward a greater focus on poverty reduction, recognizing the role of women in development and the need to protect vulnerable groups. The Bank expanded investments in basic needs, human capital, and the provision of basic services (for example, health and education) and introduced specific efforts to mitigate the potential negative impacts of large infrastructure projects on indigenous peoples and vulnerable groups more broadly. Similarly, responding to the feminist critique of development, the Bank introduced the Women in Development Program in 1977 with the aim of improving the recognition of women's contributions to development.

In the early 1980s, these concerns were codified in Bank policies and procedures, which were designed and supported by a growing (albeit relatively small) cadre of social managers and specialists. The Bank's Operations Manual was updated to recognize the needs of indigenous peoples, and special protection measures were introduced for vulnerable groups who could be affected by resettlement or displacement as a result of Bank projects. An operational policy was introduced, calling for integrating social issues into the technical and economic analysis of projects.[7] Without an explicit stand-alone requirement for social analysis, however, these initial approaches to social policy and inclusion remained focused on "doing no harm," with circumscribed efforts to acknowledge the contribution of women but limited opportunities for Bank staff to engage with borrower country governments on the broader social agenda (IEG 2010).[8]

Concerns that development was, in many cases, hurting the poor and vulnerable continued to grow into the early 1990s, as structural adjustment programs focused on privatization, fiscal austerity, and trade liberalization, which often led to cuts in social programs and higher prices for basic commodities.

Reflecting the growing operational relevance of the social dimensions of development, the Bank created a dedicated Social Development Unit in 1989, 15 years after hiring its first sociologist. The new unit stressed the importance of adopting a people-first agenda (Cernea 1991) and emphasized principles that later coalesced as inclusion and cohesion (Bhatnagar and Williams 1992; Serageldin and Steer 1994). It also spearheaded early institutional efforts, such as including more systematic social analysis in the Bank's project preparation and approval processes, in the process developing new lending instruments focused specifically on inclusion as well as establishing new diagnostic tools and guidebooks to understand and operationalize social issues across the Bank's portfolio (McPhail and Jacobs 2003; World Bank 1996).[9] These efforts supported the introduction of Social Funds as well as the later community-driven development initiatives, which emphasized participation, transparency, and local empowerment to manage resources, identify priorities, and implement projects that address community-level development challenges.[10]

In 1991 the Bank also revised its Indigenous Peoples Policy, extending its definition of indigenous peoples to include a much wider array of people vulnerable to exclusion from the development process. In 1994 it rolled out a pioneering Information Disclosure Policy, raising the bar for transparency in development. By the late 1990s, fostered by rich internal debates—focused primarily on social capital and other key concepts of that era[11]—an intellectual and operational foundation for the Bank's approach to the social aspects of development was beginning to emerge. However, these initial efforts did not include broader efforts to promote principles related to social sustainability, nor did they explicitly make the link, noted by the UN Stockholm Conference, between environmental and social sustainability.[12]

These expanding efforts paralleled similar trends outside the Bank. A confluence of global factors around the turn of the 21st century led to a more explicit focus on the people-centric dimensions of development and efforts to ensure that growth was inclusive and reached the poorest and most vulnerable. This shift was partly informed by the end of the cold war and the challenges faced by many post-Soviet states transitioning to free markets, ongoing concerns that structural adjustment policies had undermined vulnerable groups, and an expanded focus on the effectiveness of development aid in achieving poverty reduction, with increased attention on debt relief and debt forgiveness initiatives.[13] The World Summit for Social Development in 1995 was an important milestone, creating the UN Commission for Social Development and attracting high-level recognition of social development as a professional field and global priority.[14]

Such emphasis on an integrated approach to development, uniting the social and economic dimensions with a focus on poverty, continued to be reflected in the Bank's evolving approach. In 1999 President James Wolfensohn introduced the Comprehensive Development Framework (CDF), establishing a country-led process for setting development strategies that prioritized human and social development and emphasized partnerships between governments (at all levels), civil society, the private sector, and external assistance agencies. In collaboration with the International Monetary Fund and based on CDF principles, the Bank also introduced Poverty Reduction Strategy Papers (PRSPs) to strengthen the links between debt relief, development, and poverty reduction. PRSPs were not only client-owned and results-focused, but also intended to be prepared in a participatory manner that involved civil society; they represented the Bank's first explicit acknowledgment of the broad and catalytic role that civil society plays in building transparency and accountability. In 2001, reflecting the need to integrate social issues more clearly into structural reforms, the Bank developed a Poverty and Social Impact Analysis to promote more systematic ex ante analysis of the intended and unintended consequences of Bank-supported policy reforms on different social groups, particularly the poor and vulnerable (World Bank 2003a, 2005c).

At the same time, many economists grew increasingly concerned about whether the benefits of economic growth were reaching the poor, a shift in thinking that would affect the broader development paradigm. During this period, development's endgame expanded beyond growth to include nonmonetary well-being (and better access to services) as well as voice and agency. In 1999 Amartya Sen won the Nobel Prize in economics and published his seminal book *Development as Freedom*, drawing attention to the importance and intrinsic value of individual freedoms: to be free from vulnerability and danger and able to access services, influence political outcomes, and reach one's potential (Sen 1999). Reflecting this broader concept of development, the adoption of the Millennium Development Goals in 2000 went beyond monetary definitions of poverty, setting ambitious new targets for fighting poverty and hunger as well as promoting inclusion, equity, and gender equality, with an enhanced focus on results and outcomes.

The Bank played an important role in this evolution. Building on years of participatory research that underscored the intrinsic importance of voice and agency for vulnerable groups in addition to poverty reduction, Deepa Narayan and coauthors published the *Voices of the Poor* trilogy in 2000 and *Moving Out of Poverty* in 2007 (Narayan 2009; Narayan, Chambers et al. 2000;

Narayan, Patel, et al. 2000; Narayan and Petesch 2002, 2007; Narayan, Pritchett, and Kapoor 2009). Likewise, a series of *World Development Reports* deepened this thinking over the last two decades, providing the conceptual foundation to integrate agency, opportunity, vulnerability, and accountability into the Bank's approach to development. Box 1.1 explores the Bank's intellectual evolution on these issues in greater detail. Wolfensohn's priority of addressing corruption was another important driver during this period, as was the Bank's 2007 Governance and Anticorruption Strategy, which enshrined the "demand for good governance" approach and focused on citizens as the ultimate stakeholders for better governance through efforts to strengthen voice, participation, and transparency (World Bank 2007). In 2005 the Bank's then–Social Development Unit adopted a sector strategy that articulated key concepts and goals to guide the Bank's work on social issues and identified three operational principles to guide its approach: inclusion, cohesion, and accountability (World Bank 2005a). In 2011 an internal review of the Social Development Strategy recommended adding a fourth operational principle, resilience, noting its critical role in reducing vulnerability. This book, with its focus on inclusion, cohesion, resilience, and process legitimacy, builds on and updates these critical efforts (World Bank 2011a).[15]

Box 1.1
The Conceptual Foundations of Social Sustainability at the World Bank

This book's proposed definition and conceptual framework for social sustainability (see chapter 2) builds on a deep foundation of prior research and strategic efforts at the World Bank. Conceptually, the book's broad views have been reflected in five seminal *World Development Reports* over the last two decades. In 2000 the *World Development Report* on poverty explored poverty's multiple dimensions, underscoring the entwined nature of opportunity, empowerment, and vulnerability (World Bank 2001; see also Narayan 2009; Narayan, Chambers, et al. 2000; Narayan and Petesch 2007; Narayan, Pritchett, and Kapoor 2009). In 2004 the *World Development Report* on public sector accountability, especially between public service providers, the state, and service users, emphasized the importance of voice and agency for promoting equal opportunities in societies (World Bank 2003b). In 2006 the *World Development Report* on equity showed how equal opportunities contribute to economic development and documented the links between more equal societies and long-term growth (World Bank 2005d). In 2011 the *World Development Report* on conflict and fragility emphasized institutional legitimacy, citizen justice, and cohesion as drivers of social instability—concepts closely linked to social sustainability (World Bank 2011b). Finally, the 2017 *World Development Report* on governance and the law highlighted the costs of power asymmetries in society—as manifested by exclusion, elite capture, and clientelism—as well as the benefits of inclusion, greater citizen engagement, and strong coalitions for positive reforms (World Bank 2017b).

The shifting paradigm was encapsulated in 2013 when the Bank's new corporate strategy adopted the twin goals of ending extreme poverty and promoting shared prosperity (defined as income growth for the bottom 40 percent of households). To achieve these goals, the strategy prioritized sustainability's three pillars—environmental, economic, and social (figure 1.1)—so that development objectives across all three pillars are sustained "over time and across generations" (World Bank 2013, 8). The strategy defined social sustainability as a concept integrating empowerment, voice, participation, and equality of opportunities, with a particular focus on marginalized and vulnerable groups, and identified it as critical for long-term development:

> *An inclusive society must have the institutions, structures, and processes that empower local communities, so they can hold their governments accountable. It also requires the participation of all groups in society, including traditionally marginalized groups, such as ethnic minorities and indigenous populations, in decision-making processes. . . . A society that promotes equal opportunities, and is perceived by its citizens to be doing so, is more likely to be able to achieve the stability and cohesiveness needed to generate a sustainable development path (World Bank 2013, 33).*

Building on this triad of economic, environmental, and social sustainability, the adoption of the Sustainable Development Goals (SDGs) in 2015 enshrined social issues as central to the development challenge. For years, the UN and other multilateral institutions referred broadly to the importance of "environmental and social sustainability" but did not define, analyze, or develop social sustainability as a distinct concept or objective (United Nations 2012). The majority of the 17 SDGs, however, address the core principle of "leave no one behind" and reflect the importance of the social dimension: several underscore that development benefits should be shared equitably by all, including poverty eradication (SDG 1); elimination of hunger (SDG 2);

Figure 1.1 The Triad of Sustainability

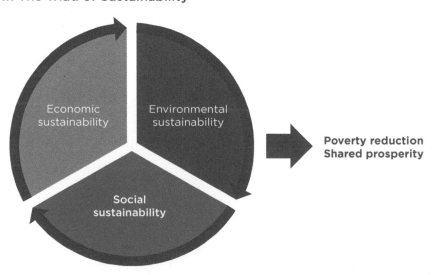

Source: World Bank.

health and well-being (SDG 3); education (SDG 4); water and sanitation (SDG 6); affordable and clean energy (SDG 7); decent work (SDG 8); and inclusive, safe, and resilient cities and settlements (SDG 11). Notably, three SDGs focus squarely on social sustainability:

- *Reduced inequalities.* SDG 10 addresses equality of opportunity and the importance of removing discriminatory laws and promoting political, economic, and social inclusion; safe and orderly migration; fiscal and social protection programs for the poor; and income growth of the bottom 40 percent.
- *Gender equality.* SDG 5 seeks to ensure women's full and effective participation and equal opportunities in political, economic, and public life; reforms to give women equal rights to economic resources; and sound policies and enforceable legislation for the promotion of gender equality and the empowerment of women and girls at all levels.
- *Peace, justice, and strong institutions.* SDG 16 calls on the international community to "promote peaceful and inclusive societies for sustainable development, provide access to justice for all, and build effective, accountable, and inclusive institutions at all levels."

These developments have helped to incorporate social sustainability into the post-2015 development agenda (United Nations 2015). In 2016 UNRISD published an extensive study on the social aspects of sustainable development, arguing that market-based mechanisms and green economy policies can only flourish if the rights of individuals and communities are protected (UNRISD 2016). Within the UN system, the United Nations Department of Economic and Social Affairs has well-developed institutions for promoting social sustainability in all its forms, including the long-running Commission for Social Development (UNDESA 2021). Many country governments have also promoted the concept or its underlying principles: for example, the European Union focuses on social cohesion, and its parliament commissioned a study of social sustainability (McGuinn et al. 2020), municipal governments in Canada have embraced social sustainability as a holistic approach to local governance (City of Maple Ridge n.d.), and China has placed renewed emphasis on "common prosperity" following a period of rising inequality.

The Bank was an important partner in shaping the post-2015 development agenda, and the institution's trajectory toward socially sustainable development has continued to accelerate in recent years. In 2017 the Bank launched the Human Capital Project to increase investments in human development, particularly social protection programming focused on poor and vulnerable populations, followed by the human capital index to track progress and spark global momentum—efforts that deepened during the COVID-19 economic and health crises (World Bank 2020b). The Bank has also made important strides to mainstream citizen engagement across its operational portfolio and focus greater attention on transparency and accountability, including the Strategic Framework for Mainstreaming Citizen Engagement (World Bank 2014) and the *World Development Report* on governance (World Bank 2017b). This framework ensures that all projects conduct consultations with beneficiaries during project preparation, design, and implementation stages.

In 2018 the Bank adopted its Environmental and Social Framework (ESF), representing a major step forward in operationalizing the role of social issues in development. For the first time, the ESF required that social analysis be conducted on every investment project, as had been Bank policy for environmental project analysis since the 1980s. The ESF incorporates key human rights principles, including transparency, accountability, consultation, participation, nondiscrimination, and social inclusion. Its vision statement explicitly states, "Social development and inclusion are critical for *all* of the World Bank's development interventions" (emphasis added), and "The World Bank's activities support the realization of human rights expressed in the Universal Declaration of Human Rights."[16]

The ESF boosted Bank efforts to protect disadvantaged or vulnerable individuals and groups and to ensure their access to project benefits. In particular, it introduced standards for nondiscrimination, universal access, and labor and working conditions, including child labor and forced labor as well as general occupational hazards. A specific ESF directive provides a comprehensive description of disadvantaged or vulnerable individuals and groups at risk of discrimination (World Bank 2016a), with guidance and due diligence requirements for identifying and mitigating the risks and impacts on such individuals and groups. This guidance led to an expanded focus on persons with disabilities, sexual and gender minorities, and ethnic minorities. A specific standard was also introduced for indigenous peoples, going even further than prior Bank policy by defining who was indigenous and calling for consistent free, prior, and informed consent for all projects affecting indigenous peoples. Other ESF standards require borrower countries to prepare stakeholder engagement plans and establish grievance redress mechanisms for all investment projects.

Going beyond the ESF, which concentrates on the Bank's investment operations, in 2021 the Bank introduced the overarching Green, Resilient, and Inclusive Development (GRID) operational framework to influence country strategies and the institution's global engagement. The "I" in GRID calls for investing in more inclusive and reliable health, housing, child care, education, water supply, and sanitation services to build stronger and more resilient communities and to reach vulnerable and disadvantaged communities (World Bank 2021a). Likewise, the two most recent replenishment cycles for the International Development Association, the Bank's fund for the poorest countries, underscored the importance of integrating persons with disabilities across the Bank's engagements as well as strengthening citizen engagement at the country level, drawing further attention to inclusion and accountability (World Bank 2020a, 2022b). In particular, 14 policy commitments in the most recent replenishment focus explicitly on inclusion, drawing on the ESF directive for disadvantaged or vulnerable individuals and groups.

The last half century has seen important progress at the Bank and across the development community to acknowledge the influence of local context on development outcomes, recognize that vulnerable groups need special protections, and advance a development paradigm that honors the intrinsic values of agency, empowerment, and nonmonetary well-being, underpinned by the principles of nondiscrimination, right to safety, and voice. However, this progress has only begun to be operationalized. The ESF is a powerful and influential framework, but with only three years of implementation, it has not yet reached its full potential to go beyond doing no harm and influence the broader social agenda. At the Bank and beyond, the reality of everyday practice has not kept pace with these sweeping aspirations, and the recognition that social factors are important has not dramatically affected the way development is done on the ground. In most development toolkits, operational approaches, and theories of practice, the social dimension remains much less prominent than its economic or environmental counterparts. These gaps partly reflect the highly complex, context-specific barriers to social sustainability, which are driven by factors that can be difficult to identify, deeply embedded in cultural practices and norms, and costly to address, but they also highlight the urgency of reforms and efforts that are long overdue as well as the costs of further inaction.

Social sustainability has not yet traveled the full distance from aspiration to effective action; in the face of today's growing list of challenges, the old tools and approaches will not suffice on their own. While social factors have always been important to the development process, they are urgently important now.

Why Now?

As the world faces an unprecedented array of challenges, the social sustainability of development can no longer be overlooked. Even before the COVID-19 pandemic, global growth and the pace of poverty reduction had slowed (Alvaredo et al. 2018; Lakner and Milanovic 2016; Schoch, Lakner, and Fleury 2020; World Bank 2016b, 2022d, 2022e). In the midst of the pandemic, extreme poverty had increased to 9.3 percent in 2020, up from 8.4 percent in 2019 (measured at 2017 purchasing power parity US dollars), increasing the number of the extremely poor from 648 million to 719 million globally (World Bank 2022c, 2022d). Likewise, while inequality between countries has been declining for decades, driven by rapid growth in large economies like China and India (see, for instance, Deaton 2013; Milanovic 2016; World Bank 2016b), it remains high, and progress may be slowing for the first time in a generation (Yonzan, Lakner, and Gerszon Mahler 2021). Moreover, recent evidence suggests that a growing share of income is going to the world's top earners, widening the gaps between the ultra-rich, the middle class, and the poor (Alvaredo et al. 2018; Lakner and Milanovic 2016). Beyond poverty and inequality, nearly one-third of the world's population is at risk of social exclusion due to economic status, gender or gender identity, race, religion, ethnicity, nationality, age, or sexual orientation (Cuesta, López-Noval, and Niño-Zarazúa 2022). These challenges are compounded by the gnawing persistence of racism, prejudice, discrimination, and social injustice; globally, billions of people face deep-rooted structural barriers to participating equally in society (box 1.2).

In recent years, the "three Cs" of COVID-19, climate change, and rising levels of conflict have enflamed these long-standing challenges, and the current global economic slowdown threatens to make matters worse. In particular, evidence suggests that each of the three Cs is constraining efforts to address poverty, inequality, and exclusion.

- ■ *Conflict.* The number, frequency, and duration of violent conflicts have all increased in recent decades (World Bank 2021b), including in middle-income countries, where the majority of people killed as a result of political violence and criminal homicides now reside (World Bank 2022a). Since 2007, the number of major civil wars has tripled (World Bank 2021b). Conflict directly undermines poverty reduction efforts: recent analysis estimates that the conflict in Ukraine along with the lingering effects of the pandemic will push another

70 million to 89 million people into poverty in 2022 (Gerszon Mahler et al. 2022; World Bank 2022d). Conflict is often driven by inequality and exclusion, which can create and exacerbate grievances (United Nations and World Bank 2018), as supported by an emerging literature exploring the empirical links between conflict and between-group inequality (see, for instance, Besançon 2005; Østby 2013; Stewart 2000).

Box 1.2
Global Estimates of the Population at Risk of Exclusion

While there are multiple estimates of global monetary and multidimensional poverty, populations at risk of social exclusion still lack a worldwide estimate, which limits the ability of national and multilateral institutions to monitor progress toward the Sustainable Development Goals, honor commitments to leave no one behind, or design effective social programs.

Filling this gap, new World Bank research by Cuesta, López-Noval, and Niño-Zarazúa (2022) estimates the size of populations at risk of exclusion based on identity, circumstances, and socioeconomic conditions, including persons with disabilities; indigenous peoples; lesbian, gay, bisexual, transgender, and intersex people; Afro-descendants; religious minorities; victims of gender-based violence; and forcibly displaced people.[a] Using a macro counting measure, the researchers estimate the number and share of populations at risk of exclusion at the country level, impute information gaps based on regional or global peer averages, and avoid double-counting across group categories. Approximately 2.3 billion people, or 31 percent of the global population, are estimated to be at risk of exclusion (figure B1.2.1). This number is larger than most leading estimates of global monetary poverty, including the 9.6 percent or 722 million people living under the recently updated international poverty line of US$2.15 (2017 purchasing power parity).

In absolute terms, the largest vulnerable populations are in the South Asia and East Asia and Pacific regions, with 1.3 billion people at risk of exclusion or 53 percent of the worldwide total (figure B1.2.1, panel b). Sub-Saharan Africa has the next largest vulnerable population (552 million people or 23 percent of the total) and the highest incidence, with 52 percent of its population at risk of exclusion, three times the rate in Europe and Central Asia (18 percent). Worldwide, the share of at-risk populations in fragile, conflict-affected, and violent situations is nearly 50 percent.

These estimates suggest that interventions to address extreme poverty need to be complemented with efforts focusing on the nonextreme poor who are at risk of exclusion. This gap reflects an estimated one-fifth of the world's population, or almost 1.5 billion people. The research also underscores the need to enhance the resilience of groups at high risk of exclusion, which are disproportionately exposed to shocks, hardships, and marginalization.

(continued)

Box 1.2
Continued

Figure B1.2.1 Global Rate of Poverty and Estimated Share and Number of the Population at Risk of Exclusion, 2017

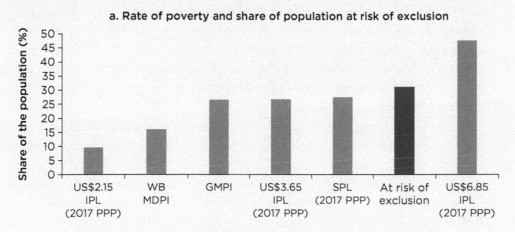

a. Rate of poverty and share of population at risk of exclusion

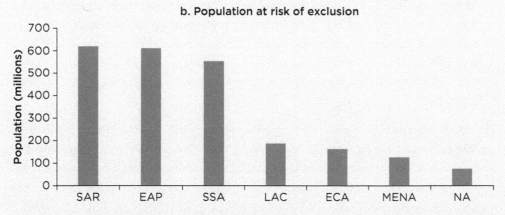

b. Population at risk of exclusion

Source: Cuesta, López-Noval, and Niño-Zarazúa 2022.
Note: Using the new 2017 purchasing power parity adjusted poverty lines, World Bank (2022c) reports global headcount rates (population) of 9.6 percent (722 million), 26.7 percent (2 billion), 48.9 percent (3.7 billion), and 27.5 percent (2.1 billion) using, respectively, the US$2.15, US$3.65, and US$6.85 poverty lines and the SPL (2017 purchasing power parity). EAP = East Asia and Pacific; ECA = Eastern Europe and Central Asia; GMPI = global multidimensional poverty index; IPL = international poverty line; LAC = Latin America and the Caribbean; MDPI = multidimensional poverty index; MENA = Middle East and North Africa; NA = North America; PPP = purchasing power parity; SAR = South Asia Region; SPL = societal poverty line; SSA = Sub-Saharan Africa.

a. These categories come from the World Bank's Directive "Addressing Risks and Impacts on Disadvantaged or Vulnerable Individuals or Groups," March 27, 2021.

■ *Climate change.* Likewise, the manifestations of climate change are growing increasingly severe, further complicating efforts to address poverty and inequality. Climate effects will push as many as 132 million people into poverty by 2030 (World Bank 2020c) and force as many as 216 million people to migrate by 2050 (Clement et al. 2021). Growing evidence suggests that climate-related shocks also worsen within-country inequality, as disadvantaged groups suffer disproportionately (Islam and Winkel 2017). Meanwhile, although reforms to address climate change are critical, if too hastily implemented they can aggravate poverty, vulnerability, and inequality in the short term (for example, emissions reduction policies that increase energy and food prices) (Hallegatte et al. 2016). Similarly, if policies are not carefully designed, the costs of climate change mitigation and transition can be unequal across groups (for example, coal-mining communities).

■ *COVID-19.* Finally, the pandemic has erased years of global progress on poverty reduction and shed harsh light on long-standing inequities (World Bank 2020c). The costs of COVID-19 have been borne disproportionately by the poor, marginalized, and traditionally excluded groups (Henson et al. 2020; World Bank 2020d; WHO and World Bank 2011). On average, the world's bottom 40 percent of earners have had worse income shocks (Furceri, Loungani, and Ostry 2020; Yonzan et al. 2022) and have recovered less of their prepandemic incomes, a trend that may be worsening amid rising inflation (Gerszon Mahler et al. 2022). As a result, the pandemic is expected to exacerbate inequality in both the short and long runs, especially between countries or inside low- and middle-income countries with limited fiscal programs to cushion the shocks (Yonzan et al. 2022), creating long-run generational effects on social mobility (Sánchez-Páramo et al. 2021). Learning losses may also have long-lasting impacts, especially on poorer families (Sánchez-Páramo et al. 2021).

The social effects of these challenges are growing harder to ignore. Poverty, inequality, and exclusion—exacerbated in recent years by COVID-19, conflict, and climate change—are making social sustainability all the more elusive. In particular, there is evidence that inequality is linked to higher social tensions, lower levels of trust, and diminished social cohesion as well as lower income growth (see, for instance, Bjørnskov 2008; Delhey and Dragolov 2014; Delhey and Newton 2005; Rodrik 1999; Uslaner and Brown 2003; Wilkinson and Pickett 2010; World Bank 2016b). These linkages may be stronger after significant shocks: a recent review of past pandemics found that the resulting increase in inequality and decrease in economic output were associated with a significant rise in social unrest. This unrest, in turn, was associated with subsequently higher inequality and lower economic output, suggesting a vicious cycle between inequality, economic losses, and social tensions (Sedik and Xu 2020).

Other forces are also deepening social tensions, driving a wedge between groups, and undermining social cohesion. Political polarization, declining trust in public institutions, unequal access to the digital economy, and the adoption of narrower, more exclusive identities are all disrupting and dividing communities, contributing to erosion of the social fabric (World Bank 2020c).

Figure 1.2 Share of Countries with Social Unrest Events, 12-Month Moving Average, by Region, 1985–2020

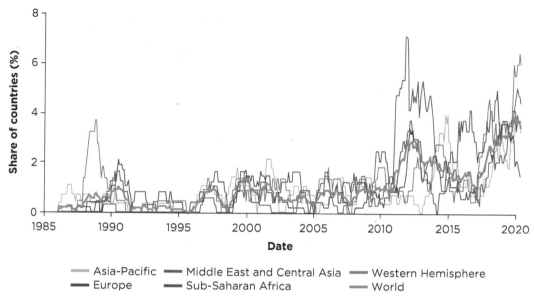

Source: Barrett et al. 2020.

For example, Barrett et al. (2020) recently constructed an index of social unrest—defined as protests, riots, and other forms of civil disorder and tension as measured by media reports—and found that the global frequency of social unrest events has increased since 1985 (figure 1.2). Likewise, public opinion surveys suggest that trust in public institutions is declining around the world. In the United States, trust in government declined from 73 percent to 24 percent between 1958 and 2021 (Pew Research Center 2021); Western Europe has seen gradual but less precipitous declines (European Union 2021), and data from surveys across 62 low-, middle-, and high-income countries show that average trust in government fell by 10 percentage points between 2006 and 2019 (Perry 2021). Emerging evidence suggests that social media and other digital technologies are exacerbating these challenges (box 1.3).

These challenges are not isolated or temporary; they will not solve themselves, and the headwinds are only growing more extreme. Addressing them will require novel solutions. While important, the old tools and approaches, such as fiscal policy, investments in human capital, or improvements in labor productivity, are insufficient to face the challenges at hand and must be complemented by new approaches. To overcome today's gaps and manage future tensions, the *social* sustainability of policies, programs, and outcomes must be central to the development agenda. The current moment highlights the need to advance social sustainability as a concept and operational imperative, while sharpening the analytical foundations on which it rests.

Box 1.3
Social Media's Effects on Social Cohesion

Social media platforms connect billions of people across the planet; during COVID-19 lockdowns, they offered many people their primary channel of communication and social connection. At their dawn, these technologies were widely believed to be a force for good, but in recent years, researchers have begun to investigate their potential negative social consequences (Haidt 2022). This research suggests that social media can erode traditional social connections, divide groups into echo chambers with homogeneous views and identities, weaken empathy, and widen the perceived gaps between the haves and have-nots (Vinnakota 2017). In particular, research has revealed that social media's effect on subjective well-being—or a person's moment-to-moment feelings and satisfaction with his or her life—is more often negative (provoking social comparisons and envy) than positive (creating social capital and stimulating feelings of social connectedness) (Verduyn et al. 2017).

Emerging evidence suggests that these potential consequences are multiplying as social media grows and evolves. Social media algorithms, where the most provocative posts spread fastest and farthest, can exacerbate the negative effects, while intensifying the spread of misinformation and conspiracy theories. Viral dynamics can amplify previously marginal political extremes and hostile provocateurs (Hawkins et al. 2018), allowing a small number of aggressive people to attack a large set of victims (Bor and Petersen (2019). Increasingly, bots and even artificial intelligence are being used to spread disinformation and falsehoods through texts, images, and deep-fake videos. In the absence of a shared sense of truth or even reality, echo chambers and the exponential spread of information can corrode people's trust in public authorities (health officials, courts, police), institutions (government, news media, universities), and fellow citizens (Gurri 2018; Lorenz-Spreen et al. 2022). In recent years, as conspiracy theories have grown in prominence, online anger and violence have increasingly spilled over into reality in countries at all income levels.

Notes

1. Even so, there was enormous diversity in how humans organized and structured their societies. See, for instance, Galor (2022); Graeber and Wengrow (2021).
2. Both Adam Smith and his contemporary, Adam Ferguson, articulated versions of these concerns. See Hill (1997).
3. This approach draws on prior efforts to define "social" and "social development" at the World Bank. See, for instance, Davis (2004); World Bank (2005a, 2005b).
4. Cited in Escobar (1993, 1). Needless to say, views of local populations and cultures vastly more disparaging than these were expressed in earlier decades and centuries by those seeking to justify imperialism and empire.
5. These concerns moved in parallel with other developments in the social sphere, such as the emergence of environmentalism, the sustainability movement, the prioritization of human

rights, the establishment of grassroots civil society nongovernmental organizations, and the women's rights movement.

6. This section draws on more extensive efforts to trace the history and evolution of the World Bank's approach to the social dimensions of development, such as Davis (2004) and Koch-Weser and Guggenheim (2021), as well as materials and recollections provided by the World Bank Archives team and other colleagues.

7. In 1982 these concerns were converted into the first operational social policies on involuntary resettlement (OMS 2.33, later updated to OD 4.30) and indigenous peoples (OMS 2.32). In 1984 a broader statement in the operational policy for project appraisal (OMS 2.20) called for social analysis alongside economic and technical assessments.

8. In contrast, an explicit requirement was introduced for all Bank investment projects to have an environmental assessment.

9. Social assessments were encouraged to support incorporating participation and social analysis into the design and delivery of operations. *The World Bank Participation Sourcebook* provided a how-to guide to help Bank staff to support participatory approaches in economic and social development (World Bank 1996).

10. However, these instruments and diagnostic tools were deployed most prevalently in fragile and conflict-affected countries with limited institutional capabilities, with some notable exceptions.

11. This focus reflected the global and internal influence of works such as Bebbington, Guggenheim, et al. (2004); Bebbington, Woolcock, et al. (2006); Putnam (1993); and Woolcock and Narayan (2000).

12. For a retrospective analysis of implementation gaps and long-term results of five of the Bank's most innovative social development loans of the 1990s, see Fox (2020).

13. The Heavily Indebted Poor Countries Initiative and Multilateral Debt Relief Initiative were created by the World Bank, the International Monetary Fund, and other multilateral, bilateral, and commercial creditors in 1996 and 2005, respectively, to ensure that the poorest countries in the world were not overwhelmed by unmanageable or unsustainable debt burdens.

14. Drawing on the work of the World Bank and others, the summit adopted 10 commitments around a people-first approach to development, including equitable access to health and education; gender equality; protection of human rights; eradication of extreme poverty; increased attention to social issues in structural reform programs; more resources and international collaboration around social issues; and recognition of the need for an integrated approach to social development across legal, economic, social, cultural, and political contexts.

15. The book is also consistent with the Bank's framework establishing the Social Sustainability and Inclusion Global Practice in 2020, which focused on inclusion, resilience, and empowerment. While empowerment in that strategy referred to citizen engagement, social accountability, and women's agency, the framework presented here integrates empowerment under inclusion (ensuring access to political and social spaces) as well as process legitimacy (ensuring that all stakeholders, especially vulnerable groups, can meaningfully contribute input and feedback into the design and implementation of policies and programs). Building on and updating these previous strategies, the book offers a more detailed vision of social sustainability and how it can be enhanced.

16. World Bank (2017a). The vision statement further states, "Through the projects it finances, and in a manner consistent with its Articles of Agreement, the World Bank seeks to avoid adverse impacts and will continue to support its member countries as they strive to progressively achieve their human rights commitments."

References

Acemoglu, D., and J. Robinson. 2019. *The Narrow Corridor: States, Societies, and the Fate of Liberty.* New York: Penguin Press.

Alvaredo, F., L. Chancel, T. Piketty, E. Saez, and G. Zucman. 2018. "The Elephant Curve of Global Inequality and Growth." *AEA Papers and Proceedings* 108 (May): 103–08.

Barrett, P., M. Appendino, K. Nguyen, and J. L. Miranda. 2020. "Measuring Social Unrest Using Media Reports." IMF Working Paper 2020/129, International Monetary Fund, Washington, DC.

Bebbington, A., S. Guggenheim, E. Olson, and M. Woolcock. 2004. "Exploring Social Capital Debates at the World Bank." *Journal of Development Studies* 40 (5): 33–64.

Bebbington, A., M. Woolcock, S. Guggenheim, and E. Olson, eds. 2006. *The Search for Empowerment: Social Capital as Idea and Practice at the World Bank.* Bloomfield: Kumarian Press.

Besançon, M. 2005. "Relative Resources: Inequality in Ethnic Wars, Revolutions, and Genocides." *Journal of Peace Research* 42 (4): 393–415.

Bhatnagar, B., and A. Williams. 1992. *Participatory Development and the World Bank.* Washington, DC: World Bank.

Bjørnskov, C. 2008. "The Growth-Inequality Association: Government Ideology Matters." *Journal of Development Economics* 87 (2): 300–08.

Bor, A., and M. B. Petersen. 2019. "The Psychology of Online Political Hostility: A Comprehensive, Cross-National Test of the Mismatch Hypothesis." *American Political Science Review* 116 (1): 1–18.

Cernea, M. 1991. *Putting People First*, 2d ed. Oxford: Oxford University Press.

City of Maple Ridge. n.d. "Social Sustainability." Maple Ridge, BC. https://www.mapleridge.ca/1779/Social-Sustainability.

Clement, V., K. Rigaud, A. de Sherbinin, B. Jones, S. Adamo, J. Schewe, N. Sadiq, and E. Shabahat. 2021. *Groundswell Part 2: Acting on Internal Climate Migration.* Washington, DC: World Bank.

Cuesta, J., B. López-Noval, and M. Niño-Zarazúa. 2022. "Social Exclusion: Concepts, Measurement, and a Global Estimate." Policy Research Working Paper 10097, World Bank, Washington, DC.

Davis, G. 2004. "A History of the Social Development Network in The World Bank, 1973–2002." Social Development Paper 56, World Bank, Washington, DC, March 2004.

Deaton, A. 2013. *The Great Escape: Health, Wealth, and the Origins of Inequality.* Princeton, NJ: Princeton University Press.

Delhey, J., and G. Dragolov. 2014. "Why Inequality Makes Europeans Less Happy: The Role of Distrust, Status Anxiety, and Perceived Conflict." *European Sociological Review* 32 (2): 151–65.

Delhey, J., and K. N. M. I. Newton. 2005. "Predicting Cross-National Levels of Social Trust: Global Pattern or Nordic Exceptionalism?" *European Sociological Review* 21 (4): 93–137.

Escobar, A. 1993. *Encountering Development: The Making and Unmaking of the Third World.* Princeton, NJ: Princeton University Press.

European Union. 2021. "Public Opinion in the European Union." *Eurobarometer* 96 (April). https://europa.eu/eurobarometer/surveys/detail/2553.

Fox, J. 2020. "Contested Terrain: International Development Projects and Countervailing Power for the Excluded." *World Development* 133 (September): 1–18.

Furceri, D., P. Loungani, and J. Ostry. 2020. "How Pandemics Leave the Poor Even Farther Behind." *IMF* (blog), May 11, 2020.

Galor, O. 2022. *The Journey of Humanity: The Origins of Wealth and Inequality.* Woodland Hills, CA: Penguin Random House.

Gerszon Mahler, D., N. Yonzan, R. Hill, C. Lakner, and H. W. Yoshida. 2022. "Pandemic, Prices, and Poverty." *World Bank Data* (blog), April 13, 2022. https://blogs.worldbank.org/opendata/pandemic-prices-and-poverty.

Graeber, D., and D. Wengrow. 2021. *The Dawn of Everything: A New History of Humanity.* London: Penguin.

Gurri, M. 2018. *The Revolt of The Public and the Crisis of Authority in the New Millennium.* San Francisco, CA: Stripe Press.

Haidt, J. 2022. "Why the Past 10 Years of American Life Have Been Uniquely Stupid." *The Atlantic,* April 11, 2022.

Hallegatte, S., M. Bangalore, L. Bonzanigo, M. Fay, T. Kane, U. Narloch, J. Rozenberg, D. Treguer, and A. Vogt-Schilb. 2016. *Shock Waves: Managing the Impacts of Climate Change on Poverty.* Climate Change and Development. Washington, DC: World Bank.

Hawkins, S., D. Yudkin, M. Juan-Torres, and T. Dixon. 2018. *Hidden Tribes: A Study of America's Polarized Landscape.* New York: More in Common.

Henson, S., U. Kambhampati, T. Mogues, W. Olsen, M. Prowse, R. Ramos, J. Rand, R. Rasiah, K. Roelen, R. Tiessen, and O. F. Yap. 2020. "The Development Impacts of COVID-19 at Home and Abroad: Politics and Implications of Government Action." *European Journal of Development Research* 32 (5): 1339–52.

Hill, L. 1997. "Adam Ferguson and the Paradox of Progress and Decline." *History of Political Thought* 18 (4): 677–706.

Hirschman, A. 1967. *Development Projects Observed.* Washington, DC: Brookings Institution.

IEG (Independent Evaluation Group). 2010. *Safeguards and Sustainability Policies in a Changing World: An Independent Evaluation of World Bank Group Experience.* IEG Study Series. Washington, DC: World Bank.

Islam, S. N., and J. Winkel. 2017. "Climate Change and Social Inequality." UNDESA Working Paper 152, United Nations Department of Economic and Social Affairs, New York.

Koch-Weser, M., and S. Guggenheim, eds. 2021. *Social Development in the World Bank. Essays in Honor of M. M. Cernea.* Cham, Switzerland: Springer.

Lakner, C., and B. Milanovic. 2016. "Global Income Distribution: From the Fall of the Berlin Wall to the Great Recession." *World Bank Economic Review* 30 (2): 203–32.

Latham, M. 2011. *The Right Kind of Revolution: Modernization, Development, and U.S. Foreign Policy from the Cold War to the Present.* Ithaca: Cornell University Press.

Lorenz-Spreen, P., L. Oswald, S. Lewandowsky, and R. Hertwig. 2022. "Digital Media and Democracy: A Systematic Review of Causal and Correlational Evidence Worldwide." *Nature Human Behavior*, November 7, 2022. https://doi.org/10.1038/s41562-022-01460-1.

McGuinn, J., E. Fries-Tersch, M. Jones, C. Crepaldi, M. Masaso, I. Kadarik, M. Samek-Lodovici, et al. 2020. "Social Sustainability—Concepts and Benchmarks." Think Tank European Parliament, Brussels.

McPhail, K., and S. Jacobs. 2003. "Social Assessment." Social Development Note 13, World Bank, Washington, DC.

Milanovic, B. 2016. *Global Inequality: A New Approach for the Age of Globalization.* Cambridge, MA: Harvard University Press.

Narayan, D. 2009. *Moving Out of Poverty.* Vol. 3: *The Promise of Empowerment and Democracy in India.* New York: Oxford University Press for the World Bank.

Narayan, D., R. Chambers, M. Shah, and P. Petesch. 2000. *Voices of the Poor: Crying Out for Change.* New York: Oxford University Press for the World Bank.

Narayan, D., R. Patel, K. Schafft, A. Rademacher, and S. Koch-Schulte. 2000. *Voices of the Poor: Can Anyone Hear Us?* New York: Oxford University Press for the World Bank.

Narayan, D., and P. Petesch. 2002. *Voices of the Poor: From Many Lands.* Washington, DC: World Bank and Oxford University Press.

Narayan, D., and P. Petesch. 2007. *Moving Out of Poverty.* Vol. 1: *Cross-Disciplinary Perspectives on Mobility.* New York: Oxford University Press for the World Bank.

Narayan, D., L. Pritchett, and S. Kapoor. 2009. *Moving Out of Poverty.* Vol. 2: *Success from the Bottom Up.* New York: Oxford University Press for the World Bank.

Østby, G. 2013. "Inequality and Political Violence: A Review of the Literature." *International Area Studies Review* 16 (2): 206–31.

Perry, J. 2021. "Trust in Public Institutions: Trends and Implications for Economic Security." Policy Brief 108, United Nations Department of Economic and Social Affairs, New York, June.

Pew Research Center. 2021. "Public Trust in Government: 1958–2021." Pew Research Center, Washington, DC, May 17, 2021. https://www.pewresearch.org/politics/2021/05/17/public-trust-in-government-1958-2021/.

Putnam, R. 1993. *Making Democracy Work.* Princeton, NJ: Princeton University Press.

Rajan, R. 2019. *The Third Pillar: How Markets and the State Leave the Community Behind.* New York: Penguin Press.

Rodrik, D. 1999. "Where Did All the Growth Go? External Shocks, Social Conflict, and Growth Collapses." *Journal of Economic Growth* 4 (4): 385–412.

Sánchez-Páramo, C., R. Hill, D. Gerszon Mahler, A. Narayan, and N. Yonzan. 2021. "COVID-19 Leaves a Legacy of Rising Poverty and Widening Inequality." *World Bank Let's Talk Development* (blog), October 7, 2021. https://blogs.worldbank.org/developmenttalk/Covid-19-Leaves-Legacy-Rising-Poverty-And-Widening-Inequality.

Schoch, M., C. Lakner, and M. Fleury. 2020. "Progress toward Ending Poverty Has Slowed." *World Bank Data* (blog), October 16, 2020. https://blogs.worldbank.org/opendata /progress-toward-ending-poverty-has-slowed.

Sedik, T. S., and R. Xu. 2020. "A Vicious Cycle: How Pandemics Lead to Economic Despair and Social Unrest." IMF Working Paper 2020/216, International Monetary Fund, Washington, DC.

Sen, A. 1999. *Development as Freedom*. New York: Random House.

Serageldin, I., and A. Steer, eds. 1994. *Making Development Sustainable: From Concepts to Action*. Washington, DC: World Bank.

Stewart, F. 2000. "Crisis Prevention: Tackling Horizontal Inequalities." *Oxford Development Studies* 28 (3): 245–62.

UNDESA (United Nations Department of Economic and Social Affairs). 2021. "Division for Inclusive Social Development." UNDESA, New York. https://www.un.org/development /desa/en/about/desa-divisions/social-policy.html.

United Nations. 1951. *Measures for the Development of Underdeveloped Countries*. New York: United Nations.

United Nations. 2012. "A Framework for Advancing Environmental and Social Sustainability in the United Nations System." United Nations, New York. https://sustainabledevelopment. un.org/content/documents/2738sustainabilityfinalweb-.pdf.

United Nations. 2015. *United Nations Global Assessment Report on Disaster Risk Reduction*. Geneva: UNDRR.

United Nations and World Bank. 2018. *Pathways for Peace: Inclusive Approaches to Preventing Violent Conflict*. Washington, DC: World Bank.

UNRISD (United Nations Research Institute for Social Development). 2016. *Policy Innovations for Transformative Change: Implementing the 2030 Agenda for Sustainable Development*. Geneva: UNRISD.

Uslaner, E. M., and M. Brown. 2003. "Inequality, Trust, and Civil Engagement." *American Politics Research* 33 (6): 868–94.

Verduyn, P., O. Ybarra, M. Résibois, J. Jonides, and E. Kross. 2017. "Do Social Network Sites Enhance or Undermine Subjective Well-Being? A Critical Review." *Social Issues and Policy Review* 11 (1): 274–302.

Vinnakota, R. 2017. "How Social Media Divides Us." *Aspen Institute Social Capital* (blog), January 24, 2017. https://www.aspeninstitute.org/blog-posts/social-media-divides-us/.

WHO (World Health Organization) and World Bank. 2011. *World Disability Report*. Geneva: WHO.

Wilkinson, R., and K. Pickett. 2010. *The Spirit Level: Why Equality Is Better for Everyone*. London: Penguin.

Woolcock, M., and D. Narayan. 2000. "Social Capital: Implications for Development Theory, Research, and Policy." *World Bank Research Observer* 15 (2): 225–49.

World Bank. 1996. *The World Bank Participation Sourcebook*. Washington, DC: World Bank.

World Bank. 2001. *World Development Report 2000/2001: Attacking Poverty*. Washington, DC: World Bank.

World Bank 2003a. *A User's Guide to Poverty and Social Impact Analysis.* Washington, DC: World Bank.

World Bank. 2003b. *World Development Report 2004: Making Services Work for Poor People.* Washington, DC: World Bank.

World Bank. 2005a. "Empowering People by Transforming Institutions: Social Development in World Bank Operations." Social Development Strategy Paper, World Bank, Washington, DC.

World Bank. 2005b. "Putting Social Development to Work for the Poor: An OED Review of World Bank Activities." Operations Evaluation Department, World Bank, Washington, DC.

World Bank. 2005c. *Tools for Institutional, Political, and Social Analysis (TIPS): A Sourcebook for Poverty and Social Impact Analysis (PSIA).* Washington, DC: World Bank.

World Bank. 2005d. *World Development Report 2006: Equity and Development.* Washington, DC: World Bank.

World Bank. 2007. *Strengthening World Bank Group Engagement on Governance and Anticorruption.* Washington, DC: World Bank.

World Bank. 2011a. "World Bank Social Development Strategy Mid-Cycle Implementation Progress Report." World Bank, Washington, DC.

World Bank. 2011b. *World Development Report 2011: Conflict, Security, and Development.* Washington, DC: World Bank.

World Bank. 2013. *The World Bank Group Goals: End Extreme Poverty and Promote Shared Prosperity.* Washington, DC: World Bank. https://www.worldbank.org/content/dam /Worldbank/document/WB-goals2013.pdf.

World Bank. 2014. *Strategic Framework for Mainstreaming Citizen Engagement in World Bank Group Operations.* Washington, DC: World Bank.

World Bank. 2016a. "Bank Directive Addressing Risks and Impacts on Disadvantaged or Vulnerable Individuals or Groups." World Bank, Washington, DC.

World Bank. 2016b. *Poverty and Shared Prosperity 2016: Taking on Inequality.* Washington, DC: World Bank.

World Bank. 2017a. *The World Bank Environmental and Social Framework.* Washington, DC: World Bank.

World Bank. 2017b. *World Development Report 2017: Governance and the Law.* Washington, DC: World Bank.

World Bank. 2020a. *Additions to IDA Resources: Nineteenth Replenishment—Ten Years to 2030: Growth, People, Resilience.* Washington, DC: World Bank.

World Bank. 2020b. *The Human Capital Index 2020 Update: Human Capital in the Time of COVID-19.* Washington, DC: World Bank.

World Bank. 2020c. *Poverty and Shared Prosperity 2020: Reversals of Fortune.* Washington, DC: World Bank.

World Bank. 2020d. "Saving Lives, Scaling-up Impact, and Getting Back on Track: World Bank Group COVID-19 Crisis Response Approach Paper." World Bank, Washington, DC.

World Bank. 2021a. *Green Resilient and Inclusive Development.* Washington, DC: World Bank.

World Bank. 2021b. "Social Cohesion and Resilience." World Bank, Washington, DC. https://www.worldbank.org/en/topic/social-cohesion-and-resilience#1.

World Bank. 2022a. *Fragility, Conflict, and Violence in Middle-Income Countries*. Washington, DC: World Bank.

World Bank. 2022b. *IDA20—Building Back Better from the Crisis: Toward a Green, Resilient, and Inclusive Future*. Washington, DC: World Bank.

World Bank. 2022c. Poverty and Inequality Platform (database). World Bank, Washington, DC.

World Bank. 2022d. *Poverty and Shared Prosperity 2022: Correcting Course*. Washington, DC: World Bank.

World Bank. 2022e. Social Sustainability Global Database 2022. World Bank, Washington, DC.

World Commission on Environment and Development. 1987. *Our Common Future*. Oxford: Oxford University Press.

Yonzan, N., A. Cojocaru, C. Lakner, D. Gerszon Mahler, and A. Narayan. 2022. "The Impact of COVID-19 on Poverty and Inequality: Evidence from Phone Surveys." *World Bank Data* (blog), January 18, 2022. https://blogs.worldbank.org/opendata/impact-covid-19-poverty-and-inequality-evidence-phone-surveys.

Yonzan, N., C. Lakner, and D. Gerszon Mahler. 2021. "Is COVID-19 Increasing Global Inequality?" *World Bank Data* (blog), October 7, 2021. https://blogs.worldbank.org/opendata/covid-19-increasing-global-inequality.

What Is Social Sustainability?

Overview and Literature Review

By its nature, social sustainability is a more elusive and complex concept than environmental or economic sustainability. When rain forests are burned down and replaced with monocrop agriculture, it is clear what has been lost; when hyperinflation wipes out entire generations of wealth, the costs of economic mismanagement are obvious and calculable. It is less clear what sustainability looks like when people and their communities are at stake: when severe inequality leads to social unrest, when marginalized groups are excluded from development planning, or when infrastructure projects destroy the communities of rural indigenous peoples, forcing them to move to cities. The vignettes in box 2.1 illustrate the nature of social sustainability and the distinctive types of challenges that failing to address it can pose for advancing inclusive development.

As noted in the previous chapter, the social dimension of development has often served as the overlooked third pillar of sustainability—an elusive goal reflecting complex sociocultural factors that are difficult to analyze empirically and fraught with normative concepts. In recent years, however, a gradual shift in perspective has elevated the importance of social factors, seeing them not just as secondary complements but as integral to the development process itself—important in their own right and inextricably linked to broader development goals. Academics and practitioners alike are increasingly seeing the three pillars of sustainability as interdependent: a lack of economic or environmental sustainability can stoke social tensions and exacerbate other social challenges, just as the presence of economic or environmental sustainability can enable and support social sustainability—and vice versa (Becker, Jahn, and Stiess 1999; Purvis, Mao, and Robinson 2019; World Bank 2013c).

Box 2.1
Vignettes to Illustrate Social Sustainability

The following four vignettes explore three interrelated questions: What does socially sustainable development mean? Why does it matter? And why is it often so challenging to achieve in practice? Each vignette highlights and connects to the key features and components of social sustainability, as defined and described later in this chapter.

- A new government in a lower-middle-income country in Latin America with a long history of conflict, corruption, social exclusion, and civil unrest achieves important reforms that result in large donor programs followed by a few years of solid economic growth, poverty reduction, and political stability. Suddenly, a series of corruption scandals leads to friction between the largest group (to which most political elites have traditionally belonged) and more marginalized groups, which have historically lacked representation in government. Isolated incidents of violence lead to protests that consume the capital, with clashes between protesters from the marginalized groups and heavy-handed police from the dominant group. Efforts at national dialogue fail, the protests spread, and the government doubles down—activating paramilitary police, blocking streets in large cities, harassing opposition members, and intimidating the media and civil society. Assistance from development organizations is put on hold, and the economy contracts, with millions pushed into poverty and a protracted political crisis that takes years to resolve.

- In an historic election, a young presidential candidate in a lower-income African country unseats the incumbent (who had been in power for decades) by appealing to the rural vote and campaigning on a commitment to improve living conditions for poor citizens in rural areas. Once in office, he launches a US$900 million rural investment program focused on transport, water, agriculture, and health infrastructure. Concerned that working through the national and regional bureaucracy would be too slow, the president's office recruits a large multinational company to deliver projects directly and quickly to communities according to a central plan, with all procurement done through large international bids. While the program delivers quick results, the process does not prioritize coordination with line ministries, subnational governments, or local communities and fails to budget for the costs of long-term maintenance. Moreover, the centrally planned projects do not fully align with the priorities and needs of many communities, raising questions about the sustainability of these important investments.

- Outside the capital in a South Pacific middle-income country, a village chief reflects on the changes brought by "development"—a word that has no direct counterpart in his local language but that carries tremendous power in his fast-growing, fast-changing country. On the one hand, as chair of the prestigious regional development board, he is proud to show off progress in his district—two

(continued)

Box 2.1
Continued

primary schools, a high school, and a hospital, where his two wives gave birth to five daughters (unlike their poorer neighbors, who give birth at home). On the other hand, since he (like most village elders) is illiterate, his educated daughters treat him as simple or even foolish. The village's youth no longer respect the elders' pronouncements, religious traditions, or local court customs and complain that women are not allowed on the village council. He dreads the day when his daughters announce that they want a "better life" and leave the village for good to "make something of themselves," in the process raising children who do not speak his language, know nothing of their heritage, and will not care for him in his sunset years. He often has to reassure anxious donors of his commitment to gender equity, but many on the village council do not believe in it; personally, he still longs for a son. He feels blessed to have experienced the benefits of "development" but often mourns what is being lost.

■ After resettling in the United States as a child refugee from a poor Central Asian country, getting a master's in business administration, and becoming wealthy at a tech company, a young man returns home to give back to his community. Having learned about the country's untapped agricultural potential, he decides to establish an agribusiness company that distributes hybrid seeds, fertilizers, and modern farming equipment and connects small-scale farms to domestic and regional export markets. The venture initially meets with resistance from individual farmers, who prefer traditional agricultural methods and resent the young new arrival, who speaks with a thick accent and does not practice the local religion devoutly. When local chiefs and regional administrators hear of the venture, they resent that their approval was not sought and insist on overseeing a new series of negotiations, in the process taking a cut of the proceeds. A few livestock die after eating fertilizer, which leads to village-level court cases across the region. When trying to set up export arrangements in neighboring countries, the entrepreneur has few connections, does not understand local business norms, and gets bogged down jumping through bureaucratic hoops and paying bribes. After three years of failed starts, he returns to the United States.

These shifting perspectives are reflected in the growing importance of social sustainability and its key features over time. Figure 2.1, for example, shows the growth in prevalence of the three pillars of sustainability between 1985 and 2019, as measured by their appearance across millions of English-language books digitized in the Google Books database (Michel et al. 2011). The prevalence of "environmental sustainability" in the database steadily increases starting in the late 1980s, and by 2019 the term is more prevalent than the other two pillars combined. "Economic sustainability" peaks in prevalence in the early 2000s—paired here with "debt sustainability," which spikes in prevalence after the debt crises of the 1980s and

Figure 2.1 Appearance of Key Types of "Sustainability" in Published English Books, 1985–2019

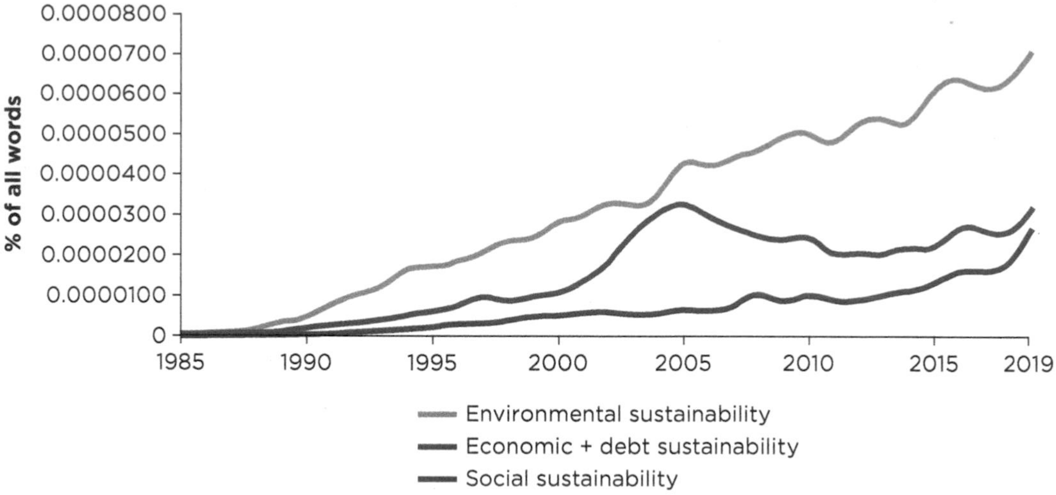

Source: Analysis using Google Ngram Viewer.

1990s—and only begins to rise again starting in the early 2010s. While "social sustainability" is still the least prevalent pillar in the Google Books database, its prevalence has accelerated in recent years, and by 2019 it has nearly caught up with economic sustainability.

As the concept has become more prevalent in recent decades, a limited but growing academic literature on social sustainability has emerged. Previously, the broader literature on sustainability often treated the social pillar as secondary to (see, for instance, Daly 1996; Kunz 2006; Locke and Dearden 2005; Partridge 2005; Vifell and Soneryd 2012) or subsumed within (Sachs 1999) environmental and economic sustainability, but a more contemporary view is that no pillar can be understood in isolation and that all three must be considered relationally. The social sustainability literature spans multiple academic and professional disciplines, with diverse applications, definitions, and connotations across the public and private sectors and the global, national, and local levels (see, for instance, Åhman 2013; Boström 2012; Boyer et al. 2016; Colantonio 2007, 2009; Eizenberg and Jabareen 2017; Griessler and Littig 2005; James et al. 2013; Koning 2001; McKenzie 2004; Sachs 1999). As a result, social sustainability emerges from the literature as a highly dynamic concept—neither absolute nor constant, but subject to change, context, and scale (Murphy 2012; Vallance, Perkins, and Dixon 2011). Nonetheless, at a high level, a certain set of broad, recurring themes emerge.

The social sustainability literature is united by an emphasis on connected communities, well-being for all, durability or resilience over time, and meaningful participation and engagement (Dempsey et al. 2011). Connected communities manifest in the literature with a frequent focus on social capital, social cohesion, and themes of identity and sense of place (Cuthill 2010; Dempsey et al. 2011; Eizenberg and Jabareen 2017; Fiszbein, Kanbur, and Yemtsov 2014; Glasson and Wood 2009; Griessler and Littig 2005; Lehtonen 2004; Schlosberg 2007; Siisiäinen 2003; Weingaertner and Moberg 2014; for a recent literature review, see Ballet, Bazin, and Mahieu 2020). Well-being for all is articulated as both a positive value (basic needs, capabilities, quality of life, equality of opportunity) and an absence of discriminatory practices (racism, xenophobia, ageism) that hinder individuals' meaningful participation in economic, social, and political life (Pierson 2002; Ratcliffe 2000). Durability and resilience focus on the stability and security of communities over time. Some literature characterizes these principles as safety, resembling but going further than resilience by emphasizing reduced vulnerability *before* shocks occur (Adger 2000). Meaningful participation and engagement reinforce the importance of connected and cohesive communities, underscoring the value of a strong social contract.

These core strands combine in the literature to describe the arrangements that enable individuals, groups, and societies to exist together in harmony through time. Given the intertemporal and future focus of social sustainability, the literature frequently connects current generations to future ones and links historical events and processes—such as chronic injustice or inclusion—with present and future considerations. Some scholars consider social sustainability to be about the process itself of moving toward a just society for current and future generations (Castillo et al. 2007; Partridge 2005). At the local level, social sustainability is conceived as a process for creating sustainable and thriving places that promote well-being, as defined by the people who live and work there (Woodcraft et al. 2011). Sustainable communities constitute a setting for long-term human activity and interaction that is equitable, inclusive, and sustainable in the broad sense of the term (including all three pillars), thus delivering democratic, diverse, and connected communities (Bramley and Power 2009). From this perspective, sustainability in communities is associated with social capital and social cohesion, as concepts that encompass social networks, norms of reciprocity, and features of social organization at that scale.

This book groups and refines these aspects of the literature to put forward a definition of social sustainability and a conceptual framework centered on four key components: social cohesion, inclusion, resilience, and "process legitimacy"—a relatively new concept that focuses on *how* policies and programs are designed and implemented.

Definitions and Conceptual Framework

As noted in chapter 1, this book uses the United Nations Brundtland Commission definition of sustainability and refers to "social" in its broadest sense: the relationships between individuals and groups and the diverse characteristics that shape those relationships—norms, values, shared identity, culture, and institutions (for early World Bank efforts to define "social" and "social development," see Davis 2004; World Bank 2005a, 2005b). As such, the book is concerned not just with the "social sectors" of development (health, education, social protection, other development efforts to improve people's welfare) or "social policies" (progressive taxation, safety nets, universal health care, other policies to address social challenges), but with how development interacts with, influences, and is influenced by a broad set of social factors and how those dynamics can support improved welfare overall.

The following definition and conceptual framework for social sustainability are grounded in the existing academic literature—both the recent literature on social sustainability and the comparatively wider literature on its constituent elements—but are also aligned with the World Bank's institutional objectives, strategic priorities, and operational frameworks, while seeking broader relevance across the development community:

Social sustainability increases when more people feel part of the development process and believe that they and their descendants will benefit from it.

Communities and societies that are more socially sustainable are more willing and able to work together to overcome challenges, deliver public goods, and allocate scarce resources in ways perceived to be legitimate and fair so that all people may thrive over time.

This definition emphasizes the aspirational nature of social sustainability: it is not a binary concept but exists on a spectrum, meant to inspire continued efforts and progress toward ever greater levels of social sustainability. Indeed, no community or society has ever achieved social sustainability absolutely and permanently. The definition, its constituent elements, and the conceptual framework are also parsimonious and intuitive by design, intended to demonstrate clearly the core components and relationships that support social sustainability. This book does not attempt to model all of the factors and dynamics that engender or constrain social sustainability or its components. Given the quantity and complexity of the issues involved (culture, norms, values, beliefs, identity) and how dramatically these issues can vary across contexts, designing such a model would be extremely complicated—if even possible—although recent efforts in the economics literature have made important initial attempts.[1] Nonetheless, while the definition emphasizes subjectivity (how people feel, what they believe), the book is also concerned with concrete, measurable objectives, such as the World Bank's new Social Sustainability Global Database (SSGD).

Unpacking the definition reveals four critical dimensions or components of social sustainability. First, it highlights *social cohesion*, linked to a sense of shared purpose and trust, which allows communities and groups to work together toward a common good and respond to challenges such as climate change, pandemics, and natural disasters in a way that avoids conflict and war and drives real solutions and sustainable compromises. Second, it underscores *inclusion*, defined as access to markets and services as well as political, social, and cultural spaces for all individuals and groups, which allows all members of society to thrive. Third, it prioritizes *resilience*, including the ability, capacity, and flexibility to avoid conflicts (including interpersonal violence) and to withstand, bounce back from, or absorb the impacts of exogenous shocks over time. Fourth, it emphasizes *outcomes* but also the *processes* by which policies or programs are designed and implemented—the "what" of development but also the "how"—highlighting the need for *process legitimacy* within the context of existing norms and values, such that the decisions made and carried out are considered fair, credible, and acceptable by all members and groups.[2]

Figure 2.2 presents a conceptual framework for the four components of social sustainability and their interlinking dynamics. The left side of the framework illustrates that a given community or society (that is, "context") has baseline levels of inclusion, cohesion, and resilience. The middle part shows that how decisions are made and implemented (that is, "process legitimacy") can result in policies and programs that promote (or not) inclusion, cohesion, and resilience. As such, the effects of these policies and programs (that is, "outcomes") can influence (positively or negatively) future levels of social sustainability, as indicated by the right side of the framework. In other words, socially sustainable development occurs when inclusion, cohesion, and resilience are enhanced gradually over time. In the hypothetical example presented in figure 2.2, the context

Figure 2.2 Conceptual Framework of Social Sustainability

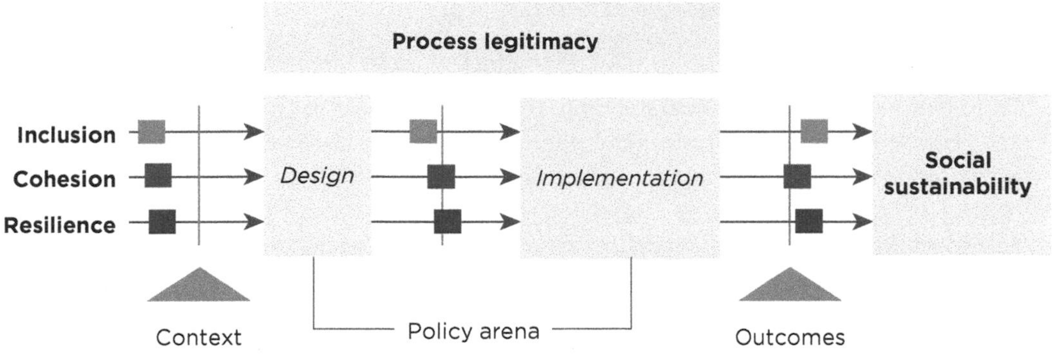

Source: World Bank.

has low baseline levels of social sustainability, but the programs and policies (and how they are designed and implemented) improve all three components.

Conceptually, the framework functions within the "policy arena," a concept developed by the 2017 *World Development Report* on governance and the law (World Bank 2017). Policy arena refers to the hypothetical forums in a given community, country, region, or global body where resources are allocated, goals are set, and decisions are made. The policy arena involves interactions between individuals, government, and stakeholder groups, often with varying degrees of power and influence and typically involving debate, negotiation, and compromise, with the potential for disagreement, tensions, or even conflict (World Bank 2017). In the framework, the design and implementation of policies and programs (and whether this process embodies inclusion, cohesion, and resilience) reflect decisions made in the policy arena. The book contends that if there is process legitimacy in a policy area—if goals are set and decisions are made in ways that are considered fair, credible, and acceptable by all members and groups in a given context—then the resulting policies and programs that get designed and implemented will enhance inclusion, cohesion, and resilience over time. In other words, inclusion, cohesion, and resilience interact and combine through process legitimacy to produce social sustainability—a broad quality that is greater than the sum of its parts and that supports and reinforces its own constituent elements.

In spite of the framework's simplicity, the interactions between its various components are, in practice, highly complex, nonlinear, and contextual, reflecting the rich dynamics at play in any given community or society at any given time. Moreover, the components operate across all levels of society, from the individual and household levels to the national and regional or transnational levels. Social sustainability and its components are important objectives in and of themselves—they are each, on their own, constituent elements of the ends of development—while also being important means or drivers. They underscore that development is not only about economic growth, although growth is very important; it is also about the social elements of life, which matter very much to people. These elements can, in turn, support broader sustainable development goals, including growth, poverty reduction, and shared prosperity. Box 2.2 highlights recent World Bank efforts to assess these links empirically, after which each component and its contributions to development are explored in turn.

Box 2.2
Social Sustainability Global Database

To advance the empirical understanding of social sustainability, its core components, and their links to key developmental outcomes, a global database was constructed with composite indexes for social cohesion, inclusion, resilience, and process legitimacy. The Social Sustainability Global Database (SSGD) comprises 71 indicators across 236 countries and territories, accounting for 98.7 percent of the global population and covering the period 2016–20.[a] The cohesion index, for example, includes indicators measuring trust at the community level and between citizens and national institutions. The inclusion index draws on variables measuring overall access to basic services and markets as well as female political participation. The resilience index is a composite of indicators examining access to assets, financial markets, and savings as well as the extent to which people have multiple sources of income. Finally, the process legitimacy index tracks indicators measuring the rule of law, access to justice, and government effectiveness. Annex 2A provides a full list of the indicators for each index and details on their construction. Indicators were chosen based on three criteria: they must (a) be unidimensional variables, (b) measure outcomes rather than inputs, and (c) reflect objective data or data directly from vulnerable groups.

The SSGD can be used to create country-level profiles and benchmarks between countries. Figure B2.2.1, panel a, for example, shows a profile of Chile using four indicators of social cohesion, illustrating that Chile's levels of interpersonal trust, confidence in government, confidence in police, and tolerance for minorities are on par with regional averages in Latin America and the Caribbean but systematically lag global averages. Figure B2.2.1, panel b, benchmarks the performance of Sub-Saharan African countries on a single indicator of inclusion: the gap between men's access to a bank account compared to women's, showing that Tunisia has the largest gap (more than 20 percentage points), while Madagascar and Namibia have almost no gap.

The database can also be used to conduct simple analytics. The scatterplot in figure B2.2.2 reflects cross-country analysis showing that process legitimacy is broadly correlated with gross domestic product (GDP) per capita but that broad dispersion exists within income levels, suggesting that other factors matter for process legitimacy. For instance, exposure to conflict could play a role; B2.2.2 shows that relatively stable countries like Ghana and Senegal are stronger on process legitimacy than countries with recent civil conflicts, such as Sierra Leone (a poorer country) or even Lebanon and the Philippines, which both have higher per capita GDP than Ghana or Senegal, while Cambodia, which underwent a genocide in the late 1970s, is weakest on process legitimacy.

More work is needed to address measurement challenges, data limitations, and methodological issues (as discussed later in this chapter and the next). Nonetheless, this research represents an important step forward in the empirical understanding

(continued)

Box 2.2
Continued

Figure B2.2.1 Indicators of Social Cohesion and Inclusion

a. Chile's social cohesion profile and regional and world benchmarking

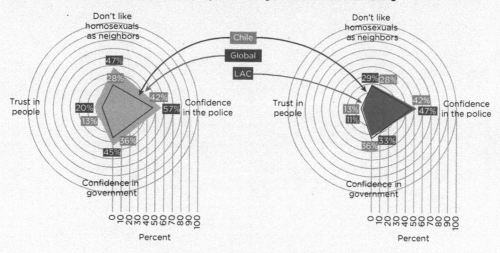

b. Gender gaps in access to a bank account in Sub-Saharan Africa

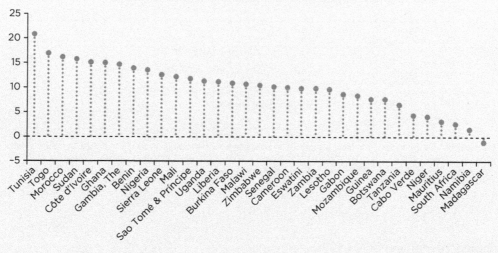

Sources: Cuesta, Madrigal, and Pecorari 2022; World Bank 2022b.
Note: On panel b, a positive number indicates that men's ownership of a bank account exceeds that of women.
LAC = Latin America and the Caribbean.

of social sustainability. For the SSGD, along with its codebook and a dashboard, see World Bank (2022b, 2022c). A companion article to this book documents the construction of the database and some of its applications (Cuesta, Madrigal, and Pecorari 2022).

(continued)

Box 2.2
Continued

Figure B2.2.2 Understanding Countries' Income Levels and Process Legitimacy

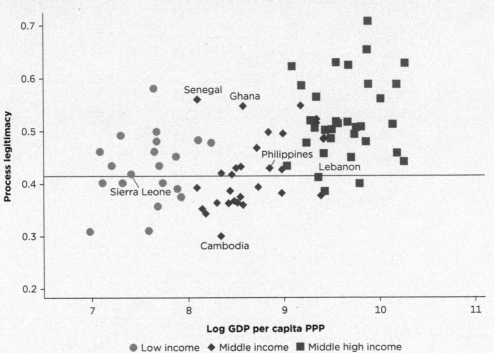

Sources: Cuesta, Madrigal, and Pecorari 2022; World Bank 2022b.
Note: GDP = gross domestic product; PPP = purchasing power parity.

a. Data sources include harmonized living standards and income and expenditure household surveys from the World Bank's Global Monitoring Database; regional databases such as the Afrobarometer, Arab Barometer, Asian Barometer, and Latinobarometer; and global databases such as the World Values Survey, World Development Indicators, the Varieties of Democracy Project, Worldwide Governance Indicators, the Armed Conflict Location and Event Data Project, and the World Justice Project.

Social Cohesion

Social cohesion is a sense of shared purpose, trust, and willingness to cooperate among members of a given group, between members of different groups, and between people and the state for a common good.

Social cohesion cultivates communities that allow people to trust each other and cooperate on behalf of a common purpose, establishing the basic social foundations for peace and prosperity (Chatterjee, Gassier, and Myint 2022; Larsen 2013). This relationship is true for every society—rich or poor, peaceful or conflict-affected, regardless of norms, politics, or system of government. Different forms of cohesion matter at different levels and according to which groups are working together. Cohesion between individuals in a community—which is necessary to set shared priorities, undertake collective action, and manage local disputes—is referred to as *bonding* cohesion.[3] Cohesion (and conflict management, when necessary) across different groups—whether between villages and regions or between broader identity collectives, such as political or religious groups—is referred to as *bridging* cohesion. Bonding and bridging are both "horizontal" forms of cohesion, but "vertical" relations between citizens and institutions in power are also critical for peaceful development to flourish and are referred to as *linking* cohesion (Loewe, Zing, and Houdret 2021). Linking cohesion is an important input for establishing and protecting a strong social contract, as it influences the citizen-state bargaining process, the resulting political settlement, and the ultimate social outcomes (Coutier et al. 2021).

While the concept of social cohesion has garnered increased attention in recent years, its roots[4] date back to French sociologist Émile Durkheim, who in the late 19th century defined it as interdependence between individuals characterized by strong social bonds and the absence of latent social conflict (Durkheim 1897). Since then, a vast literature has conceived of it in various ways: as an intragroup characteristic dependent on size, intimacy, social organization, rewards, and the roles of reciprocity and trust (Lewin 1946; Lott and Lott 1966); as an ongoing process, offering mechanisms to resolve conflict (Beauvais and Jenson 2002; Maxwell 1996); and as a society's capacity to ensure the well-being of its members, avoid marginalization, and minimize disparities (OECD 2011). Recent theoretical developments have considered societywide issues related to cohesion, while others have focused on local dynamics. The literature stresses different facets of cohesion: trust, shared identities, pressures to conform, and other mechanisms through which norms are enforced. Nonetheless, a consensus is emerging that cohesion is associated with greater capacity for effective collective action—with high levels of trust, openness toward "outgroups," and a shared perception that public institutions are legitimate.

More recently, amid rising inequality and social tensions around the world, scholars and practitioners are increasingly focused on the role that cohesion plays in development—as both a means and an end, important for strengthening the social contract, avoiding conflict, and promoting prosperity, but also in its own right (OECD 2011). As mentioned in chapter 1, an extensive literature has shown links between inequality and diminished cohesion. Building and bolstering cohesion are considered particularly vital for addressing fragility, conflict, and violence: relationships in which groups have an incentive to cooperate (or at least coexist) without violence form the basis for effective institutions and pathways toward sustainable peace (Marc et al. 2012). In 2011 the Bank's 2011 *World Development Report* on conflict, security, and development underscored that violence weakens cohesion within and between communities, that building cohesion is both a bulwark against violence and a requisite for postconflict development, and that breakdowns in cohesion can increase vulnerability to criminal networks and gangs (World Bank 2011). Likewise, a 2018 joint United Nations–World Bank study put cohesion at the center of efforts to prevent violence and solidify peace (United Nations and World Bank 2018), and the Bank's Fragility, Conflict, and

Violence Strategy in 2020 emphasized cohesion as both a means to preventing and building back from conflict and as a valuable end in itself (World Bank 2020).[5]

There is compelling evidence that cohesion has positive impacts on development, particularly in contexts of fragility, conflict, and violence. Evidence suggests that cohesion may play a significant role in preventing conflict and averting its costs and that, in times of crisis, the strength of cohesion matters (Norton and de Haan 2012; see also OECD 2011). Conflict destroys trust, fosters intergroup divisions, weakens the social contract, and increases the probability of criminality and future conflict, whereas cohesive societies are less susceptible to the influence of armed or criminal groups (Besley and Reynal-Querol 2014; Cassar, Grosjean, and Whitt 2013; Dell and Querubin 2017; Fearon and Laitin 2012; Rohner 2018; Rohner, Thoenig, and Zilibotti 2013).[6] Cohesion also offers broad development benefits, facilitating beneficial change processes and enhancing resilience for many types of crises (Aldrich 2012; Gates 2002; Migdal 2001; Staniland 2014; Townshend et al. 2015). During COVID-19, for example, people in regions of Europe that have high levels of trust were more likely than people in low-trust regions to limit their mobility in response to public pandemic prevention measures (Bargain and Aminjonov 2020). Low levels of cohesion, by contrast, are linked with social discontent, political instability, and social tensions such as strikes, demonstrations, riots, and unrest (Alesina and Perotti 1996; Esteban and Ray 2011). While cohesion is generally a positive feature, it can also be associated with negative consequences should it lead to the exclusion of certain groups (such as ethnic minorities or those with a different sexual orientation) or when it is used to build support for violent action toward a particular group (Chatterjee, Gassier, and Myint 2022).

Emerging rigorous evidence from randomized control trials, meta-analyses, and systematic reviews also shows the potential impacts of efforts to strengthen cohesion. For example, an impact evaluation of a community and local development (CLD) program in the Kyrgyz Republic found that it increased the community's sense of unity, cooperation, and perceptions of local governance and educational services, with weaker but still positive effects on addressing entrenched perceptions, changing attitudes, and building trust (Esenaliev et al. 2018). Likewise, a systematic review of peace-building interventions aimed at promoting cohesion in low- and middle-income countries experiencing fragility, conflict, and violence (intergroup dialogues, workshop-based peace education) found positive effects on trust, sense of belonging, willingness to participate and help, and acceptance of diversity, although the effects were small (Sonnenfeld et al. 2021). The findings suggest that such interventions alone may be insufficient unless broader challenges and structural or contextual barriers to cohesion are addressed.

The scatterplots in figure 2.3 show the results of SSGD analysis for the cohesion index, which includes indicators that measure trust, confidence, and participation in government and violence (see box 2.2 and annex 2A). The analysis suggests that cohesion is associated with lower poverty levels, higher gross domestic product (GDP) per capita, lower inequality, stronger human capital accumulation, and greater human development.[7] The strength of these correlations suggests that, in particular, more cohesive societies have lower poverty and are more likely to deliver learning and health outcomes.

Figure 2.3 Association between Social Cohesion and Poverty, Income, Inequality, Human Capital, and Human Development

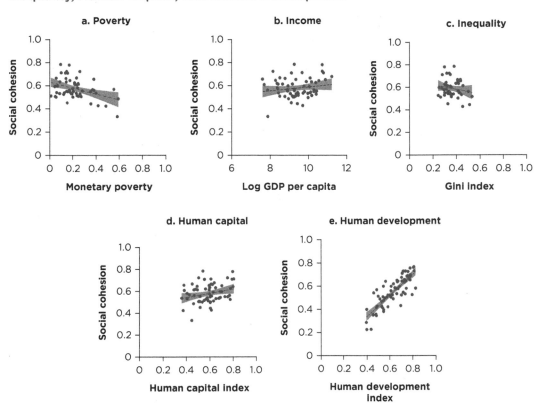

Sources: Cuesta, Madrigal, and Pecorari 2022; World Bank 2022b.
Note: GDP = gross domestic product.

Inclusion

Inclusive societies are those where everyone has access to basic services and markets as well as to political, social, and cultural spaces in order to participate in society with agency and live with dignity.

Historically, the term "social inclusion" was motivated by the observation that some groups in society face constraints to socioeconomic participation.[8] Over the past decade, however, the concept has increasingly been adapted to the context of development. During the early 2010s, the Millennium Development Goals drew to a close amid recognition that development investments had not addressed some of the deepest pockets of poverty and had produced unequal benefits across and within countries. In 2013 the World Bank report *Inclusion Matters* defined inclusion as "the process of improving the ability, opportunity, and dignity of people, disadvantaged on the basis of their identity, to take part in society," emphasizing that exclusion goes beyond poverty or even inequality (World Bank 2013b, 4). As noted in chapter 1, the 2015 Sustainable Development Goals encapsulated the core motivation of inclusion in their rallying cry to "leave no one behind." Since 2020, inclusion has gained traction as part of a call for "inclusive recovery" from the COVID-19 pandemic.

The exclusion of groups or individuals from society can take many forms and be driven by many factors, such as gender, age, location, occupation, race, ethnicity, religion, citizenship status, disability, and sexual orientation and gender identity. Exclusion is sustained through a range of formal and informal norms, behaviors, and institutions. For instance, laws can stipulate a lower status for some groups or afford fewer rights to certain members of society, such as laws that restrict women's participation in labor markets or land rights that constrain ownership by women or people of certain ethnic groups. Likewise, informal norms and behaviors can relegate some groups to inferior status, such as stereotypes of persons with a disability or a different sexual orientation, which can limit their access to and benefits from education, health care, or other services.

Exclusion can have significant costs, which have been estimated in various ways. At the individual level, the most commonly used measures of exclusion are wages, lifetime earnings, education, and employment outcomes (Buehren, Gonzalez, and Copley 2019; Lamichhane and Sawada 2013; Male and Wodon 2017; Turner 2013; Wodon and de la Brière 2018; World Bank 2014). Lower earnings or employment outcomes can be driven by human capital endowments, which may be due to prior disadvantage in education but also to discrimination in hiring or in the workplace (Buckup 2009; Lamichhane and Sawada 2013; Morgon Banks and Polack 2015). Discrimination, which typically perpetuates patterns of exclusion, can also have immediate negative impacts on physical and mental health of those affected, creating costs for individuals and society at-large (Lereya et al. 2015).

At the national level, the economic costs of exclusion can be calculated in terms of lost GDP and human capital wealth. Actual or perceived exclusion can lead to individuals opting out of education, health care, or labor markets, with costs to individuals and the economy (Burns 2012; World Bank 2013b, 2018a). For countries that rank in the bottom half of gender inequality, the economic costs of gender gaps in the labor force are equivalent to around one-third of GDP (Ostry et al. 2018). Closely related to studies that seek to quantify the costs of exclusion are studies on inequality of opportunity driven by differences at birth, such as gender, ethnicity, or parental background. Evidence suggests that inequality of opportunity is particularly detrimental to growth (Brunori, Ferreira, and Peragine 2013; Ferreira et al. 2013; Marrero and Rodriguez 2013). In the most extreme cases, exclusion can result in accumulated grievances that undermine social cohesion and lead to conflict (United Nations and World Bank 2018). Exclusionary policies and behaviors have also been identified as important causal factors in a relapse of violence (Call 2012).

Conversely, promoting inclusion can generate significant development benefits. One study, for example, attributed 25 percent of the productivity increases in the United States between 1960 and 2010 to improved allocation of talent in the labor market, largely due to the reduction of discrimination against women and Black people (Hsieh et al. 2013). Likewise, the potential economic benefit from achieving gender parity in labor markets worldwide is estimated to be as much as US$28 trillion over a decade (Madgavkar, Ellingrud, and Krishnan 2016), while eliminating exclusion based on sexual orientation or transgender identity could increase global output by as much as 1 percent (Badgett 2020). Such benefits accrue most notably to the excluded individuals and groups, but they also help society as a whole. Inclusion is often accompanied by better outcomes in terms of income, poverty reduction, and human capital endowments (Freire et al. 2020; World Bank 2013b, 2020). More equal access to basic services and markets as well as political, social, and cultural spaces can lead to more efficient human capital accumulation, thriving entrepreneurship (Rauch 1991), and better access to credit and insurance products—all boosting productivity (World Bank 2006). Countries that implement policies to foster the participation and political engagement of excluded groups have been shown to experience less conflict (Min et al. 2017; see also Fearon 2010; Fearon and Laitin 2012; United Nations and World Bank 2018).

The scatterplots in figure 2.4 show the results of SSGD analysis for the inclusion index, which consists of indicators that measure labor force participation, financial inclusion, access to public services, and gender equality (see box 2.1 and annex 2A; World Bank 2022b, 2022c). The analysis suggests that inclusion is strongly associated with lower poverty levels, higher GDP per capita, stronger human capital accumulation, and greater human development. It is also linked with inequality, although the association is weaker.[9]

Figure 2.4 Association between Social Inclusion and Poverty, Income, Inequality, Human Capital, and Human Development

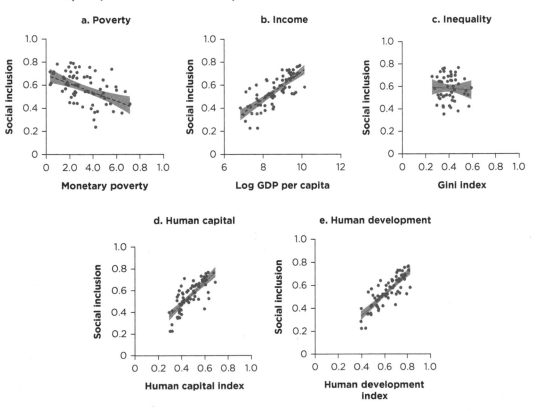

Sources: Cuesta, Madrigal, and Pecorari 2022; World Bank 2022b.
Note: GDP = gross domestic product.

Rigorous evidence has also shown the positive impacts of inclusion. For example, a series of impact evaluations in Indonesia found that a community block grant program targeting excluded geographic regions had large, sustained, and positive effects on health and education outcomes (World Bank 2018b). Likewise, another Indonesian program to improve the economic and social integration of at-risk youth—by establishing livelihood alternatives to illegal logging—was found to improve economic and environmental outcomes while also increasing participation in community groups and offering subjective benefits in terms of well-being, life satisfaction, and attitudes toward the potential benefits of environmental reforms (Paler et al. 2015). These results align with a review of Bank-financed CLD projects analyzed in impact evaluations, academic studies, project audit reports, monitoring reports, and publicly available internal evaluations building on previous similar studies (Wong 2022; previous studies include Casey 2018; Mansuri and Rao 2013; Wong and Guggenheim 2018). The review found that CLD projects can boost health, education, and economic welfare outcomes, but that their most consistent positive impacts are in delivering basic services (access, use, quality), reaching previously excluded groups (lagging regions, conflict-affected areas, vulnerable households), and increasing participation and voice (including among vulnerable groups) in the village development process.

Resilience

Resilient societies are those where everyone, including poor and marginalized groups, are safe and can withstand shocks and protect the integrity of their culture.

Resilience is a broad concept with applications across several domains in the sciences and social sciences, including engineering, ecology, psychology, disaster response, and sustainable development. In its most general sense, resilience is a system's capacity to persist amid shocks, adapt to future challenges, and transform in ways that enhance its functioning (Keck and Sakdapolrak 2013). In the social sphere, resilience is determined by the capacities of an individual, household, community, or entire society to prepare for and cope with shocks (Bowen et al. 2020; Folke 2016). Shocks can be categorized as either idiosyncratic (specific to individuals or households, such as a job loss or health crisis) or systemic (affecting large groups of people, such as food shortages, natural disasters, or violent conflict) (World Bank 2013a). They can be external (trade shocks) or internal (disease) as well as rapid (natural disasters), gradually worsening (soil degradation), or continuous (poverty, child labor, gender-based violence). More resilient households, communities, and societies are able to recover faster, regaining their well-being and wealth more efficiently after a shock or crisis. This definition builds on prior work (Chambers and Conway 1991) emphasizing that one's livelihood is sustainable when one can cope and recover from stress and shocks, maintain or enhance one's capabilities and assets, and provide sustainable livelihood opportunities for the next generation.

While resilience is important for all people, it is particularly critical for poor and marginalized groups—who are exposed to hazards more often, lose more as a share of their wealth when hit, and have fewer support systems (Hallegatte et al. 2017). Resilience at one level of a community or society does not necessarily improve resilience at another, and vulnerabilities are often distributed unequally (Cannon 2008; Glavovic, Scheyvens, and Overton 2003). Depending on social norms, for instance, women, youth, and the elderly might be more exposed or less resilient to various risks (Ajibade, McBean, and Bezner-Kern 2013; Barrett et al. 2021; Jordan 2015, 2019). For billions of poor and marginalized people around the world, lack of or weak resilience can have grave consequences when trouble strikes.

To manage risks, people rely on formal and informal strategies that can be divided into three key types of resilience. *Risk reduction and mitigation* are preparation measures that aim to lower the probability that shocks will occur or to mitigate their negative impacts if they do (Obrist 2010; World Bank 2001, 2013a). Such measures can be at the individual or household level (digging wells, diversifying assets, getting vaccinated), the community level (local informal flood infrastructure, community insurance schemes, village public health campaigns), and the national, transnational, or global level (building dams, establishing social safety nets, undertaking large-scale vaccination efforts). Sound economic and environmental policies, education and training, and other measures can also reduce a wide variety of risks (World Bank 2001, 2013a). The resilience literature often emphasizes the importance of safety (lower vulnerability *before* shocks occur) as a foundational principle related to reducing and mitigating risk (Adger 2000).

Coping measures, by contrast, aim to relieve the impact of shocks after they occur. At the individual or household level, such measures can include drawing down savings, selling assets, borrowing, or calling on support networks (friends and family, community insurance schemes, formal support and insurance mechanisms). Government efforts can support coping efforts, including through direct transfers and other social safety net programs (workfare, unemployment insurance). When such efforts are inadequate, however, individuals and households may be forced to adopt unsustainable coping measures (reducing consumption, taking children out of school, resorting to illegal activities) that can have long-term costs and consequences (Garschagen, Renaud, and Birkmann 2011; Tawodzera 2012; World Bank 2001, 2013a). Societies as a whole can also practice unsustainable coping mechanisms (exhausting finite natural resources).

Finally, *transformative* strategies—the most difficult and rare type (Moshy, Bryceson, and Mwaipopo 2015; Mozumder et al. 2018; Solórzano 2016)—reflect efforts by society to strengthen, reform, or create new institutions that improve citizens' welfare and better prepare society to weather future crises (Béné et al. 2012; Keck and Sakdapolrak 2013; Smith and Frankenberger 2018; Voss 2008). To prepare for and mitigate the shock of seasonal flooding, for example, a government might establish national and local agencies dedicated to flood preparedness and response, with adequate budgets as well as partnerships with the private sector to transform the country's capacities for managing, mitigating, and coping with risk. In a similar vein, the threat of climate change is ushering in revolutions in public transportation, green technologies, and clean energy. Risks of gender-based violence or child labor can generate important investments in legal, institutional, and normative efforts to reduce incentives for the harm to transpire.

The scatterplots in figure 2.5 show the results of SSGD analysis for the resilience index, which includes indicators that measure household assets, savings, food security, and vulnerability to the effects of climate change (see box 2.2 and annex 2A; World Bank 2022b, 2022c). The analysis suggests that resilience is associated with lower poverty levels, higher GDP per capita, stronger human capital accumulation, and greater human development. It is also linked with inequality,

Figure 2.5 Association between Resilience and Poverty, Income, Inequality, Human Capital, and Human Development

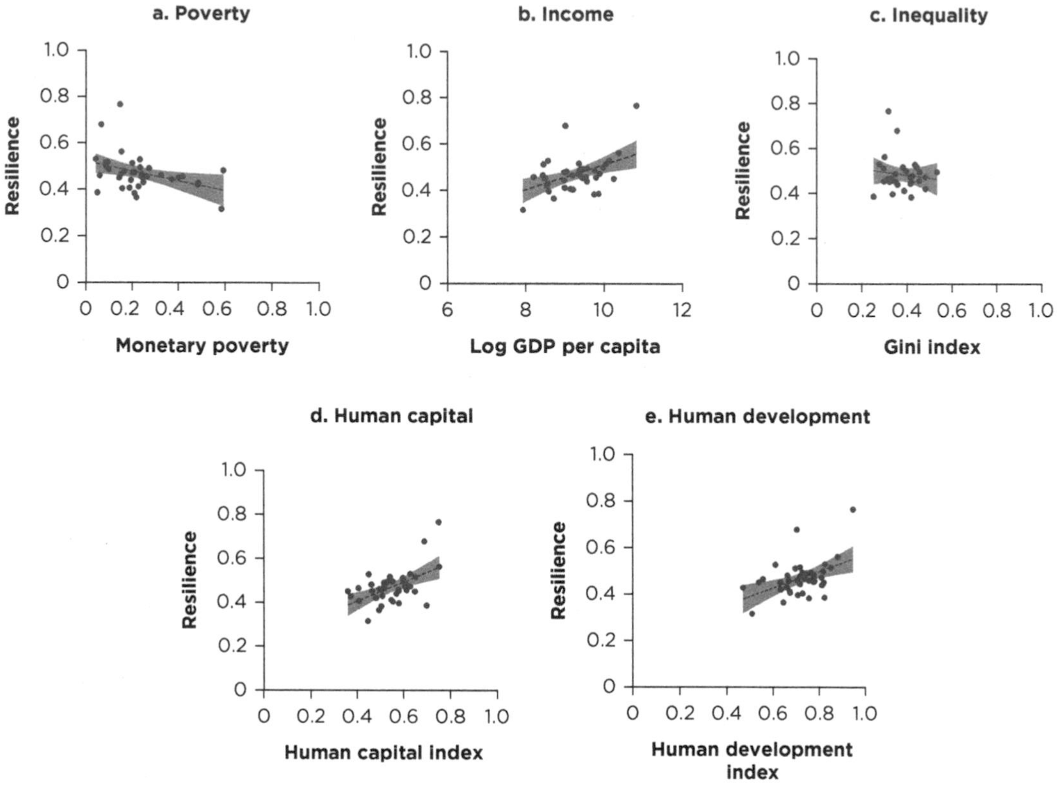

Sources: Cuesta, Madrigal, and Pecorari 2022; World Bank 2022b.
Note: GDP = gross domestic product.

although the association is weaker—partly due to insufficient data, in terms of both the number of variables in the index and country coverage. More work is needed to improve the measurement and collection of data on social resilience.[10]

A range of development interventions seek to bolster resilience, and recent rigorous evidence has shown the positive impacts of these efforts. For example, a meta-analysis of 129 impact evaluations assessing the effects of group-based livelihoods programs, such as community-based microfinance schemes, self-help groups, or savings and producer groups, often based on gender, economic, social, cultural, or ethnic affinity, found that they provided much-needed safety nets and led to reduced vulnerability in contexts of extreme deprivation and adverse events like conflict or climate shocks. Participants in group-based livelihoods programs were 26 percent more likely to have income-generating activities beyond farming, providing them with an important livelihood buffer to weather challenges (Barooah et al. 2020). Moreover, the meta-analysis found that group-based livelihoods programs systematically improved social cohesion in the form of greater access to entitlements and intra- and intergroup relationships, among several other positive development outcomes.

Other evidence also suggests that resilience has strong links to social cohesion and inclusion and that the three may be mutually reinforcing. Building and maintaining social relations and network structures are critical for resilience (Adger 2000; Bodin, Crona, and Ernstson 2006; Peiling and High 2005; Traerup 2012). For example, a study of natural disaster response across four countries found that communities with robust social networks were better able to coordinate recovery and minimize long-term consequences (Aldrich 2012). In contrast, a study of Chicago's 1995 heat wave found that various forms of social breakdown, including the physical and social isolation of senior citizens, contributed to high fatality rates (Klinenberg 2002). Similar studies have assessed resilience amid climate change and broader development efforts, especially focusing on vulnerable communities (for example, Ashwill, Flora, and Flora 2011; Mearns and Norton 2010; World Bank 2013a). Institutions and power relations, including cultural capital in the form of gender, kinship, or ethnic ties, also influence social resilience (Adger 2000; Obrist 2010).

Process Legitimacy

The framework presented here establishes cohesion, inclusion, and resilience as the core elements of social sustainability and as important development outcomes in and of themselves. However, the extent to which these elements produce social sustainability entails a transformative process that is more than the sum of its parts—just as schools, teachers, and textbooks do not generate learning on their own, and hospitals, doctors, and medicines do not enhance public health on their own. From a social sustainability perspective, a fourth element—process legitimacy—is a critical driver of this transformation.

Process legitimacy is about the "how" of policy making, program design, and implementation and the extent to which these elements are consistent with a given context.[11] Communities and societies at-large decide whether policies and programs are deemed legitimate, illegitimate, or somewhere in between, based on their own sense of and standards for fairness and credibility. While relevant for any policy or program in any given context, process legitimacy is particularly important for socially sustainable development. This book contends that efforts to support cohesion, inclusion, and resilience are more likely to be successful if they reflect process legitimacy:

> Process legitimacy is the extent to which a community or society accepts who has authority, what goals are formulated, and how policies and programs get implemented. It also encompasses the approaches for reconciling disagreements or tensions, especially among those who stand to bear the greatest cost.

Process legitimacy occurs when decisions are perceived as fair and credible by all; it is not a binary variable, but rather exists on a scale—decision-making processes may be perceived as more or less legitimate. Process legitimacy is strong when people believe that decisions are taken by credible and recognized authority figures in ways that align with their values and reflect agreed rules or processes for decision making. In addition, process legitimacy can be enhanced when decision making is transparent and participatory and when the perceived benefits for the affected population are significant. When there is disagreement, process legitimacy ensures that extensive good-faith efforts are made to engage with and ultimately accommodate the tensions between groups. This engagement is especially important for those who stand to bear the greatest costs as a result of the decisions made, goals selected, or procedures enacted (for instance, all those who may lose as a result of higher fuel prices or carbon taxes).

Process legitimacy can be derived in various ways, depending on the context and ultimately determined by the given community or society. The sources of process legitimacy are multiple, diverse, and often overlapping. In particular, five common drivers lend process legitimacy to an authority, its goals, and the ways those goals are implemented:[12]

- *Credibility of decision makers.* The power to make decisions, set policies, and implement programs gains legitimacy when it stems from an accepted source (an election, formal or informal designation, technical expertise).
- *Consistency with agreed-upon rules.* The rules followed to make and implement decisions gain legitimacy when they reflect established methods or approaches that a community or society agrees to be acceptable and credible (legal precedents, professional standards, procedural guidelines, informal traditions or customs).
- *Consistency with societal values.* The beliefs or moral convictions about what and how things should be done (religious, philosophical, and ideological convictions or widely respected but nonbinding rules, such as international laws regarding war crimes or human rights).
- *Perceived benefits for the affected population.* The acceptance and legitimacy achieved for specific policies and programs—although regarded by some as dubious or morally fraught—by convincing key stakeholders that they are (or will soon be) better off (their incomes are rising or their security is being protected). In this sense, the ends come to justify (legitimize) the means.
- *Participation and transparency.* Dialogue, engagement, feedback, and partnership between authority figures and members of a given community or society—coupled with open and transparent decision making. Such participation can generate legitimacy, especially when there are disagreements or tensions.

As illustrated in figure 2.6, the five drivers of process legitimacy are related and can reinforce one another; they also can function independently of one another. Process legitimacy is stronger when an authority has credibility, when the community or society accepts the chosen goals and their implementation as reflecting agreed-upon rules and societal values or offering perceived benefits, and when the levels of participation and transparency are high. In contrast, process legitimacy is weaker when an authority derives power through force, when its goals are rejected by the affected population and do not reflect shared principles, and when it implements policies and programs in ways that are not in line with prevailing cultural practices and rules. Figure 2.7 illustrates various possible scenarios, depending on whether particular drivers of process legitimacy are present or absent. By far the most "typical" scenarios are mixed, with varying degrees of difference between members and groups about what counts as a basis for exerting authority, what counts as a reasonable policy or program goal, and what counts as fair implementation procedures for achieving it.

Figure 2.6 Drivers of Process Legitimacy

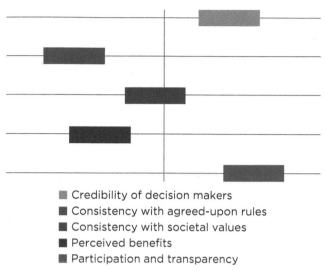

■ Credibility of decision makers
■ Consistency with agreed-upon rules
■ Consistency with societal values
■ Perceived benefits
■ Participation and transparency

Source: World Bank.
Note: The five drivers of process legitimacy are related and can reinforce one another; they also can function independently of one another. They are dynamic and change over time.

The Policy Arena: Where Process Legitimacy Is Forged

The drivers of process legitimacy are fluid and dynamic; they change over time (for better and worse) and depend on where policies and programs are formulated and implemented (parliaments, executive offices, the military, the private sector, civil society organizations, and local and community associations). Thus, a useful way of framing process legitimacy is that it concerns what happens in the policy arena—the space for collective decision making, where different groups interact and bargain over issues within the public domain, resulting in agreements that can lead to change. The legitimacy of the policy arena is critical, and it ultimately depends on all parties accepting the authority of the decision-making body, the policy goals it chooses to pursue, and the procedures it enacts for pursuing them.

The consequences of failing to achieve process legitimacy are often obvious: when the conditions of fairness and credibility are not met, outrage may follow. More often, process legitimacy is compromised in less obvious ways: when certain groups lack access to the policy arena due to high levels of inequality, when corruption or clientelism puts decision-making authority up for sale to the highest bidder, or even when well-meaning external actors create short-term incentives for policy reforms that do not reflect a transparent engagement in the policy arena. In all such cases, the social sustainability of the change process can be jeopardized and social tensions may emerge. In recent years, process legitimacy has become more challenging as the policy arena has become more fragmented, driven in part by political and cultural polarization and technologies like social media. These dynamics often undermine the credibility of information shared, and dialogue often

Figure 2.7 Process Legitimacy—Illustrative Scenarios

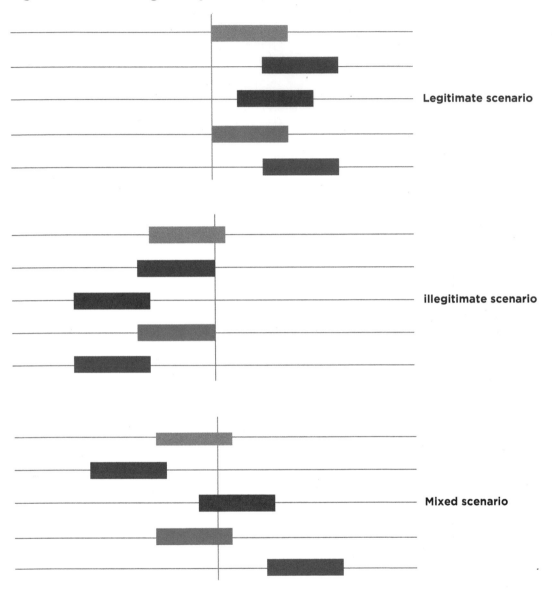

Legitimate scenario

illegitimate scenario

Mixed scenario

- Credibility of decision makers
- Consistency with agreed-upon rules
- Consistency with societal values
- Perceived benefits
- Participation and transparency

Source: World Bank.

happens between like-minded individuals in parallel but noncommunicative forums, making it difficult to build and sustain broad consensus around the legitimacy of policy-making and implementation processes.

Process Legitimacy in the Development Context

Development presents myriad challenges where the presence or absence of process legitimacy is decisive, as it shapes how stakeholders experience social change and the extent to which they accept the outcomes it generates—ultimately affecting whether the change process is socially sustainable or destabilizing. Policies to upgrade slums, for instance, are common and technically straightforward, but *how* they are implemented matters greatly. A government can arrive with bulldozers and forcibly displace residents by invoking eminent domain laws, or it can undertake extensive community consultations and implement a fairly negotiated and transparently communicated resettlement process. From the perspective of social sustainability, the latter approach—while still disruptive for the residents—is more likely to be perceived as legitimate.[13] Likewise, social norms and values often determine the dynamics of process legitimacy in development; indigenous peoples who believe that their ancestors reside within their bodies might reject a national polio vaccination decree, for example, not because they reject the government's authority or its goal, but because they believe that piercing their skin (an unavoidable aspect of implementing the vaccination program) is a violation of their venerated ancestors. In such cases, process legitimacy ensures that such beliefs are taken into account and accommodated.

Moreover, the development process often influences who has authority, what policy or program goals they pursue, and how those policies and programs get implemented.[14] Such large changes can *alter the drivers of process legitimacy* in a given context. Specifically, development often shifts the balance of power, affecting established rules, norms, values, and principles while introducing new ones. Depending on the context, it may also introduce entirely "new ways of doing things." Concerns and tensions may arise particularly over policies and programs that alter the social dimensions of development—precisely because identities, relationships, expectations, aspirations, and rules themselves are often disruptively changed. For example, gender equality, educational pedagogy, policies concerning the inclusion of traditionally disadvantaged groups, and many other aspects of contemporary development interventions may or may not accord with what is considered legitimate by national governments, let alone particular communities within and across borders. Such concerns and tensions may even erode social cohesion over time, as illustrated by the vignette in box 2.1 about incumbents (traditional leaders, religious authorities)[15] whose interests or values are challenged by newly empowered groups (youth, women).

In practice, managing these changes can be complex and contentious. Furthermore, the development process itself can either intensify or help to resolve the disagreements that arise over these issues, creating significant challenges for process legitimacy. Given the high likelihood of ongoing contention about issues of process legitimacy, establishing robust and shared overarching mechanisms (or "meta-rules")[16] by which differences can be reconciled or resolved is often important. Similarly, enhancing participation and transparency—particularly by bringing into the policy arena new groups who have tended to have less access and divergent viewpoints—often plays a crucial role in forging broad acceptance. This role is especially relevant for policies and programs that are not fully consistent with existing agreed-upon rules or shared principles; such efforts are typically most effective when the process is seen as endogenously driven. *How* tensions are resolved in the policy arena is critical for broader efforts to build legitimacy around development and the changes it brings about (intentionally or unintentionally).

For all of these reasons, process legitimacy is a critical element for promoting cohesion, inclusion, and resilience. Practicing socially sustainable development is about navigating, negotiating, and resolving these complex trade-offs in the policy arena. Routinely, however, the trade-offs cannot be anticipated in advance and are highly challenging to address when they materialize. There is also no single blueprint for promoting process legitimacy: the necessary rules, standards, norms, and procedures for managing these trade-offs are often absent, inadequate, contradictory, or compromised, thereby becoming part of the development challenge.

In light of these challenges and complexities, chapter 3 offers specific principles about effective approaches for promoting process legitimacy.

Evidence

Several types of interventions offer evidence on the positive effects of process legitimacy. Interventions that seek to strengthen social accountability, for example, have been shown to have several benefits for socially sustainable development. In Cambodia, an impact evaluation of a program designed to increase the government's capacity to implement social accountability approaches in rural regions, including the development of citizen-state feedback mechanisms, found that it empowered citizens to provide comments to community service providers on the quality of critical public services, ultimately strengthening transparency in access to information, increasing the use of health centers, and improving school facilities (Mubarak et al. 2020). In the Philippines, an economic support program reduced the number of conflict-related incidents and weakened the influence of insurgents (Crost, Felter, and Johnston 2016). In Afghanistan, the participatory and transparent community-driven approach helped to minimize conflict and tensions throughout the program, as community leaders were able to ensure that households were included that may otherwise not have been. In Colombia, an economic support program was found to have positive effects on the demobilization of combatants (Pena, Urrego, and Villa 2017; for additional references, see Chatterjee, Gassier, and Myint 2022).

The scatterplots in figure 2.8 show the results of SSGD analysis for the process legitimacy index, which includes indicators measuring the rule of law, control of corruption, accountability, and justice systems (see box 2.2 and annex 2A; World Bank 2022b, 2022c). The analysis suggests that process legitimacy is associated with lower poverty levels, higher GDP per capita, lower inequality, stronger human capital accumulation, and greater human development.[17] The strength of these correlations, particularly with lower inequality and improved human development outcomes, is noteworthy and suggests that process legitimacy plays a critical role in the development process. These "big picture" empirical findings complement the more granular vignettes presented in box 2.3.

Figure 2.8 Association between Process Legitimacy and Poverty, Income, Inequality, Human Capital, and Human Development

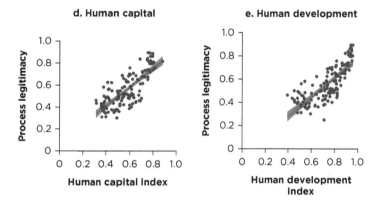

Sources: Cuesta, Madrigal, and Pecorari 2022; World Bank 2022b.
Note: GDP = gross domestic product.

Box 2.3
Four Vignettes on the Importance of Process Legitimacy in Development

The importance of process legitimacy for ensuring that development is socially sustainable plays out across all levels of society. This box considers four vignettes drawn from an array of complex cases spanning development challenges at different levels—from the global to the local. Versions of such cases are a common reality in all sectors of development.

Global Challenges: Openness, Democracy, and Sovereignty

It is increasingly understood that the sizable gains from global integration, while bringing the benefits of growth, can come at a cost, often to the most vulnerable groups (for example, those with low skills in vulnerable industries), and can lead to the decline of certain economic sectors and deep tensions in affected communities (see, for example,

(continued)

Box 2.3
Continued

Stiglitz 2007)—often resulting in protests, unrest, and political upheaval. Assessing these trade-offs, Dani Rodrik declared that democracy, sovereignty, and openness cannot be pursued simultaneously; globalization can accommodate only two of the three (Rodrik 2011). In other words, if countries wish to be open and democratic, they must cede a large portion of their sovereignty (as have members of the European Union, for example). Process legitimacy is critical: countries can only sustain these tensions if their citizens—especially those who lose from globalization—regard the policy-making process (and any redress offered) as legitimate. How compromise is reached, and on what basis, matters. The intensity of these trade-offs will vary, but countries with small populations or economies reliant on a few low-skill industries will be particularly affected (on policy strategies for responding to these challenges, see, among others, Catão and Obstfeld 2019).

National Challenges: Enabling and Constraining Central Banks

Most countries have several powerful institutions overseen not by elected public officials (who are accountable to citizens) but by political or professional appointees. A prominent example is the central bank, whose remit is vital to maintaining the nation's economic health and, by extension, shaping the fortunes of the incumbent political party. Legitimacy is paramount: central bankers must make hard decisions that prioritize the national interests over those of the party or leader that appointed them and can face pressure (including financial incentives or blackmail) *not* to do their job. Paul Tucker argues that specific forms of accountability, such as transparency and "360-degree monitoring," and central banks' willingness to be bound by these standards, are key to their credibility; such measures help to ensure that their actions are squarely "in the territory of legitimacy" (Tucker 2018, 422).

Local Challenges: Managing Peatlands in the Democratic Republic of Congo

Were it ever to dry up, a large peatlands ecosystem in rural Democractic Republic of Congo could release a "carbon bomb" equivalent to 10 years of US car emissions; as such, climate scientists insist that the peatlands must be protected (Maclean 2022). But how, by whom, and on what basis? Enduring tensions exist between two villages over which of them is the peatlands' rightful custodian, each invoking different historical maps and memories; the government system for granting logging rights is deeply compromised, and villagers see the peatlands as the sacred resting place of their ancestors, have little comprehension of what carbon is and does, and see little reason to forgo lucrative income in order to address climate change, to which they have contributed almost nothing. Process legitimacy is required to reconcile these competing claims and interests, but the tensions run deep, and few sources of authority are credible in the eyes of all stakeholders. For now, it seems that a single scientist has achieved broad legitimacy, based on his combination of linguistic, scientific, and cultural knowledge.

(continued)

Box 2.3
Continued

Personal Challenges: Reconciling Social Norms and Reproductive Health

While it is denounced as a violation of human and women's rights and a major cause of serious health problems (Efferson et al. 2015), female genital cutting is also a long-established and "sacred" rite-of-passage ritual for young women in certain countries. Various approaches have been deployed to reconcile women's rights with local traditions and found wanting (McChesney 2015 documents six failed strategies), but the programs that seem to bring about lasting change "are community led, aim to change social norms in the whole community, and empower women" (McChesney 2015, 3) as well as work with traditional community leaders (who are often male). One effective approach involves taking the time to understand communities well enough to identify women of high status who have quietly refrained from adopting female genital cutting (or from insisting that their daughters do so), enabling them to be role models, mentors (Pascale, Sternin, and Sternin 2010), and influential "positive deviants" who legitimize the change process for others. (Box 3.7 in chapter 3 expands on this vignette to illustrate one example of how process legitimacy is operationalized.)

Strengthening the Empirical Foundations of Social Sustainability

As noted in chapter 1, social sustainability and its core components have both intrinsic and instrumental value; while their value is unique and innate, they also support key development outcomes. However, efforts to understand these links empirically are still nascent. There is a small but growing body of micro-level evidence, as the examples in this chapter have highlighted. More broadly, the SSGD, described in box 2.2 and the scatterplots offer new macro-level evidence that higher levels of social sustainability are associated with poverty reduction, per capita income growth, lower inequality, human capital accumulation, and human development.

Several of the SSGD correlations are strong—notably, the links of inclusion and process legitimacy with poverty reduction and human capital and the association of process legitimacy with less inequality. Indeed, process legitimacy is among the most strongly correlated indexes, underscoring the importance of factors like the rule of law, fairness, justice, and government effectiveness for the broader development agenda. Nonetheless, some of the correlations are weaker.[18] This weakness likely reflects data shortcomings and measurement challenges, including the need to refine the SSGD indicators and the composition of its indexes.[19] There are also broader methodological issues. For instance, the SSGD correlations are based on static cross-country data over a relatively short time horizon. This approach is not ideally suited for unpacking the complex relationships between social factors and economic or environmental outcomes, which often exhibit a high degree of endogeneity, can shift quickly due to short-term country-specific events, and often reflect long-standing structural conditions. Long-term country-specific time-series data (as well as continued improvements in the core data) would improve analytical tools like the SSGD. Likewise, additional causal analyses—leveraging impact evaluations as well as experimental and quasi-experimental analyses—would help to confirm the correlations presented here.

The relatively weak correlations of social inclusion and resilience with inequality may also underscore that some of the many ways to make progress on the twin goals are more socially sustainable than others. For instance, some countries do well in terms of poverty reduction or inequality but do less well on one or several dimensions of social sustainability. This finding does not suggest, however, that social sustainability does not matter; as noted, the components of social sustainability are also important for their intrinsic value and contribution to human dignity and respect for basic human rights. Likewise, progress on the twin goals can be short-lived and is subject to reversals (including reversals driven by the lack of social sustainability). In other words, solutions that seem to deliver poverty reduction without social sustainability in a given time period may themselves not be sustainable in the long run. For example, poverty and inequality in contexts of migration can be reduced by providing cash transfers to refugees; however, failure to support host communities (who may be just as poor) or to involve them in the decision-making process may undermine the gains achieved and exacerbate social tensions.[20]

Overall, the large number of positive correlations in the SSGD suggests that inclusion, cohesion, resilience, and process legitimacy are mutually reinforcing: in other words, social sustainability will generally be strongest when all of its components are present, offering a virtuous circle that helps to drive poverty reduction and shared prosperity. In reality, of course, the components often work at cross purposes. Some of the least inclusive societies, for example, are also the most resilient and may appear cohesive only because minority groups are suppressed or marginalized. Likewise, there are often significant trade-offs: highly resilient communities can be too tolerant of adversity, while efforts to enhance inclusion can generate resentment from groups who fear losing out. Such instances can undermine social sustainability, leading to heightened tensions or conflict.

At the broadest level (and beyond the scope of SSGD analysis), the three pillars of sustainability are also mutually reinforcing but subject to consequential trade-offs. Lack of economic or environmental sustainability can exacerbate social challenges, while sustainable growth can enable and support social sustainability—and vice versa. Without cohesion, for example, societies may find it difficult to agree on policies to promote economic or environmental sustainability; such policies will be less effective if parts of the population are excluded or vulnerable. Often, the trade-offs can move both ways: failure to address climate change, for instance, can undermine resilience and worsen exclusion, but policies to address climate change (higher taxes, subsidy removals, coal exits) can often trigger social unrest. The overall sustainability of a given community or society can fall into any number of potential scenarios (figure 2.9 presents only three possible scenarios).

Figure 2.9 Sustainability Triad: Potential Scenarios

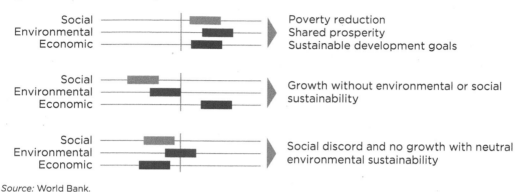

Source: World Bank.

Ideally, communities and societies would pursue all four components of social sustainability (cohesion, inclusion, resilience, and process legitimacy) and the full triad of sustainability (social, economic, and environmental) simultaneously. In practice, however, stakeholders and policy makers often choose or are forced to prioritize particular components or certain dimensions over others. This process—of balancing trade-offs and making difficult choices—unfolds within the policy arena amid the reality of competing priorities, budget constraints, and limited time frames. Process legitimacy is thus very useful—by ensuring that tensions between stakeholders are meaningfully accommodated, especially among groups that stand to lose from a given decision or trade-off.

Of course, as noted in chapter 1, the status quo for most of the last 75 years has been to prioritize economic and (more recently) environmental sustainability over social sustainability, and the increased recognition that social factors are important has not dramatically affected the way development is done on the ground. To motivate policy makers and development organizations to take social sustainability more seriously, strengthening its empirical foundations is critical, but so too is developing practical experience and operational expertise. Chapter 3 explores how to operationalize social sustainability, despite the many challenges and obstacles.

Annex 2A Empirical Annex

Table 2A.1 Variables Used in Social Sustainability Indexes

Variable	Country observations	Source
Social inclusion		
Labor force participation rate (0–1)	113	GMD
Share of population with a bank account (0–1)	105	Regional barometers, FINDEX Database
Share of households without access to adequate sanitation (0–1)	137	GMD
Share of households with access to electricity (0–1)	104	GMD
Secondary enrollment rate (0–1)	114	GMD
Proportion of seats held by women in national parliaments (0–1)	190	World Development Indicators
Social inclusion index (0–1)	73	
Resilience		
Index of average assets in household (normalized 0–1)[a]	101	GMD
Share of population that saves some money (0–1)	85	Regional barometers and World Values Survey
1 minus the share of population that has gone without enough food to eat in the past year (0–1)	110	Regional barometers and World Values Survey
Share of households with several sources of income (0–1)	113	GMD
Share of population that considers moving because of climate change reasons (0–1)	113	Gallup
Resilience index (0–1)	40	
Social cohesion		
Share of population that says most people can be trusted (0–1)	86	Regional barometers and World Values Survey
Share of population that says they have confidence in the government (0–1)	112	Regional barometers and World Values Survey
Share of population that says they have confidence in the police (0–1)	113	Regional barometers and World Values Survey
Share of population that voted in the last national election (0–1)	106	Regional barometers and World Values Survey
Share of population that are active members of organizations (0–1)	78	World Values Survey
Index of fatalities from violence (normalized 0–1)[b]	206	ACLED
Index of homicides (normalized 0–1)[c]	90	World Development Indicators
Social cohesion index (0–1)	68	

(continued)

Table 2A.1 Continued

Variable	Country observations	Source
Process legitimacy		
Rule of law (normalized 0–1)	209	World Governance Indicators
Control of corruption (normalized 0–1)	209	World Governance Indicators
Government powers are effectively limited by the judiciary (score 0–1)	139	World Justice Project
Equal treatment and absence of discrimination in the legal system (score 0–1)	139	World Justice Project
People can access and afford civil justice (score 0–1)	139	World Justice Project
Government regulations are applied and enforced without improper influence (score 0–1)	139	World Justice Project
The right of life and security to the person is effectively guaranteed (score 0–1)	139	World Justice Project
Process legitimacy index (0–1)	139	

Source: World Bank 2022b.
Note: ACLED = Armed Conflict Location and Event Data; GMD = Global Monitoring Database.
a. Average = set of assets, including computer, cell phone, radio, television, washing machine, sewing machine, car, fridge, and motorcycle, that are owned by a household in the country, normalized between 0 to 1 (1 = having all assets considered).
b. Index = number of fatalities due to violence in a country. The indicator is normalized across all countries in the sample using var-var$_{min}$/var$_{max}$-var$_{min}$.
c. Index = number of homicides per 100,000 inhabitants in a country normalized across all countries in the sample using var-var$_{min}$/var$_{max}$-var$_{min}$.

Those indicators are aggregated across each of the four social sustainability components through the following index:

$$SS_j = \Sigma_i (w\,s)_i, \tag{2A.1}$$

where, for the *j*th social sustainability component ($j = 1, 2, 3, 4$)—that is, social cohesion, resilience, and process legitimacy in each region—each *i*th social sustainability indicator, *s*, used to define the respective component is weighted by a factor, *w*. Following the most parsimonious definition, $w = 1/i$—that is, each index equally weights its indicators. In practice, the index for each component of social sustainability is defined at the national level.

Robustness checks were conducted to see the sensitivity of results to the number of indicators used in each component, alternative choices of indicators across indexes, and nonlinear functional forms for the index (figure 2A.1 and table 2A.2). Key findings regarding the direction and strength of correlations did not change after these changes. See Cuesta, López-Noval, and Niño-Zarazúa (2022) for a detailed discussion of those robustness checks.

Figure 2A.1 Pairwise Correlations between Social Sustainability Components

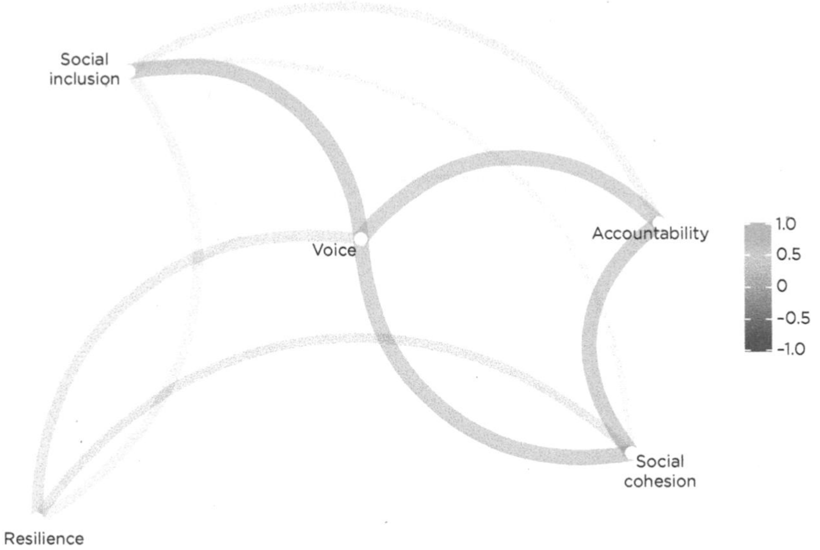

Source: Cuesta, Madrigal, and Pecorari 2022.

Table 2A.2 Correlations among the Components of Social Sustainability

	Social inclusion	Resilience	Social cohesion	Process legitimacy
Social inclusion	1.000			
Resilience	-0.088	1.000		
Social cohesion	-0.042	0.391	1.000	
Process legitimacy	0.393	0.493	0.353	1.000

Source: World Bank 2022b.

Annex 2B Social Sustainability and Developmental Outcome Correlations, Controlling for Income

This annex reports the estimates of simple linear regressions linking each component of social sustainability with the various developmental outcomes analyzed in this chapter, except for GDP per capita, which now becomes a control variable. Table 2B.1 compares the results from unconditional regressions, regressions conditioning for log per capita GDP, and, finally, regressions conditioning for income-level group dummies. As explained in the main text, controlling for either log per capita GDP or income-level category of countries included in the regressions does not alter the direction—that is, the sign—of the unconditional correlations (those graphed in the scatterplots). However, the strength—size of the coefficient—of those relationships tends to decrease and, in a few cases, stops being statistically significant. This finding indicates that income level partially mediates the relationship between social sustainability and other development outcomes, which is why coefficients change in magnitude. Table 2B.1 reports the coefficients, standard deviation, and statistical significance of all the estimates of the regressions.

Table 2B.1 Unconditional and Conditional Regressions of Social Sustainability and Developmental Outcomes

Social Cohesion

Variables	[1] SC index	[2] SC index	[3] SC index	[4] SC index	[5] SC index	[6] SC index	[7] SC index	[8] SC index	[9] SC index	[10] SC index	[11] SC index	[12] SC index
Poverty NPL last 5 years	-0.256*** [0.080]	0.242** [0.091]	-0.252*** [0.086]									
Gini past 5 years				-0.204 [0.170]	-0.198 [0.177]	-0.115 [0.18]						
Human capital index							0.196** [0.090]	0.129 [0.175]	0.218 [0.143]			
Human development index										0.181** [0.088]	-0.002 [0.299]	0.331 [0.179]
Log per capita GDP		-0.004 [0.014]			0.002 [0.014]			0.002 [0.023]			0.017 [0.039]	
High income												
Low income			0.0101 [0.0561]			0.0264 [0.0606]			0.0213 [0.0722]			0.074 [0.086]
Lower middle income			-0.0144 [0.03]			-0.0126 [0.0293]			0.00724 [0.0394]			0.034 [0.048]
Upper middle income			-0.0291 [0.0305]			-0.05 [0.0308]			-0.03 [0.0335]			-0.024 [0.033]
Constant	0.630*** [0.020]	0.661*** [0.143]	0.644*** [0.0271]	0.663*** [0.063]	0.642*** [0.160]	0.650*** [0.0636]	0.464*** [0.054]	0.483*** [0.143]	0.458*** [0.105]	0.441*** [0.067]	0.417*** [0.173]	0.321** [0.160]
Observations	58	57	58	48	48	48	65	62	65	66	63	66
R-squared	0.157	0.128	0.176	0.030	0.031	0.108	0.071	0.157	0.11	0.062	0.030	0.1297

(continued)

Table 2B.1 Continued

Social inclusion												
Variables	[1] SI index	[2] SI index	[3] SI index	[4] SI index	[5] SI index	[6] SI index	[7] SI index	[8] SI index	[9] SI index	[10] SI index	[11] SI index	[12] SI index
Poverty NPL last 5 years	-0.377*** [0.089]	0.002 [0.081]	-0.14 [0.0833]									
Gini last 5 years				-0.078 [0.203]	-0.022 [0.142]	-0.0137 [0.173]						
Human capital index							1.014*** [0.099]	0.583*** [0.148]	0.752*** [0.129]			
Human development index										0.908*** [0.072]	1.084*** [0.211]	1.042*** [0.143]
Log per capita GDP		0.124*** [0.016]			0.106*** [0.015]			0.064*** [0.017]			-0.027 [0.030]	
High income												
Low income						-0.185*** [0.0433]			-			0.05 [0.0469]
Lower middle income			0.125*** [0.0321]			-0.0994*** [0.0298]			0.0544* [0.0286]			0.031 [0.026]
Upper middle income			0.219***			-			0.105***			-
Constant	0.671*** [0.032]	-0.516*** [0.153]	0.469*** [0.0452]	0.614*** [0.083]	-0.340** [0.144]	0.715*** [0.0745]	0.068 [0.048]	-0.281*** [0.104]	0.134*** [0.0506]	-0.024 [0.046]	0.094 [0.140]	-0.134 [0.109]
Observations	69	69	69	51	51	51	70	70	70	72	72	72
R-squared	0.212	0.592	0.487	0.003	0.524	0.311	0.606	0.673	0.654	0.696	0.699	0.702

(continued)

Table 2B.1 Continued

Resilience												
Variables	[1] RE index	[2] RE index	[3] RE index	[4] RE index	[5] RE index	[6] RE index	[7] RE index	[8] RE index	[9] RE index	[10] RE index	[11] RE index	[12] RE index
Poverty NPI last 5 years	-0.210** [0.086]	-0.108 [0.103]	-0.155* [0.0886]									
Gini past 5 years				-0.131 [0.208]	-0.140 [0.197]	-0.095 [0.186]						
Human capital index							0.436*** [0.115]	0.362* [0.183]	0.419*** [0.148]			
Human development index										0.364*** [0.111]	0.289 [0.321]	0.492** [0.184]
Log per capita GDP		0.041* [0.021]			0.042** [0.020]			0.017 [0.025]			0.017 [0.045]	
High income												
Low income			-0.101 [0.0823]			–			-0.0256 [0.0851]			0.04 [0.102]
Lower middle income			-0.101** [0.0398]			0 104** [0.0387]			0 044 [0.0451]			-0016 [0.053]
Upper middle income			-0.118*** [0.0386]			-0 123*** [0.0397]			-0.0794* [0.0395]			-0.076* [0.04]
Constant	0.520*** [0.023]	0.114 [0.208]	0.605*** [0.0354]	0.534*** [0.079]	0.147 [0.200]	0.621*** [0.076]	0.231*** [0.064]	0.110 [0.172]	0.298*** [0.107]	0.208** [0.081]	0.101 [0.219]	0.157 [0.163]
Observations	38	37	38	31	31	30	39	38	38	40	39	39
R-squared	0.141	0.223	0.33	0.013	0.146	0.29	0.280	0.290	0.407	0.220	0.230	0.391

(continued)

Table 2B.1 Continued

Process legitimacy												
	[1]	[2]	[3]	[4]	[5]	[6]	[7]	[8]	[9]	[10]	[11]	[12]
Variables	PL index	PL index	PL index	PL index	PL index	PL index	PL index	PL index	PL index	PL index	PL index	PL index
Poverty NPL past 5 years	-0.475*** [0.083]	0.137* [0.079]	-0.122* [0.0618]									
Gini last 5 years				-0.728*** [0.185]	-0.129 [0.139]	0.053 [0.119]						
Human capital index							0.863*** [0.060]	0.316** [0.136]	0.026*** [0.0984]			
Human development index										0.826*** [0.056]	0.318 [0.221]	0.443*** [0.113]
Log per capita GDP		0.121*** [0.011]			0.111*** [0.011]			0.076** [0.017]			0.070** [0.030]	
High income												
Low income			-0.285*** [0.0309]			-0.298*** [0.0324]			-0.23*** [0.041]			-0.1398*** [0.0511]
Lower middle income			-0.305*** [0.0206]			-0.315*** [0.0228]			-252*** [0.0299]			-0.197*** [0.033]
Upper middle income			-0.214*** [0.0200]			-0.216*** [0.0228]			-0.163*** [0.0235]			-0.146*** [0.0219]
Constant	0.658*** [0.024]	-0.613*** [0.116]	0.770*** [0.0172]	0.847*** [0.070]	-0.445*** [0.132]	0.731*** [0.0403]	0.064* [0.036]	0.332*** [0.096]	0.556*** [0.0733]	0.049 [0.042]	0.330** [0.129]	0.348*** [0.101]
Observations	115	114	114	95	94	95	133	131	133	136	133	135
R-squared	0.225	0.631	0.75	0.142	0.613	0.744	0.611	0.656	0.758	0.618	0.644	0.767

Source: World Bank.

Note: Standard errors are in brackets. NPL = national poverty lines; PL = process legitimacy; RE = resilience; SC = social cohesion; SI = social inclusion.

*** $p < 0.01$, ** $p < 0.05$, * $p < 0.1$

Notes

1. Nunn (2022), for example, adapts conceptual frameworks from evolutionary anthropology to provide a theoretically guided discussion of the dynamics surrounding culture and tradition in society, modeling the costs and benefits of different beliefs, values, and worldviews over time. Nunn's model illustrates how decision making that relies on tradition can be an effective strategy in certain contexts—namely, stable environments where the knowledge and skills obtained by earlier generations are still relevant and useful in the present day—but may not be as beneficial when the world changes and the new environment presents challenges that require new knowledge and skills (or even policies) to overcome.

2. As noted in the brief history of social sustainability, these four components align with and further develop the operational principles in the World Bank's 2005 Social Development Strategy and its 2011 Mid-Term Review, which stated, "Development is socially sustainable when it promotes inclusive, cohesive, resilient, and accountable institutions."

3. The terms bonding, bridging, and linking are drawn from Woolcock and Narayan's work on social capital (Woolcock and Narayan 2000). Whereas social capital can refer to an individual or a community and generally refers to the extent of one's own communities or social networks, social cohesion is measured at the intra- or intercommunity and society levels and refers to trust. See also Olawole, Lichtenheld, and Sheely (2022).

4. This brief summary of the literature is adapted from Chatterjee, Gassier, and Myint (2022).

5. Recognizing the importance of cohesion, in May 2020 the World Bank established a Global Solutions Group on Social Cohesion and Resilience, which works on these issues in contexts of fragility, conflict, and violence and beyond.

6. By contrast, several authors have found that conflict might also be associated with higher political participation, more local collective action, and stronger intragroup trust (see Bauer et al. 2016; Bellows and Miguel 2009; Blattman 2009; Gilligan, Pasquale, and Samii 2014).

7. These and other figures using the SSGD show correlations rather than, necessarily, causal relationships. Nonetheless, the findings hold when controlling for income level—using either countries' log per capita GDP or income-level categories. Results are presented in annex 2B. Coefficients of these conditional regressions also indicate that the correlations between cohesion and some developmental outcomes stop being significant, as in the case of human capital and human development. This finding suggests that income level partly mediates the relationship between social sustainability and some developmental outcomes.

8. In France in the 1970s, for instance, then–Secretary of State for Social Action Rene Lenoir was one of the first to use the term "social exclusion" for persons with disabilities, single parents, drug addicts, "delinquents," and the elderly, who, he argued, all needed active state help to be able to participate in society. See Paugam (1993).

9. Controlling for the country's level of income—either through the income-level category or the per capita GDP of the country—does not change the sign of these correlations, although it typically reduces their strength (the coefficient between social inclusion and poverty stops being significant). This finding indicates that income mediates how social inclusion and poverty relate to each other. See annex 2B.

10. Both the sign and the strength of these correlations remain after controlling for income level, confirming that it is not only and not mainly income that mediates between resilience and other developmental outcomes. The only exception is the correlation with poverty, which, after controlling for income, stops being statistically significant. See annex 2B.

11. The concept of process legitimacy has deep roots in prior World Bank efforts. The concept of process legitimacy was first explicitly used in the 2017 *World Development Report* on governance and the law. It is closely related to the Bank's work on empowerment and accountability, including the bottom-up "demand for good governance" approach. The 2005 Social Development Strategy, for example, emphasized cohesion, inclusion, resilience, and accountability as the key pillars of social development, while the 2020 framework launching the Social Sustainability and Inclusion Global Practice emphasized inclusion, resilience, and empowerment. See the brief history of social sustainability in chapter 1.

12. This view extends the definition of legitimacy from classical social theory, which was understood to be secured via three primary sources: tradition (inheritance, custom), legal or rational procedures (elections, professional merit), and routinized charisma (a compelling orator and associated social movement, for example, Martin Luther King Jr.). This three-part framework was expressed most influentially by Max Weber (1864–1920). Contemporary work, especially by Tom Tyler (1990), has demonstrated that the legitimacy of decisions by authority figures is enhanced to the extent that such decisions, and the basis on which they are reached, comport with prevailing moral norms.

13. However, the very act of opening up such wrenching decisions to broad community input has the potential to raise unrealistic expectations and cause costly debilitating delays—for example, the efforts to rebuild a section of lower Manhattan after Hurricane Sandy remain unrealized nearly a decade later (see Kimmelman 2021).

14. As noted, development changes how people live, including peoples' identities, expectations, and established ways of managing resources and relations—a process that is often deeply disruptive (and sometimes overtly destructive) to the local ways of doing things. This dynamic—pursuing goals through a process of deep change—can be considered a form of "creative destruction," in the Schumpeterian sense. See Aghion, Antonin, and Bunel (2020).

15. See Berry (2015, 1) on the sociopolitical dynamics, in Rwanda, shaping the paradoxical effects on women of political empowerment, rising education levels, and labor force participation, wherein "efforts to remedy women's subordination may actually end up reinforcing it."

16. See Barron, Smith, and Woolcock (2004) for an application of the idea of meta-rules to understanding local dispute resolution procedures in rural Indonesia.

17. As with the other SSGD indexes, these findings remain after controlling for country income level or per capita GDP. The size of the correlations typically diminishes after controlling for income. See annex 2B.

18. Also, the associations among components of social sustainability are complex and intricate, as reported by their pairwise correlations. See annex 2A.

19. For example, the indicators for the inclusion index measure access rates overall, rather than only access rates for vulnerable groups. Likewise, some indicators relate to multiple components of social sustainability; access to political and civic spaces is an indicator for the inclusion index,

but it could fit in the process legitimacy index as well; similar issues exist for the social cohesion and resilience indexes. See Cuesta, Madrigal, and Pecorari (2022).

20. The need to support both host and refugee communities is a key conclusion of World Bank (2022a), which presents 26 country case studies.

References

Adger, W. N. 2000. "Social and Ecological Resilience: Are They Related?" *Progress in Human Geography* 24 (3): 347–64. https://doi.org/10.1191/030913200701540465.

Aghion, P., C. Antonin, and S. Bunel. 2020. *The Power of Creative Destruction: Economic Upheaval and the Wealth of Nations.* Cambridge, MA: Harvard University Press.

Åhman, H. 2013. "Social Sustainability: Society at the Interpart of Development and Maintenance." *Local Environment: The International Journal of Justice and Sustainability* 18 (10): 1153–66.

Ajibade, I., G. McBean, and R. Bezner-Kern. 2013. "Urban Flooding in Lagos, Nigeria: Patterns of Vulnerability and Resilience among Women." *Global Environmental Change* 23 (6): 1714–25.

Aldrich, D. 2012. *Building Resilience: Social Capital in Post-Disaster Recovery.* Chicago, IL: University of Chicago Press.

Alesina, A., and R. Perotti. 1996. "Income Distribution, Political Instability, and Investment." *European Economic Review* 40 (6): 1203–28.

Ashwill, M., C. Flora, and J. Flora. 2011. *Building Community Resilience to Climate Change: Testing the Adaptation Coalition Framework in Latin America.* Washington, DC: World Bank.

Badgett, L. 2020. *The Economic Case for LGBT Equality: Why Fair and Equal Treatment Benefits Us All.* New York: Beacon Press.

Ballet, J., D. Bazin, and F. Mahieu. 2020. "A Policy Framework for Social Sustainability: Social Cohesion, Equity, and Safety." *Sustainable Development* 28 (5): 1388–94.

Bargain, O., and U. Aminjonov. 2020. "Trust and Compliance to Public Health Policies in Times of COVID-19." *Journal of Public Economics* 192 (December): 104316.

Barooah, B., S. Chinoy, A. Bagai, P. Dubey, R. Sarkar, T. Bansal, and Z. Siddiqui. 2020. "How Effective Are Group-Based Livelihoods Programmes in Improving the Lives of Poor People? A Synthesis of Recent Evidence." 3ie Working Paper 35, International Initiative for Impact Evaluation, New Delhi. https://doi.org/10.23846/WP0035.

Barrett, C., K. Ghezzi-Kopel, J. Hoddinott, N. Homami, E. Tennant, J. Upton, and T. Wu. 2021. "A Scoping Review of the Development Resilience Literature: Theory, Methods, and Evidence." *World Development* 146 (October): 105612.

Barron, P., C. Q. Smith, and M. Woolcock. 2004. "Understanding Local-Level Conflict in Developing Countries: Theory, Evidence, and Implications from Indonesia." Social Development Paper, Conflict Prevention and Reconstruction 19, World Bank, Washington, DC.

Bauer, M., C. Blattman, J. Chytilova, J. Henrich, E. Miguel, and T. Mitts. 2016. "Can War Foster Cooperation?" *Journal of Economic Perspectives* 30 (3): 249–74.

Beauvais, C., and J. Jenson. 2002. *Social Cohesion: Updating the State of the Research.* CPRN Discussion Paper F|22. Ottawa: Canadian Policy Research Networks.

Becker, E., T. Jahn, and I. Stiess. 1999. "Exploring Uncommon Ground: Sustainability and the Social Sciences." In *Sustainability and the Social Sciences: A Cross-Disciplinary Approach to Integrating Environmental Considerations into Theoretical Reorientation*, edited by T. Jahn and E. Becker. London: Zed Books.

Bellows, J., and E. Miguel. 2009. "War and Local Collective Action in Sierra Leone." *Journal of Public Economics* 93 (1): 1144–57.

Béné, C., R. Godfrey-Wood, A. Newsham, and M. Davies. 2012. "Resilience: New Utopia or New Tyranny? Reflection about the Potentials and Limits of the Concept of Resilience in Relation to Vulnerability Reduction Programmes." IDS Working Paper 405, Institute for Development Studies, Brighton.

Berry, M. E. 2015. "When 'Bright Futures' Fade: Paradoxes of Women's Empowerment in Rwanda." *Signs: Journal of Women in Culture and Society* 41 (1): 1–27.

Besley, T., and M. Reynal-Querol. 2014. "The Legacy of Historical Conflict: Evidence from Africa." *American Political Science Review* 108 (2): 319–36.

Blattman, C. 2009. "From Violence to Voting: War and Political Participation in Uganda." *American Political Science Review* 103 (2): 231–47.

Bodin, O., B. Crona, and H. Ernstson. 2006. "Social Networks in Natural Resource Management: What Is There to Learn from a Structural Perspective?" *Ecology and Society* 11 (2).

Boström, M. 2012. "A Missing Pillar? Challenges in Theorizing and Practicing Social Sustainability: Introduction to the Special Issue." *Sustainability: Science, Practice, and Policy* 8 (1): 3–14.

Bowen, T., C. del Ninno, C. Andrews, S. Coll-Black, U. Gentilini, K. Johnson, Y. Kawasoe, A. Kryeziu, B. Maher, and A. Williams. 2020. *Adaptive Social Protection: Building Resilience to Shocks.* International Development in Focus. Washington, DC: World Bank.

Boyer, R., N. Peterson, P. Arora, and K. Caldwell. 2016. "Five Approaches to Social Sustainability and an Integrated Way Forward." *Sustainability* 8 (878): 1–18.

Bramley, G., and S. Power. 2009. "Urban Form and Social Sustainability: The Role of Density and Housing Type." *Environment and Planning B: Planning and Design* 36 (1): 30–48. https://doi.org/10.1068/b33129.

Brunori, P., F. H. G. Ferreira, and V. Peragine. 2013. "Inequality of Opportunity, Income Inequality, and Economic Mobility: Some International Comparisons." Policy Research Working Paper 6304, World Bank, Washington, DC.

Buckup, S. 2009. "The Price of Exclusion: The Economic Consequences of Excluding People with Disabilities from the World of Work." Employment Working Paper 43, International Labour Organization, Geneva.

Buehren, N., P. Gonzalez, and A. Copley. 2019. "What Are the Economic Costs of Gender Gaps in Ethiopia?" Gender Innovation Policy Initiative, World Bank, Washington, DC.

Burns, C. 2012. "The Costly Business of Discrimination: The Economic Costs of Discrimination and the Financial Benefits of Gay and Transgender Equality in the Workplace." Center for American Progress, Washington, DC.

Call, C. 2012. *Why Peace Fails: The Causes and Prevention of Civil War Recurrence.* Washington, DC: Georgetown University Press.

Cannon, T. 2008. "Reducing People's Vulnerability to Natural Hazards Communities and Resilience." WIDER Research Paper 2008/34, United Nations University World Institute for Development Economics Research (UNU-WIDER), Helsinki.

Casey, K. 2018. "Radical Decentralization: Does Community-Driven Development Work?" *Annual Review of Economics* 10: 139–63.

Cassar, A., P. Grosjean, and S. Whitt. 2013. "Legacies of Violence: Trust and Market Development." *Journal of Economic Growth* 18 (3): 285–318.

Castillo, H., C. Moobela, A. Price, and V. Mathur, 2007. "Assessing Urban Social Sustainability: Current Capabilities and Opportunities for Future Research." *International Journal of Environmental, Cultural, Economic and Social Sustainability* 3 (3): 39–48.

Catão, L., and M. Obstfeld, eds. 2019. *Meeting Globalization's Challenges: Policies to Make Trade Work for All.* Princeton, NJ: Princeton University Press.

Chambers, R., and G. Conway. 1991. *Sustainable Rural Livelihoods: Practical Concepts for the 21st Century.* IDS Discussion Paper 296. Brighton: Institute of Development Studies.

Chatterjee, S., M. Gassier, and N. Myint. 2022. "Leveraging Social Cohesion for Development Impacts: Framing Paper." World Bank, Washington, DC.

Colantonio, A. 2007. "Social Sustainability: An Exploratory Analysis of Its Definition, Assessment Methods, Metrics, and Tools." EIBURS Working Paper 2007/01, Oxford Institute for Sustainable Development (OISD), International Land Markets Group, Oxford.

Colantonio, A. 2009. "Social Sustainability: A Review and Critique of Traditional Versus Emerging Themes and Assessment Methods." In *SUE-Mot Conference 2009: Second International Conference on Whole Life Urban Sustainability and Its Assessment: Conference Proceedings,* edited by M. Horner, A. Price, J. Bebbington, and R. Emmanuel, 865–85. Loughborough University, Loughborough, UK.

Coutier, M., B. Harbone, D. Isser, I. Santos, and M. Watts. 2021. *Social Contracts for Development— Bargaining, Contention, and Social Inclusion in Sub-Saharan Africa.* Paris: Agence Française du Développement; Washington, DC: World Bank.

Crost, B., J. Felter, and P. Johnston. 2016. "Conditional Cash Transfers, Civil Conflict, and Insurgent Influence: Experimental Evidence from the Philippines." *Journal of Development Economics* 118 (C): 171–82.

Cuesta, J., B. López-Noval, and M. Niño-Zarazúa. 2022. "Social Exclusion: Concepts, Measurement, and a Global Estimate." Policy Research Working Paper 10097, World Bank, Washington, DC.

Cuesta, J., L. Madrigal, and N. Pecorari. 2022. "Social Sustainability, Poverty, and Income: An Empirical Exploration." Policy Research Working Paper 10085, World Bank, Washington, DC. http://documents.worldbank.org/curated/en/099915206132218553/IDU05fa103b00466704a130bfec06158420e23ee.

Cuthill, M. 2010. "Strengthening the 'Social' in Sustainable Development: Developing a Conceptual Framework for Social Sustainability in a Rapid Urban Growth Region in Australia." *Sustainable Development* 18 (6): 362–73.

Daly, H. E. 1996. *Beyond Growth: The Economics of Sustainable Development.* Boston, MA: Beacon Press.

Davis, G. 2004. "A History of the Social Development Network in The World Bank, 1973–2002." Social Development Paper 56, World Bank, Washington, DC.

Dell, M., and P. Querubin. 2017. "Nation Building through Foreign Intervention: Evidence from Discontinuities in Military Strategies." *Quarterly Journal of Economics* 133 (2): 701–64.

Dempsey, N., G. Bramley, S. Power, and C. Brown. 2011. "The Social Dimension of Sustainable Development: Defining Urban Social Sustainability." *Sustainable Development* 19 (5): 289–300.

Durkheim, E. 1897. *Le suicide: Étude de sociologie.* New York: F. Alcan.

Efferson, C., S. Vogt, A. Elhadi, H. E. F. Ahmed, and E. Fehr. 2015. "Female Genital Cutting Is Not a Social Coordination Norm." *Science* 349 (6255): 1446–47.

Eizenberg, E., and Y. Jabareen. 2017. "Social Sustainability: A New Conceptual Framework." *Sustainability* 9 (1): 68.

Esenaliev, D., A. Bolotbekova, G. Asylbek, K. Tilekeyev, A. Aladysheva, R. Mogilevskii, and T. Brück. 2018. "Social Cohesion through Community-Based Development in Kyrgyzstan." IPPA Working Paper 46, Institute of Public Policy and Administration, Bishkek.

Esteban, J., and D. Ray. 2011. "Linking Conflict to Inequality and Polarization." *American Economic Review* 101 (4): 1345–74.

Fearon, J. 2010. "Governance and Civil War Onset." Background paper for *World Development Report 2011: Conflict, Security, and Development.* Washington, DC: World Bank.

Fearon, J., and D. Laitin. 2012. "How Persistent Is Armed Conflict?" Working Paper 311, Economic Research Southern Africa, Cape Town.

Ferreira, F. H. G., J. Messina, J. Rigolini, L. López-Calva, M. A. Lugo, and R. Vakis. 2013. *Economic Mobility and the Rise of the Latin American Middle Class.* Washington, DC: World Bank.

Fiszbein, A., R. Kanbur, and R. Yemtsov. 2014. "Social Protection and Poverty Reduction: Global Patterns and Some Targets." *World Development* 61 (C): 167–77.

Folke, C. 2016. "Resilience." *Ecology and Society* 21 (4): 44.

Freire, G., M. E. García Mora, G. Lara Ibarra, and S. Schwartz Orellana. 2020. *Social Inclusion in Uruguay.* Washington, DC: World Bank.

Garschagen, M., F. G. Renaud, and J. Birkmann. 2011. "Dynamic Resilience of Peri-Urban Agriculturalists in the Mekong Delta under Pressures of Socio-Economic Transformation and Climate Change." In *Environmental Change and Agricultural Sustainability in the Mekong Delta,* edited by M. Stewart and P. Coclanis. Advances in Global Change Research 45. Dordrecht: Springer.

Gates, S. 2002. "Recruitment and Allegiance: The Microfoundations of Rebellion." *Journal of Conflict Resolution* 46 (1): 111–30.

Gilligan, M. J., B. J. Pasquale, and C. Samii. 2014. "Civil War and Social Cohesion: Lab-in-the-Field Evidence from Nepal." *American Journal of Political Science* 58 (3): 604–19.

Glasson, J., and G. Wood. 2009. "Urban Regeneration and Impact Assessment for Social Sustainability." *Impact Assessment and Project Appraisal* 27 (4): 283–90.

Glavovic, B. C., R. Scheyvens, and J. Overton. 2003. "Waves of Adversity, Layers of Resilience: Exploring the Sustainable Livelihoods Approach." In *Contesting Development: Pathways to Better Practice. Proceedings of the Third Biennial Conference of the Aotearoa New Zealand International*

Development Studies Network (DevNet), edited by D. Storey, J. Overton, and B. Nowak, 289–93. Brighton: Institute of Development Studies.

Griessler, E., and B. Littig. 2005. "Social Sustainability: A Catchword between Political Pragmatism and Social Theory." *International Journal for Sustainable Development* 8 (1/2): 65–79.

Hallegatte, S., A. Vogt-Schilb, M. Bangalore, and J. Rozenberg. 2017. *Unbreakable: Building the Resilience of the Poor in the Face of Natural Disasters*. Climate Change and Development. Washington, DC: World Bank.

Hsieh, C.-T., E. Hurst, C. I. Jones, and P. J. Klenow. 2013. "The Allocation of Talent and U.S. Economic Growth." NBER Working Paper 18693, National Bureau of Economic Research, Cambridge, MA.

James, P., A. Scerri, J. Thom, and L. Magee. 2013. "Reframing Social Sustainability Reporting: Towards an Engaged Approach." *Environment, Development, and Sustainability* 15 (1): 225–43.

Jordan, J. C. 2015. *Swimming Alone? The Role of Social Capital in Enhancing Local Resilience to Climate Stress: A Case Study from Bangladesh*. PhD diss., University of Manchester.

Jordan, J. C. 2019. "Deconstructing Resilience: Why Gender and Power Matter in Responding to Climate Stress in Bangladesh." *Climate and Development* 11 (2): 167–79.

Keck, M., and P. Sakdapolrak. 2013. "What Is Social Resilience? Lessons Learned and Ways Forward." *Erdkunde* 67 (1): 5–19.

Kimmelman, M. 2021. "What Does It Mean to Save a Neighborhood?" *New York Times*, December 2, 2021. https://www.nytimes.com/2021/12/02/us/hurricane-sandy-lower-manhattan-nyc .html.

Klinenberg, E. 2002. *Heat Wave: A Social Autopsy of Disaster in Chicago*. Chicago, IL: University of Chicago Press.

Koning, J. 2001. "Social Sustainability in a Globalizing World: Context, Theory, and Methodology Explored." Paper prepared for the United Nations Educational, Scientific, and Cultural Organization (UNESCO) meeting, November 22–23, 2001, The Hague, The Netherlands.

Kunz, J. 2006. *Social Sustainability and Community Involvement in Urban Planning: Lessons from the ECOCITY Project*. Tampere, Finland: University of Tampere.

Lamichhane, K., and Y. Sawada. 2013. "Disability and Returns to Education in a Developing Country." *Economics of Education Review* 37 (December): 85–94.

Larsen, C. A. 2013. *The Rise and Fall of Social Cohesion. The Construction and De-Construction of Social Trust in the USA, UK, Sweden, and Denmark*. Oxford: Oxford University Press.

Lehtonen, M. 2004. "The Environmental-Social Interface of Sustainable Development: Capabilities, Social Capital Institutions." *Ecological Economics* 49 (2): 199–214.

Lereya, S. T., W. E. Copeland, E. J. Costello, and D. Wolke. 2015. "Adult Mental Health Consequences of Peer Bullying and Maltreatment in Childhood: Two Cohorts in Two Countries." *Lancet Psychiatry* 2 (6): 524–31.

Lewin, K. 1946. "Behavior and Development as a Function of the Total Situation." In *Manual of Child Psychology*, edited by L. Carmichael, 791–844. Hoboken, NJ: J. Wiley and Sons.

Locke, H., and P. Dearden. 2005. "Rethinking Protected Area Categories and the New Paradigm." *Environmental Conservation* 32 (1): 1–10.

Loewe, M., T. Zing, and A. Houdret. 2021. "The Social Contract as a Tool of Analysis." *World Development* 145 (September): 104982.

Lott, A. J., and B. E. Lott. 1966. "Group Cohesiveness and Individual Learning." *Journal of Educational Psychology* 57 (2): 61–73.

Maclean, R. 2022. "What Do the Protectors of Congo's Peatlands Get in Return?" *New York Times,* February 21, 2022.

Madgavkar, A., K. Ellingrud, and M. Krishnan. 2016. "The Economic Benefits of Gender Parity." *Stanford Social Innovation Review,* March 8, 2016.

Male, C., and Q. Wodon. 2017. "Disability Gaps in Educational Attainment and Literacy: The Price of Exclusion." Disability and Education Series, World Bank and Global Partnership for Education, Washington, DC.

Mansuri, G., and V. Rao. 2013. *Localizing Development: Does Participation Work?* Washington, DC: World Bank.

Marc, A., A. Williams, G. Aslam, M. Rebosio, and K. Balasuriya. 2012. *Societal Dynamics and Fragility: Engaging Societies in Responding to Fragile Situations.* New Frontiers of Social Policy. Washington, DC: World Bank.

Marrero, G. A., and J. G. Rodriguez. 2013. "Inequality of Opportunity and Growth." *Journal of Development Economics* 104 (September): 107–22.

Maxwell, J. 1996. "Social Dimensions of Economic Growth: E. J. Hanson Memorial Lecture." University of Alberta, Edmonton, January 25, 1996.

McChesney, K. Y. 2015. "Successful Approaches to Ending Female Genital Cutting." *Journal of Sociology and Social Welfare* 42 (1): 3–24.

McKenzie, S. 2004. "Social Sustainability: Towards Some Definitions." Hawke Research Institute Working Paper Series 27, Hawke Research Institute, University of South Australia, Adelaide.

Mearns, R., and A. Norton. 2010. *Social Dimensions of Climate Change: Equity and Vulnerability in a Warming World.* New Frontiers of Social Policy. Washington, DC: World Bank.

Michel, J.-B., Y. K. Shen, A. P. Aiden, A. Veres, M. K. Gray, W. Brockman, The Google Books Team, et al. 2011. "Quantitative Analysis of Culture Using Millions of Digitized Books." *Science* 331 (6014): 176–82.

Migdal, J. S. 2001. *State in Society: Studying How States and Societies Transform and Constitute One Another.* Cambridge, UK: Cambridge University Press.

Min, E., M. Singh, J. N. Shapiro, and B. Crisman. 2017. "Understanding Risk and Resilience to Violent Conflicts." Background paper for *Pathways for Peace: Inclusive Approaches to Preventing Violent Conflict.* Washington, DC: World Bank.

Morgon Banks, L., and S. Polack. 2015. "The Economic Costs of Exclusion and Gains of Inclusion of People with Disabilities: Evidence from Low- and Middle-Income Countries." International Centre for Evidence in Disability and London School of Hygiene and Tropical Medicine, London.

Moshy, V. H., I. Bryceson, and R. Mwaipopo. 2015. "Social-Ecological Changes, Livelihoods, and Resilience among Fishing Communities in Mafia Island Marine Park, Tanzania." *Forum for Development Studies* 42 (3): 529–53.

Mozumder, M. M. H., M. A. Wahab, S. Sarkki, P. Schneider, and M. M. Islam. 2018. "Enhancing Social Resilience of the Coastal Fishing Communities: A Case Study of Hilsa (Tenualosa Ilisha H.) Fishery in Bangladesh." *Sustainability* 10 (10): 3501.

Mubarak, K., E. Johnson, A. Beath, M. Latif, and X. Luo. 2020. "Impact Evaluation of Cambodia's Implementation of the Social Accountability Framework." World Bank, Washington, DC.

Murphy, K. 2012. "The Social Pillar of Sustainable Development: A Literature Review and Framework for Policy Analysis." *Sustainability: Science, Practice, and Policy* 8 (1): 15–29.

Norton, A., and A. de Haan. 2012. *Social Cohesion: Theoretical Debates and Practical Applications with Respect to Jobs*. Washington, DC: World Bank.

Nunn, N. 2022. "On the Dynamics of Human Behavior: The Past, Present, and Future of Culture, Conflict, and Cooperation." *AEA Papers and Proceedings* 112: 15–37.

Obrist, B. 2010. "Multi-Layered Social Resilience: A New Approach to Migration Research." *Progress in Development Studies* 10 (4): 283–93.

OECD (Organisation for Economic Co-operation and Development). 2011. *Perspectives on Global Development 2012: Social Cohesion in a Shifting World*. Paris: OECD.

Olawole, I., A. Lichtenheld, and R. Sheely. 2022. *Strengthening Social Cohesion for Violence Prevention: 10 Lessons for Policymakers and Practitioners*. Washington, DC: Mercy Corps.

Ostry, J. D., J. Alvarez, R. A. Espinoza, and C. Papageorgiou. 2018. "Economic Gains from Gender Inclusion: New Mechanisms, New Evidence." Staff Discussion Note, International Monetary Fund, Washington, DC.

Paler, L., C. Samii, M. Lisiecki, and A. Morel. 2015. *Social and Environmental Impact of the Community Rangers Program in Aceh*. Washington, DC: World Bank.

Partridge, E. 2005. "Social Sustainability: A Useful Theoretical Framework?" Prepared for the Australasian Political Science Association Annual Conference, Dunedin, New Zealand, September 28 and 30, 2005. http://auspsa.anu.edu. au/index.html.

Pascale, R., J. Sternin, and M. Sternin. 2010. *The Power of Positive Deviance*. Boston, MA: Harvard Business Press.

Paugam, S. 1993. *La societé française es ses pauvres [French Society and Its Poor]*. Paris: Presses Universitaires de France.

Peiling, M., and C. High. 2005. "Understanding Adaptation: What Can Social Capital Offer Assessments of Adaptive Capacity?" *Global Environmental Change* 15 (4): 308–19.

Pena, P., J. Urrego, and J. Villa. 2017. "Civil Conflict and Conditional Cash Transfers: Effects on Demobilization." *World Development* 99 (C): 431–40.

Pierson, J. 2002. *Tackling Social Exclusion*. London: Routledge.

Purvis, B., Y. Mao, and D. Robinson. 2019. "Three Pillars of Sustainability: In Search of Conceptual Origins." *Sustainability Science* 14 (3): 681–95.

Ratcliffe, P. 2000. "Is the Assertion of Minority Identity Compatible with the Idea of a Socially Inclusive Society?" In *Social Inclusion: Possibilities and Tensions*, edited by P. Askonas and A. Stewart, 169–85. New York: Macmillan.

Rauch, J. E. 1991. "Productivity Gains from Geographic Concentration of Human Capital: Evidence from the Cities." NBER Working Paper 3905, National Bureau of Economic Research, Cambridge, MA.

Rodrik, D. 2011. *The Globalization Paradox: Why Global Markets, States, and Democracy Can't Coexist.* New York: Oxford University Press.

Rohner, D. 2018. "The Economics of Conflict: A Literature Review and Practitioner's Guide for the Foreign Aid Community." *Revue d'Économie du Développement* 26 (4): 5–25.

Rohner, D., M. Thoenig, and F. Zilibotti. 2013. "Seeds of Distrust: Conflict in Uganda." *Journal of Economic Growth* 18 (3): 217–52.

Sachs, I. 1999. "Social Sustainability and Whole Development: Exploring the Dimensions of Sustainable Development." In *Sustainability and the Social Sciences: A Cross-Disciplinary Approach to Integrating Environmental Considerations into Theoretical Reorientation,* edited by T. Jahn and E. Becker. London: Zed Books.

Schlosberg, D. 2007. *Reconceiving Environmental Justice: Global Movements and Political Theories.* Oxford: Oxford University Press.

Siisiäinen, M. 2003. "One Concept, Two Approaches: Bourdieu and Putnam on Social Capital." *International Journal of Contemporary Sociology* 40 (2): 183–204.

Smith, L. C., and T. R. Frankenberger. 2018. "Does Resilience Capacity Reduce the Negative Impact of Shocks on Household Food Security? Evidence from the 2014 Floods in Northern Bangladesh." *World Development* 102 (C): 358–76.

Solórzano, A. 2016. "Can Social Protection Increase Resilience to Climate Change? A Case Study of Oportunidades in Rural Yucatan, Mexico." IDS Working Paper 465, Institute of Development Studies, Brighton.

Sonnenfeld, A., J. Doherty, M. Berretta, S. Shisler, B. Snilstveit, J. Eyers, K. Castaman, et al. 2021. "Strengthening Intergroup Social Cohesion in Fragile Situations." 3ie Systematic Review 46, International Initiative for Impact Evaluation, New Delhi.

Staniland, P. 2014. *Networks of Rebellion: Explaining Insurgent Cohesion and Collapse.* Ithaca, NY: Cornell University Press.

Stiglitz, J. 2007. *Making Globalization Work.* New York: W. W. Norton.

Tawodzera, G. 2012. "Urban Household Survival and Resilience to Food Insecurity in Crisis Conditions: The Case of Epworth in Harare, Zimbabwe." *Journal of Hunger and Environmental Nutrition* 7 (2-3): 293–320.

Townshend, I., O. Awosoga, J. Kulig, and H. Fan. 2015. "Social Cohesion and Resilience across Communities That Have Experienced a Disaster." *Journal of the International Society for the Prevention and Mitigation of Natural Hazards* 76 (2): 913–38.

Traerup, S. 2012. "Informal Networks and Resilience to Climate Change Impacts: A Collective Approach to Index Insurance." *Global Environmental Change* 22 (1): 255–67.

Tucker, P. 2018. *Unelected Power: The Quest for Legitimacy in Central Banking and the Regulatory State.* Princeton, NJ: Princeton University Press.

Turner, A. 2013. "The Business Case for Racial Equity." W. K. Kellogg Foundation and Altarum Institute, Battle Creek, MI.

Tyler, T. R. 1990. *Why People Obey the Law.* New Haven, CT: Yale University Press.

United Nations and World Bank. 2018. *Pathways for Peace: Inclusive Approaches to Preventing Violent Conflict.* Washington, DC: World Bank.

Vallance, S., H. C. Perkins, and J. E. Dixon. 2011. "What Is Social Sustainability? A Clarification of Concepts." *Geoforum* 42 (3): 342–48.

Vifell, A. C., and L. Soneryd. 2012. "How 'the Social Dimension' Gets Lost in Sustainability Projects." *Sustainable Development* 20 (1): 18–27.

Voss, M. 2008. "The Vulnerable Can't Speak: An Integrative Vulnerability Approach to Disaster and Climate Change Research." *Behemoth: A Journal on Civilisation* 1 (3): 39–56.

Weingaertner, C., and A. Moberg. 2014. "Exploring Social Sustainability: Learning from Perspectives on Urban Development and Companies and Products." *Sustainable Development* 22 (2): 122–33.

Wodon, Q., and B. de la Brière. 2018. *The Cost of Gender Inequality Unrealized Potential: The High Cost of Gender Inequality in Earnings.* Washington, DC: World Bank.

Wong, S. 2022. "Evidence Note on Community-Driven Development (CDD): A Summary of Key Findings on World Bank-Financed CDD Operations." World Bank, Washington, DC.

Wong, S., and S. Guggenheim. 2018. "Community-Driven Development: Myths and Realities." Policy Research Working Paper 8435, World Bank, Washington, DC.

Woodcraft, S., N. Bacon, T. Hackett, and L. Caistor-Arendar. 2011. *Design for Social Sustainability: A Framework for Creating Thriving New Communities.* London: Young Foundation.

Woolcock, M., and D. Narayan. 2000. "Social Capital: Implications for Development Theory, Research, and Policy." *World Bank Research Observer* 15 (2): 225–49.

World Bank. 2001. *World Development Report 2000/2001: Attacking Poverty.* Washington, DC: World Bank.

World Bank. 2005a. "Empowering People by Transforming Institutions: Social Development in World Bank Operations." Social Development Strategy Paper, World Bank, Washington, DC.

World Bank. 2005b. "Putting Social Development to Work for the Poor: An OED Review of World Bank Activities." Operations Evaluation Department, World Bank, Washington, DC.

World Bank. 2006. *World Development Report 2006: Equity and Development.* Washington, DC: World Bank.

World Bank. 2011. *World Development Report 2011: Conflict, Security, and Development.* Washington, DC: World Bank.

World Bank. 2013a. *Building Resilience: Integrating Climate and Disaster Risk into Development—The World Bank Group Experience.* Washington, DC: World Bank.

World Bank. 2013b. *Inclusion Matters: The Foundation of Shared Prosperity.* Washington, DC: World Bank.

World Bank. 2013c. *The World Bank Group Goals: End Extreme Poverty and Promote Shared Prosperity.* Washington, DC: World Bank.

World Bank. 2014. *Youth Employment in Sub-Saharan Africa.* Washington, DC: World Bank.

World Bank. 2017. *World Development Report 2017: Governance and the Law.* Washington, DC: World Bank.

World Bank. 2018a. *Engaging Citizens for Better Development.* Washington, DC: World Bank, Independent Evaluation Group.

World Bank. 2018b. "Indonesia: Long-Term Impact Evaluation of Generasi." World Bank, Washington, DC.

World Bank. 2020. *World Bank Group Strategy for Fragility, Conflict, and Violence 2020–2035.* Washington, DC: World Bank.

World Bank. 2022a. *Social Cohesion and Forced Displacement: A Synthesis of New Research.* Washington, DC: World Bank.

World Bank. 2022b. Social Sustainability Global Database 2022. World Bank, Washington, DC.

World Bank. 2022c. "Social Sustainability Global Database Codebook." World Bank, Washington, DC.

3

Closing the Implementation Gap

Introduction

The previous chapters made the case for why, to respond to the most urgent crises of the moment and meet the challenges of the 21st century, development needs to embrace social sustainability as a core objective. Building on this background and the book's definition, conceptual framework, and empirical evidence, this chapter discusses key areas for development cooperation to enhance its impact on social sustainability. A wealth of experience has been accumulated on how to design and implement successful projects, programs, and policies to support social cohesion, inclusion, resilience, and process legitimacy, translating aspirations for social sustainability into action. Yet there is a need to integrate social sustainability more systematically and consistently across all areas of development.

This chapter begins by outlining five common operational challenges that need to be factored into programming for social sustainability. It then provides an overview of interventions, from World Bank experience as well as that of other development organizations, that have proven effective at fostering cohesion, inclusion, and resilience. While not comprehensive, the examples highlight some of the most effective and innovative efforts to date, with the understanding and expectation that new insights will emerge in the years to come. The chapter closes by drawing out three high-level, overarching priorities for supporting process legitimacy, in order to ensure that efforts to promote social sustainability work within the context of existing norms and values and are considered fair, credible, and acceptable by all members and groups in a society.

Challenges in Operationalizing Social Sustainability

Progress toward social sustainability can be fostered, and this chapter provides some insights on how to advance it. However, five common challenges must be taken into account in efforts to promote and support inclusion, cohesion, resilience, and process legitimacy.

73

Progress is often nonlinear and time-consuming. The change process can be contentious and sometimes violent, with achievements often followed by setbacks. This dynamic is discussed in depth in the academic literature, for example, on racial justice in the United States[1] and on advances in women's labor market participation globally.[2] In particular, policies and projects that target deeper change, such as behavioral or normative transformation, take longer to show measurable results. As such, the time horizon for social change is often longer than the typical project horizon for development practitioners and other change makers. Moreover, while the four key components of social sustainability often mutually reinforce each other (that is, inclusion can promote trust and cohesion, which together can foster resilience—all supported by process legitimacy and further enhancing it in turn), they do not always move together. Societies often make progress on one dimension (or certain aspects of a dimension), while failing on others. A country might improve access to education for people with disabilities, for instance, but experience greater interethnic conflict or have high levels of resilience to climate shocks alongside high levels of exclusion.

The factors that drive or impede social sustainability are nonuniform and context-dependent. Inclusion, cohesion, resilience, and process legitimacy are shaped by local context and vary across countries and communities. Depending on the specific stressors experienced by a community and its particular needs, efforts to bolster resilience will need to take a different focus. While strengthening social protection systems may help communities to cope with recurring income shocks, improving early warning systems and providing better information may be more critical for communities facing the threat of natural disasters. Likewise, fostering cohesion can involve programs to increase trust in the police, strengthen interethnic connections in schools, or promote nonviolent conflict resolution between communities; in other situations, cohesion may best be supported as part of programs with broader objectives such as improving livelihood opportunities or access to public services (Chatterjee, Gassier, and Myint 2022).

The obstacles are often complex, multidimensional, and entrenched. Social sustainability is first and foremost about people, and the obstacles to it cut across many areas of people's lives. Therefore, solutions must be multidimensional and work across sectors to foster new opportunities by lifting constraints where they exist. Job schemes to promote women's inclusion in labor markets, for example, may only work if women also have access to quality child care, water, and electricity (to free their time to engage in income-generating activities), if gender norms are conducive, and if they have agency to take up employment (Barca 2019; Barros et al. 2011; Berlinski and Galiani 2007; Buvinic and O'Donnell 2019). Likewise, making buildings physically accessible may improve access to education for some children with disabilities, but others will continue to be left out unless teachers know how to teach children with different learning needs and learning materials are accessible (Alasuutari et al. 2020). In the most vexing cases, obstacles are so entrenched that much broader issues will need to be tackled (structural inequality, elite resistance, vested interests) before any social sustainability efforts can thrive.

Progress may involve normative changes, which can be difficult to generate. Deeply embedded social and cultural norms, values, and behaviors can also impede social sustainability and undermine the effectiveness of policies and programs to enhance it. While a core aspect of process legitimacy is working within existing contexts, promoting positive norms is important and can sometimes require influencing or counteracting negative ones. Such efforts are challenging, however, and can be unpredictable and potentially destabilizing—often aggravating deep-rooted social tensions and increasing the risks of unrest or conflict.

The context is always evolving. As certain goal posts for social sustainability are reached, new challenges arise, partly due to the nature of the issues associated with social sustainability. Resilience, almost by definition, is about coping with the unforeseen; the complex and diverse impacts of climate change, for instance, are still being understood and can be highly unpredictable.[3] For cohesion, while several models exist to forecast social tensions and violent conflict, it is impossible to predict their onset, location, intensity, and timing accurately (on the challenges of predicting violent conflict, see United Nations and World Bank 2018, 241). For inclusion, sexual orientation and gender identity (SOGI) are now well-recognized aspects of inclusivity in a growing number of countries, but were not widely acknowledged until recent decades and are not (yet) recognized in other countries. Likewise, new technologies create new ways of interacting and doing things; the COVID-19 pandemic, for example, suddenly made digital inclusion in education a mainstream challenge where it had previously been a frontier issue. As such, social sustainability will, in part, always remain aspirational and continue to inspire progress as societal values, behaviors, and norms change and societies evolve (box 3.1).

Box 3.1
Social Inclusion in Uruguay

The case of Uruguay illustrates the aspirational nature of social sustainability and its key components. In a region where inequality is common, the country has made significant progress on inclusion; it stands out for its robust middle class, near absence of extreme poverty, high levels of job formality, and near universal access to basic services. Over the past two decades, poverty in Uruguay has declined by roughly 75 percent, and the country has low levels of corruption as well as social spending that is on par with levels in the Organisation for Economic Co-operation and Development countries.

These achievements have been supported by a strong social compact and a long history of inclusive legislation. During the first decades of the 20th century, Uruguay enacted far-reaching labor reforms, becoming the first country in the world to adopt an eight-hour workday. The government universalized access to primary education and health care, legalized divorce, and offered strong unemployment benefits. In 2007 Uruguay was the first Latin American country to legalize same-sex civil unions.

Important gaps remain, however. Stigmatization and disadvantages in education and health are still linked to gender, race, sexual orientation, disability, age, and geographic location. Female-headed households, for example, are still twice as likely to be poor as households headed by males. Likewise, despite Uruguay's affirmative

(continued)

action policies, Afro-descendants are still 2.5 times more likely to live in poverty than the national average. Uruguay's experience provides two lessons. First, investment and policies aimed at social inclusion pay off, making societies more equitable and resilient to shocks in the long run. Second, gaps in income, well-being, and access to opportunities among social groups are persistent, often driven by complex and long-standing structural barriers and norms. Even a regional leader in social inclusion such as Uruguay cannot afford to be complacent.

What Has Worked to Promote Cohesion, Inclusion, and Resilience?

Cohesion, inclusion, and resilience are broad concepts that encompass a wide range of relationships, social groups, and dimensions of socioeconomic life. This section provides examples of successful and innovative projects, programs, and policies that have been implemented effectively to propel progress. Many of the interventions discussed here cut across multiple or all three dimensions; as noted, the key components of social sustainability can often be mutually reinforcing.

Fostering Cohesion—What Works?

As described in chapter 2, cohesion encompasses relations between people in a given community (bonding cohesion), across different communities (bridging cohesion), and between people and state structures (linking cohesion). Consequently, the kinds of interventions used to foster cohesion span a broad range. At a high level, efforts to strengthen cohesion often have overarching goals to reduce violence (or the potential for violence), repair inter- or intragroup dynamics, improve perceptions of and trust in government, and strengthen local institutions. Such efforts have been achieved with measurable success in contexts both with and without fragility, conflict, and violence. The most effective interventions can be grouped into three broad categories: the establishment and strengthening of local and community platforms, efforts that integrate economic support with mechanisms for collaboration, and efforts that integrate social accountability mechanisms.

Local and community platforms comprise a broad array of efforts; when intentionally designed and implemented with a view to fostering cooperative behaviors, they have successfully contributed to strengthening cohesion (Barron 2011). In particular, local and community platforms can help to build cohesion between different ethnic or religious groups (box 3.2), including between host and migrant communities, and can strengthen dispute resolution mechanisms (box 3.3).

Box 3.2
Strengthening Community Bonds: Insights from Indonesia

In 1998 the government of Indonesia launched the Kecamatan Development Program (KDP), a large national effort to train facilitators to elicit active participation from community members at the village level, a demographic whose voice had long been marginalized. Initially targeting the poorest subdistricts, KDP covered a quarter of the country's 70,000 villages; over a 15-year period, it was expanded to reach almost half of all Indonesian villages.

An in-depth study of both KDP and comparison villages suggests that the program and its collective decision-making processes had positive effects on intergroup relations (World Bank 2018c). In one of the provinces studied, 39 percent of respondents reported improved relations between religious groups (compared to an average of 15 percent in comparison sites). The longer KDP had been in place in a village, the larger these effects became. Furthermore, the program also appears to have democratized debates within villages, increasing the participation of marginalized groups.[a]

a. The share of respondents reporting that marginalized groups were coming to village meetings was 50 percent higher in KDP villages than in comparison villages. This share reached 75 percent in villages where KDP had been in place for at least four years. See Barron, Diprose, and Woolcock (2011).

Box 3.3
Strengthening Cohesion and Resilience in Nigeria

Nigeria's population has quadrupled in the last 50 years, while climate change and environmental degradation have led to increased competition over natural resources. Two current World Bank projects (the Agro-Climatic Resilience in Semi-Arid Landscapes Project and the Livestock Productivity and Resilience Support Project) explicitly combine elements that aim to foster cohesion with technical efforts to improve the resilience of agricultural livelihoods.

The projects seek to improve sustainable natural resource use (for example, by implementing remote-sensing technologies to assess the status of water and feed and by facilitating the dissemination of this information to key users). At the same time, the projects aim to increase local capacity for conflict resolution. This effort involves establishing and training local committees for conflict prevention and resolution within and between communities. These committees aim to build on existing institutions and mechanisms. To promote process legitimacy, they map stakeholders, identify sources of conflict, and consider ideas to address them.

In Colombia, for instance, a rural program was found to be highly effective at improving cooperation within communities, with increased cooperative behavior observed in both program beneficiaries and nonbeneficiaries alike (D'Exelle, Coleman, and Lopez 2018). In postconflict Liberia, a community-focused program requiring men and women to address collective action challenges together improved levels of cooperation.[4] In North Central Nigeria, training local leaders in interest-based mediation improved their ability to resolve disputes and significantly reduced the share of community members who recently experienced a violent incident, which improved participants' overall sense of security (Chatterjee, Gassier, and Myint 2022). In Israel, randomly assigning Jewish patients to Arab doctors in medical clinics facilitated intergroup contact and improved majority-group perceptions of minorities (Weiss 2020). In Türkiye, an early childhood program preparing Turkish and Syrian children for primary school led to the formation of inter-ethnic friendships, improved the Turkish language skills of Syrian children, and reduced primary school absenteeism for Syrian children (Boucher et al. 2021).

Efforts that integrate economic support with mechanisms for collaboration have also shown promise at fostering cohesion. On their own, cash transfer or livelihood support programs—even when successful at providing targeted economic support—can generate feelings of unfairly excluding nonbeneficiaries, often increasing tensions within communities (Pavanello et al. 2016). When such efforts explicitly integrate mechanisms for encouraging collaboration, however, they have been shown to foster bonding (within communities) as well as bridging (between communities) and linking (citizen-state relations) types of cohesion.

In Malawi, for example, combining cash transfers with training and participation in a savings group was found to improve cohesion among participants more than providing cash transfers on their own, according to a study that attributed the impacts to the fact that participation in the savings group improved within-community relations (Burchi and Roscioli 2021). Economic and livelihood support interventions have also been shown to improve bridging cohesion through intergroup contact and collaboration.[5] In Jordan, a vocational training program was targeted toward both Jordanians and Syrian refugees, encouraging contact between the groups. An evaluation found that persons enrolled in the program showed less in-group favoritism as a result of the interactions, with greater trust in others and less bias toward other nationalities (Mercy Corps and Ministry of Foreign Affairs of the Netherlands 2020).

Integrating social accountability mechanisms can also support cohesion. When paired with economic support programs—for example, training beneficiaries or civil society organizations to monitor funds—social accountability can improve linking cohesion at the level of citizen-state relations (linking) (Fox 2015). Likewise, mechanisms to enhance the transparent provision of information can improve trust in governments when combined with adequate service delivery.

In Uganda, training the beneficiaries of a community program to report misuse of funds led to improved monitoring, project quality, and trust in the central government (Fiala and Premand 2018). Likewise, during the 2014–15 Ebola epidemic, the government of Liberia's door-to-door canvassing campaign to encourage voluntary compliance with disease containment policies was effective at improving safety-related behaviors, generating support for public health policies, and increasing trust in the government (Blair et al. 2021). In Pakistan, a government agency used social media during the COVID-19 pandemic to communicate with citizens, increasing trust and creating positive perceptions of the government's management of the crisis (Mansoor 2021). Also in Pakistan, providing accurate information about shorter delays in state courts increased citizens' support for the state and reported likelihood of using the courts, as measured in lab games. Moreover, this intervention led to less support for nonstate actors (Acemoglu et al. 2020).

Fostering Inclusion—What Works?

Inclusion involves expanding access to markets (labor, land, financial markets) and services (health, education, social protection services) as well as fostering the voice and agency of groups at risk of exclusion. The types of interventions that support inclusion are as diverse and multifarious as the types of exclusion they seek to address, including efforts to address the exclusion of indigenous peoples from land markets, tackle gender gaps in labor markets, improve education for persons with disabilities, ensure that refugees can access quality health care, and promote the voice of lesbian, gay, bisexual, transgender, and intersex people, to only name a few (Das and Espinoza 2020; World Bank 2013). Some of the most effective interventions for supporting inclusion fall into six categories: legal reform, affirmative action or quotas, efforts to target particular groups, efforts to involve groups at risk of exclusion in the design of policies and programs, efforts to foster the voice and agency of formerly excluded groups, and normative change.

Legal reform can be a powerful driver of inclusion. Laws and institutions provide the framework for all areas of social life. They can affect whether individuals and groups can access and benefit from education, health care, social protection, and other basic services; they set the rules for individuals to participate in labor markets; and they determine who can inherit or own land, who is considered a citizen, and who gets a say in political decision-making processes. Legal reforms can have far-reaching impacts. For instance, changes in property law that give formerly excluded groups title to land or the right to inherit can be effective beyond land ownership and have been shown to improve labor market participation and livelihoods. In Rwanda, for example, land reforms had significant positive impacts on women's access to land markets as well as their rights to mortgage or lease land. Perceived rights for women to be registered as a claimant (alone or jointly) on parcels owned by married couples, for instance, increased from only 33 percent in the baseline to about 94 percent after land tenure was regularized (Ali, Deininger, and Goldstein 2011; Ali et al. 2015). In Ethiopia, reforms in family law[6] significantly strengthened women's bargaining position within the household and increased the rates of women working outside the home, with women's participation in work outside the home 24 percent higher in reforming areas than in nonreforming areas (Ali, Deininger, and Goldstein 2011; Ali et al. 2015; Das and Espinoza 2020; Hallward-Driemeier and Gajigo 2013).

Affirmative action or quotas for groups who have historically faced discrimination or exclusive social norms, while sometimes politically controversial, can be effective at addressing entrenched group-based disparities in several countries (Das and Espinoza 2020; Langer, Stewart, and Schroyens 2016). For example, a recent reform in Colombia provides Venezuelan migrants with temporary protection status, providing formal access to the labor market (box 3.4). In Vietnam, community and local development programs have increased the participation of women and ethnic minorities by including participatory mechanisms in their project designs, such as mandates for gender parity in community councils (Beath, Christia, and Enikolopov 2013; World Bank 2019b).

> **Box 3.4**
> **Strengthening the Integration of Migrants in Colombia**
>
> The government of Colombia approved temporary protection status (TPS) for Venezuelan migrants in 2021 as part of a broader shift in the government's approach to the migration crisis from emergency response to a longer-term strategy supporting the integration and inclusion of Venezuelan migrants in Colombian society (World Bank 2021).
>
> By permitting Venezuelan migrants to stay and work in Colombia for up to 10 years, the TPS facilitates access to basic services and the labor market. The government also created a Single Registry of Venezuelan Migrants (Registro Único de Migrantes Venezolanos) to facilitate the identification, socioeconomic characterization, and targeting of migrants eligible for education, health care, emergency shelter and disaster response, and social protection programs. In addition to the TPS, the government is implementing further policies to facilitate the access of Venezuelan migrants to critical services, including COVID-19 vaccines, housing subsidies, and financial services.
>
> To foster cohesion between migrants and Colombians and build public support for these efforts, the government implemented a broad communications and social media campaign to promote positive and fact-based reporting on the benefits of migration and to counter negative stereotyping of migrants.

Ensuring that universal access programs (health or education) reach groups at particular risk of exclusion is another way to foster their inclusion (World Bank 2019a). Some groups face additional barriers to accessing quality services or benefiting from programs that are intended to increase overall service provision. To ensure that children with disabilities can access and benefit from quality educational opportunities, for example, they may need targeted support to address discriminatory enrollment practices, insufficiently trained teachers, or school infrastructure and services that are not universally accessible (safety procedures, play areas, hygiene and sanitation, laboratories, extracurricular activities, educational materials).[7] Likewise, children from ethnic minority backgrounds may need language instruction to benefit from education, while children and youth who belong to sexual and gender minorities may face discrimination from teachers or fellow students, causing them to drop out from education early. Infrastructure can play an important role in facilitating inclusion; ensuring that roads reach remote areas, for example, can help lagging regions to have better access to schools, health centers, or markets.

Efforts to involve groups at risk of exclusion in the design of policies and programs can also foster inclusion across different types of interventions. Traditionally excluded groups can help to diagnose and develop solutions to overcome barriers (box 3.5). In health programs, for instance, they can be involved in the surveillance of the availability and quality of health services, or service providers may be given incentives to reach and stay in remote areas (Das et al. 2017). This aspect of inclusion also pertains to process legitimacy, which is discussed in more detail below.

Box 3.5
Social Inclusion of Persons with Disabilities in Nigeria

During preparation of the World Bank's Nigeria Digital Identification for Development Project, persons with disabilities were involved in extensive stakeholder consultations to ensure that their perspectives were taken into account and that the resulting project would be inclusive. Targeted consultations highlighted systemic, long-entrenched barriers to accessing a means of identification (ID) for Nigerians with disabilities, including the inaccessibility of enrollment centers, high indirect costs for completing complex procedures, and difficulties obtaining accessible transport. In addition, frontline staff responsible for processing IDs are often not trained in addressing the needs of persons with disabilities, while stigma and misconceptions often dominate how services are provided.

Recommendations from these stakeholder consultations shaped differentiated measures in the design of the project, including (a) using civil society organizations such as disabled peoples' organizations to facilitate outreach to persons with disabilities and (b) ensuring exceptional data capture and processing requirements for any persons unable to provide the required biometrics (such as iris scans due to visual disabilities or fingerprints due to physical disabilities).[a]

a. Insights also informed a global guidance note on creating disability-inclusive ID systems with proposed actions for a comprehensive approach to overcoming barriers to ID enrollment and use for persons with disabilities (World Bank 2020).

Fostering the voice and agency of formerly excluded groups can tackle a key barrier to inclusion. In the area of gender and gender-based violence, for example, empowerment programs providing cross-sectoral assistance can effectively promote the voice and agency of women. The Sahel Women Empowerment and Demographic Dividend Program combines access to quality reproductive, child, and maternal health services while working with religious leaders, legislators, and health workers to change norms regarding child marriage, family planning, and gender-based violence (Das and Espinoza 2020, 130).

Normative change is often a critical component of efforts to strengthen inclusion, as norms typically play a role in sustaining exclusion over time. Some interventions have successfully triggered normative changes. Legal reform, in addition to the benefits mentioned above, can often lead to changing norms, particularly in contexts where institutions enjoy high levels of trust and the changes are relatively small or gradual (Banerjee, La Ferrara, and Orozco-Olvera 2019a; Bicchieri 2016; Bicchieri and Mercier 2014; Gauri, Rahman, and Sen 2019). Media-based solutions, like progressive soap operas or nudging information campaigns (Banerjee, La Ferrara, and Orozco-Olvera 2019a, 2019b), have also achieved measurable changes in social norms, as have deliberation efforts (that is, allowing individuals to discuss taboos openly). Likewise, iterative and participatory engagement with communities can be a powerful driver of normative change, which is most sustainable when it is consistent with the community's broader values and vision for improved well-being (box 3.6).

Box 3.6
Stopping Female Genital Cutting and Other Harmful Practices by Building on Community Values and Leaders

Tostan is a local nongovernmental organization in Senegal committed to supporting communities to define and enhance their own well-being. It partners at the community level on inclusive approaches to critical development challenges. The following describes its work to end female genital cutting and other harmful practices.

In many remote, rural African communities, people carry out their daily lives in accordance with a system of inherited beliefs and social rules that define relationships, interactions, and power structures. Many of these beliefs and rules are the result of wisdom and traditions handed down through the centuries to help communities to function in their resource-poor contexts. Others, however, are drivers of marginalization, exclusion, and poverty. Justified by inherited beliefs, they condone and perpetuate gender discrimination and its many forms of violence and inhibit the growth of individual and community aspirations for better lives.

After Tostan arrives in a community and explains its approach, the community agrees to establish a community management committee (CMC) composed of at least 50 percent women. The community also selects a group of adults and a group of youths to follow the program's classes in the local language. A facilitator begins by encouraging participants to discuss and define their vision of well-being. The groups then embark on an exploration of human rights and responsibilities, connecting these ideas to their own deeply held inherited values and enabling the emergence of a shared commitment to dignity and respect for all. Information on health and reproductive health, hygiene, sanitation, and child development is also shared and discussed. The participatory and respectful methodology fosters questioning of some existing practices that prevent the fulfillment of human rights, especially among women and children, such as the lack of participation of women and youth in decisions affecting them as well as female genital cutting, child marriage, and the use of violence to discipline children. Participants, who also acquire skills in problem solving, discuss and identify what they need to do in order to abandon these practices. They share the results of this process with other community members and work with CMC leadership to participate in social mobilization activities. When such efforts are successful, the community reaches a point whereby the harmful practices are no longer considered acceptable, and most agree to abandon them.

The Tostan model is premised on the notion that social norms change from within. Rather than being imposed from the outside, the changes build on and interweave with previous and concurrent community-led efforts to improve well-being and are consistent with the community's broader vision of improved well-being. As a result, they are more likely to be sustained.

For an additional example of how the Tostan approach supports social sustainability, see box 3.11.

Fostering Resilience—What Works?

Several approaches have been shown to strengthen all three forms of resilience—coping, adaptive, and transformative. Interventions to strengthen resilience seek to ensure that communities not merely cope with shocks but also overcome adversity without resorting to unsustainable strategies,[8] that they anticipate and reduce risk, and that they strengthen or create new institutions to prepare for future adversity. Three categories of resilience efforts have proven to be particularly effective: improving people's livelihoods, reducing their risk exposure, and promoting agency and self-organizing capacity building, including through better access to information.

Improving people's livelihoods through investments in cash transfers, education, and health care can directly enhance resilience (Barrett and Constas 2014). Financial inclusion efforts (access to finance, digital finance, financial education) have also been found to be effective at improving the immediate capacities of individuals and groups to cope with shocks (Moore et al. 2019). In Kenya, for example, the widely used mobile-based money transfer service M-PESA has dramatically reduced the cost of sending money across long distances, increased households' ability to weather negative income shocks (such as those from illness or agricultural losses), and enhanced the availability of income support from social networks during shocks (Suri and Jack 2016). After a disaster, access to credit can help with recovery and reconstruction (Hallegatte et al. 2017).

Reducing risk exposure has also been found to bolster resilience through a diverse range of projects and programs for individuals and communities. Many of these efforts seek to change underlying institutional structures—including police protection, disease-resistant seeds, insurance programs, and employment guarantee schemes (Barrett and Constas 2014). Certain financial inclusion efforts (for example, savings through risk sharing and diversification mechanisms) also help individuals and households to anticipate and mitigate their exposure to risks or make their wealth less vulnerable to natural disaster shocks.

Agency and self-organizing capacity building can help to identify key strengths at the community level that enable resilience (GFDRR, forthcoming). For example, in conflict zones in the Philippines, sustained engagement of the state through organizing regular meetings with community leaders led to increased delivery of services to at-risk communities (Haim, Nanes, and Davidson 2021). Along the same lines, *strengthening access to information* can support both coping and adaptive capacities. Actively involving citizens in the government's collection and sharing of information can have the added benefit of creating stronger collaborative connections between government, citizens, and civic organizations, contributing to greater cohesion (Myers 2021).

Leveraging Process Legitimacy: *How* Things Are Done Matters

A key take-away from this book is that *how* development is done matters. How goals are formulated and how policies and programs are designed and implemented can often mean the difference between success and failure. Explaining in an accessible way how reforms are needed to fight climate change—for example, introducing green transport options—can make environmental policies more socially accepted (box 3.7). Promoting positive social norms and behaviors is an important part of this puzzle.

Box 3.7
Resilience—Kenya's Financing Locally Led Climate Action Program

The Bank's Kenya Financing Locally Led Climate Action (FLLoCA) program establishes the first national-scale model of devolved climate finance (Arnold and Soikan 2021). The program is based on the premise that locally led adaptation can be more effective than top-down interventions, as local communities are more familiar with their context and what is needed to drive change. FLLoCA supports partnerships between local governments and their citizens to assess climate risks and identify socially inclusive solutions tailored to local needs. With communities across Kenya also dealing with the impacts of the COVID-19 pandemic, the program takes a broad view of resilience and recognizes that communities are aware of their vulnerabilities and are experienced in managing multiple risks simultaneously. For example, investments may focus on activities that support livelihood diversification or community-level preparedness. Depending on what communities prioritize, investments may also promote water conservation and more efficient use of water, support natural resource management, rehabilitate degraded lands, or promote early warning systems. The program supports government fiscal transfers to local governments and aims to strengthen social cohesion by strengthening the interactions between communities and local governments. The program supports the government's fiscal decentralization initiative and strengthens the links between national ministries for water, sanitation, urban development, agriculture, and communities, working through local governments.

Social norms affect what is considered acceptable behavior, whether individuals and groups trust each other, whether they are willing to engage and cooperate, and whether they face stigma or discrimination in their daily interactions. In fragile contexts, social norms can even shape people's motivations and incentives to engage in violent behavior (United Nations and World Bank 2018). Interventions thus need to be sensitive to the social and normative context in which they are implemented.

Advancing socially sustainable development requires the promotion of process legitimacy in practice, which involves a certain mind-set as much as an operational tactic. At the highest level, engaging with process legitimacy requires all development actors—from government ministers and World Bank country directors to nongovernmental organization (NGO) managers and community leaders—to consider meaningfully their own role in shaping it. A useful starting point is acknowledging the potential for development efforts to be socially disruptive, no matter how well intentioned. Likewise, it is useful to recognize that mainstream professional development discourse and practice—grounded in numbers, written documents, and analytical abstractions—is but one way among many of comprehending the world. In reality, the professional discourses and practices of development are often at odds with the prevailing beliefs and ways of doing things in a given context. In such cases, development actors must realize that they *lack* legitimacy and must earn (rather than impose) it in order for their efforts to be socially sustainable.

The concerns or grievances generated by development interventions and policies should thus not be regarded as mere annoyances to mitigate, but as challenges to be addressed proactively. Indeed, a key aspect of the development process is for societies to build robust domestic policy arenas incrementally—including capable administrative and judicial institutions, citizen engagement mechanisms, local government decision making, and civic spaces that provide voice to civil society—that can "manage" the increasingly large, complex, and contested tasks that development itself brings about (Andrews, Pritchett, and Woolcock 2017). This process involves strengthening systems for accountability (open government, public sector user feedback mechanisms, participatory or civil society monitoring); supporting groups traditionally excluded from the policy arena or lacking the means, confidence, vocabulary, or information to participate fully; and bringing groups with differing views together to explore solutions for common challenges.

Three high-level and overarching priorities are critical for putting these principles into practice. To foster process legitimacy and ensure that social sustainability is promoted in a way that works within the context of existing norms and values—such that decisions are considered fair, credible, and acceptable by all members and groups in a society—development actors should:

1. *Understand the policy arena.* Identifying the key aspects and contours of a given policy arena helps in assessing the viability of a specific policy or program and in gauging its chances of success. To be socially sustainable, interventions must be designed to work alongside (or in spite of) existing power structures, incentive systems, vested interests, and political or policy realities. As such, it is important to understand who the actors in the arena are, what their objectives are, what authority they have (and where it is derived from), and what the prevailing norms are that guide access to the policy arena as well as behavior and decision making within it. In some cases, shortcomings can be addressed; in others, it may be better for development actors to avoid direct investment and find alternative ways to engage.

2. *Work with all key stakeholders.* It is particularly critical to understand, engage with, and adapt to the needs of those who stand to lose from the reforms, investments, or policies being pursued, as they are often the stakeholders who are most familiar with the factors that may affect the effectiveness of the project or program. Programs promoting social sustainability should put explicit focus on engaging with groups who are at risk of being excluded from voice and decision making. Engagement also creates opportunities for real-time feedback loops, emergent learning, and efforts to promote positive norms and behaviors through iterative and participatory efforts (Appiah 2010).

3. *Engage for the long haul.* Since the right moment for change cannot always be anticipated, and because norms and values as well as institutions take time to change, engagement for social sustainability must be for the long haul. Staying engaged, investing in relationships, and building trust typically pay off. Doing so can pose challenges for development actors, who often face pressures to deliver more results in shorter time frames amid incentives for growth, efficiency, and measured effectiveness, but it enhances the social sustainability of their efforts.

These three core priorities for fostering process legitimacy are discussed in more detail below.

Understand the Policy Arena

Understanding the context-specific drivers of inclusion, resilience, and cohesion is a critical first step for social sustainability (box 3.8). To design interventions for inclusion and resilience, it is

Box 3.8
Social Sustainability and Inclusion Country Diagnostic

The Sustainability and Inclusion (SSI) Country Diagnostic is a World Bank analytical tool that improves the understanding of social sustainability in a given country (Madrigal, Cuesta, and Pecorari 2022). It brings together evidence on key excluded groups, their numbers, and the drivers of exclusion. It also provides an in-depth profile of the main gaps in terms of inclusion, cohesion, and resilience and (to the extent possible in that country) how those gaps manifest between vulnerable groups, across locations, and over time. Ultimately, these diagnostics can help the Bank to identify entry points, key priorities, and the most meaningful operational and knowledge engagements with country clients on issues of social sustainability (figure B3.8.1).

The Cameroon SSI core diagnostic identified women, youth, and residents of former conflict areas as being most at risk, with climate variability as the main driver of vulnerability. The diagnostic influenced prior actions (policies) for a development policy loan on financial access and labor regulations for women and informed a vulnerability analysis conducted as part of Cameroon's Country Climate and Development Report.[a]

Figure B3.8.1 What Is an SSI Country Diagnostic?

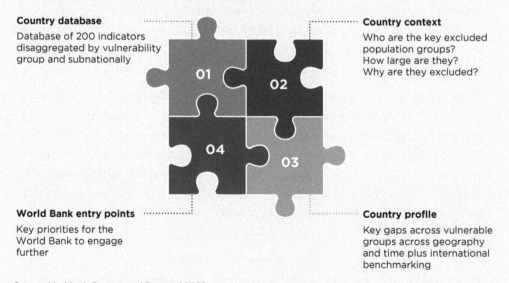

Country database
Database of 200 indicators disaggregated by vulnerability group and subnationally

Country context
Who are the key excluded population groups?
How large are they?
Why are they excluded?

World Bank entry points
Key priorities for the World Bank to engage further

Country profile
Key gaps across vulnerable groups across geography and time plus international benchmarking

Source: Madrigal, Cuesta, and Pecorari 2022.

a. The World Bank Group's Country Climate and Development Reports are diagnostic reports that integrate climate change and development considerations. See https://www.worldbank.org/en/publication/country-climate-development-reports.

important to understand who is at greatest risk of not benefiting from (or even being adversely affected by) interventions and what are their specific needs and constraints. What works to enhance inclusion in higher education or labor markets for urban women from majority ethnic groups is typically not the same as what works for rural women from discriminated ethnic minorities. Resettling households from flood-prone coasts to inland villages may increase resilience for those whose livelihoods are transferable to the new environment, but it may be disastrous for fisher people or others who depend on the coastal economy. Similarly, social tensions or conflict can derail even the best development interventions, so a thorough understanding of what drives conflict—who the different parties and decision makers are as well as how tensions can be mitigated and addressed—is essential to promote effective and sustainable solutions.

Moreover, it is critical for development practitioners to understand what constitutes process legitimacy in a given context to ensure that interventions function within local rules, principles, and authority structures. Without this understanding, interventions are likely to be resisted and may not be implementable. This understanding requires deep engagement with local power dynamics. Even if politicians and other decision makers seek development progress, they may struggle to pursue these goals effectively, manage coalition governments, navigate fiscal problems, or respond constructively to public discontent because of the need to maintain the support of vested interests, including pressures for favors from family members or close allies (Fritz, Levy, and Ort 2014).

The insight that politics and the political economy of countries matter to the success of reforms is not new (see, for example, Fritz, Kaiser, and Levy 2009; Woolcock 2014; World Bank 2017), but it has not been translated consistently into action. Understanding the policy arena also includes a broader understanding of a given context's social norms and values, which can undercut the effectiveness or sustainability of projects and programs. Even with the best of efforts, it can be challenging for outsiders to grasp or navigate the often-complex social dynamics at play in low- and middle-income countries, especially in contexts of weak governance or fragility. Moreover, the capacity to pursue a socially sustainable development agenda (including technical and financial resources) matters greatly. In some cases, shortcomings in the policy arena can be addressed once they have been identified and understood; in others, it may be better for development practitioners to engage analytically and support dialogue where possible, but not invest directly. In many contexts, certain sectors or areas of engagement will be more conducive and have higher capacity than others. Box 3.9 presents a simplified typology for assessing the viability of social sustainability efforts.

Box 3.9
Typology for Social Sustainability

When social sustainability is challenged in one area, there may be openings in another. If a given country has political sensitivities around promoting the inclusion of a specific group, for instance, there may still be openings around strengthening resilience for all vulnerable groups; similarly, where the policy arena around the energy sector is very narrow, the education sector might be highly transparent, open, and inclusive. In such cases, development actors may achieve more results by investing in resilience or education efforts rather than targeted work on inclusion or energy, respectively.

A typology can help development actors to navigate these trade-offs and make judgment calls regarding what to prioritize in the face of time and budget constraints. Figure B3.9.1 illustrates a simplified typology for mapping the potential social sustainability of development efforts along two key dimensions: *context* and *capacity*. Context, as

(continued)

Box 3.9
Continued

Figure B3.9.1 A Typology for Social Sustainability

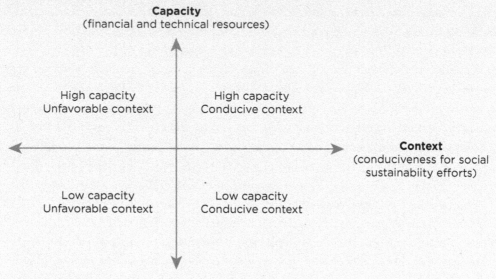

Source: World Bank.

discussed throughout this book, is the full set of social factors that characterize a given community or society and its policy arena (including norms, behaviors, and beliefs), which can be conducive or not conducive to change. Capacity, by contrast, refers to the capability of development actors, including governments and other authorities, to get things done (establishing and maintaining peace, setting compliance mechanisms for revenue collection, enforcing rights). Such capacity can be technical (level of staff expertise, administrative resources) or financial (resources to undertake large-scale citizen engagement efforts).

The potential success of any policy or program (in terms of its social sustainability) depends on a combination of context and capacity. In figure B3.9.1, the far corner of the top-right quadrant represents the most promising potential for socially sustainable development, the far corner of the lower-left quadrant represents the least promising, and the areas closer to the axes represent moderate viability. Considering this typology, it is not surprising that high-income economies are often more inclusive, cohesive, and resilient and have higher levels of process legitimacy than fragile or conflict-affected countries. Even so, some high-income countries still have less favorable contexts (for example, those with persistent levels of social exclusion, lack of gender equality, or political or social dynamics that deprioritize efforts like climate change adaptation or mitigation). As with the examples above, within a given country one sector may also have more or less capacity or a more or less conducive context than other sectors.

(continued)

Box 3.9
Continued

Of course, as this book has emphasized, *how* development is done also matters greatly. A given policy or program is unlikely to succeed if the affected community or society does not support it, does not accept the authority who designed it, or does not see its implementation as legitimate—or if there is no process for reconciling the potential concerns, disagreements, and tensions that may arise. In other words, process legitimacy determines what is seen as acceptable or desirable within a given country, both in terms of what to support and how to support it. This will differ widely across countries—and within countries, it may differ widely across sectors, demographics, or even individual policies and programs.

Although assessing process legitimacy cannot be reduced to a simple rubric, some classic examples of challenging cases are described below.

■ *Fragmented legitimacy* can occur where different sections of a population have deeply divided views on what is acceptable or desirable—which will always be the case to some extent but is more pronounced and difficult to resolve in certain contexts (for example, countries with ethnonational conflict or significant differences on development pathways between groups, such as farmers and pastoralists). In these cases, development actors can help by creating space for contentious discussions and participatory processes to occur, particularly at the local level, where the tensions or conflicts often play out. Community and local development instruments, for example, can be effective.

■ *Challenged legitimacy* can occur when existing rules, norms, or values are threatened by an emerging challenge, crisis, or the development process itself. A classic example is gender equity in places where some groups oppose efforts to promote girls' education, female participation in the workforce, or access to contraception—thus challenging the legitimacy of traditional views about gender. To overcome such challenges, development actors can incentivize particular reforms or projects, such as offering technical assistance and supplemental concessional financing (for example, to strengthen transparency in governments struggling with corruption or to support communities hosting refugees if they develop sustainable integration strategies). Supporting different perspectives to play out in the policy arena can also be helpful here.

■ *Displaced legitimacy* can occur where governments are not supported by most of society (for example, after some coups or where democratic institutions do not function). In these cases, there is often still some degree of consensus among the population about what to do and how to do it, and development actors can support such efforts through nonstate bodies rather than the government, often also working at the community level.

This book does not aim to provide detailed and customized guidance on all the potential interventions and engagements across different types of communities and societies. Rather, it emphasizes the importance of being aware of how context and capacity interact with social sustainability to drive outcomes. Any typology or assessment of social sustainability (including this one) is time-sensitive and fleeting, and, as noted previously, development itself can alter both the context and the capacity for social sustainability.

Work with All Key Stakeholders

Development actors must foster space for all stakeholders (especially those at risk of exclusion) to be meaningfully and regularly involved in the policy arena, such that all groups can provide feedback, feel that their concerns are taken seriously, and perceive the change process as legitimate. It is critical to understand whether certain norms or rules keep specific groups outside the arena; if they do, a key concern is how to enlarge the policy arena and foster greater contestability. Are there openings for more engagement, consultations, participatory budgeting and monitoring, feedback loops, or programs to influence norms? If necessary, can support be provided to allow excluded groups to engage in these openings? Emergent learning approaches for project management, as well as meaningful engagement that allows stakeholders to voice concerns and shape the design of policies and programs, can provide the flexibility needed to try out new approaches to reach groups at risk of exclusion, taking into account feedback from communities in real time.

In recent years, there has been broad recognition of the importance of concepts like citizen engagement and social accountability, which are about creating spaces for stakeholders to engage in policy and project processes and supporting the participation of civil society. However, there is still much progress to be made to ensure that engagement is fully representative of all groups in society, that there is genuine support from key decision makers for transparent and participatory processes, and that such engagement meaningfully informs the design and implementation of projects (Masud, Kumagai, and Grandvoinnet 2019; World Bank 2018a). At the World Bank, the 2018 Environmental and Social Framework represents an important leap forward in this regard (box 3.10).

Box 3.10
Fostering Process Legitimacy through the Environmental and Social Framework

The World Bank Environmental and Social Framework (ESF) recognizes that sustainable development requires effective collaboration with everyone who has a stake in the outcome of a project. The ESF makes it mandatory for borrowing country governments to engage with stakeholders (including communities, groups, or individuals affected by proposed projects) and other interested parties through information disclosure, consultation, and informed participation. A growing number of Bank projects leverage the ESF to ensure that groups who are otherwise excluded from decision making can participate more actively in the policy arena, strengthening their inclusion but also fostering process legitimacy more broadly.

In Türkiye, for example, ESF consultations highlighted constraints that prevented many women, youth, refugees, and host community members from engaging in income-generating activities, including the shortage of local child care options and the lack of soft skills. These findings shaped the design and implementation of the Türkiye Social Entrepreneurship, Empowerment, and Cohesion Project.

(continued)

Box 3.10
Continued

Similarly, the Tajikistan Socio-Economic Resilience Strengthening Program used a wide range of stakeholder engagement approaches and methods to cover a diverse range of project beneficiaries. These approaches helped to motivate local authorities to support participatory monitoring of project activities.

In Guatemala, the ESF consultation process for the Modern and Resilient Agri-Food Value Chains Project (designed in response to COVID-19) specifically included engagement around how the project could foster the participation of persons with disabilities, indigenous peoples, and women, which led to an expansion of beneficiaries to include indigenous peoples and women producer organizations. For the Early Childhood Care and Education Project in El Salvador, the ESF provided the space to develop differentiated strategies for the inclusion of children with various educational needs, including children with disabilities, children whose parents are in jail, and children from ethnic minorities.

Participation of stakeholders also has to be iterative—in other words, it must be regular and continuous, and stakeholders need to see that their involvement makes a difference (World Bank 2018a). It is also important to consciously and continuously engage groups at risk of exclusion to ensure that they can participate meaningfully in consultations and provide feedback throughout the project cycle. This effort necessitates concern for timing, location, and appropriate support (disability-accessible locations, provisions for child care). All participants need to feel that they are treated with respect and that their feedback and inputs are considered based on their merit and relevance, which may require specific support or training for women, youth, or members of specific racial, religious, or ethnic groups (box 3.11) (Masud, Kumagai, and Grandvoinnet 2019). Often, simple modifications to development operations can go a long way to promoting process legitimacy (box 3.12).

Engage for the Long Haul

As noted at the start of this chapter, processes of social change happen slowly and over time, and this protracted time frame can pose challenges in the face of pressures to deliver more results in shorter timelines. Development actors, including governments, international financial institutions, NGOs reliant on donor funding, and other stakeholders, often operate on project timelines that are too short to achieve measurable results in terms of social change. Even among policy makers and development actors with the best intentions, institutional incentives for growth, efficiency, and measured effectiveness often pose challenges for conducting rigorous stakeholder engagement and participation up-front and can distract attention away from the importance of social factors.

Box 3.11
Strengthening the Links between Communities and Elected Officials

In 2013 the government of Senegal sought to harmonize its decentralization and local governance efforts. In support of these efforts, starting in 2018, Tostan piloted an innovative approach called Strengthening Democracy and Civic Engagement (SDCE) in collaboration with the United Nations Children's Fund. Following positive results in eight Senegalese districts, Tostan is currently integrating the SDCE in all of its community programs in the country.

SDCE training modules engage communities through Tostan-facilitated community management committees (CMCs) (see box 3.6) as well as elected officials at the district level. The training modules are offered in local languages and use Tostan's human rights–based approach and participatory methodology, paying special attention to enabling women's participation. Through their CMCs, communities in the district become aware of the roles and responsibilities of their elected officials, reinforce their own engagement toward community well-being, and are better placed to collaborate with decentralized government structures and hold them accountable.

Through these engagements, SDCE enhances community capacity to advocate and collaborate with local government in pursuing a collective vision of well-being. At the same time, it builds the capacity of elected officials in decentralized government structures to manage resources and carry out their community development mandates. By contributing to stronger relationships between communities and decentralized government officials, the program is building trust and contributing to social cohesion.

Box 3.12
Working with Civil Society for Third-Party Monitoring in Tajikistan

National development projects financed by external organizations are often implemented and overseen by a small group of government workers in a given country, typically with limited requirements for ongoing engagement with civil society. This situation can sometimes lead to a shortage of process legitimacy because information is not shared publicly. Social accountability approaches seek to involve civil society throughout the implementation and monitoring process. In Tajikistan, to promote social accountability in a project providing temporary social assistance for vulnerable households in response to COVID-19, the Bank hired a consortium of Tajik civil society organizations (CSOs) to help to ensure that the project continues to be accountable and effective.[a]

The CSO consortium is leading a coalition of eight other grassroots organizations that engages local authorities, health providers, and users to monitor project implementation in 16 hospitals across the country. Their participatory approach employs various innovations, including mobile-enabled household surveys to track the receipt

(continued)

> **Box 3.12**
> **Continued**
>
> of cash transfers, verification of assets in hospitals, public hearings for community members to ask questions or raise concerns, an online platform to facilitate two-way feedback between the government and citizens, and the use of "mystery customers" to monitor health grievance redress mechanisms. By integrating local grassroots organizations at the forefront of results monitoring, third-party monitoring helps to foster process legitimacy by providing feedback loops between citizens and the state and builds capacity and experience in locally led social accountability between CSOs and government representatives.
>
> a. The World Bank's Global Partnership for Social Accountability Trust Fund provided a US$320,000 grant to hire the CSO consortium as part of the World Bank's Tajikistan Emergency COVID-19 Project (TEC-19).

However, some moments in time are more amenable to positive social change than others. Likewise, windows of opportunity can often emerge suddenly due to country-specific or global events (for example, the election of a reform-oriented administration, rapid economic growth, or even shocks like COVID-19) that necessitate drastic changes in the way things are done. Development actors cannot always anticipate the right moment for change, but investments in building relationships and trust tend to pay off. Staying engaged, building trust, making connections, and generating coalitions and partnerships can help development actors to detect and be prepared to act as windows of opportunity emerge (see box 3.13) (Green 2016, especially ch. 1).

This book has argued that increasing social sustainability is critical for designing and implementing programs that lead to poverty reduction and shared prosperity. To meet the challenges of the 21st century, "business-as-usual" will not suffice. The book aims to advance the concept of social sustainability and sharpen the analytical foundations on which it rests; it is not, however, meant to be the final word on social sustainability. Its broader goal is to inspire greater commitment to social sustainability, leading to more investments and more research and helping to refocus the development agenda on this critical pillar.

As noted in chapter 2, more efforts are needed to address key data, measurement, and methodological challenges. Among other benefits, better data and measurement would help to build the evidence base for what works for social sustainability and to address some of the implementation challenges. Developing a suite of indicators or dashboards with data relevant to social sustainability could help to capture trends over time as well as disaggregated analytics, focused on each of the key components of social sustainability and specific groups at risk of exclusion (due to gender, age, disability status, SOGI, displacement, religious or ethnic status, and other indicators of vulnerability and marginalization). While the Social Sustainability Global Database (SSGD) and the Global Sustainability Global Dashboard developed as companions of this book are steps in that direction (Cuesta, López-Noval, and Niño-Zarazúa 2022; Cuesta, Madrigal, and Pecorari 2022), more work

Box 3.13
The Panama Indigenous Peoples Plan

In 2012 members of the Ngäbe and Buglé groups protested the government of Panama's proposed dilution of their rights to consultation over extractive and hydroelectric project development within their territories. In confrontations with the government, two Ngäbe were killed and 89 were injured. To promote peaceful engagement between the government and Ngäbe leaders, a Conciliatory Dialogue was established and resulted in an agreement to prepare a National Plan for the Integral Development for the Indigenous Peoples of Panama. After two years of community consultations, the dozen traditional congresses and councils for indigenous peoples in the country approved the plan, calling for it to be adopted as national policy with an annual budget allocation.

In 2015 the World Bank systematic country diagnostic for Panama identified the stark inequalities still faced by indigenous peoples, suggesting that the plan was not being implemented effectively (Koehler-Geib and Scott 2015). The Bank team leveraged its dialogue with the government to include support for the plan within the 2016 country partnership framework and to ensure that new lending in Panama would contribute to its implementation, including a development policy loan series with prior actions to legally recognize the National Indigenous Peoples Roundtable and advance the implementation of the plan.

While these actions were not initially successful, continued dialogue with the government advanced awareness and appreciation of the plan. The Bank provided technical assistance on international good practice, and in 2016 the government requested Bank financing to implement the plan. The Bank's indigenous peoples loan to Panama would be the first of its kind in 20 years. All of the critical design decisions were carried out with the roundtable, the government, and the Bank in a triparty process—designing *with* indigenous peoples instead of *for* them. The Bank's continuous engagement also contributed to the creation of the National Council for the Development of Indigenous Peoples in 2018 (formerly the National Indigenous Peoples Roundtable). The council provides a structured platform for coordination between the 12 indigenous congresses and councils and government agencies to execute a coordinated development agenda in indigenous peoples' territories that is in line with the plan. This council is a unique structure that significantly strengthened the voice and participation of indigenous peoples in policy making.

Indigenous authorities noted during project negotiations the significant transformation in their participation at the table with the Ministry of Finance and the Bank since the days when powdered milk was dropped from helicopters on their communities. The investment project to implement the plan was approved in 2018 and served as a catalyst for other development organizations to contribute financing, including the Food and Agriculture Organization and the Inter-American Development Bank, which prepared a complementary loan of US$40 million.

(continued)

Box 3.13
Continued

The investment in relationships and trust building is paying off as the Bank continues supporting the government's commitment to strengthen the participatory policy-making process and the allocation of public resources to indigenous communities. The Bank accompanied the government in the preparation of Law 301, which establishes measures for the Integral Development of Indigenous Peoples in Panama and was unanimously approved in 2022. This new law sets an important precedent for the region and aligns with international best practices. Some of the elements that make this legislation innovative include (a) the adoption of the National Indigenous Peoples Development Plan; (b) a framework for the inclusion of all indigenous peoples, both within and outside indigenous territories, in planning and implementation of policies and public investments; and (c) a monitoring system to keep track of policy commitments and targets. There is still much work to be done, but the Bank's continuous engagement is helping Panama to tackle the structural exclusion of indigenous peoples.

remains. More efforts are also needed to use the increasingly available sources of big data (social media, commercial information, telecommunications, remote-sensing data) and more sophisticated artificial intelligence methods that complement traditional household data and administrative records.

In addition to supporting operations, better analytics can help to strengthen the case for why social sustainability matters. In addition to macro-level tools like the SSGD, more micro-level analysis can help to estimate the costs of exclusion and vulnerability, quantify the impacts of lack of cohesion or resilience on development outcomes, and understand the broader effects of interventions that support social sustainability. A stronger empirical understanding of these issues will help to persuade and motivate policy makers and key stakeholders, including governments, World Bank staff and leadership, and other development institutions, to take social sustainability more seriously.

As this book has made clear, however, operationalizing social sustainability involves much more than conducting empirical analysis or generating and replicating evidence on "what works." In practice, socially sustainable development is about navigating a complex set of challenges and trade-offs, which often cannot be anticipated and for which there is no blueprint or guidebook. Promoting cohesion, inclusion, resilience, and especially process legitimacy is critical for sustainable development, but it also presents unique challenges and requires its own set of tools and approaches to advance. Crafting those tools and approaches—and improving them over time through research and experience—is central to meeting today's development challenges and those of tomorrow.

Notes

1. For example, the passage of US civil rights legislation in the 1960s was an important step toward racial equality but also triggered backlash from its opponents. See Boussac (2021); Patterson, Santiago, and Silverman (2021); World Bank (2013).

2. In many countries, women who pursue an economic role may be sanctioned, including through domestic violence, if they are perceived to be challenging the status quo. See Boudet et al. (2013).

3. The *World Development Report* on development and climate change noted that accepting uncertainty is "inherent to the climate change problem" (World Bank 2010).

4. By contrast, the program did not improve levels of cooperation in communities where women worked independently, suggesting that these programs induce improvements in cooperative capacity by providing the space or trigger to do so. See Fearon, Humphreys, and Weinstein (2015).

5. Valli, Peterman, and Hidrobo (2019) looked at cohesion in refugee-host settings while examining a short-term transfer program targeting Colombian refugees and poor Ecuadorians in urban and periurban areas of northern Ecuador. They found improvements in cohesion among Colombian refugees in the host community through enhanced personal agency, attitudes accepting diversity, confidence in institutions, and social participation, without any negative impacts among Ecuadorian counterparts. The authors attribute the impacts to the joint targeting of Colombians and Ecuadorians, the interaction between nationalities at monthly nutrition sessions, and the messaging around inclusion by program implementers. Cited in Chatterjee, Gassier, and Myint (2022).

6. The family reform introduced a requirement for both spouses' consent in the administration of property, abolished the right of spouses to deny permission to the other spouse to work outside the home, and raised the minimum age of women to marry. See Hallward-Driemeier and Gajigo (2013).

7. This list is not exhaustive and merely illustrates some of the constraints. For more information, see World Bank (2018b).

8. Negative or unsustainable coping strategies include drawing down savings, selling assets, skipping meals, taking children out of school, resorting to illegal activities, or exhausting natural resources. See the discussion in chapter 2.

References

Acemoglu, D., A. Cheema, A. Khwaja, and J. Robinson. 2020. "Trust in State and Nonstate Actors: Evidence from Dispute Resolution in Pakistan." *Journal of Political Economy* 128 (8): 3090–147.

Alasuutari, H. K., C. J. Thomas, S. M. Powers, L. S. McDonald, and J. Waite. 2020. *Inclusive Education Resource Guide: Ensuring Inclusion and Equity in Education.* Washington, DC: World Bank Group.

Ali, D. A., K. Deininger, and M. Goldstein. 2011. "Environmental and Gender Impacts of Land Tenure Regularization in Africa: Pilot Evidence from Rwanda." Africa Region Gender Practice Policy Brief 2, World Bank, Washington, DC.

Ali, D. A., K. Deininger, M. Goldstein, and E. LaFerrara. 2015. "Empowering Women through Land Tenure Regularization: Evidence from the Impact Evaluation of the National Program in Rwanda." Development Research Group Case Study, World Bank, Washington, DC.

Andrews, M., L. Pritchett, and M. Woolcock. 2017. *Building State Capability: Evidence, Analysis, Action.* New York: Oxford University Press.

Appiah, K. A. 2010. *The Honor Code: How Moral Revolutions Happen.* New York: W. W. Norton.

Arnold, M., and N. Soikan. 2021. "Kenya Moves to Locally Led Climate Action." *World Bank Blogs*, October 27, 2021. https://blogs.worldbank.org/nasikiliza/kenya-moves-locally-led-climate-action.

Banerjee, A., E. La Ferrara, and V. H. Orozco-Olvera. 2019a. "The Entertaining Way to Behavioral Change: Fighting HIV with MTV." Policy Research Working Paper 8998, World Bank Group, Washington, DC.

Banerjee, A., E. La Ferrara, V. H. Orozco-Olvera. 2019b. "Entertainment, Education, and Attitudes toward Domestic Violence." *AEA Papers and Proceedings* 109 (May): 133–37.

Barca, V. 2019. "Gender Sensitive Public Works: Literature Review." High-Quality Technical Assistance for Results (HEART), Oxford.

Barrett, C., and M. Constas. 2014. "Toward a Theory of Resilience for International Development Applications." *Proceedings of the National Academy of Sciences* 111 (40): 14625–30.

Barron, P. 2011. *Community-Driven Development in Post-Conflict and Conflict-Affected Areas: Experiences from East Asia.* Discussion Paper 61225. Washington, DC: World Bank.

Barron, P., R. Diprose, and M. Woolcock. 2011. *Contesting Development: Participatory Projects and Local Conflict Dynamics in Indonesia.* New Haven: Yale University Press.

Barros, R. P., P. Olinto, T. Lunde, and M. Carvalho. 2011. "The Impact of Access to Free Childcare on Women's Labor Market Outcomes: Evidence from a Randomized Trial in Low-Income Neighborhoods of Rio de Janeiro." Washington, DC: World Bank Group. http://documents.worldbank.org/curated/en/672391468231860498/The-impact-of-access-to-free-childcare-on-womens-labor-market-outcomes-evidence-from-a-randomized-trial-in-low-income-neighborhoods-of-Rio-de-Janeiro.

Beath, A., F. Christia, and R. Enikolopov. 2013. "Randomized Impact Evaluation of Afghanistan's National Solidarity Program: Endline Report." World Bank, Washington, DC.

Berlinski, S., and S. Galiani. 2007. "The Effect of a Large Expansion of Pre-Primary School Facilities on Preschool Attendance and Maternal Employment." *Labour Economics* 14 (3): 665–80.

Bicchieri, C. 2016. *Norms in the Wild: How to Diagnose, Measure, and Change Social Norms.* Oxford: Oxford University Press.

Bicchieri, C., and H. Mercier. 2014. "Norms and Beliefs: How Change Occurs." In *The Complexity of Social Norms*, edited by M. Xenitidou and B. Edmonds, 37–54. Cham: Springer International Publishing.

Blair, R., M. Moscoso, A. Vargas, and M. Weintraub. 2021. "Preventing Rebel Resurgence after Civil War: A Field Experiment in Security and Justice Provision in Rural Colombia." *American Political Science Review* 116 (4): 1258–77.

Boucher, V., S. Tumen, M. Vlassopoulos, J. Wahba, and Y. Zenou. 2021. *Ethnic Mixing in Early Childhood: Evidence from a Randomized Field Experiment and a Structural Model.* IZA Discussion Paper 14260. Bonn: Institute of Labor Economics.

Boudet, M., A. María, P. Petesch, C. Turk, and A. Thumala. 2013. *On Norms and Agency: Conversations about Gender Equality with Women and Men in 20 Countries.* Directions in Development. Washington, DC: World Bank.

Boussac, T. 2021. "Conservative Populism and the American Welfare State since the 1960s." In *The Faces of Contemporary Populism in Western Europe and the US*, edited by K. Tournier-Sol and M. Gayte, 181–201. London: Palgrave Macmillan.

Burchi, F., and F. Roscioli. 2021. *Can Integrated Social Protection Programmes Affect Social Cohesion? Mixed Methods Evidence from Malawi*. Discussion Paper 3/2021. Bonn: German Development Institute.

Buvinic, M., and M. O'Donnell. 2019. "Gender Matters in Economic Empowerment Interventions: A Research Review." *World Bank Research Observer* 34 (2): 309–346.

Chatterjee, S., M. Gassier, and N. Myint. 2022. "Leveraging Social Cohesion for Development Impacts: Framing Paper." World Bank, Washington, DC.

Cuesta, J., B. López-Noval, and M. Niño-Zarazúa. 2022. "Social Exclusion: Concepts, Measurement, and a Global Estimate." Policy Research Working Paper 10097, World Bank, Washington, DC.

Cuesta, J., L. Madrigal, and N. Pecorari. 2022. "Social Sustainability, Poverty, and Income: An Empirical Exploration." Policy Research Working Paper 10085, World Bank, Washington, DC.

Das, M. B., and S. A. Espinoza. 2020. *Inclusion Matters in Africa*. Washington, DC: World Bank.

Das, M. B., T. G. Evans, T. Palu, and D. Wilson. 2017. *Social Inclusion: What Does It Mean for Health Policy and Practice?* Discussion Paper. Washington, DC: World Bank.

D'Exelle, B., E. Coleman, and M. C. Lopez. 2018. "Community-Driven Reconstruction in Colombia: An Experimental Study of Collective Action beyond Program Beneficiaries." *World Development* 101 (C): 188–201.

Fearon J., M. Humphreys, and J. Weinstein. 2015. "How Does Development Assistance Affect Collective Action Capacity? Results from a Field Experiment in Post-Conflict Liberia." *American Political Science Review* 109 (3): 450–69.

Fiala, N., and P. Premand. 2018. "*Social Accountability and Service Delivery: Experimental Evidence from Uganda*." Policy Research Working Paper 8449, World Bank, Washington, DC.

Fox, J. 2015. "Social Accountability: What Does the Evidence Really Say?" *World Development* 72 (August): 346–61.

Fritz, V., K. Kaiser, and B. Levy. 2009. *Problem-Driven Governance and Political Economy Analysis: Good Practice Framework*. Washington, DC: World Bank. https://openknowledge.worldbank .org/handle/10986/16777.

Fritz, V., B. Levy, and R. Ort. 2014. *Problem-Driven Political Economy Analysis: The World Bank's Experience*. Directions in Development. Washington, DC: World Bank.

Gauri, V., T. Rahman, and I. Sen. 2019. "Measuring Social Norms about Female Labor Force Participation in Jordan." Policy Research Working Paper 8916, World Bank, Washington, DC.

GFDRR (Global Facility for Disaster Reduction and Recovery). Forthcoming. "Building the Social Resilience of Vulnerable Communities to Climate Change in Solomon Islands." Research Note 1, World Bank, Washington, DC.

Green, D. 2016. *How Change Happens*. Oxford: Oxford University Press.

Haim, D., M. Nanes, and M. Davidson. 2021. "Family Matters: The Double-Edged Sword of Police-Community Connections." *Journal of Politics* 83 (4): 1529–44.

Hallegatte, S., A. Vogt-Schilb, M. Bangalore, and J. Rozenberg. 2017. *Unbreakable: Building the Resilience of the Poor in the Face of Natural Disasters*. Climate Change and Development. Washington, DC: World Bank.

Hallward-Driemeier, M., and O. Gajigo. 2013. "Strengthening Economic Rights and Women's Occupational Choice: The Impact of Reforming Ethiopia's Family Law." Policy Research Working Paper 6695, World Bank, Washington, DC.

Koehler-Geib, F., and K. Scott. 2015. "Panama: Locking in Success; Systematic Country Diagnostic." World Bank, Washington, DC. https://openknowledge.worldbank.org/handle/10986/22035.

Langer, A., F. Stewart, and M. Schroyens. 2016. "Horizontal Inequalities and Affirmative Action: An Analysis of Attitudes towards Redistribution across Groups in Africa." WIDER Working Paper 119, World Institute for Development Economic Research (UNU-WIDER). Helsinki.

Madrigal, L., J. Cuesta, and N. Pecorari. 2022. "Social Sustainability and Inclusion (SSI) Country Diagnostic Guidelines Note." Social Sustainability and Inclusion Global Practice, World Bank, Washington, DC.

Mansoor, M. 2021. "Citizens' Trust in Government as a Function of Good Governance and Government Agency's Provision of Quality Information on Social Media during COVID-19." *Government Information Quarterly* 38 (4): 101597.

Masud, H., S. Kumagai, and H. Grandvoinnet. 2019. "Mainstreaming Citizen Engagement through the World Bank Group's Country Engagement Model." World Bank, Washington, DC.

Mercy Corps and Ministry of Foreign Affairs of the Netherlands. 2020. "Key Findings of the Innovative Research that Measures the Vocational Training Impact on Social and Economic Cohesion. The Effects of Vocational Training on Bias towards Hosts and Refugees: Findings from Jordan and Lebanon." Mercy Corps, Portland, OR. https://jordan.mercycorps.org/sites/default/files/2021-08/Key-Findings-of-the-Vocational-Training-Research.pdf.

Moore, D., Z. Niazi, R. Rouse, and B. Kramer. 2019. "Building Resilience through Financial Inclusion: A Review of Existing Evidence and Knowledge Gaps." Brief. Innovations for Poverty Action, New Haven, CT.

Myers, N. 2021. "Information Sharing and Community Resilience: Toward a Whole Community Approach to Surveillance and Combatting the 'Infodemic.'" *World Medical Health Policy* 13 (3): 581–92. https://doi.org/10.1002/wmh3.428.

Patterson, K., A. M. Santiago, and R. M. Silverman. 2021. "The Enduring Backlash against Racial Justice in the United States: Mobilizing Strategies for Institutional Change." *Journal of Community Practice* 29 (4): 334–44.

Pavanello, S., C. Watson, W. Onyango-Ouma, and P. Bukuluki. 2016. "Effects of Cash Transfers on Community Interactions: Emerging Evidence." *Journal of Development Studies* 52 (8): 1–15.

Suri, T., and W. Jack. 2016. "The Long-Run Poverty and Gender Impacts of Mobile Money." *Science* 354 (6317): 1288–92.

United Nations and World Bank. 2018. *Pathways for Peace: Inclusive Approaches to Preventing Violent Conflict*. Washington, DC: World Bank.

Valli, E., A. Peterman, and M. Hidrobo. 2019. "Economic Transfers and Social Cohesion in a Refugee-Hosting Setting." *Journal of Development Studies* 55 (S1): 128–46.

Weiss, C. M. 2020. "Curing Prejudice through Representative Bureaucracies: Evidence from a Natural Experiment in Israeli Medical Clinics." University of Wisconsin, Madison, January 8, 2020.

Woolcock, M. 2014. "Culture, Politics and Development." Policy Research Working Paper 6939, World Bank, Washington, DC.

World Bank. 2010. *World Development Report 2010: Development and Climate Change.* Washington, DC: World Bank.

World Bank. 2013. *Inclusion Matters: The Foundation of Shared Prosperity.* Washington, DC: World Bank.

World Bank. 2017. *The World Bank Environmental and Social Framework.* Washington, DC: World Bank.

World Bank. 2018a. *Engaging Citizens for Better Development.* Washington, DC: World Bank, Independent Evaluation Group.

World Bank. 2018b. "Environment and Social Framework for IPF Operations: Non-Discrimination and Disability." Good Practice Note, World Bank, Washington, DC.

World Bank. 2018c. "Indonesia: Long-Term Impact Evaluation of Generasi." World Bank, Washington, DC.

World Bank. 2019a. *Equity and Inclusion in Education in World Bank Projects: Persons with Disabilities, Indigenous Peoples, and Sexual and Gender Minorities.* Washington, DC: World Bank.

World Bank. 2019b. "Vietnam: Second Northern Mountains Poverty Reduction Project; Implementation Completion and Results Report." World Bank, Washington, DC.

World Bank. 2020. "*Creating Disability-Inclusive ID Systems.*" World Bank, Washington, DC. World Bank. https://openknowledge.worldbank.org/handle/10986/34848.

World Bank. 2021. "Supporting Colombian Host Communities and Venezuelan Migrants during the Covid-19 Pandemic." Results Brief, October 31. World Bank, Washington, DC.

Conclusion

A Perfect Storm

As the world moves deeper into the 21st century, a perfect storm has gathered force in which the overlapping crises of COVID-19, climate change, rising levels of conflict and social tensions, and a global slowdown are inflaming long-standing challenges and exacerbating inequality, persistent structural barriers, and deep-rooted systemic inequities. How these trends manifest is heavily social, and their consequences are having intense social repercussions. A range of socially destabilizing forces are accelerating in many places, including polarization, declining levels of trust, and social unrest. When certain individuals and groups perceive that they are systematically excluded from progress, when they are unable to cope with climate shocks, or when groups in society do not trust the state or each other, this situation can translate into grievances, into human capital losses, and eventually into social tensions and even conflict. These tensions, in turn, pose risks to economies and economic sustainability, as social unrest has been shown to lower gross domestic product in countries that experience it (Barrett and Chen 2021).

These challenges are making it harder to sustain the progress that humanity has already achieved and call for placing a greater focus on social sustainability. For much of the last 75 years, social sustainability has taken a backseat to growth and, more recently, the environment, relegating social factors to the important but narrow concerns of "do no harm" or the fringe of interesting but marginal and noncritical goals. However, addressing the challenges of the 21st century in ways that promote poverty reduction and shared prosperity will require communities and societies to come together to find, agree upon, and deliver socially sustainable solutions. Oftentimes, the policies that are needed are clear, including less regressive taxation, more social expenditures and better-quality service delivery for all, fewer nontargeted subsidies, more competitive markets that regulate monopoly power and protect consumers, or low-carbon growth strategies. Yet getting these policies adopted and implemented is challenging. A greater focus on process legitimacy, inclusion, cohesion, and resilience can be an important force to put policies in place for environmental and economic sustainability. Without a focus on social sustainability in the policy arena, there is also a risk that policies will only benefit the few, leading to more inequality and potential social unrest.

Another key message from this book is that social sustainability can be defined and measured. While indicators for environmental and economic sustainability are better established, an emerging and diverse literature provides the foundations for measuring the social dimension of sustainability. Future work is needed to address data, measurement, and methodological issues, but recent research has made important progress toward an empirical understanding of social sustainability. In particular, the World Bank's new Social Sustainability Global Database offers a critical new tool for analysis, with indexes for inclusion, cohesion, resilience, and process legitimacy built on 71 global indicators measuring factors like community connections, trust within and between groups, early signs of tensions or violent conflict, well-being disaggregated across social groups, and participation in social activities or political and decision-making processes (Cuesta, Madrigal, and Pecorari 2022). In short, while further work is needed to refine and develop such indicators, it is feasible to measure and assess the necessary arrangements for individuals, groups, and entire societies to exist and work together in harmony through time.

Meeting the challenges of the 21st century requires prioritizing social sustainability as a key pillar of sustainable development, alongside economic and environmental sustainability. In practice, this means integrating social sustainability into the forefront of development discourse, theory, and implementation. It means giving the social dimension of development equal consideration as its economic and environmental counterparts in analyses, strategies, and operations. It means making broader efforts and a deeper commitment to bolstering social sustainability's key components: putting a cohesion lens, an inclusion lens, and a resilience lens on all projects, programs, and policies. It means promoting process legitimacy by understanding the policy arena, fostering space for all stakeholders within it, and engaging for the long haul even when progress slows or completely reverses. Above all, it means elevating social sustainability as a local, national, corporate, and global priority and committing the time, resources, and collective energy to pursue it.

References

Barrett, P., and S. Chen. 2021. "Social Repercussions of Pandemics." IMF Working Paper 2021/021, International Monetary Fund, Washington, DC.

Cuesta, J., L. Madrigal, and N. Pecorari. 2022. "Social Sustainability, Poverty, and Income: An Empirical Exploration." Policy Research Working Paper 10085, World Bank, Washington, DC.

HOW TO DRAW PLANTS

The techniques of botanical illustration

KEITH WEST

Foreword by Wilfrid Blunt

TIMBER PRESS
in association with
The British Museum (Natural History)

Published in North America in 1996 by
Timber Press, Inc.
The Haseltine Building
133 S.W. Second Avenue, Suite 450
Portland, Oregon 97204, U.S.A.
1–800–327–5680 (U.S.A. & Canada only)

Reprinted 1997

ISBN 0–88192–350–8

Designed by Pauline Harrison
Printed and bound in Hong Kong by
South China Printing Co.

FRONTISPIECE Creeping buttercup,
Ranunculus repens. Pencil, continuous tone.

Contents

Acknowledgements 6

Foreword by Wilfrid Blunt 7

Introduction 9

1 The past 12

2 Basic equipment 21

3 Concepts 25

4 Plant handling 27

5 Plants in detail 33

6 Pencil 64

7 Ink 78

8 Scraper board 92

9 Water-colour and gouache 98

10 Acrylics 127

11 Photography 140

12 Preparing for the printer 144

Glossary 146

Selected bibliography 149

Index 150

Acknowledgements

I would like to thank Mr John Cannon and Mr Robert Cross, British Museum (Natural History), for encouragement from the beginning – and the former for critically reading the text and for helpful suggestions; Mrs Brenda Herbert, The Herbert Press, for her sensitive editing; and Mrs Judith Diment, British Museum (Natural History), for professional advice about the bibliography and for her help in selecting illustrations from the Museum's archives.

For permission to use illustrations I would like to thank the following: the Graphische Sammlung Albertina, Vienna (fig. 1); the British Museum (Natural History) (figs 2-8 and pp. 105-108); Mary Grierson and The Bentham-Moxon Trust, Royal Botanic Gardens, Kew (fig. 9); Anne Ophelia Dowden and Harper & Row, Publishers, Inc. (fig. 10); Department of Lands and Survey, New Zealand (frontispiece and figs 54-6); Stella Ross-Craig and Bell & Hyman (fig. 58); Dr Peter H. Raven, Director, Missouri Botanical Garden, USA (fig. 65); and Botany Division, Department of Scientific and Industrial Research, New Zealand (fig. 72 and p. 118, top).

With the exception of figs 1-10, 58 and the colour plates on pp. 105-108, all illustrations are by the author.

Foreword

Over the past thirty years there has been a tremendous revival of interest in the drawing and painting of flowers by amateurs. Some of these artists, though frankly admitting small knowledge of botany, have managed to produce extremely accurate portraits of plants; others have been content to discover an absorbing hobby which affords them the same satisfaction that this occupation gave to Victorian maidens combatting boredom in remote country houses. Given reasonable eyesight and a tolerably steady hand, the drawing of plants can be pursued into oldest age, and I recall with pleasure the pride with which an old lady in Bath showed me a bunch of anemones that she had painted – and none too badly – on her hundredth birthday!

Yet, inexplicably, to the best of my knowledge there has never until now been a really *thorough* book supplying the answers to all those technical questions that I am still constantly being asked by people wishing to take up botanical illustration, either professionally or as a hobby: 'What pencils, what pens, what inks do you recommend?', 'How do you "fix" a drawing?', 'What papers are best for watercolour painting?', 'How does one handle acrylics?' – and a hundred others. So it was with eager anticipation that I learned that that admirable botanical artist, Keith West, had produced what promised to be exactly what was required, and when I received a copy of the typescript and was asked if I would write a foreword, I realized at once that here, at long last, was just what we had all been waiting for.

The book is, perhaps, primarily directed at the would-be professional, but the bulk of it also gives invaluable help to even the most humble and struggling amateur. Would that I myself had had access to such a mine of information when, many years ago now, I too was striving, unaided, to draw and paint flowers!

In short, Keith West's timely book cannot be too highly recommended, and I hope it will have the great success that it undoubtedly deserves.

Wilfrid Blunt

For Margaret

Introduction

This book is intended as a guide for those who would like to portray plants with regard for botanical detail. I hope that it will help not only those whose aim is to provide plates for the scientific press with its disciplined requirements, but also students aiming to become artists and illustrators partly or wholly devoted to botanical topics, amateur and professional botanists wishing to illustrate their own works, artists looking for an extension of their range, and those with a keen but less focused interest in art and natural history who want to record accurately flowers that have given them pleasure.

Detailed botanical portraits intended for publication are generally referred to as 'illustrations', a word sometimes used pejoratively as if 'illustration' should inevitably be placed in a lower category than 'art'. Though many plant illustrations inform while possessing little or no aesthetic content, there are others which, in spite of the constraints imposed by the format of the printed page and the requirements of an author, have been long accepted as works of art. The splendid work of Dürer's, 'Das Grosse Rasenstück' (fig. 1) remains splendid whether it is thought of as fine art, illustration, or the first ecological study. In this book 'illustrator' and 'artist' are therefore used for the most part without hierarchical intent.

Books of general botanical interest are now often illustrated by photographs. This may be no bad thing for the artist in that anything that promotes botany to the public is in the long term likely to provide more creative opportunities – and ultimately the whole study of botany rests upon public support. Superficially it might appear that the artist and the photographer are in competition; sometimes they are, but there are limitations to each endeavour, and where these are recognized the strengths of each may be exploited. Given the great variety of plant life, to say nothing of the diversity of ability in illustrators and photographers, there would be little sense in trying to generalize here about one form of illustration versus the other. Nevertheless the finest works of the botanical artist have an individual character and style not to be seen in acres of photographs.

The artist can often interpret in a way that is beyond the capacity of the camera; for example, certain characters such as hair-type and pigment may have much greater botanical relevance in some groups than others, and the illustrator can reflect this significance. This view is supported by George H. M. Lawrence in his *Taxonomy of Vascular Plants*: '... in the photographic rendition the features of particular structures often are obscured by less relevant aspects – as vesture or overlapping parts, features readily de-emphasized in the line drawing. There is little question but that a well and accurately executed drawing is superior to and more satisfactory than the best photographic reproduction.'

1 Albrecht Dürer *Das grosse Rasenstück* (1503)

Currently the main media used for botanical illustration are those described in the following chapters, but this is not to slight the excellent productions of those who happen to work in other ways. A catalogue of a recent International Exhibition of Botanical Art and Illustration held at the Hunt Institute (see p. 20) reveals artists using the following means of expression in addition to those discussed here: woodcuts and wood engravings; lead cuts; copper and steel engravings; dry point; etchings; lithographs; serigraphs; aquarelle pencil; colour pencil; crayon; pen and wash; oils; and egg tempera. Lino cuts are also featured, though, as might be expected, these appear more concerned with broad decorative elements than with accuracy of detail.

The past year or so has seen the introduction of alkyd resin paints in which the pigments are bound by oil-modified synthetic resins instead of linseed oil. No doubt these paints, and other new products, will also find their way into the armoury of the botanical artist. So far there is no medium that suits all tastes and all purposes; each is limited. These limitations provide part of the stimulus: without the constant striving to overcome deficiencies in skill, the complexity of the subject and the disadvantages of the chosen medium, there would be small satisfaction in success.

You should be cautioned about cutting plants and, more seriously, about digging them up. In some countries and in some areas, particularly with common species, little harm is done, but it is important to know the conservation status of the plant and the legal position before taking plant material. Even though as illustrator you may be assisting in a scientific inquiry, this will not excuse decimation of a rare plant population. The end results are the same whether plants are gathered with scientific aims in mind or for the most frivolous reasons.

Anyone long employed in illustrating plants can scarcely fail to develop an appreciation that may in some approach nature-worship. Goethe and Ruskin, for instance, drew plants as a means of getting to know them better. The latter wrote of flowers, 'It is difficult to give them the accuracy of attention necessary to see their beauty without drawing them.' (*Proserpina*, 1874-86.) This view has doubtless been echoed by others, including scientists who have found that the 'accuracy of attention' needed to depict a plant's parts is also a path to knowledge. Ruskin's aim was to 'see their beauty' and he seems largely to have been exasperated or even disgusted by scientific interest; at the other extreme there are botanists who flinch at an aesthetic emphasis – a scan through a recently published study describing numerous species, many of which happen to be cultivated for their loveliness, discloses the one epithet 'showy', used in a single instance.

I feel confident that most, if not all, botanical artists would join me in saying that *all* plants can be brought to yield artistic and intellectual pleasure – some in great bounty, others sparingly. I have not yet found a plant that completely lacked rewards for the searching mind and eye. This is not to say that the illustrator's life is all sweetness and light – some species are so complex in form that they test the resolve of even the lionhearted; and financial gains are modest. Yet the botanical artist may be envied – each day is spent absorbingly, skills are challenged, tangible results are produced that are pleasing to most and harmful to none, the work neither pollutes nor guzzles the earth's resources. The aim is *to illuminate*, in the sense both of *to enlighten* and *to adorn*, and success is measured by the extent to which this is achieved.

1 The past

Botanical art dates from the roots of civilization. Though the first known gropings in art are largely concerned with hunting, early man did leave a few traces of his awareness of plants. And by 1500 BC, in the Great Temple of Thutmose III at Karnak, a sophisticated appreciation of plant life was reflected in a realistic stone relief figuring some 275 species.

From this promising beginning little more than fragments remain, until curiosity about the medicinal properties of plants led to the production of the first illustrated herbals by, among others, Krateuas the physician. Such works were described by Pliny the Elder in the first century AD, but unfortunately the prototypes are lost and, instead of building upon this classical foundation, workers copied the original illustrations again and again. The copies themselves were copied and at each remove small misrepresentations accrued until plates often passed beyond the point where they could be clearly related to particular species, or even in extreme cases to any portion of the plant kingdom.

It was not until the Renaissance that the arts again returned to naturalism and this movement was also to be seen in the portrayal of flowers. Though plants were mostly used as embellishments in larger compositions, a few separate studies are known from artists such as Bellini, Pisanello, da Vinci, and Dürer. The artistic climate of this period, coupled with the means of reproduction available from the woodcut, made possible the refined illustrations of Brunfels' *Herbarum Vivae Eicones* published in Strasbourg in 1530. It is from this work that scientific botanical illustration is said to date. Further advances were made in the publications of Fuchs a few years later, and of his immediate successors.

The texts of Brunfels and Fuchs were derived from earlier writers. Their main merit lies in the inclusion of accurate and lovely woodcuts made from *living* models. Ironically, although the names of Brunfels and Fuchs have long been honoured, their artists, respectively Hans Weiditz and Albrecht Meyer, remain obscure.

With growing botanical knowledge came greater demands upon illustrators for yet finer detail than was obtainable from the woodcut (it was not until the nineteenth century that the virtuosi of the wood engraving flourished). At the close of the sixteenth century the copper plate provided for these new requirements by permitting minute structures to be recorded and printed.

The development of travel in the seventeenth century led to countless opportunities for artists working both overseas and in the many gardens, founded about this time, ablaze with new introductions from abroad. Horticulture joined botany and medicine as an outlet for plant artists.

The binomial system of classification evolved by Linnaeus in the eight-

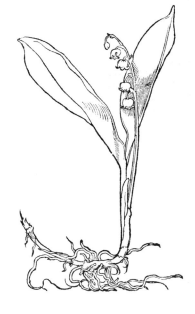

2 Hans Weiditz *Convallaria majalis* L. from *Contrafayt Kreüterbuch* . . . Strasszburg, 1532–37

eenth century, together with fervid botanical exploration, introduced a golden age of magnificent botanical art which persisted well into the next century. At this time Georg Ehret found favour with noble patrons in England, and Gerard van Spaëndonck and Pierre-Joseph Redouté worked in Paris. Through modern printing techniques the paintings of the latter artist are if anything more widely known now than in his own day; particularly the plates of *Les Roses*. This wave of talent peaked with the achievements of two brothers born near Vienna, Franz and Ferdinand Bauer. Their lives make a strange contrast. Though he worked mainly in England, Ferdinand travelled widely, even voyaging to Australia with Matthew Flinders, while Franz, on reaching Kew in his thirty-second year in 1790, stayed there contentedly until his death fifty years later.

It was in 1787 that the *Botanical Magazine*, still flourishing today, was founded by William Curtis. This journal has through almost 200 years provided support for a roll-call of notable artists. An intriguing curiosity is that from its inception until February 1948 (but for the 1921 volume) all the printed plates were hand-coloured.

With a swelling interest in botany during the eighteenth and nineteenth

BELOW LEFT
3 Georg Dionysius Ehret (1708–70) *Iberis semper-florens* L.

BELOW RIGHT
4 Gerard van Spaëndonck (1746–1822) *Solanum macrocarpon* L.

Gesse à larges feuilles.   *Latyrus latifolius*

5 Pierre-Joseph Redouté
(1759-1840) *Latyrus latifolius*
L. from *Choix des plus belles
fleurs et des plus beaux fruits*
by P.-J. Redouté, Paris,
1827-33

OPPOSITE
6 Franz Andreas Bauer
(1758-1840) *Epipactus
palustris* (L.) Crantz

centuries, many countries produced their first illustrated Floras. This en-
thusiasm was nowhere more intense than in Britain where it grew until
botany could be described as a popular recreation. Floricultural journals
abounded, plant-hunters brought in hosts of new wonders, and flower
painting was regarded as a social grace.

Scientific monographs of the period were often opulent – James Bateman's *Orchidaceae of Mexico and Guatemala* (1837-41) was said to be the
largest book ever produced with lithographic plates. The artists for this
work were the otherwise little-known Mrs Withers (fl. 1827-64) and Miss
Drake (fl. 1818-47) 'of Turnham Green'. The lithography was done by a
master noted simply as Gauci, and the anonymous hands that added the
colouring were also highly skilled.

Shortly after the death of Franz Bauer, Kew again became the setting
for an extraordinary figure in the annals of botanical illustration. Whereas

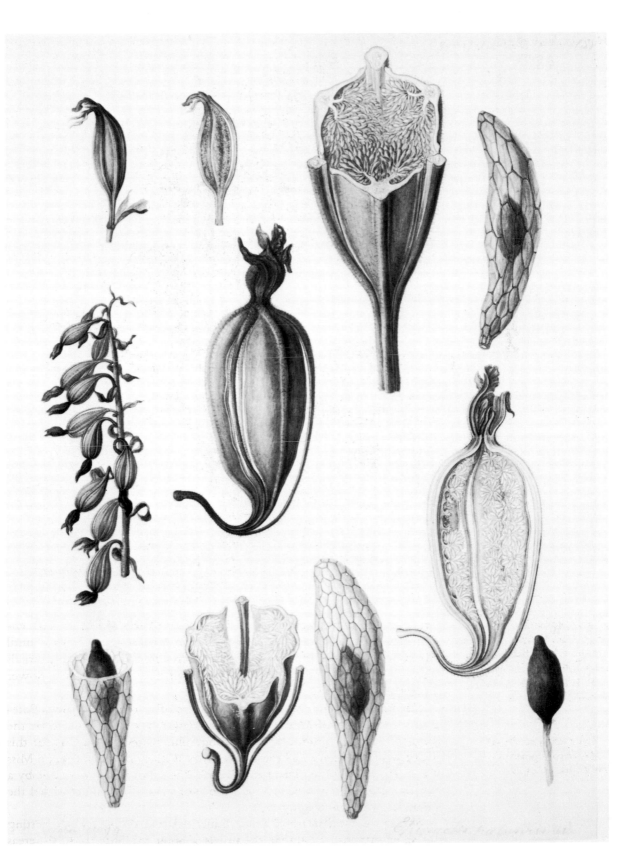

7 Walter Hood Fitch
(1817–92) *Selenicereus
hamatus* (Scheidweiler)
Britton & Rose

Bauer's work was exceptional in quality, the output of Walter Hood Fitch (1817–92) was all but incredible in quantity. No less than 9960 drawings by him are recorded as having been published; taken as an average of four plates weekly over a span of fifty years, this figure indicates not only his industry but also the awesome fluency that he must have developed.

Fitch, together with his nephew, John Nugent Fitch, stood almost alone in England in maintaining a high standard of lithography. While the skilled use of this medium tended to decline, together with engraving on metal, interest in wood engraving had gradually grown under the stimulus

Ornunda maderiensis

T:62 Madeira

8 Sydney Parkinson (1745–71) *Pteris serrulata* drawn in Madeira on Captain Cook's first voyage (1768–71)

imparted by Thomas Bewick earlier in the century. This growth continued in all areas of illustration until at the close of the nineteenth century wood engraving dominated. At first the process was used for simple, cheap text figures, but greater and greater virtuosity was developed until, with the arrival of photography, engravers were able to simulate its tonal range. Sometimes botanical artists engraved their own works but more often a specialist was used to reproduce every delicate nuance upon the wood-block. Sadly, the craft was swept away when photomechanical methods of reproduction flooded in during the first decades of this century.

Initially this technical advance could scarcely be called a step forward for the botanical artist – drawings reproduced by the new process had to approach the boldness of the early woodcuts to be assured of success. However, developments in printing techniques were rapid, and today it is

9 Mary Grierson (1912–)
Crocus baytopiorum Mathew.
In *Curtis's Botanical
Magazine* 1974 Vol.
CLXXX Part 1 N.S. t. 664

possible for a good printer to reproduce the artist's work in colour or in black and white almost in facsimile.

Only a scattering from the names of those who have contributed to the great legacy of botanical art can be included here; a complete record would be a lifetime's study. Current interest has led to the publication of the works of several botanical artists of the past – these include Franz Bauer and, oddly, Marianne North (1830-90) of whom Wilfrid Blunt tartly writes, 'Botanists consider her primarily as an artist; but artists will hardly agree, for her painting is almost wholly lacking in sensibility.' This criticism cannot be applied to the accomplished water-colours of Sydney Parkinson (*c.* 1745-71) which will be seen in a volume shortly to be produced from the archives of the British Museum (Natural History). The bright promise of this young man ended on the 1768 world voyage of Cook, Banks and Solander.

Botanical artists of today include some who are no less gifted than the best of the past: Stella Ross-Craig, Mary Grierson and Margaret Stones in England; Anne Ophelia Dowden, Priscilla Fawcett and Lee Adams in the

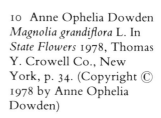

10 Anne Ophelia Dowden *Magnolia grandiflora* L. In *State Flowers* 1978, Thomas Y. Crowell Co., New York, p. 34. (Copyright © 1978 by Anne Ophelia Dowden)

United States; Claus Caspari and Martin Zahn of West Germany; Carlos Riefel in Austria – the list could be extended almost indefinitely from all countries fostering botanical study. Those who wish to know more about botanical artists around the world should purchase the catalogue of the most recent International Exhibition of Botanical Art and Illustration from the Hunt Institute of Botanical Documentation, Carnegie-Mellon University, Pittsburgh, Pennsylvania, USA. Each artist featured is introduced by a potted biography and one or two reduced reproductions of work in the exhibition. This publication indicates that botanical artists flourish through a variety of outlets: positions in Botanical Gardens, Universities and other institutions; freelancing and gallery exhibits; and more than a few both illustrating and writing their own work.

In this bare outline of the evolution of botanical illustration there are inevitably gaps – for instance, the influence of Dutch flower-pieces; or botanical art in the East where realistic flower painting emerged as an independent art form in China in the seventh and eighth centuries AD when, in the West, artists were still slavishly copying debased remains passed down from classical herbalists. For a detailed, erudite, and entirely fascinating account of the history of plant illustration from remote beginnings to the 1950s, I recommend *The Art of Botanical Illustration* by Wilfrid Blunt. This book has been a constant companion for over twenty years, and I am in Mr Blunt's debt not only for the pleasure that his researches have given over such a long period, but also for much of the information in this chapter.

It is hard to imagine what future trends in the field might be, though as the development of botanical illustration has been closely linked to printing, its future may be tied in some degree to information technology. For all that, if a worker of classical times were to be transported to a seat at my drawing table, he would without doubt be able to take up where I left off. He would have no difficulty in recognizing brushes and pigments, though he might marvel at the extended range of the latter. Acrylics might puzzle him, but I am sure that he would quickly feel at home with water-colours and would delight in the quality of the illustration board under his hand. It would not be hard to find him a plant that he would know. Could you or I expect to cope similarly if placed at a botanical artist's desk two thousand years ahead? Will there still be botanical artists? desks? paints? ... plants?

2 Basic equipment

Equipment and materials used with each medium are discussed in the relevant chapters. However, certain basics are needed no matter what you choose to work in.

WORK SPACE A separate room is desirable; failing that, a space giving some privacy and freedom from interruption, and large enough to allow free movement back from the work in progress to see it as a complete unit. This is especially helpful with larger pieces – in concentrating at close range it is easy to sacrifice the overall effect for the detail. Although in botanical illustration detail is often of prime importance, aesthetic standards and scientific accuracy are rarely at odds, and by viewing occasionally from a distance it is usually possible to meet both requirements. If surroundings are cramped, the effective viewing distance can be doubled by using a mirror. This has the bonus of reversing the image so that the design can be seen in a new way and weaknesses are often shown up. A reducing lens may also be used to see the work as a whole.

LIGHTING The workroom or studio should have good natural lighting, but without bright sunlight. At the least direct sun should be kept from the immediate working area, even if this means putting up a screen of some kind through part of the day. Also, the plant being portrayed should not be backed by a sunlit wall as this will distort tonal structure.

If you are lucky enough to have daylight from windows overhead, together with light from a window at the side to provide modelling for the subject, then you will probably need artificial light only in the early morning and evening. If not, then aim for a good bright system as close to daylight as feasible. Fluorescent lighting overhead coupled with an Anglepoise-type lamp for side-lighting provides an excellent combination. Side-lighting should be from the left if you are right-handed, and vice-versa.

Whatever arrangement is used, there are two essentials: the illumination of the work area must be bright enough for you to see the finest details without strain, and you should be fully aware of colour distortion stemming from the light source. Standard electric lighting is biased towards the yellow to red end of the spectrum; so the effect of yellow or red blooms will be enhanced under artificial light and diminished in daylight. A blue that sparkles in daylight becomes as lead under the lamp, while a poisonous green becomes a pleasing moss hue. The closer daylight is approached, the fewer colour problems will be encountered. It is true that your paintings are going to be seen in artificial light anyway, but tomorrow artificial light may rival the sun.

WORKING SURFACE The working surface can be as primitive as a piece of coreboard (fiberboard) or a similar flat plane, inclined against a pile of books or blocks to give a slope, but a smallish adjustable drawing-board on a large office desk with capacious drawers is more comfortable. Plants in pots can stand on the desk top along with paints, water, brushes etc. A steady table serves the same purpose as a desk, but lacks the useful drawers.

A desk-top adjustable stand may be purchased, to support a drawing-board of any inexpensive material such as plywood or coreboard which will not warp or crack but which can be screwed to the stand. A manufactured drawing-board covered with a white veneer is more expensive. The disadvantage of this system is that the stand will not reliably support a board larger than about 60 × 50 cm (24 × 20 in.). If you are likely to need a bigger surface a drawing- or drafting-stand should be used.

The drawing-stand (fig. 11) has two major advantages and several minor disadvantages. It provides a large working surface which may be raised or lowered and inclined through all positions from the horizontal to the vertical. Against this, there are no drawers except in the more elaborate and very expensive models, all paraphernalia must be moved to a table, and the plant you are working from also has to be put on a separate stand. For large-scale paintings these small irritations must be accepted as it is vital to be able to adjust the board towards the vertical in order to reach the upper portion without discomfort.

Ideally, I would recommend both an adjustable drawing-board and a drawing-stand, the former for most projects, the latter for large-scale work.

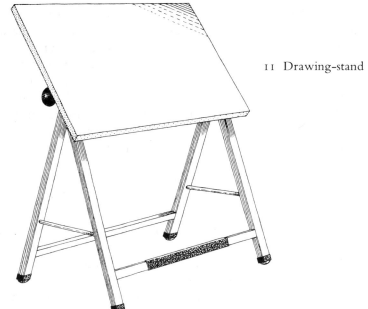

11 Drawing-stand

SEAT Choose a seat which is steady, at the correct height, and comfortable. A drawing-stand is usually, even at its lowest setting, too high for a standard chair, so the alternatives are to stand, to place the chair on a box, or to use a tall stool or a swivel chair (but this can be unsteady). The perfect work seat is one that you are not conscious of using.

PLANT-STAND In portraying plants of all different shapes and sizes, the problem is to position each one at eye-level (unless a high or low viewpoint is needed for a specific reason). I have used many sorts of clamps and stands but no single one has suited every situation. A handyman might consider making a multi-purpose stand similar to the one sketched in fig. 12.

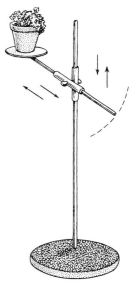

HAND-LENS This is indispensable. It should magnify by about eight to ten diameters. Though details seen through the lens may not appear in completed drawings, it is essential to understand how plant parts fit together to avoid suggesting ambiguities. And, as a bonus, unexpected wonders and beauties are revealed. A novice often holds the lens close to the object with the eye at some distance; this gives a tiny field of view and is much less satisfactory than putting the lens to the eye and raising the object until it is in sharp focus.

DISSECTING MICROSCOPE Work requiring the use of a microscope is usually done at a scientific institution; but if you can afford a microscope for work at home be sure, first, that you purchase an instrument suitable for working on topics such as seeds or flower dissections. A capacity of ×20 to ×80 or ×100 is sufficient; higher magnification than this moves into the specialized field of cell-structure which is outside the scope of this book. Even at 100 diameters the depth of field becomes wafer-thin and a lesser enlargement is usually more useful. Secondly, a choice has to be made between an instrument with a zoom-lens and the turret type in which different lenses are moved into position for each of the several set magnifications. If the *stated* magnification is the same as the *actual* magnification (and it rarely is), the turret type might be preferred; by a small movement of the hand you can select the desired setting, read off the micrometer eyepiece scale (an essential accessory) and multiply for transfer to the drawing. But if the stated magnification is inaccurate by even a small amount, a complex conversion has to be made for every measurement taken. The advantage of a zoom-lensed model is that a mark can be made on the instrument where the required settings actually occur.

CAMERA In some situations it is necessary to turn to the camera as an aid. You may want to portray rare plants that it would be criminal to pick, and though fairly simple line drawings may be carried out *in situ*, a detailed study is often impracticable. Or lack of time may prevent individual plates from being completed – though to some extent this problem can be eased by keeping plants in the refrigerator or by potting them up for later use.

The point to be stressed is that photographs should be used only where there is no other sensible means of access to the necessary information. And never – or almost never – use photographs taken by anyone else unless they are taken in your company or you have an intimate knowledge of the species concerned. I can recollect only four occasions in over twenty years when I have had to use a photograph taken by another's hand. In each instance the fact that the illustration was based on a photograph was noted in a caption, as I felt slightly uneasy that something might have been missed that would have been clear had I been able to see the living flowers.

For hints on photographing plants and choice of camera, see chapter 11.

DIVIDERS Used to take dimensions directly from the model; and by 'walking' the points across the paper, magnifications of up to × 5 or so may be rapidly recorded. Dividers are faster to manoeuvre through foliage than a ruler.

PROPORTIONAL DIVIDERS Many botanical illustrators favour this instrument. By a pre-selected setting, a dimension described by the distance between the points of the two larger arms is reflected in a correct reduction between the points of the two smaller arms (a reversal of the dividers will provide magnification when needed). You may want to reduce a plant or its parts by, say, half: move the setting device to the appropriate reading and separate the major points until they match the dimension to be taken; the minor points will then be at half scale and can be applied to the paper. To avoid leaving ugly scratches or holes in the work, the tool should be placed flush or parallel with the surface, with the long blades facing away for safety; a slight pressure towards the tips will then record the dimension on the paper as two small dots – alternatively, pencil marks may be used.

POCKET CALCULATOR This is invaluable, especially when drawing flower dissections or converting measurements from a photograph.

PRICKER A needle-like steel rod set in a holder, useful for transferring traced drawings with precision (see p. 94). The instrument may be purchased, or you can use a dissecting-needle or other sharp point.

SCALPEL AND DISSECTING NEEDLES A scalpel is the only sensible cutting tool to use for flower dissections.

Dissecting needles hold the plant part firmly in place while the scalpel is being used. I like to use two forms, one bent at an angle to its holder and the other straight. The angled kind is perfect for holding tissues in place without actually piercing them, and the straight one may be used for delicate probing.

Scalpel blades and dissecting needles should not contact the stage of the microscope as they will mar the surface. All operations should be carried out over glass such as microscope slides or petri dishes.

CRAFT KNIFE A heavy-duty craft knife (mat knife) will serve for pencil sharpening, cutting paper and illustration board etc. The kind with a retractable blade is safer than the fixed variety.

FEATHER A feather is ideal for brushing away eraser particles.

INVISIBLE MENDING TAPE Excellent for holding paper firmly in place on the drawing-board; it may be pulled away after use without lifting the fibres of the paper surface or tearing its edges. Masking tape and sellotape (Scotch tape) are far less satisfactory. An eraser will remove sticky traces left by tape.

3 Concepts

Perspective

This topic is too lengthy to cover here, and I would refer you to any good general art book. However, you need only master the essential principles: botanical illustration rarely requires anything more involved, but shaky perspective can ruin an otherwise convincing plate.

Colour-mixing

Most readers will already have some understanding of colour-mixing. The main problem will be in mixing colours to match precisely what you see in the plant. For instance, you may know that blue mixed with yellow yields green, but this is only the first step in trying to match the hue of a particular leaf. A touch of red or a hint of crimson may be needed, and perhaps a little of another blue or a different yellow. An analysis has to be made of each colour to be matched. This skill develops through experience, and before long you should be able to carry out a colour breakdown unconsciously as you are mixing. Specific suggestions are given in chapters 9 and 10.

Tone-values

Except for work done in pure outline, insufficient attention to tone-values often spoils a painting or drawing of a plant. The tone-value of a colour refers to its quality of 'lightness' or 'darkness'. If a plant is photographed in black and white, the resulting print will represent colours by a range from white to black. If the same plant is then photographed in colour it will be seen that each colour on the photograph is recorded on the black and white print as a patch of 'tone' in 'value' anywhere from white, through all the greys, to black. Fig. 13 illustrates the range of tone-values broken into ten steps. Take a piece of leaf or any pigmented material and move it along the diagram until the 'lightness' or 'darkness' is matched, and there you will have its tone-value.

13 Tone-values

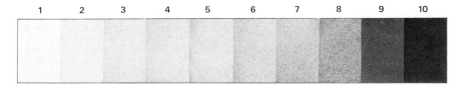

Botanical knowledge

Your effectiveness as a botanical artist, and your pleasure in your work, will be enhanced by building a background of plant-lore. There are excellent 'outline' books available such as Peter Raven's *Biology of Plants* or J. M. Lowson's *Textbook of Botany* (see Bibliography).

It is satisfying to know every species of a genus, to be aware of the characters by which one species may be distinguished from another, to look for a representative of 'your' genus in suitable habitats, and to compare details of minute form and structure.

As well as having common names, plants also have Latin names based on the binomial system invented by Linnaeus and developed since. Here I wish only to point out the advantage of using scientific names in gaining an understanding of relationships. The use of 'common' or 'vernacular' names alone can easily be misleading. For example, *Erythronium americanum* is also known as trout–lily and as dog-tooth violet, yet it is neither trout-like nor a violet, though it is a lily. Common names also vary according to locality, whereas scientific names are stable (excepting when new studies change the interpretation of relationships, as in the recent merging of the genus *Zauschneria* into the genus *Epilobium*).

Self-criticism

Each painting, each drawing, each illustration should be better than the last. Measure yourself against your own work and that of others. When starting on a project, try to find something similar by another artist, see how he has solved like problems, and then strive to go one better. This examination of the attempts of fellow artists is very worth while – one can learn from, and share their pleasure.

Accuracy

In working for taxonomic purposes, each plant portrayed is not only an individual, distinct and apart, it must also be seen as a representative of a particular *taxon* (form, variety, subspecies, species etc.). In other words it represents a group. It is necessary to be sure that the individual portrayed has all the characteristics associated with the group. These are easily checked in detail if there are published descriptions to compare with the specimen, or, if the illustration is for a new monograph or revision, the author may like you to use his manuscript. Though the author may have a number of the plants that you are illustrating growing in the experimental garden, or available from the wild, there is no guarantee that every one of them will conform to the description for the group. You and your work, not the plant, are more likely to be blamed for deviation from the printed word. Let me give an example. I had drawn a dissection of the *corolla* of a small heath showing internal hairs. A botanist, looking at the species afresh after some years, examined my drawing and commented that the corolla should not show hairs on the inside surface. There was no convincing answer to this other than to find the plant long forgotten and to demonstrate the veracity of the study. The same heath was found in the experimental garden carrying the same identification as the drawing – even though the tag had almost faded away after ten years or so. Flowers were present and so were the disputed hairs.

4 Plant handling

Plant portraits may give problems of two main kinds apart from those caused by deficiencies in the artist: some arise from the medium or the style chosen; others are inherent in the plants themselves.

Phenotypic variation

One source of difficulty is *phenotypic* variation. All living organisms may be thought of in terms of their *genotype* or genetic structure, and their *phenotype* or appearance due to the response of the genotype to external factors. Two plants of the same genotype grown in the same conditions will look much alike; but grown under entirely different regimes, their phenotypic responses may be such as to make them appear to be separate species. This is an oversimplification; the interested reader will find that these terms represent the tip of a very large iceberg.

Problems may arise when, for example, a plant which normally grows at a high altitude is gathered and grown on for a period. It will often develop characteristics quite other than those shown on its rocky peak. There, in response to higher levels of solar radiation, its leaves would have a reddish or coppery pigmentation, and harsh conditions might impose a compact form. At a lower elevation, the leaf pigmentation would probably revert to green, and the form of the plant might become tall, lush and open. This kind of change is not unusual – though some species will vary little through a broad spectrum of growing conditions. You may be embarrassed in faithfully recording the plant in hand if you know little of the same plants in the bush. To avoid distortion from phenotypic plasticity, the best approach is to use authentic fresh material from the subject's typical habitat.

Growth-phase

Distortion can also occur when plants either have not reached maturity or are in decline. In both phases flower size may be affected – the first and last flowers are often smaller than those of the plant in full prime. Again, in the *ontogeny* (life-history) of an individual, juvenile leaves – often less toothed or dissected – may be very much in evidence before maturition, remaining or partly present at maturity, absent or decaying in senescence.

Models

Subject to the reservations mentioned above, the ideal plant model is one growing healthily in a pot. With some species it is possible (depending upon their conservation status – see pp. 11, 31) to take a plant from the wild complete with roots and soil, pot it up, allow it to stabilize (twenty-four hours in a water bath sometimes helps, plus a couple of days in the shade) portray it, and then make it into a voucher herbarium specimen (p. 30). Other plants wilt when lifted and these have to be drawn immediately if this is feasible, or must be grown from seed. If neither course is practicable it may be necessary to use photography allied with dried specimens, field notes etc. Naturally the dimensions of the plant also have some bearing upon treatment.

Sometimes a plant which collapses after potting will revive for long enough to be drawn if it is placed in a container of water after washing out the roots.

A flowering branch, or a single flower or other detail, can be placed in a jar of water. For the tiny portion, a small shallow receptacle – a petri dish or similar – with cotton-wool or blotting paper soaked in water, will create a micro-climate of moist air, essential when working with delicate membraneous tissues in a warm dry atmosphere. The upper section of a petri dish can be placed over the lower to increase the greenhouse effect if you have to leave the work for some minutes. If the plant material is light in tone, stain the cotton-wool or blotting paper with ink or paint to obtain enough contrast between the subject and the background. This is also useful when examining plant parts carrying hairs which may not be visible against a light ground.

Dissections

Often the technique of flower dissection is clothed by a certain amount of humbug. A dissecting needle or two, a sharp scalpel, a good eye and a steady hand are all that are generally required. For minute organs the dissecting microscope will also be used. Small objects are more easily handled if they are embedded lightly in a low-temperature wax or other malleable substance. Scalpel blades lose their edge quickly: rather than replacing them after little use, I prefer to maintain sharpness by frequent use of a fine-grained stone. Resistant tissue is sometimes more amenable if a moistened blade is used. A dissecting needle is used to hold the object still while cutting. Speed is important as tissues rapidly deteriorate during dissection – with flowers, for example, though all measurements should be taken from one specimen, it is worth while to have others available to provide supplementary information. Details of a typical dissection are given in chapter 7.

Sometimes a botanist will need to make a dissection in order to point out special features, but it is usually better to use this only as a guide. In my experience, the illustrator will make an improved dissection to draw from, having perhaps a clearer understanding of the requirements for illustration. It is a pleasurable experience to remove an organ, a pistil perhaps less than a millimetre tall, cleanly and without damage and to place it in a position for drawing; but the dissection of small flowers etc. calls for the greatest patience as well as dexterity. So often, within reach of success, required material will be damaged by an inadvertent movement.

Lighting and placement

Plant illustrations are in the main shaded on the right-hand side, suggesting light falling from the upper left which, for the right-handed artist, will not throw a shadow from the working hand on to the drawing. The reverse is true for the left-hander who will find it more convenient to have the light source on the right. With individual plates it does not matter which side the light appears to be from, but for a set of illustrations it is better if the lighting is consistent. The same is true for plant details surrounding a habit study (fig. 65).

The plant model should stand in correct relation to your eye; normally the portion being worked on should be kept at about eye-level. This means that with a tall specimen, starting with the *inflorescence*, it may be necessary to raise the plant two or more times, giving a view of separate sections on the illustration. One point worth emphasis is that the specimen should be viewed from exactly the same point while each section is being drawn: as the model will be close - ideally, 30-60 cm (12-24 in.) from the eye - even small movements of the head will change what can or cannot be seen and will render a complex structure almost impossible to manage. For the same reason it is best to favour one eye in viewing; the other should briefly be closed or covered. With especially difficult topics, choose a specific point on the plant which may be aligned with a mark on the background. Make sure from time to time that the original viewpoint is being held, by checking that the spot on the plant and the mark behind are superimposed. The background mark must be made by someone else, while you sit comfortably in the exact working position and select the two points by eye.

With a simple subject the foregoing tactic is not needed. However, for both simple and complex items you should not be over-hasty in starting to draw. Once the specimen is at eye-level, turn it around slowly a couple of times before selecting the best aspect. If the plant has just been brought indoors it may also be advisable to allow it time to adjust to new light conditions. With a rigid species such as a cactus or a succulent no period of adjustment is needed, but with non-woody flexible models it is surprising how much twisting and turning occurs. In some species virtually all parts move to present themselves to the brightest source of light. This is another reason for blocking direct sun from the studio - it is more than annoying when a light-sensitive plant swings away from an artificial light to track a moving band of sunshine.

A plant should be allowed an hour or so for settling in the studio since, as well as moving towards the light, flowers sometimes react strongly to a new regime - commonly petals flex open more widely, buds burst, and anthers *dehisce* (open to expose pollen).

Storage

Frequently plants are held over from one day to another. If your model is growing in a pot it may be left with safety overnight, but if, for instance, another growth phase is required which may occur some days later, it is usually best to return the plant to its usual situation to avoid distortion from growth indoors. When fragments or cut stems are held they often freshen if they are placed, still in their container, overnight inside a plastic bag: this should be of stiffish quality to ensure that it will stand free of its contents - petals and other delicate parts may otherwise cling to condensation on the inner surface. Many specimens also benefit (bagged or not) from a stay in the refrigerator – the chill moist air has a rejuvenating effect.

If you have more cut plants than can be managed for several days, decay may be inhibited by placing them in the refrigerator. Some species will stay in excellent condition for a long time in this way – alpine plant cuttings have stayed in prime condition for approaching six months. Flowers usually deteriorate before foliage, so they should be given priority for drawing. Note that chilling, not freezing, is the aim – the tissues of frozen plants break down quickly upon thawing.

For realistic plant portraits without specific scientific intent, pressing and drying (see below) will also preserve material for later access. The professional botanical illustrator, however, will inevitably need to use to a greater or lesser extent the organized facilities of an herbarium.

Herbarium specimens

Herbaria are collections of dried and pressed plants, filed alphabetically or according to an accepted system of classification, for reference and study. They range in size from the small, perhaps home-based, special-purpose assemblage to the herbarium of a great scientific institution holding millions of specimens from all parts of the world. Botanical illustrators employed by scientific establishments may spend a large proportion of their time working directly from herbarium specimens. And, when live plants are illustrated, these also are generally processed into 'voucher' specimens as a matter of routine. In either case an illustration will be associated with a preserved plant, and a caption should record the plant's sheet identification – a number prefixed by the international code letters assigned to the herbarium.

The value of a plate is enormously enhanced when it is cross-referenced to a particular herbarium sheet: the specimen may serve to confirm the veracity of the drawing, and botanical workers are enabled to examine both the illustration and the specimen as required throughout the several hundred years that they may be extant. If the illustration was made solely from a dried specimen, it can show only those characteristics retained after processing; yet many details may be illuminated that otherwise could be deciphered only by intensive study. And if the illustration was made from a living plant, it may convey information no longer present or obscured in the dried specimen – features such as natural posture of leaves and flowers, secreting hairs, glossiness, succulence and so on.

Professional botanical artists will not normally be called upon to prepare herbarium specimens, but there may be occasions when it may be helpful to preserve a plant for later examination. Detailed instructions on the many methods used for drying can be found in books dealing with botanical collecting. All the methods have in common the objective of drying the specimens as quickly as possible without the use of more than a very gentle heat. Excessive heat causes severe discoloration and results, at best, in very inferior specimens.

The simplest method consists of pressing the plant material between sheets of absorbent paper – old newspaper will do nicely – and then changing the papers every day until the specimens are quite dry. Pressure can be provided by any convenient heavy object, such as old books or, if the papers are sandwiched between boards, by straps.

The artist will appreciate more than most people the qualities needed in a good botanical specimen. Ideally, the specimen should illustrate all the features of the species. This may be easy with small species as the whole plant, or even a sample of the population, can conveniently be pressed. But with large herbs, not to mention trees and shrubs, only a small part of the whole plant can be preserved. The missing information can, to some extent, be provided by careful notes, e.g. height, branching pattern, bark colour and texture; and, for all specimens, notes on flower colour and scent and any other features that are difficult to preserve, should be made. Photographs, carefully coordinated with dried specimens, can be of particular value to illustrate the general appearance of plants that are too large to preserve as normal specimens.

Before collecting any specimens in the wild, you should be familiar with local legislation governing conservation, and in any case you should never collect specimens unless the species concerned is plentiful in that particular area.

Herbarium specimens are intended for use, and the scientific illustrator should consult additional sheets as background, whether working from living or dried specimens. Each herbarium has its own rules and these should be carefully observed: their main intent will be to ensure that each specimen is preserved for as long as possible consonant with its function as a botanical tool.

Lichens, mosses and liverworts (usually housed in packets in the herbarium), ferns, grasses, many conifers, and other groups, are often little altered as dried specimens from their appearance in life. Apart from slight difficulties which may be found in translating pressed parts into realistic perspective, such plants should not test the illustrator more than they would have done in life. But species with delicate, easily damaged tissues may well give problems – flowers for example are vulnerable to distortion during drying and pressing. Sometimes flowers from the same collection will have been preserved in spirits, and then it is usually straightforward to use a substitute in drawing, as these blooms will appear in structure much as they did in life. If this solution is not available, dessicated tissues of crushed flowers etc. may be partially re-inflated by detaching them from the sheet (where this is permissible) and immersing them in boiling water for a minute or two. After use the fragments should be restored to the sheet in one of the small envelopes or packets used by the herbarium.

Though drawing from herbarium specimens has disadvantages, there are some gains. A major one is that the model is fixed in time at whatever point in its cycle it was collected: it can be put aside and picked up again unchanged years later if necessary, while with live plants a number of needed species may flower at around the same time. Also, the actual handling of herbarium specimens in comparison with live models is usually easier. The sheet can be conveniently placed on the working surface and may easily be manoeuvred under the dissecting microscope.

As a rule, some direction will be given as to which features on the sheet are of special botanical interest, and the artist will ensure that these are clearly shown. Beyond this it will often be useful to introduce an element of tonal emphasis, particularly when the material to be drawn is poorly differentiated. Emphasizing some parts in greater detail and darker tone than their surrounds will give the drawing a slightly three-dimensional quality and make the work easier to 'read'. Sharp photographs or colour slides may be used as aids, but do not rely on reportage or on others' illustrations.

Since many features are modified in drying and pressing, a restrained illustrative treatment is best, relying mainly on line, with tone kept to a minimum. Ink is the ideal medium for this purpose (chapter 7).

Experienced botanical illustrators are able to reconstruct the appearance of a living plant from a herbarium specimen by calling on their background knowledge and 'feel' for their subjects – even though often they will not have seen the plant in its live form. This accumulated experience is different from that of the scientist but complementary; and when the two are brought together, the best possible results are seen.

5 Plants in detail

This chapter contains observations about various kinds of plants, plant parts, and their characteristics. Apart from the first model, it is biased towards flowering plants as they are more familiar to most readers and the nomenclature of their parts is less esoteric than for some groups. Nevertheless, the structures detailed have their counterparts elsewhere, and information given here may be used in drawing like forms wherever they occur.

The plants in fig. 14 demonstrate the variety of combinations that exist. Here we will look at some of the items helpful to the artist confronted by this diversity and at the basic steps of transferring data about the plants to paper – before tone, ink or water-colour etc. are used.

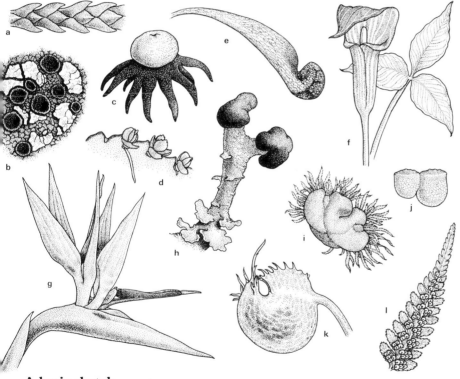

14 A selection of diverse plant structures: **a** *Libocedrus bidwillii*, a detail of closely appressed conifer leaves; **b** *Rhizocarpon geographicum*, crustose lichen (enlarged); **c** *Astraeus hygrometricus*, earth star fungus; **d** *Kalenchoë daigremontiana*, the maternity plant – margin of leaf with plantlets; **e** *Sarracenia psittacina*, pitcher plant – prostrate pitcher; **f** *Arisaema triphyllum*, Jack in the pulpit; **g** *Strelitzia reginae*, bird of paradise plant – inflorescence; **h** *Cladonia* sp., magnified portion of lichen; **i** *Ricciocarpus natans*, a water-dwelling liverwort; **j** *Wolffia arrhiza* var. *australiana*, of the duckweed family (enlarged); **k** *Utricularia novae-zelandiae*, bladder wort – magnified bladder trap; **l** *Dryopteris felis-mas*, male fern – frond underside

A basic sketch

Several general principles emerge in drawing a fungus species – one of the simplest forms (fig. 15).

The model was placed at eye-level, examined from all sides, and the most pleasing aspect chosen. Initially I intended to draw only one specimen, but as the underside *gills* must also be seen, I included another, tilted to expose the required detail.

SIZE AND SCALE Pencil and paper were selected with the finishing medium in mind and need not be discussed here except for one point – paper size. A common error is to cut a sheet so that the subject extends to the edges. This may create problems of handling, especially if the work is to be printed. Plan your plate layout first. For this exercise it was assumed that the plants were to be drawn life-scale. I took the outside dimensions with dividers, taking care that measurements were made on one plane (see below); these were used to work out an arrangement leaving ample margins. Sometimes it is not easy to reach a prior determination of size, or you may be unsure of just how much of the subject is needed on paper until it is sketched in. In these cases, work on an over-sized sheet until dimensions are settled.

If plates are to form a set, all of the same scale on the same sized sheets, you may have to juggle to fit the subject on the paper within fixed dimensions. When working on a series of such plates, perhaps portraying a genus, you may find that, with the exception of one or two species, all fit life-size within the framework. The over-sized species may be drawn life-size, showing less of their habit than those of the other plates; or be reduced in scale and still remain within the existing frame; or be drawn still at life-size, and showing the same proportion of the subjects as the rest of the series, yet within a larger framework on a larger sheet. Either of the first two choices should be made if there is no measurable loss of botanical worth. Occasionally the last possibility has to be chosen; then, if there is an appreciable difference in size from the other plates, the increased reduction on publication is usually visible – no matter what care is taken in adjusting line-thicknesses, detail etc. – so breaking the consistent appearance of the set.

I decided that the margins for the fungus plate should be 3 cm (*c.* $1\frac{1}{4}$ in.) at the top and sides and 3.5 cm ($1\frac{3}{8}$ in.) at the bottom (nearly all art works appear optically centred if a slightly wider space is left at the lower edge). These margin sizes will serve for the smallest plate up to an image height of around 30 cm (12 in.); you will see when wider ones are needed.

STARTING TO DRAW At this stage I had a sheet of appropriate size with margins, marked in very lightly, based on the outside dimensions of the fungi. The next step was to decide where to start drawing. I usually lightly block-in the whole drawing to establish that it is going to work as planned, and then move to and fro, strengthening and correcting until completion. The procedure for blocking-in is to take the major element of the composition – in this instance the fungus on the left – and to build around it. An appraisal of the form (see also p. 36) was made, and salient points were selected for measurement; these are shown on fig. 15 as small crosses connected by broken lines (in an actual drawing the broken lines would not be put in and the crosses would be made very faintly).

As the drawing was life-sized, dimensions were transferred to the paper by means of dividers, taking care to avoid sloping the dividers away from an imaginary vertical plane passing through the model. For instance, placing the point of one arm at point *A*, the other arm must be held in the same vertical plane and adjusted until it is level with point *B*. If to do this

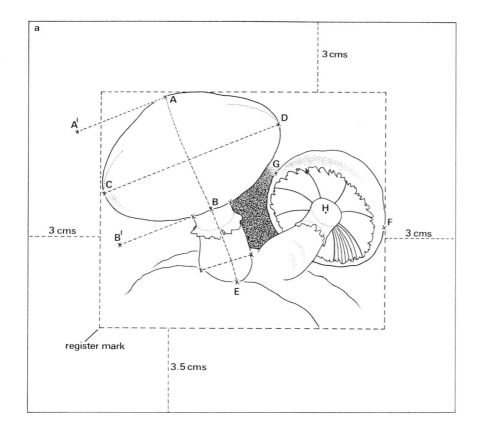

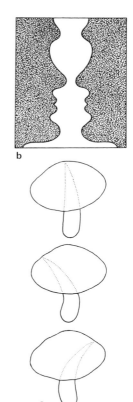

the lower arm had been tilted forward until point B was touched, the measure obtained, though life-size, would have been uncorrected for perspective and would introduce a considerable error. In this case it was necessary to move the divider arms out to points A^1 and B^1 to make a measurement free from obstruction.

Unless you are working on a complex topic such as a flower dissection, few measurements are required. For the present subject only the total height, width of the cap, width of the stem where it moved from view under the cap, and the thickness of the stem at the base were used. In practice one tends to sketch in more or less as the measurements are made – there is no rigid sequence.

PERSPECTIVE After the major component, the left-hand fungus, was drawn, the fungus on the right was put in; and this serves to illustrate a small difficulty. You will notice that the right-hand form is slightly to the rear of the other, i.e. further from the observer; so in order to show it correctly in perspective its actual dimensions were reduced by careful assessment by eye against the measured and drawn-in dimensions of the first fungus.

To avoid distortion one eye was used to view from a fixed position. Next, point F was defined where the curve of the cap intersected the line of the margin on the right. The ellipse passing through F and G was sketched in and particular care was taken in estimating the positions of G and H. Placing the stem and the exposed underside was then easy.

15 **a** basic sketch;
b 'balustrade/profile' effect;
c siting of caps on stems

35

ANALYSIS OF FORMS AND SPACES For the second fungus another concept was helpful. The pattern of the toadstool forms implied a pattern of space – an appreciation of the interplay of forms is gained by considering the shapes between them. This is illustrated by the well-known illusion in fig. 15*b* – a white balustrade or human profiles? A white form creates two black patterns of space – two black forms create a white space pattern. In fig. 15*a*, stipple indicates one pattern of space; it is abstract, so the eye tends not to be led astray by a subjective appreciation of the way it ought to appear – perspective and foreshortening do not apply.

Though the forms of the fungi are simple, they may provide a number of further pointers. Earlier it was noted that 'an appraisal of the form was made'. This mental analysis becomes automatic with practice. Complex shapes are broken down into their basic components – ellipses, cones, circles, squares etc. – in order that they may be more easily handled. In the present example the components were two dome shapes and two cylinders – not difficult forms provided care is taken with the ellipses.

When placing one unit upon another – domes on cylinders, caps on stems, flowers on stalks – it is easy to create a wrong impression by even a tiny deviation from accuracy around the section where one component joins the other. This is because the eye tends to follow an indicated subjective line. If lines are projected as shown in fig. 15*c* such errors should not occur.

The gills of the right-hand fungus radiate around the point of entry of the stem (H). To show this – and any other types of radiating lines or forms – it is helpful to mark in a hypothetical point from which they originate. Then the positions of several key-lines are drawn (see heavier lines on the sketch) and the rest can be placed with confidence.

Recorded subtle fluctuations in outline are one of the marks of careful observation. At a glance the curve of the cap of the left-hand fungus in fig. 15*a* might appear smooth, but a closer examination shows small but distinct variations in outline. The same kind of detail is seen about the rim of the cap of the second fungus along the outer edge of the gills.

STEP BY STEP SUMMARY The procedure outlined above should be useful for most types of botanical illustration: (*a*) place model carefully, choosing the most pleasing and useful aspect; (*b*) select sheet-size using overall dimensions of subject; (*c*) lightly mark in margins; (*d*) measure off and put in key-points; (*e*) establish background and other material by eye using the measured major components as guides; (*f*) move over drawing, adding detail, strengthening and correcting. The drawing can then be finished in the chosen medium.

We can now move from basic procedure to an examination of some of the more common plant structures and the challenges they present. Botanical terms are used sparingly – it is not intended that each section should provide a guide to nomenclature, or that the complete range of forms should be covered; for these topics botanical texts should be consulted.

Leaves

There are features common to virtually all leaves and the characteristic expression of each feature may be of importance.

OUTLINES As you look at a plant stem you will often see that the leaves at the bottom have a different outline from those at the top, and you should watch for such changes as well as for differences characteristic of the leaves of separate species. Taking a simple outline first, fig. 16a, there are several items of interest even in this uncomplicated shape. The widest measure is slightly oblique, falling from left to right, and the dimension of the widest part of the leaf on the left of the midrib is less than that on the right. The leaf tip attenuates to a fine point and the base of the *lamina* or blade passes smoothly into the *petiole* or stalk. The petiole is one-fifth of the length of the lamina.

16 Leaf forms: **a** simple; **b** palmate; **c** dissected; **d** pinnate

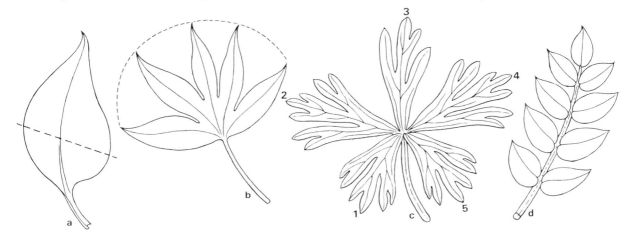

Quite small variations will alter the character of a leaf, changing its appearance and its botanical description. Several likely variations are shown in fig. 17. These emphasize the care that should be taken in drawing, as such differences are sometimes stable enough in separate species to be used as part of the process of identification. Note that the only differences between *a*, *b* and *c* are those imposed by moving the widest portion of the

17 Significant changes in leaf morphology brought about by small variations in outline

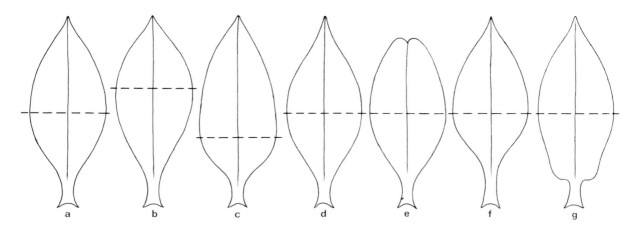

lamina from a line through the mid-section to above and below it. In *d* and *e*, the leaf apices alone are changed – all other characters remain as in *a*. In *f* and *g* only the leaf bases have been altered. By tinkering with three characters – the position of the widest portion of the leaf and the shape of the leaf apex and base – seven quite distinct outlines have been made. In nature, the widths of the leaves and the lengths of the petioles might also be varied (sometimes petioles will be absent and such leaves are termed *sessile*). These and other characters may be shuffled to give a tremendous number of possibilities.

This section started with a discussion of the leaf outline in fig. 16*a*. In the more complex shapes of *b*, *c* and *d*, it is clear that much the same questions should be asked in analysing the basic shapes and noting key dimensions (as in the fungus sketch); taking special care with the leaf bases and apices; noting the length of the petiole; and any other particular characteristics. Two further general points will be treated in more depth later: first, note the form of the base of the petiole where it attaches to the stem or branch; second, the angle at which the leaf joins the stem – its posture – may also be characteristic.

A third component may or may not be present with the lamina and the petiole. This is the *stipule*, which may be found (usually paired) at the petiole base (fig. 18). It ranges from being a leafy appendage as shown here to being hair-like or a minute scale, or absent.

Though *pinnate* leaves such as that shown in fig. 16*d* may look complex, their structure really is quite simple. The more difficult palmate leaf shape at *b* has been reduced to its basic outline; in nature it might appear as shown, or be complicated by various secondary toothing (*serration*) or dissection. In these forms it is often advisable initially to reduce the outline to its basic elements as at *b*; the points of the lobes of this leaf fall helpfully along a curve (this is not uncommon). It may also be useful to measure off the distances between these points, especially when working on leaves such as *c* where one would measure the lengths of the radiating lobes and the distances between the numbered points.

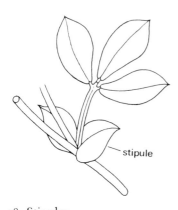

stipule

18 Stipules

LEAF MARGINS After considering basic leaf outlines, look closer at their margins. In essence, leaf margins may be simple or *linear* (without teeth); toothed in a variety of ways; hidden by being turned under or *revolute*; or wavy, *undulate*.

The main task is to discern the pattern and then to represent it accurately. Usually this is straightforward, though some margin types are difficult owing either to complexity of detail or to ambiguities introduced in portraying three dimensions upon a two-dimensional surface. This latter problem is typified by the leaf with an undulate margin (fig. 19*d*). Unless the greatest care is taken it may appear in a drawing that the blade becomes wider and narrower – moving in and out in relation to the midrib, as in *c*, rather than up and down in the vertical plane. Close observation with judicious use of shadows and highlights will avoid this impression.

In illustration, leaf margins display degrees of hairiness rather better than leaf surfaces where hairs may be obscured. Also, the thickness of a leaf may be revealed by touches along the edges.

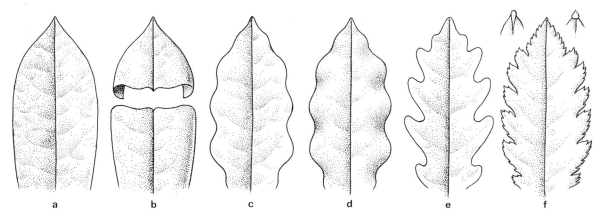

a   b   c   d   e   f

Leaves may show a tiny protruberance, *mucro*, at the tips of the margin teeth, and/or at the leaf apex. These are often different in texture from the rest of the leaf and should be shown where feasible (fig. 19*f*).

VENATION AND SURFACE MODELLING Leaf *venation* is often responsible for the surface patterning of the lamina. This influence is direct when the veins are clearly seen against the body of the leaf due to differences in tone and/or colouring, and indirect when the veins remain indistinct with their positions revealed by rucking and modelling. Often the conditions are present together – distinct venation and a sculpted surface as in fig. 20*c*.

Patterns of venation are distinctive in many groups. Parallel venation (fig. 20*e*), for example, is seen in most *monocotyledonous* plants, though even within this fundamental design there is room for variety; *dicotyledonous* taxa show a great variety of veining. Note whether veins oppose or alternate with each other along the midrib, or whether they originate at the leaf base. The ways in which the veins terminate are also important – sometimes they will follow through to a tooth tip, or they may join another major vein just inside the leaf margin and then swing away to the apex. Major veins should be accurate as to numbers and arrangement. Sometimes the minor veins are seen just as distinctly, forming a complicated reticulation. You may be sufficiently skilful to show the whole network on each leaf, but if this were done, one species might absorb the time assigned to many. Also, curiously, if an attempt is made to put in each tiny vein to scale and with no extra emphasis, the overall effect is more often than not unconvincing – a generalized impression usually appears more realistic. Avoid over-emphasizing main veins and midribs if they are obscure in life: an exception might be made for work done from

19 Leaf margins: **a** entire; **b** revolute; **c** sinuate; **d** undulate; **e** lobed; **f** serrate – in this instance, as the larger divisions carry secondary toothing, the condition is more precisely described as 'double-serrate'

20 Venation and surface modelling: **a** surface smooth, veins obscure; **b** surface smooth, veins distinct; **c** surface modelled, veins distinct; **d** surface modelled, veins obscure; **e** parallel venation

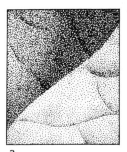

a   b   c   d   e

herbarium specimens. Although drying often obliterates surface modelling, it sometimes exposes venation, which may be illustrated since a somewhat diagrammatic version of the plant is inevitable when using dried material.

LEAVES IN PERSPECTIVE Walter Hood Fitch expressed good sense on this subject in 1869 in an article in *The Gardeners' Chronicle:* 'Leaves have been subjected to more bad treatment by the draughtsman than perhaps any other portion of the vegetable kingdom; they have been represented, or rather misrepresented, in all kinds of impossible positions. Numerous are the tortures to which they have been subjected: dislocated or broken ribs, curious twists, painful to behold – even wretched veins have not escaped; and all these errors in perspective arise from inattention to the simple fact, that in a curved leaf, showing the underside, the midrib should be continuous, and the veins should spring from the midrib.'

Drawing leaves in perspective in all their varied postures is largely a matter of observation. As Fitch implies, the midrib is the prime structure; once this is established the rest is less testing. Complex toothing or serrations are more challenging when leaves are twisted or viewed from the side or below – it is helpful to sketch the margins in very lightly, after placing the midrib, and then to use the main veins as guides to position teeth, serrations or lobes. Fig. 21 shows several common situations.

21 Leaves in perspective:
a–d steps in progression;
e some common forms in perspective

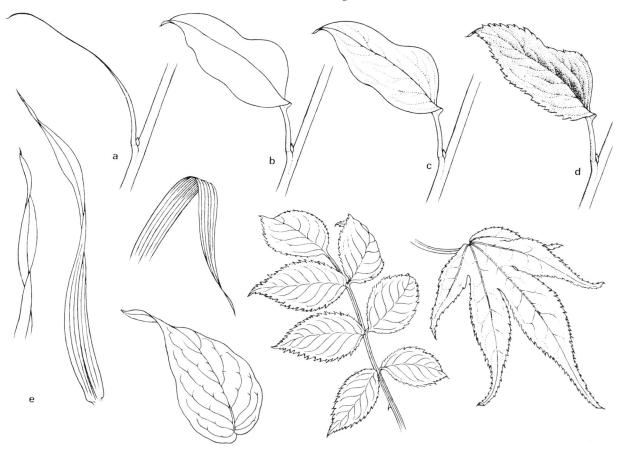

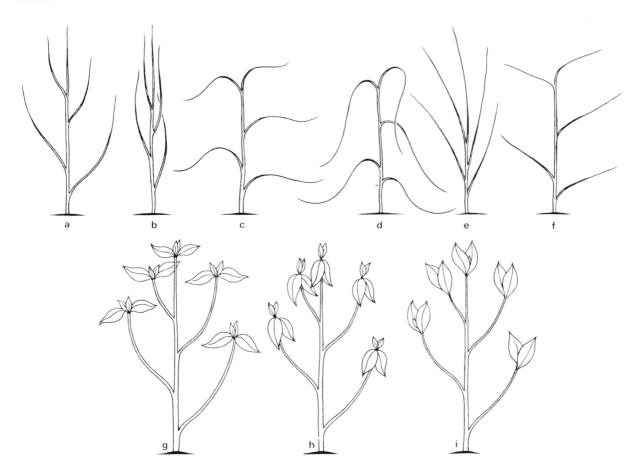

POSTURES OF LEAVES, BRANCHES AND STEMS Posture is related to *habit*, that is, the general appearance of the plant due to the particular way in which the stem or stems emerge from the ground, the mode of branching (if any), the way the leaves sit, and the type of inflorescence etc.

Posture is vital in capturing the character of a species. It may be analysed in terms of angles. The angles which stems and branches maintain in relation to each other and to the ground may be constant. This is less true of many leaves since their posture is more likely to change according to their stage of development, water stress, whether it is day or night, position in relation to the sun, etc. The above points are demonstrated in fig. 22. A simple hypothetical plant form is shown and its four bare branches are moved through several plausible postures (*a–f*). The stem stays upright – making the point that the appearance of a plant may be vastly altered by the stance of the limbs alone, though of course in life the stem itself might also contort. In *g*, *h* and *i*, stems and branches remain identical but the angles at which the leaves are held are radically altered, creating what might be three different species.

The way in which leaves are angled to the branch will also affect the working sequence: if they are more or less erect in relation to the stem (fig. 23*a*) it is easier to work from the lowest upwards, using the first as a guide for placing the others; if leaves are reflexed as in *b*, the upper ones determine the positions of the rest. Pairs of opposite leaves emerging from the stem at something like a right-angle are more clearly and pleasingly presented if shown as in *c* rather than as in *d*.

22 Posture: **a–f** effects of moving limbs through postures seen in nature; **g–i** different effects achieved by altering angles at which leaves are carried

41

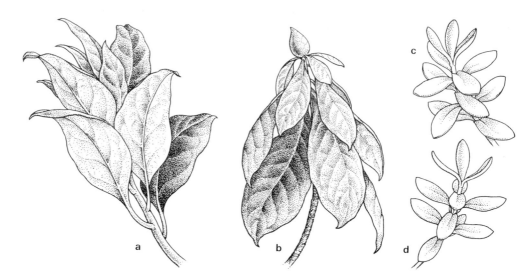

23 Leaf postures

a　　　　b　　　　d

LEAF ARRANGEMENTS Though there are ample botanical terms to describe the ways in which leaves are arranged upon stems, there are just a few basic themes, which allow great variation. Leaves may be *opposite*, *alternate*, *whorled* or *spiralled*; they may also be in groups or clumps – though even in the tightest grouping a definite pattern can usually be found.

Trichomes – hairs, bristles and prickles

Trichomes (fig. 24) are defined as outgrowths of the epidermis but this does not begin to suggest their beauty or interest. Botanically they may be categorized by structure, by density upon leaves, stems, petioles etc., and by size. For instance, a surface is *puberulous* when it is evenly covered (density) in hairs (structure) so minute (size) as to be just visible to the naked eye.

Problems often arise from trichome density, as when long erect hairs thickly cover a stem – a situation almost impossible to depict with accuracy in ink. A workable solution is merely to suggest them in a habit study (though still keeping the length and the posture correct) and to give more detail in an inset. (See also chapter 7 under *Dissections*.)

24 Trichome types (not to scale)

Trichomes range from simple single-celled hairs to the poisoned needle of the nettle, the thorn of the rose, and the elaborately sculpted leaf-scales of some rhododendrons. As always, watch for patterns – certain organs may carry hairs absent from other parts; there may be an admixture of various trichome types; hairs are sometimes organized in lines along mid-ribs, margins or from nodes.

A plant or part of a plant is described as *glabrous* where there are no hairs, and it is just as important to show this condition as it is to draw hairs where they are present. Be cautious – it is not uncommon for hairs to be invisible against some surfaces, only to be revealed by a raking side light as being present in some density.

Cactus spines have special characteristics. First, a warning: aside from the clear threat presented by large and often easily detached spines, watch out for the minute, sometimes almost microscopic spines known as *glochids*. For example, some species of *Opuntia* carry white to rust-coloured pads which are composed of aggregations of glochids – and even brushing against them can implant thousands of barbed darts which may cause severe irritation.

A spine-covered cactus may look baffling, but once you have understood the various patterns, the challenge is only to dexterity. In fig. 25 a step by step approach is shown which can be applied to many if not most, cactus species. First the overall shape *a* is worked out by ignoring the spines and examining the outline described by the raised *areoles* or *tubercles*. The way in which the areoles are disposed will help you to establish the foundation shown at *b*; loose to tight spirals will often be present as shown in the shaded areas. A count of the areoles visible along the shaded strips will ensure that the double spiral framework is accurate. The tubercles and areoles may then be drawn as at *c*. The numbers and types of spines present in each group, *d*, must be decided; there will often be a sequence from immature spines at the apex to a mature armature at a lower level. Finally, the spines are placed in perspective upon the understructure. Measurements are taken throughout as described on pp. 34–5. As may be seen from the sketch, any attempt to show a heavily armed cactus in detail in black ink would fail. White on black may be used as in scraper board, but the best approach is to use opaque pigments such as acrylics or gouache.

Surface ornament of stems and branches

Stems and branches have been mentioned in connection with posture and trichomes; now they are examined more closely. The term 'stem' is used here to include trunk, *rachis*, branch, branchlet etc. Variety is as wide for stem surfaces as it is for leaves; yet because the eye tends to be drawn to flowers and leaves, stems often receive less attention. This is especially so with trees, where foliage, flowers and fruit may be illustrated and distinctive bark designs ignored. Stems even of fleeting annual species carry patterns of pigmentation and/or structural developments such as fluting and keel-like projections.

Look for stem features such as buds (see p. 48), *leaf scars* and *lenticels* (fig. 26). Leaf scars often have quite specific shapes corresponding to the form of the petiole at the point of contact with the stem. Within the leaf scars,

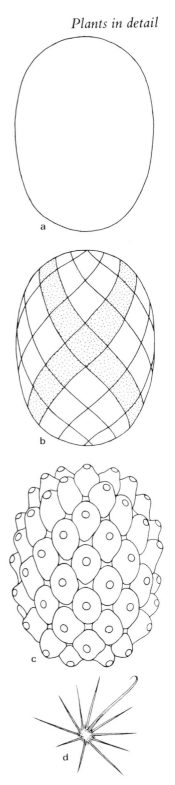

25 Cactus structure

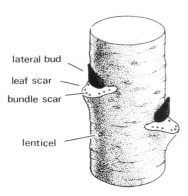

lateral bud

leaf scar

bundle scar

lenticel

26 Woody stem features

bundle scars may also be detected – these represent the *vascular* strands which pass up through the leaf petiole prior to leaf fall (*abscission*). Though often minute, the bundle scars (where visible) will be seen to have a definite arrangement. Terminal bud scales also leave characteristic scars. Lenticels are small spongy openings in surrounding impermeable tissue that allow interchange of gases between internal tissues and the atmosphere. They are often seen as lens-shaped markings, either parallel with the *axis* or placed horizontally. Frequently lighter in tone than their surrounds, they are often prominent on stems, though they may also be found on other plant parts. Lenticels may be of importance to the artist in three ways: they are likely to have a size, shape and colour consistent within a group; the surrounding tissue is often ridged or otherwise modified by their presence; and although lenticels are not usually orientated in distinct lines, spirals etc. their placement is only apparently random, as their overall distribution may contribute to characteristic stem patterns.

Some forms of stem ornamentation are shown in fig. 27 where, in the first three examples, the upper and lower cut surfaces help to reveal structure. Sometimes in a drawing the stem end is allowed to fade out; this can give a quite pleasing effect, but information of value and interest is lost.

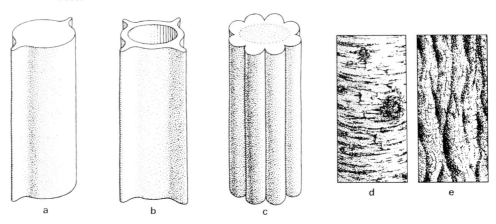

27 Stem ornamentation:
a, b flanges; **c** fluting;
d, e common bark types

Shading and the representation of surface markings on stems can suggest a surprising amount – certainly more than simply the direction of the light and the kind of ornamentation. It should be possible to indicate whether viewing is from above or below, whether the surface is receding from, or advancing towards the observer, and the rate at which this movement occurs, from a slow curve to a sharp kink. Changes in direction are more easily shown if the stem is seen from the side, but for a front or back view a technique for recording these effects is useful.

Even the smallest marks can be significant and, except where this would mislead, fortuitous markings which run counter to the trend should be omitted. Fig. 28 illustrates some of the possibilities. In *a*, the crudest drawing of a stem is shown – though further data could have been included by varying line strength etc. Here nothing more is implied than a straight smooth stem. The same parallel lines enclose the next three stems, yet by shading and directional trends indicated by lenticels and surface modelling

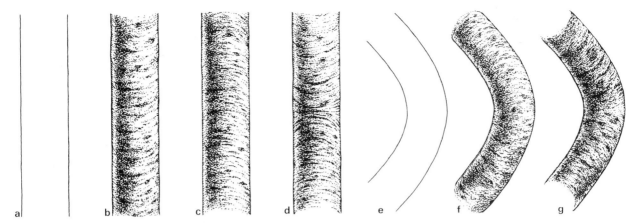

a   b   c   d   e   f   g

it was easy to convey more information. In *b*, the stem is viewed from above, and in *c*, from below. When the two kinds of surface are placed together as in *d* it can be seen that they may be used to indicate an abrupt change of direction in the stem at around midpoint. This change could have been slowed by a less rapid move from one mode to the other. In a larger context, if *b* and *c* were portions of a plant shown in its entirety, the former might be seen as moving towards the viewer from the bottom to the top, and the latter from the top to the bottom.

Similar implications are made in the remaining stems: in fig. 28*e*, two lines illustrate a bend in one plane alone, yet the same lines in *f* and *g* give curves not only from top left to bottom right but also, respectively, forward and back.

28 Shading and stem markings

Storage organs

Tubers, bulbs and *corms* are all food storage organs – adaptations of stems or leaves. The swollen petioles of plants such as celery and rhubarb function similarly. Enlarged stems of cacti and other succulents act as water reservoirs.

The *tunic*, the loose tissue surrounding a bulb or corm, will often appear almost as if woven, and an effort should be made to record the fibrous pattern. Some bulbs have membraneous translucent tissues which allow pigmentation to show through from one layer to another. Fig. 29*a* shows the way in which the tone of the colouring is modified where the tissues overlap. Layers wrap over each other in a particular sequence and this should be indicated wherever it is visible – sometimes the fine *hyaline* margins are impossible to pick out without dissection.

One characteristic common to all storage organs is dictated by their function – they are receptacles and so tend towards rotundity. In the potato form, fig. 29*b*, only preconception suggests that it is not discoid. Line thicknesses and directions in *c*, and a better choice of 'eye' placement, help to create the required effect, and with the addition of shading (*d*) plumpness results.

Look carefully at surface markings on storage organs – they may be the remnants of past processes, or precursors of coming events – as in the 'eyes' of the potato: these depressions, containing groups of buds, represent the axils of scale-like leaves and they are definite in structure.

45

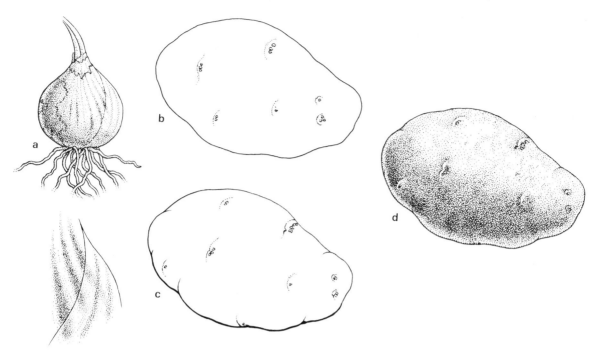

29 Storage organs: **a** bulb with detail showing overlapping translucent tissues; **b, c, d** indicating rotundity (see text)

Roots

When illustrating a whole plant, do not neglect the root system. Sometimes all species in a genus may have like roots and there would be small gain in showing them other than in perhaps one example. In other cases a portrayal of the underground parts may be of special interest.

Roots may be too long, massive or spreading to fit at anything like life-size on a plate. They then may be suggested with a minimum of detail at a reduced scale; treated diagrammatically; or photographed. Occasionally quite small plants will be found to possess extraordinarily long and spreading roots. It may be sensible in such instances to show the relationship between the parts above and below ground by an inset showing a much reduced outline of the entire plant. This will supplement the detail given in the body of the illustration where the roots may be shown as terminating abruptly in an artificial line.

As always, the first step is to try to understand what is happening – to analyse the underlying structure. Often this may be quite obscure even after all soil has been gently removed under running water. It is helpful to suspend the roots in water and view them through the walls of a glass container, but allowance should be made for the magnifying effect.

Up to this point mention of a specific medium has been avoided. Yet roots require a decision as to whether to work in pencil, ink, water-colour, gouache etc. as the medium modifies the method. The most difficult (though the most common) medium for this subject is ink. As it is used for so much scientific illustration, I am assuming here that the work is in this medium.

For present purposes I am also assuming that the subject has no definite, helpful form such as a single taproot or even an agglomeration of several large roots accompanied by subsidiaries, but consists of an amorphous fibrous mass. The difficulty is not just that of drawing the specimen accurately, which alone might be challenging enough, but also of presenting the information so that the reader may absorb it without becoming confused. Fig. 30 outlines procedure.

In *a* the overall dimensions of the root system are taken – note that the average length and width of the mass are the most useful, though the extremes are also recorded. Next, the appearance of a single root is examined (*b*): what is the thickness at the point of emergence? – does it branch? – do the branches themselves branch? – does it taper slowly or abruptly? – are root hairs prominent? – and so on.

At stage *c* several typical roots are pencilled lightly as a framework, showing thickness, length, number of branches, twists and turns, etc. They are then inked in, leaving small breaks where other roots cross them, to be filled in later. The upper sides of roots and lateral branches are inked first, then the remainder using the first lines as guides. Right-handed artists will find it easier to start with the left-hand line of vertical branches; for left-handers the reverse is true.

For step *d* the pencil is left aside; it would be time-consuming and of no value to attempt to draw the whole meandering tangle in both pencil and ink. As long as the roots are accurate in character it doesn't matter how they wander, and at this stage direct work with the pen is more appropriate. The specimen and the established guide roots are referred to constantly.

Watch for the moment when the addition of a few more lines would make the structure too dark and heavy. You will probably be aware of this well before the actual number of strands has been depicted. Then, as

30 Roots: sequence of drawing

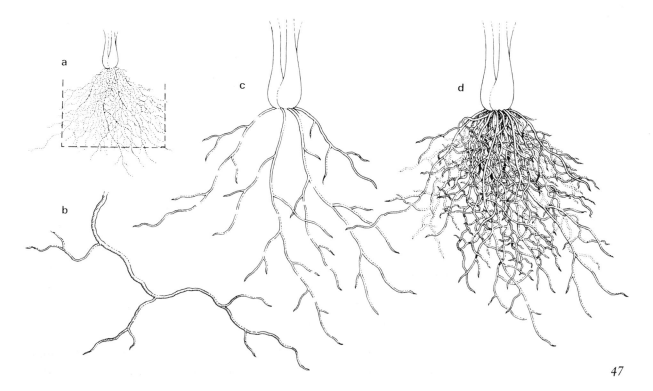

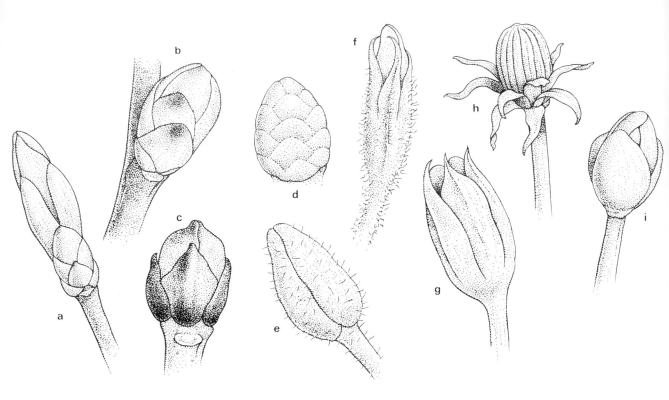

31 Buds: leaf buds –
a sycamore, *Acer pseudoplatanus*; **b** hazel, *Corylus avellana*; **c** ash, *Fraxinus excelsior*; **d** oak, *Quercus robur*. Flower buds – **e** poppy, *Papaver* sp.; **f** primrose, *Primula vulgaris*; **g** foxglove, *Digitalis purpurea*; **h** dandelion, *Taraxacum officinale*; **i** lesser celandine, *Ranunculus ficaria*

shown in *d*, the rest can be suggested by lighter broken and dotted lines. Finally, touches of shadow may be added: this should not be at random, but without misleading may be used to give a more pleasing aspect and greater clarity.

Buds

Buds may enfold developing leaves and/or flowers (fig. 31). Those which overwinter are insulated by scales which may be arranged in a variety of ways; in drawing them the patterns in which the scales fit together or overlap should be unravelled. With flower buds the emerging *corolla* will unfold in a particular style and often this will be suggested by the modelling of the bud at quite an early phase: a beautiful example of this is seen in *Kalmia*, mountain laurel, in which the smallest flower buds are distinctively spiralled; in contrast, the poppies, *Papaver* spp., appear to have their *petals* cramped into the enveloping *sepals* in an apparently haphazard way not indicated by the form of the developing bud. Where the *calyx* opens to expose the flower the lines along which opening will take place may be discernible and should be drawn.

Fruits

Here the term 'fruit' is used loosely, to include not only the ripe *ovary* or group of ovaries containing seeds but also the reproductive bodies of other groups of plants.

It is not always possible to show fruits, as plants are generally illustrated during flowering. Some species generously display flowers and fruits together, though more often this is not the case. Naturally both should not be shown on the same branch when this would not happen in life, though it is often worth reserving a portion of a plate to include the fruit later. It may be shown as an inset, or as one of several features surrounding a habit study; or perhaps a separate branch may be inserted at a later date (noted in the caption or text).

For convenience, fruits may be divided into broad and informal categories: dry – *follicles, capsules, nuts* etc., and wet – *drupes, berries, pomes* and so on. Dry fruits may be further subdivided into those that *dehisce* – peas, mustards, poppies etc., and those that are *indehiscent* – buttercups, grasses, walnuts etc. A selection is shown in fig. 32.

There are scores of botanical descriptive words for fruits and their parts in addition to those mentioned above, but they need not concern us here. But there are some non-specific factors to bear in mind for illustrating.

It is essential that the fruit should be mature – with familiars such as blackberries and strawberries the ripe and the unripe are easily distinguished, but with unfamiliar or exotic species maturity may not be so obvious. Sometimes the final phases of ripening bring about dramatic changes in appearance. Wherever unripe and ripe fruits occur together it may be appropriate to illustrate a sequence.

32 Several fruit types:
a legume, *Sarothamnus*;
b berry, *Lycopersicon*;
c capsule, *Viola*; **d** capsule, *Papaver*; **e** schizocarp, *Myrrhis*; **f** schizocarp, *Acer*; **g** drupe, *Daphne*; **h** achene studded aggregate fruit, *Fragaria*; **i** follicle, *Aquilegia*; **j** nut (acorn), *Quercus*

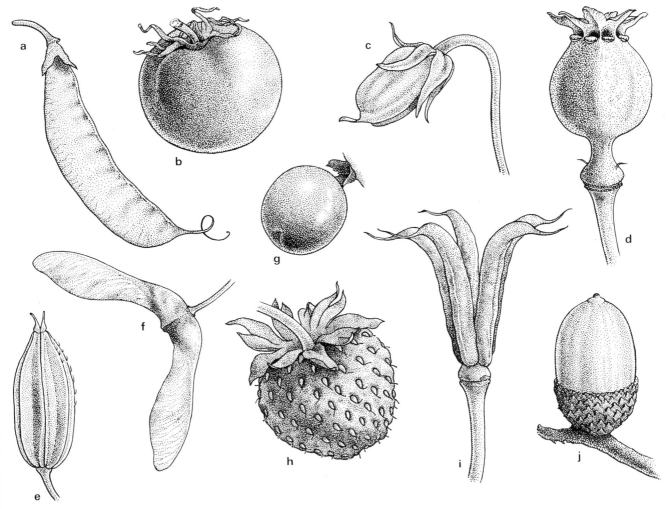

The methods by which seeds or spores are distributed are reflected in the structure of the fruits which carry them. It is often readily seen where seeds will be carried by the wind, as with the dandelion, or where the whole fruit will be windborne – the ash and the sycamore spread in this way. Succulent fruits carrying hard pips are generally distributed by birds and animals.

Some fruits show lines of dehiscence along which opening will occur. Watch for such lines, as they will be characteristic at least of the species involved; sometimes they remain indistinct up to the time of rupture, in other cases they may be obvious throughout development or on maturity. As noted earlier, mature fruits should be shown, but a later phase where they open to expose seeds may also be figured.

Many fruits have a spiralled structure similar to that shown in the cactus diagram, fig. 25. A common example is the strawberry, *Fragaria* spp., where the 'seeds' (achenes containing seeds) are studded upon the fleshy body in a spiralled arrangement. The unrelated pinecones and pineapples also share this feature. The spiral occurs throughout nature – in animals (think of shellfish) as well as plants and inanimate matter; the pattern is seen from the double helix of DNA to nebulae wheeling in space.

Seeds

Though the dissecting microscope is necessary for most seed illustration, seeds do range in size from tiny dust-like particles to those which may be examined with the hand-lens or the naked eye (fig. 33). Some are highly ornamented, and once again patterning tends to be characteristic and of significance botanically.

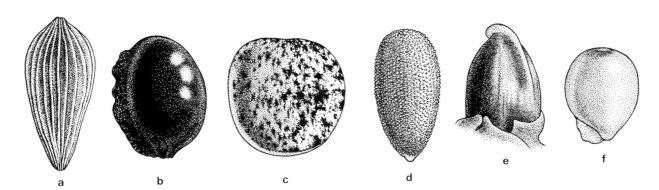

33 Seeds: **a** *Lactuca*;
b *Narcissus*; **c** *Vicia*;
d *Epilobium*; **e** *Dacrydium*;
f *Viola*

Bigger seeds usually have a fairly obvious morphology: it is the minute seed requiring microscopic examination that often provides a challenge. At a high level of magnification even the smallest seeds may reveal extraordinary surface sculpting – and this is best recorded by a scanning electron microscope (SEM). However, only the smallest detail need be treated in this way; the whole seed (of say 1 mm upwards) is still best handled by the artist as follows.

When selecting a seed for illustration you will see that examples vary as the parent plants do, and, although after examining twenty or thirty seeds it will be possible to see the 'ideal' approached in varying degrees by each, it will also usually be clear that no single seed is representative of the species. Often it will be possible to pick out from the sample many that will come close to the mean in shape and size; yet rarely will there be one among these that has in full all the characteristic marking and modelling present in some put aside as otherwise imperfect. In portraying one seed you will have to select from others to show all the important characters. One specimen might be typical in overall shape, yet the *papillae* may be obscure on part of the surface and this may be atypical, so this feature must be taken from another seed. Again, on the seed with perfect papillae their arrangement may break down – longitudinal lines may merge or be distorted in a fashion seen only in a few, and perhaps papillae at the base and apex of the seed may be less enlarged than in their fellows – so other seeds will be chosen for these qualities. In this way you can make a kind of amalgam that will come close to the truth, whereas a single electron micrograph cannot entirely succeed.

There are three main considerations in illustrating seeds and other minutiae: first, as noted above, representative characteristics must be defined and selected. Second, measurements from the micrometer eyepiece scale in the microscope must be taken with scrupulous accuracy: a 0.1 mm error is significant when scaled up in drawing a subject only 1 mm in length. Third, extra care has to be taken over the placement of lighting – for example, longitudinal corrugations seem to all but disappear from a seed coat when the light source is placed towards top or bottom (fig. 34).

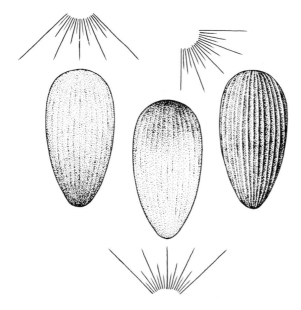

34 The effect of light placement in obscuring or revealing details of seeds

Flowers

A complete survey of flowers would fill volumes. Here I will simply define what a flower is, with a diagram of a 'typical' form with parts named, as this elementary botanical information is a must to any aspiring illustrator from the beginning. Next, a few useful categories of flowers will be noted, and types for these groupings will be illustrated and discussed.

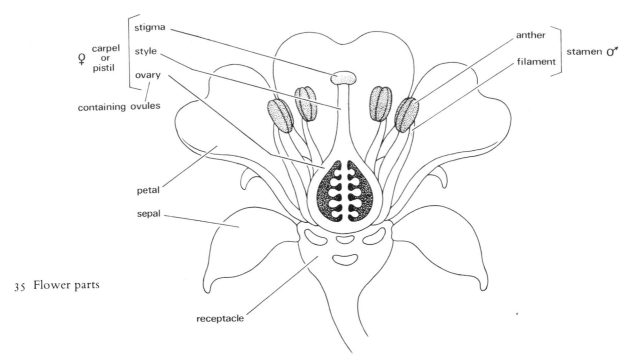

carpel or pistil ♀
stigma
style
ovary
containing ovules
petal
sepal

anther
filament
stamen ♂

35 Flower parts

receptacle

A concise definition of the term *flower* appears in *Biology of Plants*: 'The reproductive structure of angiosperms; a complete flower includes calyx, corolla, androecium (stamens), and gynoecium (carpels), but all contain at least one stamen or one carpel' (fig. 35).

For the botanical artist flowers may be divided into two main categories: *actinomorphic* (*radially symmetrical* or *regular*) – where the petals radiate from the centre of the flower and are more or less equidistant each from the other; and *zygomorphic* (*bilaterally symmetrical* or *irregular*) – flowers that may be divided into two like-parts along only one plane (see fig. 36). A few groups have flowers that are not divisible into like-parts.

The above concepts are useful to remember as they affect dissections, methods of measurement etc. The botanist uses a host of other descriptive floral terms and these are also needed by the artist who wishes to communicate fluently. In addition to knowing something of floral parts it is also helpful to be able to recognize the various modes in which the flowers are arranged on the stems, the *inflorescences*. There is no great gain in describing inflorescence types in detail here though an exception can be made for the *capitulum*.

In essence a capitulum is a tight inflorescence of usually *sessile* (stalkless) flowers which are of two kinds: *ray florets* and *disc florets*, the former being disposed about the perimeter of the latter (fig. 37). This type of inflorescence is commonly met with, as it is present in the enormous *family* Asteraceae (Compositae, composites). Though inappropriate in a biological sense, it is logical in terms of form to place composite capituli here with actinomorphic flowers.

Oddly, this apparently simple composite form is not easy to draw well. As demonstrated in fig. 38 there are several difficulties. One is that identified in the fungi (fig. 15), of sitting the heads upon the stems convincingly, which is solved by projecting the line of the stem through the capitulum

(*a*). The next stage is to put in the massed disc florets in outline (*d–g*). These often describe a dome, though the centre may be somewhat flat or even concave. These features break down into an arrangement of ellipses which must be placed in correct relationship. The key ellipse is that at the base of the 'dome', where the disc florets meet the *receptacle* hidden beneath; once this is correctly sited the rest follow.

36 Flower examples.
Zygomorphic –
a *Cypripedium*; **b** *Digitalis*;
c *Mimulus*; **g** *Delphinium*.
Actinomorphic –
d *Aquilegia*; **e** *Rosa*;
f *Geranium*; **h** *Meconopsis*

37 Generalized structure of a capitulum

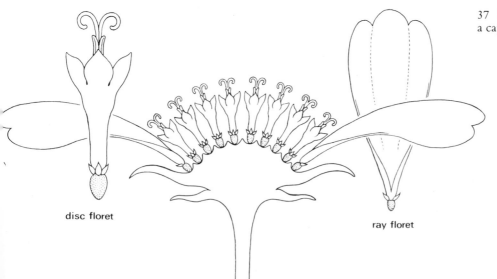

disc floret

ray floret

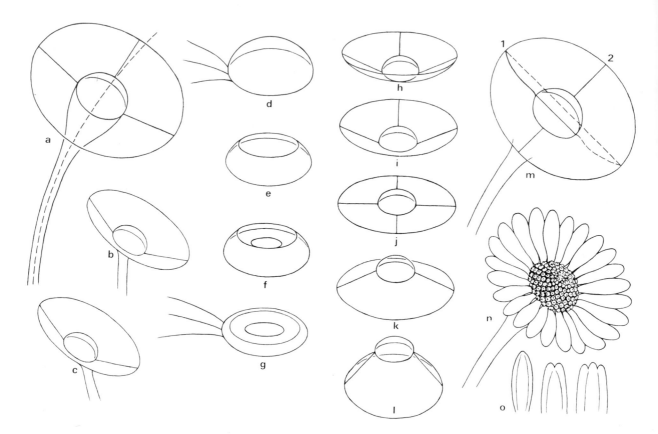

38 Drawing composite
flower heads: **a** correctly
sited head; **b, c** incorrectly
sited heads (exaggerated);
d–g generalized outlines of
disc florets; **h–l** generalized
outlines of ray florets;
m key lines in drawing a
capitulum; **n** generalized
head showing disc florets
and radiating ray florets;
o ray floret apices

The ellipse of the ray floret tips is rarely in the same plane as the ellipse
at the base of the disc florets. The ray florets may form a saucer-shape or
even a flask-shape (according to how far open they are) through all degrees
of concavity from deep to shallow, until, when the rays are horizontal, the
'flower' becomes discoid; from that point the form becomes convex –
through inverted saucer to inverted flask (*h–l*). Throughout this range
there are just two key lines: the first describes the angle of the ray florets in
relation to the disc, and the second depends upon the placement of the
'flower' in relation to the viewer – this was established in drawing the
ellipse at the base of the disc florets. For clarity these two lines are shown
in fig. 38*m*, with the lines that follow indicated by dashes.

Once the framework is established the ray florets may be drawn in and
the disc details added. Remember that, as with the mushroom gills, the
outer florets radiate from a central point. They also may overlap in layers,
and some may bend away from the others. Note the ray floret tips – they
are frequently divided and these divisions can affect the modelling of the
floret surface.

A spiralled arrangement of disc florets is often evident, especially in
larger heads. This may be distinct when the ray florets are in bud, but the
pattern can be confused as they open. In some plants such as the big
sunflowers, *Helianthus* spp., the spirals are striking, though even in the
common (English) daisy, *Bellis perennis*, the same arrangement may be
picked out.

The completed drawing in fig. 38*n* shows the character of the flower-head insofar as the upper parts are exposed, yet the receptacle, hidden in this case, may also be of importance. It is often covered by *phyllaries* (*bracts*) which are disposed and ornamented variously. As with all flower illustration, a range from 'flower'-bud to fruiting-head should be shown where this is feasible.

The next flower, alkanet, *Pentaglottis sempervirens* (fig. 39) is also actinomorphic – the same principles are involved as in the composite flower, though here their application is more straightforward. At the centre of the lobes of the *corolla* is a dark orifice or throat, and this is the point from which the drawing should originate. It is placed along the line of the projected stem (*pedicel* in this case) and from it the length of a non-foreshortened lateral lobe is taken, to set the limits for the broad ellipse which defines the flower outline. Here the corolla lobes fuse towards the flower centre (see p. 57). Lines radiating from this centre follow the twists of the corolla lobes and intersect the outer ellipse at almost equidistant points. The flower is placed so that a portion of the densely hairy calyx and pedicel may be seen.

The *Iris* (fig. 40) is another actinomorphic flower, though contrasting strongly with the two previous examples. The snag here for the novice is that this kind of flower appears at first to be a jumble of disparate parts, though on analysis only three units are found and these are each in triplicate. The example on the right has been 'exploded' to show the components clearly: *a*, is the *standard*; *b*, the *fall*; *c*, the *petaloid style*-branch. Flowers that appear intricate should always be dissected or gently unravelled to expose their workings.

Though the flowers in fig. 40 resemble each other, two different species

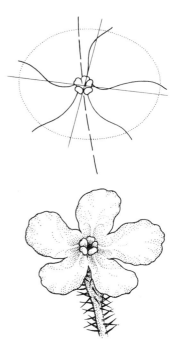

39 Actinomorphic flower: alkanet, *Pentaglottis sempervirens*

40 Actinomorphic flower: *Iris*, structure

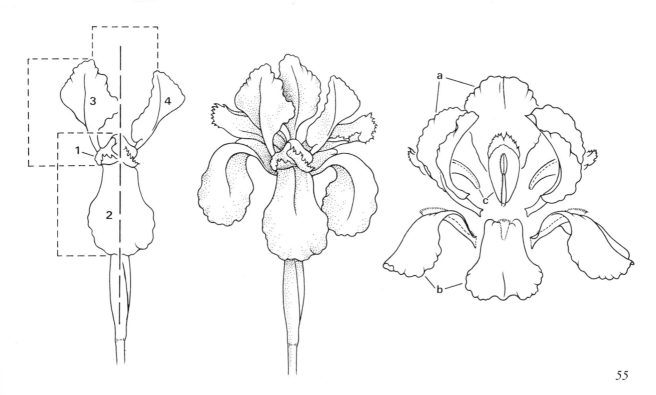

are represented; from this you will see that once the basic components and the way in which they fit together are assimilated, you can then decode other species in this genus. If the *Iris* flower is looked at with the foregoing in mind, a working sequence will resolve itself. This is shown in the diagram at the left. The first proposition is that the flower is balanced along a vertical axis (indicated by the heavy broken line). Next it can be seen that the unit to start on is comprised of the components numbered 1 and 2 on the diagram – the petaloid stigma and the fall. Once these are drawn, the two standards (3 and 4) can be erected, and, remembering the lessons of the fungus (pp. 33–6), the rest may be completed confidently – using the established parts as guides. Important dimensions are indicated by dotted lines on the sketch and it may be helpful to take others. Decorative markings have been left off for this exercise as they would have obscured the forms. Whatever the medium used, the characteristic pigmented venation would be added in the later phases of the study.

The iris in fig. 40 was orientated for ease of explanation; in an actual plate it would be useful to show at least one bloom with one of the standards more or less facing the front so that the base of the flower, in *Iris* the *spathe valves*, would be seen.

The next subject (fig. 41) is a zygomorphic (irregular) flower from the Papilionaceae – like Compositae, one of the largest of the families of flowering plants. The bilateral symmetry of this form is not helpful unless the flower is facing you – then measurements are more easily made and proportions assessed. In illustrating an inflorescence of this pea-type plant a bloom thus orientated may be included to show the standard complete, but the full-frontal position is usually not ideal in that much is obscured.

41 Zygomorphic flower: broom, *Sarothamnus* cultivar – **a** lateral view; **b** three-quarter view; **c** exploded view of parts

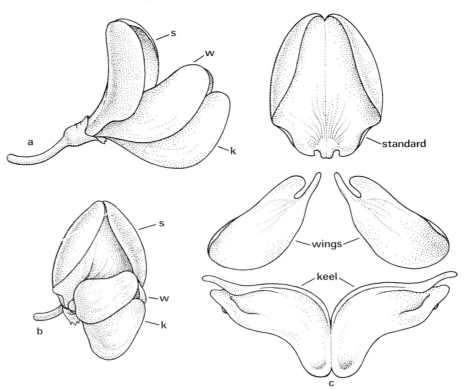

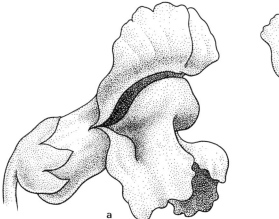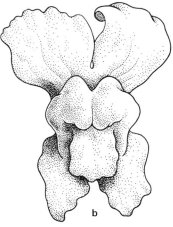

Often an inflorescence can be placed to show flowers from various angles, including a hind view.

Apart from the hidden sex organs, this flower, like the iris, breaks down into three components, known as the *standard*, the *wings* and the *keel*. Though the parts may vary in size they will still be recognized in common plants such as peas, beans, clovers, vetches, brooms etc.

Bilateral symmetry along a vertical axis is evident when zygomorphic flowers are viewed from the front, but the same flowers seen from the side are generally aligned obliquely or diagonally. This side view is often difficult to draw as appropriate measuring points tend to be placed at angles to the axis, and these angles may be awkward to estimate with accuracy. Dimensions should be taken where possible but with zygomorphic flowers a good eye is especially valuable.

An oblique posture is also seen in the snapdragon, *Antirrhinum* sp. (fig. 42); in this flower the corolla is fused into a tube without separate parts (*gamopetalous* – with the petals united, at least at the base – as distinct from *polypetalous*, where the petals are entirely separated). Though the parts are united, this does not inhibit variety; the families and genera that have flowers of this kind – the mints, sages, lavenders, foxgloves, pentstemons etc. – testify to this.

Gamopetaly and polypetaly are found in both actinomorphic and zygomorphic flowers. The two modes are of botanical significance so you should try to show the points at which the petals unite; and to make it clear if they do not. Naturally this applies not only to petals but also to calyces and all other parts that may or may not fuse.

In the snapdragon, the lower lip of the 'dragon's mouth' provides a good example of *inflation*. Many flowers possess this feature to some degree; sometimes the shapes do resemble inflated bladders or sacs, more often they appear as if moulded over a three-dimensional form.

The final zygomorphic flower for discussion is from the family Orchidaceae – which consists of some 17,000 species. Depending upon who is doing the counting, this is either the second or third largest family of the *angiosperms* (flowering plants). A knowledge of the parts of the orchid flower will help you to recognize the basic structures, in spite of their many cryptic and flamboyant forms.

42 Zygomorphic flower: snapdragon, *Antirrhinum* cultivar, **a** lateral and **b** frontal views

Walter Fitch, after illustrating at least six volumes of works on the family, speaks with authority: 'Perhaps there are no flowers more varied in size, form, and colour, than those of orchids, and I think I may add more difficult to sketch, if the artist has not some general knowledge of their normal structure . . . Indeed they almost seem to have been created to puzzle botanists, or to test an artist's abilities, and consequently they are all the more worthy of a skilful pencil in endeavouring to do justice to them . . . It is impossible to lay down any rules for sketching these protean plants, but if the structure is not correctly rendered in a drawing it is worse than useless, as no colouring will redeem it.' (From articles in *The Gardeners' Chronicle*, 1869.)

To help you understand the drawing of an orchid flower in fig. 43 a botanical description is useful. 'In the orchids, the three carpels are fused, and, as in the composites, the ovary is inferior. Unlike the composites, however, each ovary contains many thousands of minute ovules; consequently each pollination event may result in the production of a very large number of seeds. Usually only one stamen is present (in the lady's slipper orchids, there are two), and this is characteristically fused with the style and stigma into a single complex structure, the column. The entire contents of the anther are held and distributed as a unit, the pollinium. The three petals are modified so that the two lateral ones form wings and the third forms a cuplike lip that is often very large and showy. The sepals, also three in number, are often coloured and petal-like in appearance. The flower is also irregular.' (Raven, Evert and Curtis, *Biology of Plants*.)

In spite of Fitch's strictures, a few general indications should nevertheless prove worth while.

Most orchids show the double 'Y' pattern seen in fig. 43, though in some this design is almost completely hidden. The double 'Y' is formed

43 Zygomorphic flower: generalized orchid structure – frontal and lateral views; inset demonstrates the establishment of a 'ruffled' margin

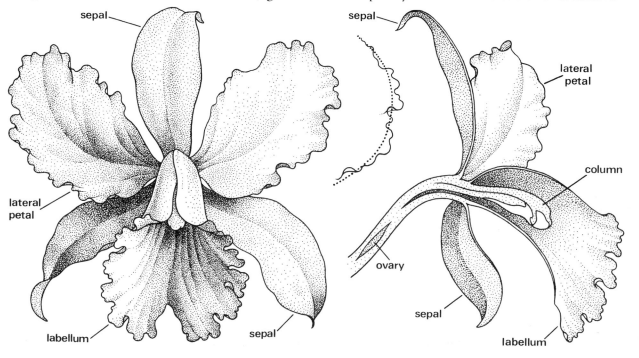

sepal

sepal

lateral petal

lateral petal

column

ovary

labellum

sepal

sepal

labellum

by the way in which the petals and sepals are arranged – a 'Y' is described by the lateral petals and the *labellum* or lip, and this is imposed upon the inverted letter form seen in the sepals. This formation is also clear in numerous other *monocotyledonous* species.

In an actual illustration, for better information and for aesthetic appeal it is usual to site subjects in a three-quarter view, tilted left or right. However, the frontal view shown here demonstrates the 'Y' forms well, and also suggests that the sequence to be followed in working on flowers of this kind is really closely related to that described for the iris. The key dimension here is from the apex of the labellum to the base. Once this petal is established, the tip of the *column* should be accurately placed and further dimensions taken from this point. The two lateral petals should be drawn after the labellum, and these three elements will serve as guides for the positioning of the sepals.

Do not be misled by the undulate margins of the petals (or similar features in other flowers). In wandering along such a complex outline one tends to stray from the main route: as for leaves, the solution is lightly to pencil in an approximate margin before tackling the frills in detail.

Many species in this family show all but incredible designs. Their bizarre formations earn orchids such epithets as 'man', 'monkey', 'lizard', 'bee', 'spider' etc.; this kind of patterning can help the artist by striking a responsive chord in his mind. It is surprising how much easier it becomes to draw a shape when you find something familiar in it.

Sex expression

Botanical illustrators often work mainly with flowering plants, though most will also make excursions into the *gymnosperms* (pines etc.) and other groups on occasion. It is therefore appropriate to look specifically at reproductive organs in angiosperm flowers.

The sexual organs of flowers show almost as much variety of form and colour as the corollas that enfold them. Their characteristic disposition is also of fundamental interest to the botanist, in spite of John Ruskin's admonition: 'With these obscene processes and prurient apparitions the gentle and happy scholar of flowers has nothing whatever to do.' (*Proserpina*, 1874–86)

In thinking about male and female parts of the flower it is useful to absorb several terms. In fig. 35 the male organs, the *stamens*, surround the female organ, the *carpel* or *pistil* (single in this instance, but commonly – as in buttercups – present in numbers). The male organs are known collectively as the *androecium*, 'house of man', and the carpel or carpels as the *gynoecium*, 'house of woman'. Flowers containing stamens and carpels are termed *perfect*. Sometimes either stamens or carpels are absent and the flower is *imperfect* and either *staminate* or *carpellate*. Various sexual groupings are described by a complicated terminology.

The way in which the stamens and carpels are situated in relation to each other, and to the surrounding floral envelope, is important. In flowers with few stamens and carpels, any errors in their placing would be glaring to the informed eye. Where stamens and carpels are numerous (as in roses) it is often possible to pick out spiralled or whorled arrangements. Occasionally the siting of male and female parts will be puzzling, as in the Orchidaceae and Stylidiaceae where *anthers* and *stigmas* are borne on a single column; but more often the structures will be quite distinct.

Stamens (fig. 44*a–d*) consist of two portions: the anther bearing pollen in sacs (one to four in number) is carried on a *filament* (stalk). In addition to the size and shape of the anther, you should also try to show the way in which it dehisces to expose the pollen grains. Most anthers split longitudinally (*b*), though some have other modes – in *Rhododendron*, for instance, twin apical pores open (*c*) allowing pollen to spill out in viscid strands.

Anthers pose three small problems: first, they often shrink drastically as they open, and so wherever practicable some should be shown unopened. Second, in different breeding systems anthers open before, at the same time as, or after the stigma becomes receptive. This sometimes means that a choice has to be made between mature anthers or mature stigmas. With inflorescences it may be that a sequence of development will be apparent. The third point about anther dehiscence is that the process is often initiated by a change from moist outside air to the dry air of the studio.

Anthers are fixed to filaments in two ways: they may be *basifixed* with the anther sitting on top of the filament (*a*); or they may be *dorsifixed* with the filament attached to the 'back' of the anther (*b*) – the anther may then be *versatile* and swing freely, or it may be held rigid. Anthers are seldom highly ornamented though they may have spurs or projections as in *Euphrasia*. Sometimes they are joined at their margins to form a cylinder or ring.

Relative to the size of the flower, anther filaments show a huge range in length: in wind-pollinated plants such as grasses, and many common tree species of temperate zones, the anthers hang on long filaments well clear of the rest of the flower; in other species with different methods of pollination, filaments may barely be visible; in some families (Leguminoseae, Malvaceae) they may be united for at least part of their length to form a tube. Watch for the characteristic curves that filaments describe, they are often of subtlety and beauty.

Filament cross-sections range from cylindrical to more or less strap-shaped; filaments of the former type are usually rigid or springy whereas the latter may be flaccid. In dissections it is important to show the points from which the filaments arise: for instance, where the stamens appear in two distinct sets – one set emerging above the other in the *floral tube*; they may also emerge from the same level but be different in length – a longer set from between the petals and a shorter one from each petal base. Many other kinds of arrangements are seen. Sometimes filaments will carry hairs, especially towards the base (*d*).

The female flower parts, the gynoecium, may, as shown in fig. 35, be a single basic unit, a carpel, though the carpels may also be paired, or they may be several to numerous. Where present in numbers, they may be spirally arranged (fig. 44*e*) or whorled. Each carpel consists of three parts: stigma, *style*, and *ovary*. The ovary eventually becomes the fruit, or a section of a composite fruit, and it contains one to many *ovules* which ripen into seeds.

The stigma is composed of specialized tissues, often with minute papillae

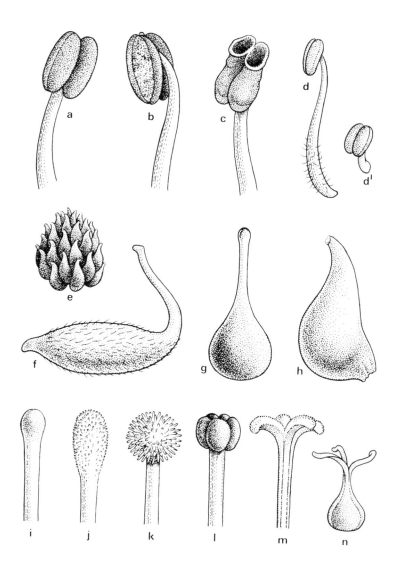

and/or sticky exudates, which capture pollen, initiating fertilization. A stigma may be little more than a moist swelling at the apex of the style or it may be lobed, branched or otherwise elaborated. Often the structures are of the greatest interest to the *taxonomist* and slight variations may be helpful in defining species. Some stigma types are shown in fig. 44 *i–m*.

The style is an outgrowth of tissue from the ovary, bearing the stigma at its apex. It may be an unbranched column, or variously branched as in fig. 44*n*; it is sometimes poorly differentiated (*h*) or even absent – the stigma then rests upon the ovary and is termed sessile. The style may be upright in relation to the ovary, or it may be flexed into one of several positions. It may be constant in position throughout development or it may change markedly to thrust the stigma into place for pollination, lengthening quickly as the stigma matures; sometimes it is angled to one side, or *reflexed* to avoid self-pollination. Or, if self-pollination is the mode,

44 Sexual structures (representative forms): **a–d** stamens; **e–h** carpels; **i–m** stigmas; **n** composite ovary with partially fused styles

the style will be of a length to allow the stigma contact with the anthers within the same floral envelope.

Even within one species there may be several different pollination stratagems. Where this is so it is often feasible to show the range – depending upon the purpose of the illustration. It may also be useful to do this where, as mentioned above, there is a distinct developmental sequence.

Ovaries, fig. 44 *e–h*, enclose the ovules (potential seeds) and so are variously container-shaped. An ovary may be simple or derived from several fused carpels. In the latter form, the styles also may have fused for all their length, as indicated by lobing of the stigmatic area and fluting of the column (*l,m*). In other cases each fused element of a composite ovary may retain its separate style, or the styles may be fused in part (*n*). Often the composite condition is also suggested by markings or modelling of the ovary itself. Ovaries may carry various surface ornamentations as well as hairs and other trichomes.

The arrangement of ovules within ovaries is botanically important, but the topic is complex and for information the interested reader should consult more specialized texts.

The position of the ovary in relation to the disposition on the floral axis of the other flower parts is important. The ovary is *superior* (fig. 35) when it is attached to the receptacle above the sepals, petals and stamens; it is *inferior* (fig. 67*c*) when it is attached below these parts. (In the former condition the flower is termed *hypogynous*; in the latter the flower is *epigynous*. A third form is recognized where a cup-shaped extension of the receptacle will bear petals and stamens about its rim above the superior ovary – this type of flower is known as *perigynous*.) Each mode should be visible in an illustration when it is clearly seen in a flower: it is easy to allow a superior ovary to be obscured by petals, but if one bloom is slightly inclined, the position of the ovary becomes obvious. Inferior ovaries may be hidden by enveloping foliage – as in some evening primrose (*Oenothera*) species where the floral tube is long and often greenish towards the base, so that in both form and colour it may resemble a *peduncle* (flower stalk) and the point where the often not strongly differentiated ovary is reached may be well down among leaves.

In the definition of a flower on p. 52 it was stated that all contain at least one stamen *or* one carpel, indicating that some flowers may be male and others female; yet the situation is more complicated than this. Some species display both male and female parts, yet are functionally either male *or* female. In these the non-functional organs (sometimes partially functional) may be smaller in size than their fully functional counterparts, or may be absent altogether, or be much reduced or otherwise modified in form – as in *staminodes* (sterile stamens or structures resembling them). The above possibilities give rise to complex situations where diverse breeding systems may operate within a single species or even within a population.

The calyx is the outermost whorl of the floral envelopes; it may appear quite separate (sometimes green and leaf-like) and be indistinctly to distinctly lobed – the lobes being known as sepals; or it may not be clearly differentiated from the rest of the *perianth* (the calyx and corolla together) in which case each unit of the perianth is referred to as a *tepal*. A distinct calyx is shown in fig. 42. In the orchid (fig. 43) the sepals of the calyx are petaloid – in some flowers the sepals equal the petals in showiness. Sometimes the sepals may be the more visible structures, with the petals being reduced, as in *Delphinium* where petals are negligible. There is often a pattern of calyx lobing – one lobe may be longer than the rest, two may be placed close together, or there may be other arrangements. The placement of the calyx lobes in relation to the petals should also be noted.

Glands within the flower (or, in some species, on other parts of the plant body) that secrete nectar, *nectaries*, are occasionally large enough to be shown, particularly if the subject is being drawn at larger than life-size (fig. 45). Excess nectar should be removed if the form of the nectary is obscured.

45 Nectary (*Ranunculus enysii*)

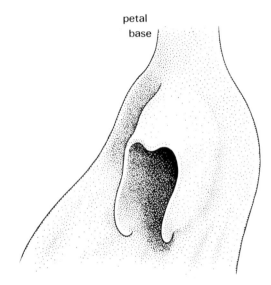

petal
base

Though the foregoing should help you when working upon mainstream subjects, you are sure to come across forms not covered here – even the most extraordinary cannot be excluded. Space precludes a treatment of grasses (Gramineae): though also flowering plants, they have a separate vocabulary of terms, more particularly for their floral parts; but the principles outlined here, with additional guidance from a volume such as C. E. Hubbard's *Grasses*, should help you to achieve a working knowledge.

6 Pencil

When plants are to be drawn in black and white, the main choices for media are ink, scraper board or pencil. Any of these media are suitable for reproduction by photolithography (offset lithography) which is the process now used for almost all printed books – although there can be a slightly greying effect in the reproduction if printing is not of a high standard. For letterpress reproduction, ink or scraper board drawings are usually more suitable.

A printing process known as 'duo-tone', which often gives a single-colour enrichment in reproductions of photographs, may also be used with fine effect for reproducing pencil drawings, when cost or other considerations prohibit the use of full colour.

Though work in pencil may be suitable for much scientific illustration in its ability to record minute elements and to give a full tonal range, the use of ink is so entrenched in this field that pencil tends to be reserved for less formal use – interpretative guide books, etc. For these purposes pencil is often an excellent choice: though its capacity is in fact greater than ink, it suggests a softer, more relaxed approach. But once you have explored the techniques of both media, you will find that a skilled pencil study may demand more work than a similar drawing in ink, because it is possible to reveal a wholly different level of detail. Where a slightly sketchy style is suitable, pencil is again ideal.

Equipment

PENCILS are graded from 6H, hard and light in tone, to 1H, then HB, and through the Bs to 6B which is soft and black. There is no hard black pencil in the above range; and though hard black pencils are available outside the H and B designations, those I have used have had waxy substances in their makeup which render them almost non-erasable. A compromise has often to be made: fine details require a hard point maintained for a reasonable period, and a drawing with a broad tonal range will require strong blacks in shadowed areas. The obvious solution is to use several grades of pencil; but work done with a soft pencil smears easily – and in a detailed drawing this may be disastrous. A fixative spray prevents smudges, but in tonal illustrations as described below the option of erasure must be retained to the finish; and, since also commercial fixatives cannot be guaranteed against eventual discoloration or other undesirable behaviour, their use is not recommended for any work where the subject matter may be of lasting importance.

How, then, is an unsmudged drawing obtained? First, by using pencils from around the middle part of the range – I find an HB the best; second, by ensuring that when the work is stored it is protected at least by tissue paper; third, by making sure that in storage there is no lateral or rubbing movement. Folders are helpful (see chapter 12).

The ordinary HB pencil can achieve minute detail and subtle effects when used on a suitable paper. It does not smear over-easily and a point may be retained for a useful time. Its one disadvantage is that it cannot produce a deep velvety black.

All pencils should conform to the grade stamp they carry – marks made by one category should be consistent and should remain distinct from those made by the other grades. In general this is the case, though brands may differ slightly in the depth of 'blackness' obtainable, and occasionally a gritty texture is found in the lead – where this occurs the pencil is best discarded.

The pencil must be kept sharp, which means constant trimming and consequently a short life, especially if it is discarded as soon as it is too short to rest comfortably in the fold between the thumb and first finger. A pencil-extender (fig. 46) allows a pencil to be used to within the final inch of its length. So far I have not been able to find this device for sale in Britain (I have one of German make, bought in the United States), but it could be improvised from a tube of springy metal split partly up one side to allow a pencil to be inserted.

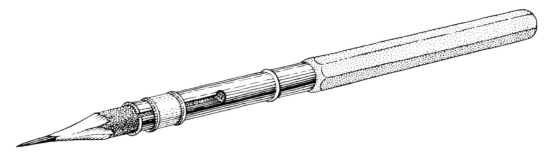

Although many people prefer a mechanical device for sharpening pencils, I would recommend a craft knife with changeable blades. For economy, the blade can be kept keen-edged with a fine-grained sharpening stone.

46 A pencil extender

Some believe that a pencil should be sharpened to a chisel-shaped tip, but I prefer a long point; this may be touched up numerous times before it becomes necessary to cut into the wood again (fig. 47). A long lead also

47 Pencil sharpened as described in text

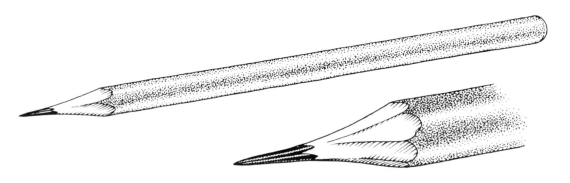

allows good visibility around the point. A piece of emery paper may be used to re-point pencils, but it tends to become a graphite reservoir to mark everything around.

PAPER Suitable paper is at least as important, perhaps even more so, than the right pencil. For a detailed plant portrait, the surface should be smooth, and not only in appearance – test it by rubbing an HB pencil over a small area, and if the grain or texture of the paper shows as in fig. 48 then the surface is unsatisfactory. On the other hand it may be so smooth and hard that the graphite particles are not retained; though the mark made may be uniform throughout, it will also be light in tone and however hard the lead is pressed against the surface, nothing beyond a mid-grey will result. Also undesirable is a soft slightly textured paper that may be flattened by hard pressure but will still allow texture to show through medium or light pressure.

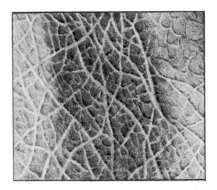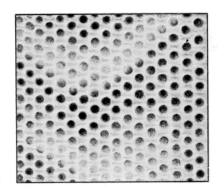

48 Pencil used on textured papers (an HB simulation of highly magnified surfaces)

The perfect surface is one that will absorb a maximum amount of graphite with a reasonable pressure; it should also be strong enough to remain intact after fairly vigorous use of a soft eraser.

Thickness or weight is a matter of individual preference; the paper should not be so thin as to cockle or deform when working over it, though it may be as thick as the heaviest board if you prefer. The heavier papers or boards are expensive.

Colour, although the least important factor, is worth consideration: for most botanical work you will find that glaring white is best avoided; given other essential qualities, the ideal is faintly off-white with a hint of warmth rather than tending towards the blue end of the spectrum.

The final criterion is that of durability. Paper should be made of rag; a wood based paper will discolour in time, and this process can be rapid with exposure to bright light.

ERASERS An eraser should be selected with care. Some which perform perfectly on one type of surface may leave ugly smears or be less effective on others. The use of two erasers (or more) is recommended – one should be fairly soft, yielding elastically and very slightly under firm finger pressure; the other hard and abrasive, yet not gritty or capable of leaving scratches. For the former kind a plastic eraser is ideal – it is uniform in texture with no small air-spaces or lumps (important for reasons explained below). In use it should not crumble, as the old-style gum eraser does; small particles should aggregate in rubbing to form spindle-shaped rolls which can be cleanly swept away, leaving no fine specks to catch under the pencil lead. Before any rubbing-out, always clean off the eraser by applying it to a sheet of spare paper.

FEATHER Using the eraser for white-line (see below) and for removing guide-lines or other unwanted material may produce a lot of debris. Blowing will remove only the larger particles, sweeps of a brush or hand may smudge – and the hand can leave traces of perspiration and/or oil. A couple of flicks with a feather will remove all crumbs without detrimental effect to either drawing or paper. A strong wing-pinion from a big bird such as a goose, swan or turkey will last for years in daily use. A wing feather is rather better than one from the tail, as the pinnules along the leading edge, being shorter, are more rigid than those of the trailing surface and so can be used when an occasional stubborn fragment resists removal. Nevertheless a handsome tail feather is not to be sneezed at. A dark feather is preferable to a light one as the latter will pick up a grey cast – though this washes off to some extent.

Equipment for general use as outlined in chapter 2 will also be needed when making pencil drawings.

Techniques

To reduce the risk of smudging, and to avoid transferring other substances to the work, a sheet of paper, of the same quality as that being drawn on, should always be between the hand and the actual working surface. As well as absorbing sweat and grease it serves as a useful area on which to try out a newly-sharpened lead or tricky shading. The best size for this sheet seems to be about 20 × 15 cm (8 × 6 in.); anything much smaller does not protect a large enough area, and a larger piece tends to blot out too much.

There are two basic ways of using a pencil – to make a line, or to make an area of tone.

LINE Before you start a drawing in line, a few preliminary strokes (fig. 49) will accustom your hand to the feel of the pencil and allow some appreciation of the qualities of the graphite line.

The pencil lines in the figure were drawn freehand without independent movement of the fingers or wrist. It is infinitely less cramping and tension-inducing to draw all lines, no matter how short, by movements originating from the shoulder or elbow, rather than from the wrist or fingers. You will find that long lines flow much better and even minute ones, such as those describing hairs, are not demanding when drawn in this way. The pencil should rest easily in the hand without the fingers being clenched.

Beyond a certain line length, varying with the individual, the whole arm becomes involved. Few are capable of completing very long lines accurately with single strokes; it is necessary to continue in a number of

49 'Doodling', exploring effects in pencil *line*: tonal variations achieved by changes in line-spacing and/or fluctuations in pressure on the pencil

comfortable movements. Each completed long line should have at least the *appearance* of resulting from one sure stroke.

The lines in fig. 49 are slightly uneven. Freehand work retains an organic or natural feeling – a vastly different quality from that of lines drawn with a set square or ruler. These aids should be reserved for diagrams, where a mechanical feeling is often an advantage.

When long lines, or a series of short ones, are drawn, the pencil blunts fairly quickly. The process is slowed noticeably by slowly rotating the pencil shaft in the hand to allow a new part of the graphite to touch the paper every so often. As the pencil is held at an angle, this gives an almost self-pointing action.

In a drawing done in line alone, the keynote should be simplicity, with an emphasis on qualities of tonal range (within the line) and delicacy. The line-drawing of the dog rose, *Rosa canina*, fig. 50, demonstrates something of these aspects, while falling short in other regards.

The procedure was basically that described on pp. 33–6. The drawing was started with the group of stigmas seen at the centre of the flower; with this established, the first key dimension was the rear petal, estimated by eye since the distance from stigmas to petal-tip would have been distorted by foreshortening. This petal was lightly drawn in before following with the other four, beginning with the one on the left, for which a measurement was taken with dividers as the apex of the petal fell in virtually the same plane as the stigmas. Especial care was taken with the foreshortened petal at the bottom left of the flower: it is difficult to resist the inclination to draw any foreshortened object as it would appear without the distortion due to perspective; here I was tempted to show the vertical distance between the base of the stigmas and the base of the petal as my intelligence insisted was correct, rather than as my eye saw it. It is a help to think momentarily of such forms as being abstract and without a third dimension. Again, it is useful to relate a puzzling object to adjacent forms that pose no problems; in this instance it is clear that the base of the petal does not extend as far down as the base of the dominant leaf on the far right.

The leaves were first drawn in as barely visible generalized outlines which were used as guides for the serrations before being removed by a gentle touch of the eraser.

The whole drawing was completed in outline before any parts were given emphasis. At that point the study was even in tone and dull in appearance. The final stage of a line drawing can be gratifying: the ground work is complete and all that remains is to give a feeling of life and interest by subtle additions. Here strengthening of the veins about the midribs indicates a light source from about the top right; this impression is re-inforced by minute dark areas under the flower and a darkening of the left side of the stem.

There are at least two weak points: the first (which could easily have been altered without misleading) is the positioning of two leaves on either side of the flower with their midribs suggesting a strong horizontal line, even though the mid-section of this line is missing under the flower. This

50 Pencil line: dog rose, *Rosa canina*

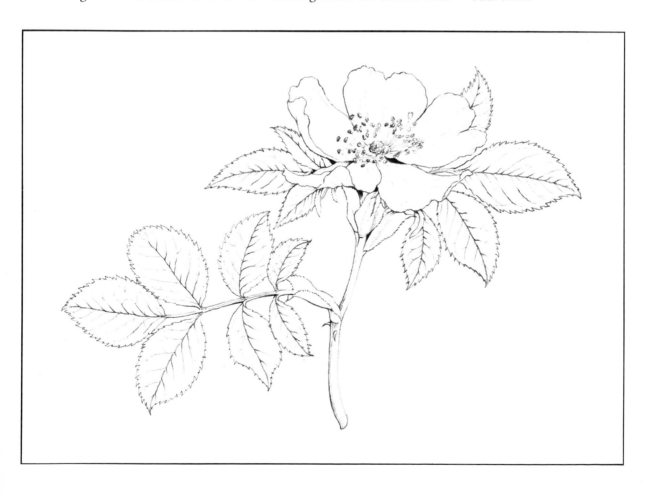

kind of effect, termed *subjective* or *implied* line, may be of great value in a composition, or, as can be seen in this illustration, a distinct minus. If the left-hand leaf were moved so that the tip stood slightly below its present position, the subjective line would be broken and the drawing much improved.

The second weakness was caused by impatience. I did not allow the plant enough time to settle before it was drawn, and after the specimen was completed several other blooms opened to expose their petal forms altogether more agreeably.

HATCHING The use of hatched lines for tone predates the invention of the graphite pencil; the technique was used by artists working in silver-point. Hatching can give an aesthetically pleasing unity; but its almost invariable use until recent times seems at least partly due to the fact that continuous tone (see below) had to wait until papers were manufactured with flaw-free surfaces. With hatched line a few catches or lumps in the paper are not seen.

The hatched leaf in fig. 51 shows that the shading is made up of individual small strokes. Even though the darkest shadows appear solid, the effect is built up with single strokes all sloping the same way. The diagonal along which to shade will depend on whether you are left- or right-handed. The drawings of Leonardo da Vinci have strokes that run from top left to bottom right, the characteristic of a left-hander.

Though consistency in the direction of hatching seems best, this should not be so rigid as to give a mechanical feeling – a look at the works of master draftsmen will confirm that though hatched lines more often than not run in the direction comfortable for the artist, there will be some shifting in angle and often it can be seen where the paper has been moved around. This is especially necessary where the hatching, if consistent throughout, would become clumsily parallel to the enclosing lines of a stem or other feature.

The method used in drawing fig. 51 was as follows: three measurements were made – the total length and the widths of the widest parts on each side of the midrib. The last two dimensions were the same in this case, though often they may differ; even in leaves with one part considerably smaller than the other this is not always as clear as might be expected, venation and serration may confuse the eye. The next step was to put in a generalized outline, taking care to position the widest parts of the leaf on each side of the mid-vein correctly in relation to the base and the apex. In this leaf the widest dimensions are opposite, and a line drawn from one to the other would be at right-angles to the midrib. This is commonly not so (fig. 16a); a line running through the widest portions will not be at right-angles to the centre vein, and the leaf will have an oblique appearance.

After completing the lightly pencilled outline, plus the midrib, the main veins were added – those on the left of the leaf, looking towards the apex, were established first, and were guides for those on the right. Notice whether veins are opposite, or alternate as in this leaf. You will see that though the venation forms an almost regular pattern of more or less parallel curves, there are small variations. At one point two veins diverge from the axis much closer together than the others, and the minor veins are not entirely regular especially towards the margins. Yet overall the impression is one of consistency.

The most stretching task was to draw the serrations; this mode is described as *double-serration*, as most of the main teeth bear smaller ones on their flanks. Each serration is the end-point of a vein, and it was necessary to adjust the lightly sketched vein ends to accommodate each with a tooth.

After the main veins, the more obvious of the minor ones were put in. As the leaf surface at this phase was divided into segments by the larger veins, it was only a question of reproducing the pattern within each area. Next, the first layer of hatched shading was drawn to indicate the broad structure of light and shade, moving from the apex of the leaf to the base.

To make a hatched stroke, place the pencil point firmly upon the appropriate spot – here, along the shadowed side of a vein – and with a flicking motion of the forearm, pivoting from the elbow, make a mark while at the same time lifting the lead from the surface. The marks will be wedge-shaped with the bases describing deeper shadow tapering away towards the apices and the light. After the first run over a drawing the

51 Leaf in pencil hatching

a

b

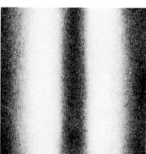

c

d

52 Continuous tone:
a, b, c basic technique;
d application

result may be disappointing – much as with the line drawing of the rose at the penultimate stage. A final application of more hatching to the areas of deepest shadow, using very short strokes and continuing until the darkest portions are as close to black as an HB pencil can reach, will add contrast and provide the missing vibrancy and range.

CONTINUOUS TONE Areas of continuous tone are made without using separate strokes. The pencil lead is applied with an elliptical motion, moving from dark areas to light and back until the required densities are achieved. As with the previous style, the most satisfactory method of working is to go over the whole drawing establishing broad areas of light and shade, and then to move to and fro over the surface adding emphasis until a full tonal range is represented. There is a freedom and flexibility about this approach which is enjoyable, yet it is entirely suited to studies demanding the greatest discipline and skill. At its worst the use of continuous tone will help the inept, since superficially pleasing results are not hard to produce. And at its best the technique will test the adept.

When applying continuous tone the movement should originate at the shoulder. This seems odd, but as the motion becomes sub-conscious you will find it relaxed and not tiring; when the same results are attempted by moving the fingers alone, the hand tends to clench more and more tightly until muscular tension affects much of the body.

The entire foundation of the technique is seen in the simple gradation exercise in fig. 52*a*: once you are proficient in moving smoothly from black to white, exciting results may be created. Figs. 53-56 (and the frontispiece) show this basic principle in practice.

You will find that in moving from dark to light, over and back again and again, revolving the lead slightly as suggested earlier, a stage will be reached where the darkest area will not absorb more graphite even though it remains a mid-grey. This is because both surfaces in contact – the lead on the pencil and that already on the paper – become so polished that insufficient friction remains to continue the process. Freshening the lead with the craft knife will provide enough new rough surface to give a much deeper tone to the wanting area. Sometimes it is appropriate to give an area an all-over coat of grey, either to be left as it stands, or to be darkened or lightened later. To keep the grey completely even in tone it is worth exploiting this tendency of the lead to become polished with use: holding the pencil at a shallow angle to the paper (20-30 degrees) and revolving it as you proceed, work over a small area on the protective paper under your hand until the tip has stopped depositing on the graphite-loaded surface. The shallow angle and the turning motion will ensure that most of the exposed lead is polished. (To hold the shaft at this slope, with the fingers well back from the point, you will need a long lead.) The polished lead can then be applied to the area to be shaded, holding the pencil at the same shallow angle and using gentle pressure, but for this type of even, feature-less toning the tip should *not* be turned but should be held in the same position throughout. An elliptical movement of the tip will give the most even results: each ellipse should be shallow and about 5mm from side to side. The movement should be continuous, without the lead leaving the paper until the area to be shaded is complete. An ellipse is preferable to a circle, which tends to leave small unshaded areas that have to be filled; horizontal or vertical strokes are not used as they leave discernible lines.

53 Continuous tone, pencil: lichen, *Stereocaulon* sp. (much enlarged)

Restrain the impulse to blend the tones by rubbing with a finger-tip, as this produces a subtle change in quality to a bland and greasy slickness. If too much tone has been added, the solution is to apply the slightest touch of the eraser, but be sure to use an unsullied part or the flaw will be worsened.

Much of fig. 53 was worked over initially in the above fashion. The drawing is based upon a lichen, *Stereocaulon* sp., and for once carries no

54 Continuous tone,
pencil: *Ascarina lucida*

OPPOSITE
55 Continuous tone,
pencil: forest interior, New
Zealand (1)

guarantee of accuracy. My original drawing, at five times life-size, was
only 58 mm (2¼ in.) high, and was rather poorly reproduced as an inset at
that scale; the present study was loosely reconstructed from the published
version for this demonstration.

The method of work was first to make a light outline drawing. Then a
mid-grey was added, covering the whole illustration except those portions
that were to remain white. Finally the drawing was brought to life by the
slow evolution of the shadowed areas through to the deepest parts among
the 'columns' and under the 'altars'. Though the mid-grey was put in by
the method outlined above, it would be misleading to suggest that an
entirely even tone was attempted except in a few areas. In this instance it

was appropriate to vary the pressure on the lead to capture the subtle variations in tone from off-white to around the middle range. The darkest tones were left until the end. Up to that point a continual process of adjustment and balance was made – a darker tone here was balanced by another there and so on until all the options were used up.

For the darkest tones the pencil should be lifted from the shallow angle used for the light areas and held at an acute angle to allow full pressure on

56 Continuous tone, pencil: forest interior, New Zealand (2)

the point. If this is kept sharp the deepest tones will be easier to realize and crisp edges can be maintained.

With experience, you will be able to plan a series of steps towards the completion of a drawing, though the effect of each, as it qualifies earlier work, may also modify steps that follow. Results rarely match completely those anticipated, and continual re-appraisal is needed.

WHITE LINE For fig. 53 the process was one of addition from the beginning, making little use of the eraser other than on the initial outline and to lift off excess tone. In figs 55 and 56 the eraser was used as a drawing instrument to create white line. Until the manufacture of plastic erasers the technique of cutting out fine white lines from a dark area could not be practised with precision and, as it may be unfamiliar, I will describe it here in full.

A plastic eraser of uniform texture, as described on pp. 66–7, lessens the likelihood of crumbling or of the uneven cutting out of tone. The edge should be cut to a sharp chisel form (fig. 57a) with the craft knife (if much of this work is intended, make sure you have a good stock of erasers as the process is fairly wasteful). A few experimental exercises should be tried before using the method on a drawing. Establish an even area of tone with the pencil, then apply the edge of the eraser with a firm even pressure in a series of lines and curves as shown in fig. 57b. You will find that the width of the eraser will not permit a really tight arc so convoluted shapes cannot be followed; also, the edge will rapidly fail, leaving a blurred trace, and this means constant trimming. In spite of these limitations, the results can be well worth while. In fig. 55 the grass-like clumps of epiphytes towards the bottom right could not have been drawn in such detail without this technique. This is also true for fig. 56 where the mosses and ferns, especially those along the base of the plate, could not have been taken out of the dark areas of tone. The delicate white veins on the kidney-shaped ferns were also done in this way. The technique was applied on and off throughout the two forest illustrations.

Fig. 57 shows the evolution of a white-line drawing. To start, an area of mid-grey has several white lines cut out by the eraser. Some of these are blurred in parts, especially where tight curves have been attempted – despite the eraser having been turned to follow the line. In c, an extra layer of tone has been added while firming up the edges of the lines. Lastly, the white lines become leaves by the addition of midribs and shadows. It is perfectly feasible to put in or take out leaves during the final stages – the epiphytes in fig. 55, for instance, were established layer after layer. In using this white-line method together with continuous tone very fine detail is possible.

A white pigment could be used for white lines – but there are at least two major objections to doing so: first, any pigment would be over-visible and so would destroy the unity of the drawing; and second, the picture surface would be ruined for further development, since the handling quality of pencil over paint is quite different from that of pencil over paper.

a

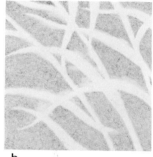

b

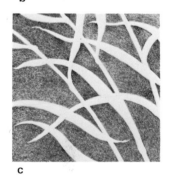

c

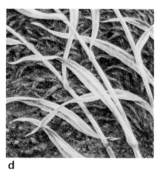

d

57 White-line drawing:
a eraser trimmed for use;
b mid-grey tone with white lines taken out; **c** addition of another layer of tone;
d addition of details

7 Ink

OPPOSITE
58 Stella Ross-Craig
(1906-) *Ranunculus
bulbosus* L. In *Drawings of
British Plants* Vol I, Bell &
Hyman, London, plate 31

Ink is nowadays the medium most commonly used to illustrate professional or 'serious' botanical publications. Photolithography will reproduce the most detailed pen drawings, but letterpress line blocks may be less satisfactory; so if your work is to be printed, try to find out in advance what process is to be used, and, if necessary restrict the use of minute detail.

Reduction of ink drawings generally should not exceed one half linear (that is, a quarter of the original image area). I prefer to aim at reproduction at two-thirds of the original length and width – a reduction of one-third linear. If an ink drawing is over-reduced, lines disappear, tonal effects achieved by stippling etc. tend to clog into black splodges in the darker parts and in the lighter areas to burn out altogether. A continuous-tone pencil drawing or a painting will be less affected by reduction than drawings in ink: large paintings, for example, have often been enormously reduced for reproduction as postage stamp designs.

From the above, the use of ink for botanical illustration might well be queried. But the technique is so firmly entrenched in the scientific press that is it hard to imagine its displacement unless information sharing changes radically. In some quarters this position has become a tradition of some rigidity – line drawings are used because line drawings have always been used. However, some botanical journals accept works in other media – including colour when the higher costs are justified. The second reason why ink is used so extensively for scientific illustration is that for the most part it is peculiarly suitable. It is possible to hover somewhere between the realistic and the diagrammatic, and this facility is frequently ideal. In working from living models one may move towards realism (though not as convincingly as with pencil or paint), moulding and texture may be indicated by the addition of tone in stipple or hatching, yet this may be done discreetly so that relevant forms are not obscured. In drawing from dried herbarium specimens it is a distinct advantage to move a step further from realism to concentrate on pure line, or line with the addition of very little tone, in order to avoid misleadingly implying qualities that have vanished with the death of the plants.

Equipment

PENS I would suggest that you try out several kinds of pen – preferences tend to be idiosyncratic and many automatic-type pens are on the market. As for the now old-fashioned nib, my long-term choice has been the Gillott number 290 (in the United States the type is known as a 'crow quill').

There is a certain human quality to the old-style pen, stemming as it does from the quill used over many centuries. There is also a feeling of

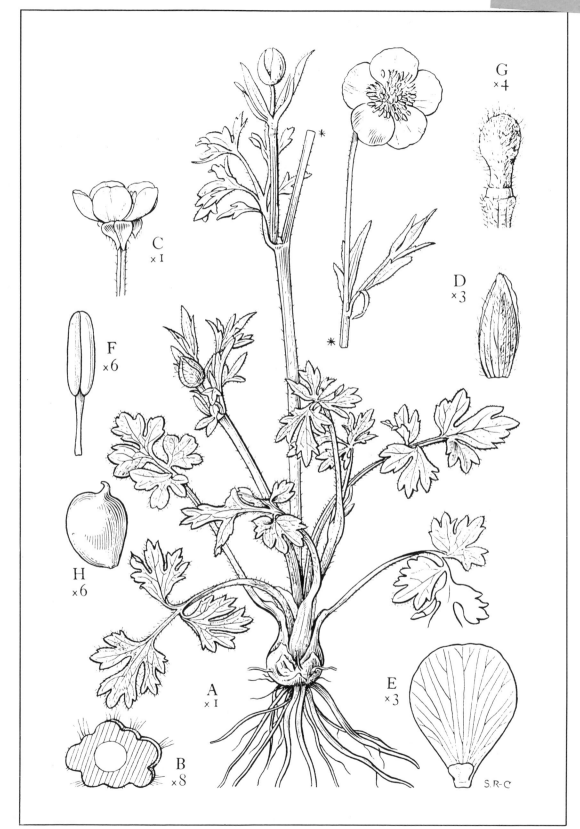

C ×1

G ×4

D ×3

F ×6

H ×6

A ×1

E ×3

B ×8

S.R-C

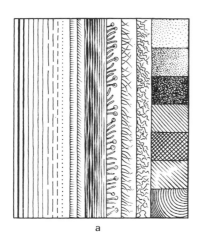 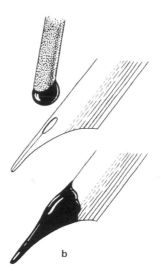 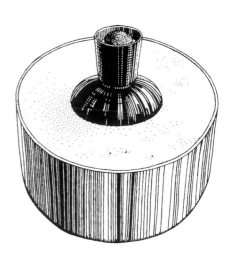

a   b

ABOVE AND CENTRE
59 Variety of marks made
by the pen, and method of
loading a nib

RIGHT
60 Stabilized ink bottle

virtue in having conquered a difficult technique: and one is reluctant to let this go in turning to an easier way of achieving an almost identical effect. Objectively, the steel-nibbed pen's continued use for botanical illustration cannot sensibly be defended; all that it can do is more readily managed with the most recent generation of fibre-tipped pens with spirit-based permanent ink which are in a category far removed from that of the earlier felt-tipped models.

A fibre-tip pen of this kind was used to draw many of the illustrations in this book. The pen is a throw-away model, which seems wasteful, but it has a surprisingly long life-span. As shown in fig 59, line-width can be varied as needed by increasing or easing pressure, and by lifting the tip gradually lines can be trailed off. With many earlier re-loadable automatic pens it was difficult to achieve this effect as lines ended in a truncated fashion when the pen was raised. Owing to the protrusion of the fibre-tip, the barrel may be held at an angle as one would a pencil, in contrast to earlier automatic pens which function best only when held close to the vertical. The ink in disposable fibre-tip pens is entirely satisfactory, provided that they are labelled 'permanent'.

For those who would still like to use a nibbed pen, a few hints can be given. The nib should be loaded by pipette (or brush) on the upper side only as shown in fig. 59, in preference to dipping into the bottle, and dried ink should not be allowed to build up on the blades. To prevent this, frequent wiping with a cloth is advised, giving extra attention to the line where the two blades of the nib meet – dried ink in this fissure gradually force the points apart, causing a thickening of the line and a loss of quality.

The past ten years or so have seen a vast improvement in the qualities of drawing inks. Black ink should be truly black and should dry waterproof with a semi-matt finish – all brands that I have used recently satisfy these criteria. The ink sold for use in re-loadable automatic pens is sometimes a fraction less opaque than it should be and this should be watched for. Some inks for nibbed pens have a built-in pipette in the bottle cap, a great convenience for loading.

When using a pen with a nib, the ink bottle should be positioned near enough to allow frequent loading to be done without stretching, but it should be below the level of the drawing surface and out of range of swinging elbows. For those who have a tendency towards clumsiness I recommend the device shown in fig. 60: a greased ink bottle is placed in a shallow container to which you then add plaster of Paris; when the plaster is dry the bottle will slide free to permit easy replacement. This simple tactic renders major spills unlikely.

PAPER As for pencil work, paper should be made of rag. Several rag papers and boards are available with surfaces designed for the use of ink. Some artists like to work on plastic drafting film; this permits easy erasure but otherwise seems to me to be unsympathetic, feeling cold and artificial. 'Board' is the term applied to paper of a certain thickness – as in 'Strathmore' board. There are also various types of 'illustration board' available, consisting of a paper mounted upon a heavy card backing. Boards are expensive (though pleasant to use), and many will prefer to use lighter weight papers which may have the added advantage of being translucent enough to allow one to trace off material where required.

Generally, boards and papers offer at least two kinds of surface, abraded and smooth. The former gives a slight 'tooth' or drag to the pen and the latter allows the nib to skim easily. The difference is subtle and you should give a fair trial to both before deciding which you prefer.

Whatever paper you choose, it should have a hard finish that will not allow an ink line to bleed (spirit based inks are particularly demanding in this respect). A good quality line is fully black with clean margins and no holes. Fig. 61 shows, in magnification, the kind of line to aim for (top); the second line is the result produced by a soft fibrous absorbent surface; and the third is the kind of line yielded by a hard over-textured finish.

61 Ink lines (magnified) on different surfaces

Paper composition should be sufficiently homogeneous and non-fibrous to allow erasure without much 'furring'. Plastic drafting film is perfect in this respect: areas can be removed with a sharp blade, and the surface can then be renewed to *almost* the original condition by gentle use of an abrasive eraser. 'Strathmore'-type boards will permit a certain amount of erasure without much destruction of the surface layer, although whenever an eraser has been used to remove an ink line an attempt should be made to repair any damage by burnishing with a clean pebble or like material. This will help, though line quality will suffer over an erased area to some degree no matter what corrective action is taken. Lighter-weight papers may allow little erasure; it may be preferable to complete a preliminary outline separately and to transfer this to another sheet for the final work. This course may be used as routine where much erasure is needed and where a light-table is available, or where paper is translucent enough to permit a direct tracing.

As with pencil drawing, the colour of the paper is probably most agreeable in light cream or ivory rather than brilliant white.

ERASERS For removing preliminary pencil drawing after inking, the resilient plastic eraser recommended in the last chapter is ideal, but to take out ink a more robust type is needed; it should be very finely abrasive but without scratching or scoring. Abrasive erasers are usually coloured, and in some kinds pigment may be ground into the paper when rubbing is prolonged.

A good hard eraser should last for years: I have a pink one of which about a third remains after use on and off for more than a decade. The main reason for long life is that removal of ink is a time-consuming chore which perhaps makes one doubly wary of making errors. Yet some mistakes are inevitable and it is as well to know how to make corrections effectively.

For erasing ink, a fairly gentle even pressure should be applied in an elliptical or circular movement covering a few centimetres with each sweep. The process will at first appear ineffective, but after a while lines will thin and eventually break before dissolving away. If initially too much weight is placed on the eraser, loosened ink particles may be pounded into the paper; though as lines fade more pressure can be safely applied. With patience, all traces of ink may be taken out: particles should be cleared with a feather, then, as mentioned earlier, the worked-over surface should be burnished with a pebble or similar object, taking care to avoid touching the remaining inked areas.

Paint can be used to cover errors, but for me this is not acceptable as the painted area is always obtrusive and lines which pass over it will change in quality. Though an ink drawing is more often than not intended mainly to be seen as a reproduction, and in this form corrective paint will not be visible, the original will be spoiled. It is a question of pride in the integrity of the work; a sloppy production will give little pleasure to creator or recipient.

Another technique – cutting away – may be used almost without leaving a mark for *tiny* flaws such as hairs that are a fraction too long, or small wavers and blemishes on otherwise good lines. A sharp scalpel should be used to pierce only the top layer of paper around the fragment to be taken, then a corner may be teased up in order to roll the piece away as shown in fig. 62. On no account should these small areas be burnished as ink will crumble from the adjacent cut edges and will be ground into the paper.

PENCILS The surfaces used for ink are often more resistant than those used specifically for pencil drawing, and where this is so, harder grades of lead are appropriate: 3H to 6H pencils perform well applied with light contact. Soft pencils lose their points too quickly on such surfaces and smear when erased. The hard pencil used properly leaves a faint line which erases easily. A natural error is to use more and more pressure in establishing a correct line, when a complex shape gives difficulty, until the paper starts to furrow. Erase gently before anything like this stage is reached. On the completed ink drawing there should be no trace of preliminary pencil work.

62 Removal of small errors

Techniques

Ink, like pencil, may be used for pure line, or in a combination of line and tone. However, there is one major difference between the two media: black ink can make only black marks, and tonal effects are made by hatching and stippling – whereas pencil can be made to range from the faintest grey to almost black by increasing pressure on the lead.

LINE As shown in fig. 61, ink lines will vary on different kinds of paper surface. But necessary as it is to find a suitable paper or board, your most important aim should be to develop the capacity and skill to produce an ascetic precision in line. This is not simply a discipline but also a source of keen pleasure. Once limitations are appreciated, refining and evolving the process may last a lifetime. Pure line is less commonly used than a combination of line and tone; even when working from herbarium specimens it will be found that a *sparing* addition of stipple or hatching will enhance and clarify.

A careful outline is first put in lightly with a hard pencil. Some artists prefer to use only the merest guide lines – a single skeletal line for the stem etc; but by making a precise preliminary drawing with correct measurements before adding ink, you will be able to concentrate entirely upon the inked line.

To ink in a long pencil line with perfect accuracy is demanding. The pencil guide, being drawn with a fine point, should have no width in practical terms, but the ink line does have a discernible thickness and this influences its placement. The eye judges the distance between the inside margins of parallel inked lines (as in stems etc.) rather than from their middles or outer edges, so inking should follow the outsides of pencil lines. How closely this ideal is approached will depend on your ability, especially over a lengthy line.

A worthwhile practice exercise is to draw lightly pencilled curves in parallels and then to attempt to follow them accurately in ink. The use of

63 Ink line drawing of rosebud reproduced at two-thirds and half original size

parallel curves is sensible, as much time is spent on stems, petioles, peduncles and other structures of this character. A drawing of a long linear leaf, stem etc. should appear to have been drawn with unerring strokes in a relaxed hand. This is the impression to strive for, though in truth I have never had the fortune to possess such skill or even to meet it in others. Unhappily, work done with broad gestures, though sometimes pleasing to the eye, cannot satisfy the stringent requirements of botanical reportage. Precisely inked lines, especially when of some length, are usually made in a number of movements, lifting the pen from the surface as each terminates, and gradually replacing it as the next span is started. You may find it necessary to change position or to move the paper as the sequence progresses. Each section should be completed in a fairly slow, even flowing motion and the pen should be lifted smoothly without flicking as the tip leaves the surface. The pen is re-applied just prior to where the last section begins to tail off. Joins between segments when done with skill are undetectable. As noted earlier, when drawing and inking parallel lines, the left-handed will find that the right line is best done first to serve as a guide for the one on the left, and the right-handed will be served best by the opposite approach.

A relaxed attitude is vital to the creation of good work. It is not easily cultivated or maintained, and a constant guard must be kept against the intrusion of tenseness. Muscle tension often originates in the fingers and can be avoided by remembering to work from the shoulder or elbow.

An ink line drawing may not necessarily be enhanced by tone – which should always be employed with a particular artistic or botanical aim, and not used simply to fill blank spaces. Also, when drawings are going to be much reduced in reproduction, an uncluttered work will, if boldly done, stand up to the process better than one hatched or stippled. As with pencil, it is surprising how much information can be conveyed by line alone. The small rosebud in fig. 63 shows how pure line may record essential form and how this kind of line will reduce. The sketch is shown here at two-thirds and at half the original size. Appropriate reduction helps to minimize irregularities and gives a general improvement in appearance.

TONE Few ink studies are done in pure line; more often tone is used to add information. Fig. 64 shows how a tonal effect in ink is based upon dots (stipple) and lines (hatching). Areas of tone are shown magnified so that differences in technique are apparent. Viewed with half-closed eyes, the result is broadly the same throughout; but in close-up the stipple as in *a* and *b* gives a quite different appearance from the hatching of *c* and *d*. The last two leaves look somewhat coarse and casual in contrast to the pair on the left. With stippling a far greater control is retained and fine detail may be shown.

Most botanical artists appear to settle into being either stipplers or hatchers. In my own case I started as a hatcher and became a stippler as frustration pushed me into a technique better suited to recording minute detail. A rational approach is to skip from one mode to the other depending upon the requirements of the moment – where simple bold drawings are needed use hatched tone, and reserve the use of stipple for subtle modelling.

Time may also be a factor – to complete a delicately modelled form, a stippled drawing may take twice as long as a hatched version, though it may also be twice as satisfactory.

To work faster in stipple without sacrificing quality I often use a modification as in *b*. Moving from light to dark I start by using dots quickly replaced by minute strokes which gradually move closer together until they fuse into black. A rhythmic movement is established which does not seem to work for pure dots; transitions from grey to black are accomplished more smoothly and reproduction seems marginally improved. Small dots remain preferable for use on structures such as petals which require a very light touch.

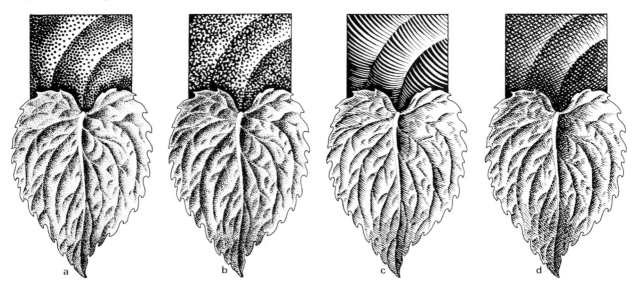

The illustration of *Epilobium latifolium* (fig. 65) indicates further how tone may be used in ink. The layout of the insets, the use of instant transfer type and the grouping of the scales (see also p. 145) may also be of interest. In this plate, drawn with a Gillott 290 nib, a method of showing the shaded sides of stems etc. is illustrated; this may be thought pernickety, yet especially where narrow parallel lines are concerned it is not easy to gain the same effect in any other way. A detail is shown in fig. 66a[1]. This type of shading is faster to do than it might appear; a press and flick movement is used and all stems and branches can be covered in minutes to add finesse.

Take care not to allow the drawing to become too dark. This can be avoided if tone is used to reveal form, not simply to fill space. With experience an over-dark plate will not occur. If an illustration as a whole has become too dark it may even be appropriate to repeat the work, as correction of large areas is a lengthy process with often not entirely satisfactory results. Small portions may be erased as described on p. 000, but areas exceeding a few centimetres in diameter should be blotted out with acrylic or other waterproof paint (bearing in mind reservations expressed earlier). For the finished appearance of the drawing it is as well to attempt to match the paper colour. The painted area will not have the same agreeable working surface as the untouched paper and even if great

64 Shading: **a** stipple; **b** modified stipple; **c** lines following leaf surface contours; **d** lines following leaf surface contours plus hatching

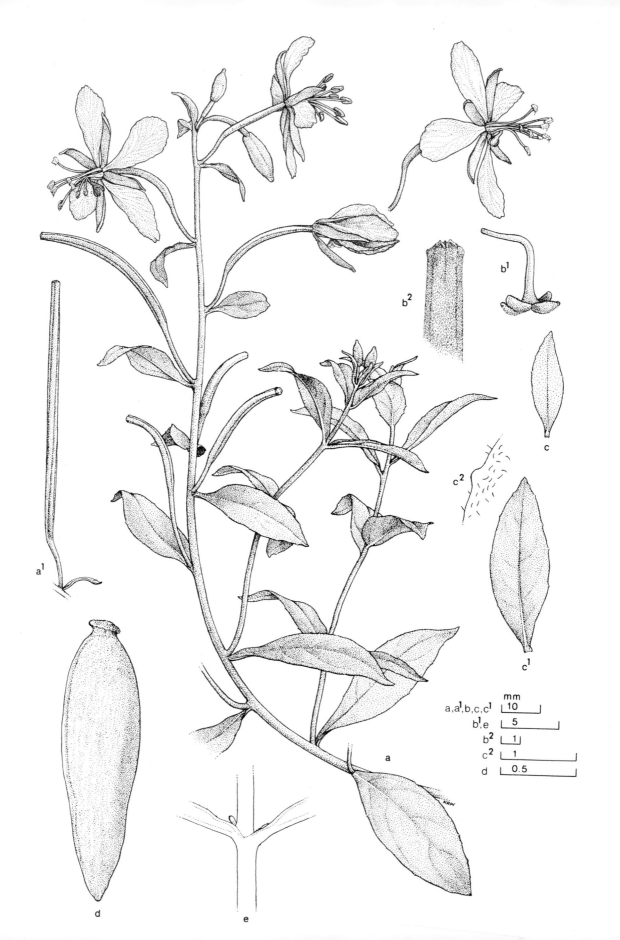

a,a¹,b,c,c¹ $\begin{array}{c}\text{mm}\\ \underline{10}\end{array}$

b¹,e $\underline{5}$

b² $\underline{1}$

c² $\underline{1}$

d $\underline{0.5}$

skill is used the repair will be to some extent visible – at least to the artist. To avoid getting into this position, beginners should err on the cautious side and make their work rather too light to start with, as this condition can easily be corrected by an extra layer of tone.

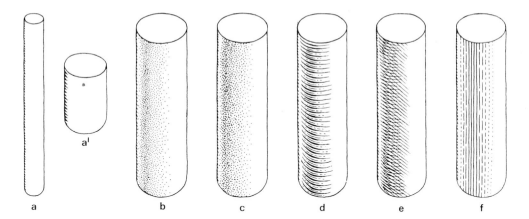

Dissections

Flower dissections are usually portrayed in ink. A high degree of accuracy is required and it may be necessary to use more measurements than are usual for whole plant or habit studies. Here scale becomes of prime importance. Sometimes, with larger flowers, it will be sensible to work at life-size, examining detail with a hand-lens; dimensions may be transferred directly, using dividers or a ruler. More often than not flowers will be too small to handle in this way and then a dissecting microscope is used. Generally, as in fig 65, there will be an area of the plate set aside for the dissection: this governs the scale used. It is helpful to have an even magnification where this is to be mentioned in the text (but see p. 145) – in other words ×2, ×5, ×10 etc., rather than an enlargement by, say 2.65. If a bar scale is to be used, and if you have a pocket calculator, an uneven magnification is no problem; on the contrary, it may be of advantage – especially when fitting the flower snugly into an allocated space. With the memory function of the calculator, each dimension – derived by reading from the micrometer eyepiece scale of the microscope – can be multiplied in the blink of an eye. Further hints on working with magnification are given below as drawing a flower dissection is described step by step.

To start, a discussion usually takes place between artist and author as to what should be shown and what should be emphasized. Emphasis does not imply exaggeration, rather clarification; for example, pollen clumps might obscure a stigma and the shape should be revealed by their removal; or perhaps hairs about the bases of the stamens migh be seen only by moving the light source; again, a minute feature such as the shape of the connective tissue between the pollen sacs might be of special interest. Sometimes it may be necessary to take out particular characters to be placed in separate detail studies.

In selecting a flower, a number of specimens should be looked over before deciding what is typical. It is not rational to aim for an absolute in

66 Stem shading: **a** 'flick-shaded' side of stem as described in text; **a**^{1} enlargement of **a** to show detail; **b** stipple; **c** modified stipple; **d** lines following stem contour; **e** lines following stem contour plus hatching; **f** vertical parallel lines

OPPOSITE
65 Ink study: *Epilobium latifolium*. a × 1, habit; a^1 × 1, capsule; b × 1, flower; b^1 × 3, stigma/style; b^2 × 5, ovary apex; c × 1, upper stem leaf; c^1 × 1, lower stem leaf; c^2 × 20, leaf detail; d × 40, seed; e × 3, axils

this respect, you can only reflect what is true in a specific place and time. Nevertheless, through consultation and perhaps prior reading you should know of special circumstances. For example, a species might be *monoecious* – where anthers and carpels are borne on separate flowers on the same plant; or there may be a developmental sequence with changing relative proportions of the sexual parts.

A decision will also have to be made as to how much of the flower tissues are to be excised in order to reveal essentials. In a single study the organs removed can be noted in a caption, though in a series this information may be conveyed once in the text rather than by constant reiteration. In the hypothetical flower of fig. 67, three stamens and one petal have been taken.

It is a natural assumption that the flower should first be taken from the plant. As noted earlier, flowers often collapse rapidly after major surgery; this is more true of blooms removed completely from the plant body, the process of deterioration is slowed if the operation can be managed on the flower *in situ*. This solution occurred to me after several years of petals etc. browning and distorting almost too fast at times for adequate recording. The technique can be used only where it is feasible to manoeuvre the flower, still on its stem, under the microscope; for this the plant must be growing in a pot and must be flexible. Any opportunity of working in this way should be taken, as drawing may then be at a more considered pace.

If the flower has to be taken from the plant its useful life may be extended by placing it on a bed of moist cotton-wool or blotting-paper in a petri dish or similar shallow container. The cut surface of the flower stem should not be exposed to the air but tucked away in the 'bed'. With flowers that break down quickly, it is helpful to draw as much as is practicable before dissection. In a specimen such as that in fig. 67 all the exterior portions may be completed in pencil before exposing the interior.

Despite all precautions, some flowers will not stay usable long enough for completion. When this happens, make a note of all dimensions before going on to finish from other specimens of the same stock. It is more acceptable to do this than to add in measurements from a second bloom, as, though shapes and structures should be the same, even slight differences in flower size will result in distortion. Almost always it should be possible to finish the pencil drawing – a second specimen may then be used for reference and checking while inking in.

Once the flower has been selected and is in place, drawing should proceed as rapidly as is compatible with accuracy. It is sometimes worth making a quick preparatory sketch. This might be done when you lack experience and wish to note all the parts to be measured in an orderly way before starting, or if the flower is extremely complex and an analysis will help in determining procedure; or it may be that an irregular scale, as mentioned above, is to be used, and it will be found time-saving to calculate all conversions in one operation. Such a rough working sketch, need bear little resemblance to the finished study – it is enough to show the parts that are to appear. In fig. 67a, the initial sketch has been made before full dissection has taken place. Here, the front petal and the upper

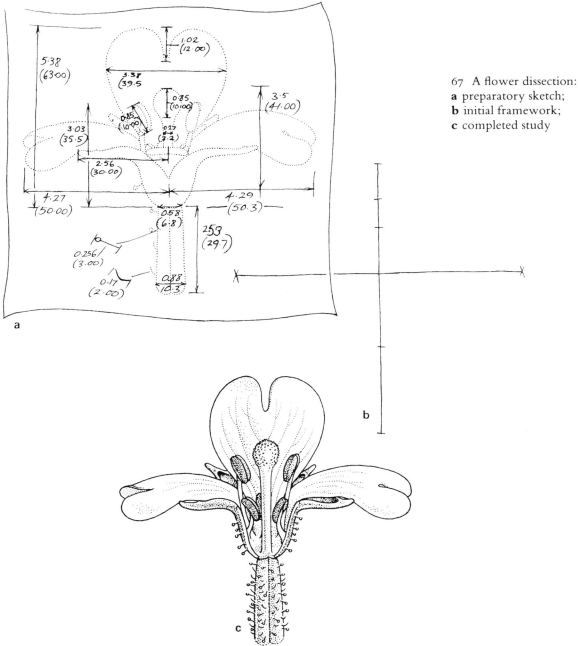

67 A flower dissection:
a preparatory sketch;
b initial framework;
c completed study

parts of two stamens have been trimmed back (using small scissors) without cutting into the calyx or floral tube. Flowers often tolerate this amount of interference without visible response. Comparison with the final version shows the few further measurements that have to be taken after full dissection.

For measurements to be read without confusion, the rough sketch is done in pencil, the figures are entered in ink, and the conversions are in ink of another colour. This sounds fussy but it is simply a matter of having a couple of pens of differing ink colours to hand.

In fig. 67*a*, the upper figures are in millimetres as read directly from the micrometer eyepiece scale (see p. 23). It has been assumed for this demonstration (reduced by one-third linear) that a space of *c.* 105 mm wide was left on the original for the flower dissection, and so each dimension has been multiplied by a factor of 11.7 in order to fit the drawing in comfortably. The upper figures are arbitrary in this example and bear no necessary relation to any real plant.

In the finished study, fig. 67*c*, a number of fairly subtle details have been shown clearly. Features will differ from species to species, but several items here indicate the kind of detail to watch for. These include: the depth of notching on the petals; the shape of the stigma and the extent to which the stigmatic papillae descend the style; the points from which the stamen filaments arise and the way in which the anthers join the filaments; the distinctive moulding of the apices of the calyx lobes; the types of hairs and their distribution; the faint pattern of venation on the petals; the cross-section shape of the ovary as suggested by the line at the base; and so on. You may notice that the rear petal is in an unnatural position in relation to the others: this posture accurately reveals the shape of the petal which otherwise would have been hidden by foreshortening. When flowers lie flat under the microscope, it is usually easy to move a rear petal to show its shape. Where this is not feasible, it may be desirable to remove and detail one separately.

Notice also that the hairs on the calyx and some of those on the ovary are glandular as shown by the secretions at their tips. This is the kind of feature that disappears from dried material.

In fig. 67*b*, the initial steps in establishing the flower are shown. It was assumed that a certain width was available with a less critical limit to the height of the flower, so the horizontal axis was entered first. A measure was then established from the extreme left to the vertical axis: the dimension runs from the left petal-tip to the line which runs conveniently through the ovary, calyx lobes, style and stigma, and the notch in the rear petal. In an actual flower it would be unusual for all these points to line up quite so neatly. However, in flowers of this type the columnar style provides an obvious key line, and generally this will at least be aligned with the ovary as in this instance. With the vertical axis in place, procedure became straightforward. Care was taken to place the dimension from the apex of the ovary to the tip of the rear petal in a pleasing position in relation to the rest of the plate, as this measure fixes the flower. Next the stigma, what was seen of the style, and the notch at the petal apex were entered. These were followed by the rear petal width; then attention was turned to the anthers and all parts visible of the upper and lower sets were drawn. (As noted elsewhere, anthers have the disconcerting habit of dehiscing on exposure to the warm dry air of the studio, though this process may be slowed where the flower is backed by a moist pad.) After adding the lateral petals, the calyx lobes and other external features, the floral tube was cleanly sliced to remove the petal stub, two remaining cut-back stamen filaments and one complete small stamen. From dissecting several flowers before the final selection, you will know just what will be revealed when the interior is exposed; often, as in the present example, this is simply a question of drawing in the base of the style together with the points from

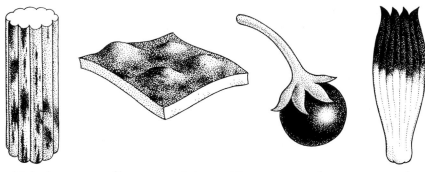

68 Use of tone to suggest pigmentation

which the stamen filaments originate. Nectaries may be seen, or perhaps hairs will be arranged in a particular pattern, etc. Sometimes it is necessary to use a brush to clear the base of the floral tube of nectar.

It would be more usual to draw a complete ovary, though here I have followed a practice used in an extended series illustrating the genus *Epilobium* where it was considered that little would be gained by showing the whole ovary in each species.

As mentioned above, by the time a dissection has been drawn in pencil, the flower itself may be wilted and a similar bloom may be used to refer to while inking in. When the lines have been inked, stipple is used, with extreme restraint, to reveal and clarify detail. In fig. 67c, stipple helps in defining such features as the anthers; the concave areas of the calyx lobes; and the ovary – note especially the way in which the sinus runs down the centre. Venation is also shown by extra-light stippled lines on the petals.

A useful tactic is shown in the way in which hairs break through the line of the ovary. The hairs look more convincing if they are inked first so that the line describing the edge of the ovary may be broken to leave minute gaps where they emerge or cross; this is related to the convention of breaking lines where structures cross one over the other – used by some in a rather affected form. Breaks in the line should be used only to avoid ambiguity – and even then they should not be obtrusively large.

As noted above, the anthers in fig. 67c are differentiated from surrounding tissues by the addition of stipple. Had they been in fact of the same tone as the background there would still have been sufficient reason for treating them in this way, though probably less stipple would have been used. This raises a problem. It is almost axiomatic that one should not try to represent colour and colour changes in black ink. Yet there are times when it is more misleading if an attempt is not made. Perhaps a petal will carry strong markings, or the stems of one species may contrast with others by being dark. The one criterion to apply is that of ambiguity – if tone is applied in a particular area, could it be taken to represent shadow indicating moulding of the surface? And, just as important, if tone is used to show pigmentation in one sector, this must not lead to doubt about other parts where its use is intended to interpret structure.

In fig. 68 this concept is put to the test; forms are treated as if they are strongly pigmented. There is no problem about recognizing where tone represents colouring except in the leaf section (second from the left) where one cannot be sure where shadows end and pigment begins: a situation where it would be wise to confine attention to structure.

91

8 Scraper board

Scraper board (scratchboard in the United States) allows a drawing to be made in white by removing portions of a black ink film with an engraving tool to expose a white underlayer.

Advantages are that a highly dramatic effect may be achieved with some ease; white detail may be placed against a dark ground; gradual modulations of tone from white to a true black are possible without difficulty; extremely fine lines may be drawn; and corrections are not tedious. Scraper board is flexible: I have used it for anatomical studies appearing in scientific journals, plant illustrations for interpretative works such as plant guides for National Parks etc., and also for cover designs.

There are drawbacks. The technique is time-consuming, and, when used for illustration, the text may easily be swamped unless care is taken to maintain a pleasing balance of black and white. One has constantly to blow away black powdery detritus as each mark is made – though this is a minor irritation, and the action becomes automatic. A small technical snag with ready-primed (black) scraper board is that the main design is best drawn separately before transferral by tracing. Also, scraper board use may become over-facile, a quality seen sometimes in advertising examples.

Notes in chapter 7 about printing ink drawings apply equally well to scraper board.

Equipment

SCRAPER BOARD is comprised of a card faced with a white china-clay preparation. Upon this a fine layer of black ink is added by the manufacturer or the artist. The ready-primed blacked board is used when most of the surface is to be worked over and few large areas of solid white are to remain. White board is preferred where considerable areas are to be left white: black ink is then added to the appropriate sections as required.

Though scraper board appears quite thick and robust it is in fact brittle. Bending should be avoided and edges treated gently as they chip; corners are especially vulnerable. Board is available in a wide variety of sizes. Unless large-scale works are definitely planned, it is better to buy small to middle-sized sheets.

69 Scraper tools

SCRAPER TOOLS (fig. 69) may be bought, though many artists find that they evolve and make instruments to suit their own styles. Whatever your eventual preference, cutting points and edges must be kept extremely sharp by the frequent use of a fine-grained stone.

MISCELLANEOUS ITEMS Apart from a whet-stone, little else is needed other than an HB pencil for direct drawing, or red-crayoned paper for transferring designs from preliminary drawings to the board. Though the commercial red-transfer paper is useful, a satisfactory substitute can be made by rubbing pencil lead over a sheet of thin paper. HB to 2H pencils are best, as anything much harder does not transfer clearly, and softer grades spread surplus graphite around too freely. A fine sable brush is useful for adding ink to white scraper board.

Techniques

Before doing a finished plant portrait in scraper board, a certain amount of preliminary doodling and sketching will help you to gain control over the tools and to appreciate the variety of marks, lines and textures that are easily made. Fig. 70 shows this kind of exercise on both black and white board. Rather different effects are obtainable from each style of board so at this stage they are discussed separately.

In starting with the ready-primed black board it will be found that parallel lines may be incised with almost mechanical precision. This facility allows the use of parallel hatching for indicating light areas in a manner similar to the way in which pencil and pen hatching is used to show shadow; though for finest detail a modified stipple is better.

Although, as illustrated, the effect changes with each doodle, the line is in fact the only basic component: even the apparent dots are minute wedge-shaped lines (in contrast with true round dots possible in pen stipple). Marks made with a vertical up and down motion will be almost invisible; to make anything approaching a dot stipple, the scraper tool is applied to the surface in a flicking motion. The resulting tiny wedges are useful in imitating many plant surfaces. These small flicks tend to run in one direction: random movement is not easily accomplished on scraper

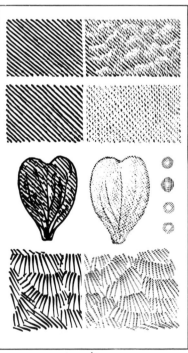

70 'Doodles' on ready-primed (black) and user-primed (white) scraper board

a   b

board as the tip of the instrument digs in or catches when direction changes are attempted.

White, unprimed scraper board may be treated in exactly the same way as ready-primed board if Indian ink is first brushed on in an even, thin layer and allowed to dry thoroughly.

An advantage of white board is that it allows one to use the method shown in fig. 70*b*. The doodles here were first made in Indian ink with a pen or fine brush (as shown on left) before being worked over with the scraper tool: some untouched portions are included for comparison. This demonstrates, as noted above, that white board is especially useful where large white areas are to remain.

The pencil for preliminary drawing should be an HB or similar medium grade as harder leads will damage the surface. Even with an HB, pressure should be light; erasures can be made in the normal fashion with the type of eraser recommended for pencil. Pen lines will be wider than when working on ordinary paper – the extra smooth surface of scraper board allows the ink to spread very slightly. This is disconcerting initially, though the extra width gives more scope for the scraper tool.

For some topics on white board it is sensible to make an ink drawing much as described in chapter 7, excepting that tone will be more freely used to exploit the properties of scraper board. Stipple or hatching can be added in the usual way and built up until the drawing overall is darker than the usual pen-and-ink botanical illustration. Be careful to build the ink up evenly, otherwise the cutting tool will incise clearly in those areas where the ink is applied thinly but will leave rough edges where application has been over-lavish. Experiment will show just how much ink is too much.

When using unprimed board, I prefer to apply ink with a brush to an area just exceeding that of the projected design outline; the area required is decided by tracing off an approximation as shown in the inset in fig. 71. Two coats applied thinly are usually sufficient to give an opaque and even covering, with the first layer being touch-dry before the second is added. The plant drawing is then transferred to the prepared ground in either of two ways. If the initial drawing has been made solely as a step towards a scraper board study, and if it is on thin paper, it can be placed over the inked area, with red-crayon or leaded paper interposed, and traced over with a well-pointed hard pencil. The original should be firmly held in place by tape. For an original containing extremely fine detail, the hard pencil is best replaced by a dissecting needle, pricker, or similar sharp point. This may cut through the drawing in places but the resulting line will have greater clarity. Each line described by the sharp point should be placed exactly where required as it will be lightly engraved into the ink and will only be removed by the scraper tool; for most originals the use of a hard pencil is a better practice as a pencil trace may be removed by gentle use of the eraser.

The second method of transferring the design should be used where the original drawing is not to be damaged. This may happen quite often, as for instance when work completed in another medium also has potential for scraper board. If the original is to remain untouched, fix tracing paper over the top and trace off a copy using the lightest practicable pressure; then continue as described above. This preliminary tracing can be omitted if you have access to a photo-copier, as the copies are thin enough to be used for the first method.

71 Leaf study, *Rubus*, on user-primed (white) scraper board; (inset) excision of leaf margin from outline

With the design transferred, cutting can begin – but check first that the ink is completely dry: even a slightly damp surface will result in an ugly mess rather than a crisp line. Experience will indicate how long ink takes to dry under different conditions. A test can be made in an area to be trimmed away, and if this is satisfactory, the unwanted ink areas extending just beyond the design boundaries may be removed.

In doodling you will have noticed that tool *points* incise thin lines that increase in width as more pressure is used, and *edges* take out areas. Consequently a sharp *edge* is best used to trim away outside the design. Tools will only perform effectively on scraper board as long as they are

72 Scraper board: *Bignonia* hybrid

kept really sharp. As the design is revealed, start blowing, as mentioned earlier, with the lips puckered to form a funnel, and continue until cutting is completed. A continuous air-stream should be directed at or about the point of the instrument – an undirected occasional puff is not enough. Even a small area of ink will yield a surprising amount of debris which quickly obscures the work if blowing is not kept up.

In releasing the design from its surrounds, the sweeping cuts made to take out the unwanted areas should be kept shallow and smooth. This is an insurance in case it is later decided to extend the original concept – not easy to do if deep scratches are present.

If you have difficulty in following a finely traced-off line, use a raking light shining almost horizontally across the board. The pencil line will then shine as if inscribed in silver. Going over the pencil line with the very tip of a pointed tool will render it still visible when the side light is removed.

Once the extraneous surround is cut away, work may commence on the exposed plant silhouette. The sequence should be from medium light to dark – that is, areas catching the light are engraved first with the 'flick-stipple' or hatching tailing away into the dark, but no attempt is made at this phase to show bright highlights or wholly white areas. These should be saved for the final touch when the drawing will spring to life as the brightest portions are shown. This does not mean that lighter parts should be left completely black until the last stages; on the contrary, the overall tonal structure is best established early, followed by a gradual working towards the lightest state at the end.

With pencil and pen caution has to be used to avoid work becoming over-dark – but with scraper board you should try to avoid any part becoming lighter than intended; hence the strategy of *slowly* strengthening all the lighter areas until the finish. If an area becomes lighter than intended, more ink may be added – but reworking is never as satisfactory.

Fig. 72 shows a completed scraper board study done on ready-primed black board. This was used as a cover design. Note the way in which different texturing is used for various parts of the plant body.

There is a similarity in appearance between wood engravings and some scraper board drawings. The former medium is sometimes consciously imitated, but most would agree that scraper board is best exploited for its own strengths.

9 Water-colour and gouache

Water-colour has been the medium preferred for plant portrayal over many centuries. Pliny the Elder mentions the names of several who painted herbs, including Krateuas whose work was copied and recopied: his paintings were used to illustrate Dioscorides' *De Materia Medica* of the first century AD. Probably the earliest versions were unillustrated but it was not long before the paintings of Krateuas were incorporated. None of his original work survives, though something of its quality may be gauged from copies in one of the better-known versions of Dioscorides' manuscript, the *Codex Vindobonensis* made for Juliana Anicia, daughter of Flavius Anicius Olybrius, Emperor of the West in the year AD 472. This dates from about AD 512 and the water-colour illustrations, even though they were imitations, remained a high-water mark for almost a thousand years. They were probably done using the opaque water-colour known as body-colour or gouache, rather than the transparent style now preferred by many.

Despite the discovery that oil could successfully be used as a binding agent for pigments, botanical artists have in the main continued to work in water-colour. Oil paints have never been serious contenders except for works such as the Flemish and Dutch flower-pieces. There are a few painters of botanical subjects in oils today, whose work indicates that the medium is not unsuitable, but it is still true that most prefer to use the simpler, more direct medium of water-colour.

Most of the pigments in artists' quality water-colours are transparent. The advantage of this is that coats of different colours may be applied, each qualifying its successor in much the same way as would occur in layering stained glass, and the white of the background paper shows through to give highlights or a translucent glow. Painting in this vein is often termed 'pure' water-colour.

In contrast, gouache or body-colour (the terms are synonymous) is opaque water-colour which may be obtained by mixing a little white pigment into transparent colours, or can be purchased ready for use as gouache, designers' colours or poster colours. Its opacity makes gouache much easier to use than transparent water-colour – mistakes are obliterated by an extra coat or so, and an area may be worked over several times. Lighter tone may be placed over dark with confidence, which also allows gouache to be used on toned or tinted paper. In spite of these properties, there are also losses to consider. These are not easily defined, as they are not absolute but matters of degree. Without transparency there is a little less brilliance (though this difference is lessened in reproduction) and sometimes a slight chalkiness and an altogether heavier quality than in 'pure' water-colour. For some the disadvantages are unimportant compared with added flexibility; others find the drawbacks important but use opaque colour here and there; and there are purists (myself included) who generally spurn opacity except to show white hairs, venation and similar details that cannot be completed by other means. You will discover with experience which approach suits you best, but it does seem that the term 'water-colour' should be reserved for work that is in the main transparent.

In discussing opacity versus transparency it should be mentioned that where a subject demands something of each quality - for instance, light stems painted over a deeper background, with the whole modified by transparent washes or glazes - then thought might be given to working in acrylics (chapter 10).

From this point 'water-colour' refers to the transparent form. Gouache is discussed on pp. 124-6.

Equipment

WATER-COLOUR PAINTS come in two forms: tubes or pans. People seem to have strong preferences. My own choice is definitely for pans, though this may be a minority view. Pan colours are immediately available as required - one can survey the ranks and move from pan to pan swiftly, pausing only to wash and squeeze out the brush to avoid contamination. A marred pan can be cleaned with a stroke of a wet brush. It is sometimes argued that pans of paint can become tough and hard when not in constant use, but this is true only of poor quality paints. Whether you choose pans or tubes, make sure that you buy 'artist's quality' water-colours.

Once you have decided which of the several excellent brands to use, thought should be given as to which colours should be included. This question is largely decided for you when buying a paint-box set, as each company prepares ranges - from 'beginners' outfits to truly opulent selections. If water-colour pigments included a pure cyan blue, a primary yellow and a good transparent magenta, it would be possible to mix virtually any colour from these - just as the printer does with his inks (though for demanding works the printer adds grey and sometimes other colours). However, all pigments fall short: it seems axiomatic that, in searching for a primary hue, if the colour is more or less as required then its handling qualities will be inferior - it will not be transparent or it will not be entirely compatible with other colours in mixing, so several different blues, yellows and approximations of magenta are required. This last hue gives the greatest problems to the botanical artist - so many flowers have petal colours from this part of the spectrum, yet it seems impossible to find pigments to depict them accurately without tolerating deficiencies in the paint itself.

Foxglove and thyme are two common flowers that nicely illustrate the difficulty. Each species has blooms that are near magenta with a touch of blue - the hue referred to as rose-purple in botanical literature. Cobalt violet, with a hint of carmine or alizarin, will reflect this handsome colour but it contains about the worst handling features of any pigment. It is muddily opaque and does not mix well with other hues. There are occasions when nothing else will do - but its use is kept to the very minimum, and from time to time I try new colours in the hope of finding a replacement with a better character.

To some degree all pigments have faults: these may be clear on first use, or they may emerge slowly. Probably it is best to start off with a nucleus of good quality colours, and to add to these over the years to solve particular problems. A capacious container will allow for supplementary purchases.

In the following list of essential colours for the botanical artist some, such as the cobalt violet noted above, violet lake and the earths are more often used in minute amounts to modify other colours. White is there to make body-colour for hairs etc. Black is excluded because an excellent black may be mixed in the palette. As detailed on p. 116, reds, blues and yellows in correct proportions make a black somehow darker than the manufactured ivory or lamp black, and this same mixture in dilution gives a wide range of greys – varying from warm to cool to neutral depending upon the relative amounts of each ingredient.

Recommended hues are: 1 lemon yellow; 2 cadmium yellow; 3 vermilion; 4 alizarin crimson; 5 *carmine; 6 cobalt violet; 7 *violet lake; 8 cobalt blue; 9 French ultramarine; 10 Prussian blue; 11 viridian; 12 *sap green; 13 burnt sienna; 14 Chinese white. These should cover most needs though the enthusiast will certainly be driven to try more. Asterisked colours are rated as being only moderately durable and they should not be used in works intended to provide a permanent record.

Experience in using each colour will give an understanding of its physical properties. Each differs in some respect, usually slight, from its fellows. For example, pigment grain sizes are not always constant from one colour to the other, and this factor explains why, in colour washes derived from an equal mixture of two components, one often dominates on drying. Again, some colours are not absorbed by paper to the same extent as others and tend to lift when an attempt is made to add another layer.

There are too many variables to attempt to catalogue the peculiarities of all pigments used individually and in combination – each maker's pigments sold under the same colour names differ slightly; responses to various papers may not be the same; colours in combination may behave differently from when they are used singly, and so on. The only advice that one can responsibly give about the handling qualities of water-colours, is to try them all out singly and in mixtures in the kinds of exercises suggested below.

BRUSHES are no less important in the production of a fine plant portrait than are high quality colours. There are many choices including several synthetic fibres as well as traditional ox-ear, squirrel, sable and others.

The qualities to watch for when purchasing brushes are their capacity for holding liquid and retaining their shape, and – especially important for the botanical artist – that when wet they come to a good point without any tendency to split. Suppliers allow the prospective buyer to wet brushes in order to check this feature and often provide a water-container for this purpose.

For brushes, as for paints, it is not hard to suggest an essential few, and they too will grow in number, though for a different reason. Most top quality brushes are close to perfection, until they start to wear; and then all but the steel-willed buy replacements without throwing out the old.

The first decision is what type of brush to buy. There are round-tipped and flat-tipped, both with either long or short handles. The choice for botanical work has to be for round tips and short shafts; a round tip is best suited for most organic subjects and a short shaft is more comfortable for working at close-quarters. There is little to separate reputable makes carried by artists' suppliers, but hair type offers several options. The best brushes, without doubt, are sable. These are expensive, but if the cost is weighed against useful life, probably the dearest are in the end the cheapest per mile of paint. Have at least the smaller grades in sable. I have tried several 0-1 grade synthetic fibre brushes, because of the difference in price between these and sable, but they proved unsatisfactory – the final half millimetre or so was too flexible and would not hold a consistent point for long. I have not used the larger sizes in synthetics – these may well be suitable for washes and broader treatment. At the time of writing, brushes of mixed synthetic fibre and sable have been introduced and these seem promising. Ox-ear and squirrel hair are also best kept for less detailed work.

You will manage perfectly well for most botanical topics with four sizes. Two of grade 0 are needed because one should be reserved for use with white paint for hairs etc. – white paint seems to wear a brush more rapidly than other pigments. This is also a function into which a grade 0 brush may be retired as it starts to lose a few hairs, as one fined down in this way may be perfect for handling delicate white detail. Grades 1, 3 and either 8, 9 or 10 make up the other essentials. The brush most in use is grade 3, though for mixing large amounts of wash I use grade 8 or 10, and for minute subjects 0 and 1 are ideal.

Brushes are precision tools and should be properly cared for. Pigment must not be allowed to dry on the hairs, especially where they enter the ferrule. If paint is allowed to accumulate in this area, it forces the hairs apart. Even after a spoiled brush has been thoroughly cleaned it may refuse to point well.

If brushes are to be stored for a long period it is as well to put them into an air-tight tube with a moth-ball. And whether brushes are stored or in daily use, points should not touch the sides of the container or anything else for that matter; contact gives a tip a bias or breaks it up, and restoration takes some time.

PAPER A sensible tactic is to try as many rag-based papers as you can, noting the good and the bad features of each. A final choice should not be made too swiftly, as some features are not necessarily appreciated at first.

Many papers can be discarded at a glance, others may have to be put aside on the grounds of expense – some French papers for example are far too costly for most day-to-day work. Paper with a rough grain or texture should be avoided for botanical illustration as this may show in reproduction and it makes detail more difficult to capture. A slight 'tooth' is helpful in holding pigment – entirely smooth hot-pressed paper is not satisfactory. An eventual choice may well be between a surface that is minutely too rough and one that is fractionally too smooth. Weight is also of some importance in that the heavier grades, 140 lb (*c.* 63 kg) weight and above do no have to be stretched (weight refers to a ream). This small advantage is offset by the greater cost of heavier types and the fact that the process of stretching paper (see below) renders it more responsive. Lighter weight paper must be stretched to prevent cockling or buckling which otherwise is inevitable when washes are laid down. Illustration board – fairly light paper, ready mounted on cardboard and so pre-stretched – is also available, though again expensive.

PALETTES The depressions on the lid of the paint-box are usually quite sufficient to hold pigment and water mixtures for washes etc. but there are times when these will not be enough. There are ample palette forms to suit personal tastes, and there is probably little to choose between them for effectiveness. My preference is for a porcelain variety that may be stacked and so kept dust-free.

WATER-JAR The perfect water-container is glass, squat, capacious and with a fairly narrow mouth. Glass allows the state of the water to be monitored: when painting dark areas muddiness can be tolerated, but light and subtle topics such as flower petals require clean water. Squatness signifies stability – a tall container may look elegant but will beg to be tipped over. Capacity should be large to minimize the number of water changes. A fairly narrow opening lessens the scope for spillage, but it should be wide enough to allow the brush entry while your attention remains partly on the model or the painting: for some operations in water-colour it is imperative to move swiftly, with the action of washing out the brush being semi-automatic. It is a help to keep the jar in the one position. The brush may then be placed blindly; with a smallish opening, entry is confirmed by the first wiggle clicking on each side.

GUMMED BROWN PAPER STRIP Used in stretching paper, as described below; it should be no narrower than 5 cm (2 in.) or the stretching paper may pull free.

LIGHT-WEIGHT DRAWING-BOARD A light-weight board placed upon the regular drawing-board gives so much extra flexibility that it is hard to imagine working without it. Water-colour paper stretched on to a light board may then be picked up, turned around, and worked on from any direction. The angle of the working surface may be changed by adjusting the regular board underneath or by tilting the light board by hand. This supplementary board may be of any stable material that will not stain the paper – 5 mm ($\frac{3}{16}$ in.) thick plywood or hardboard (masonite in the US) is ideal, cut to about 50 × 40 cm (20 × 16 in.). For small subjects a piece about 40 × 30 cm (16 × 12 in.) will provide even more ease of movement. If necessary you can work solely on the light board without a regular drawing-board or drawing-stand underneath provided that some means is devised for tilting the light board to various angles. When painting on heavy illustration board a light-weight board is superfluous.

MISCELLANEOUS ITEMS Absorbent rag or paper towelling is used for taking excess water from the brush each time it is washed. The material should be lint-free and should be hung between your lap and the drawing-board on whichever side is most convenient. This, like the water-jar, is often used automatically without looking. For the rest only a plastic eraser, pencils HB, H, 2H, and a feather for brushing away eraser particles are needed.

Techniques

Volumes appear yearly on painting in water-colour, but the methods of realistic plant portraiture are to some extent the reverse of those advised for landscape and the like. For the latter style of painting one works broadly in washes, and fine detail is thought of as niggling and not to be indulged in. Botanical art demands a disciplined precision giving maximum information; yet the aim is still to avoid an over-laboured effect by using simplicity and economy in each phase.

Before working on a plant, try the exercises below as a means of getting to know about the behaviour of each pigment and the ways in which different papers respond. Some papers will not need stretching for this preliminary work as, for the most part, each area worked on will be too small to make cockling a problem. However, it seems sensible to explain the stretching method first.

STRETCHING This is best done near a bath or sink to speed the sequence. Although the instructions may seem lengthy and complex, the operation will take only about a minute from wetting the paper if you are deft. Before starting, lay out what is needed on a cleared table-top or bench. Cut the paper to fit with ample margins on the light-weight board placed close by; cut gummed brown paper strips to allow an overlap around the sheet (fig. 73), and put a tea-towel or small hand-towel to one side. The sink should have enough water in it to cover the paper.

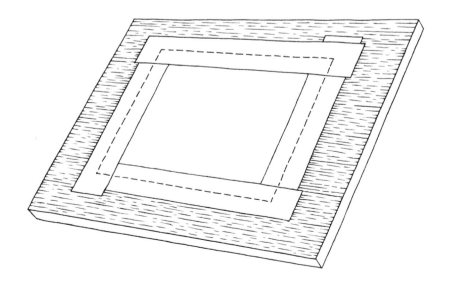

73 Stretched paper on drawing-board

1 Submerge the paper. Some recommend that it should remain under water for three or four minutes, but I have always found that thirty seconds or less gives complete wetting; in fact, some papers are slightly damaged by longer immersion.

2 Place the sheet on the drawing-board, holding it by two corners (top or side – not diagonal) and allowing the bottom edge to contact the board first, to be pulled into position as the rest of the sheet is laid down.

3 With the paper in place, cover it with a towel to absorb surplus water – dabbing so that the two materials are touching more or less throughout. Rubbing or horizontal movement will harm the paper surface. The smallest delay will allow the paper to start cockling. Sometimes this step is omitted but removal of the excess water ensures adhesion of the gummed tape.

4 Apply the gummed paper strips in turn, holding them at each end by finger and thumb and passing them through the water in one motion, and then placing them in position while held taut to present a non-sagging surface. Each strip should have about half its width on the drawing-board and half on the paper.

5 Finally, touch the gummed tape gently with the towel to remove free water, using minimal pressure to avoid squeezing gum over the paper.

Stretching paper should be left lying flat so that drying will be even over the entire surface. A tilted board may allow water to seep towards the bottom giving an uneven drying rate – uneven pressures over the paper may then cause it to tear or to pull free. Accelerating drying by the use of a heater or direct sunlight may have the same result.

The paper should be left to dry for some hours. The length of time varies depending upon room temperature and humidity. It is rash to work on an incompletely dry surface as preliminary pencil drawing leaves score marks, erasure is impossible, and paint will be absorbed too freely, blurring out over margins. As a rule I make a practice of being if anything over-careful with drying, usually stretching paper at the end of one day to use on the next. The paper must remain under tension until the painting is completed; then it may be cut free with a scalpel or craft-knife. The way the paper then pulls aside from the blade shows how much tension is involved in the process.

From the time the paper is placed wet on the board to when the completed painting is cut free, take care not to rest your hands on the area to be painted over. Grime, perspiration and body-oils do not mix well with water-colour. At some stage everyone discovers the irritation of putting down what is intended to be an even wash only to have it broken by speckles of grease. A protective sheet of paper under the hand (recommended earlier for use with pencil and pen) is equally helpful here for trying out colour mixes and brush strokes; to see how a particular wash mixture will dry; and to see how one colour will behave when laid over another and so on.

OPPOSITE
Gerard van Spaëndonck (1746-1822) *Campsis radicans* (L.) Seem

OVERLEAF LEFT
Pierre-Joseph Redouté (1759-1840) *Paeonia suffruticosa* Andrews from *Description des plantes rares cultivées a Malmaison et a Navarre* by A. J. A. Bonpland, Paris, 1813

OVERLEAF RIGHT
Franz Andreas Bauer (1758-1840) *Strelitzia reginae* Banks from *Strelitzia depicta*, London, 1818

Pæonia Moutan. Var. b.

To avoid having to replace this practice-cum-protective sheet frequently, take a piece about A4 size and fold it in half. When the half under the hand is filled up, open the sheet and fold back in the opposite direction for further use. When this exposed area is full, the sheet may be folded again to give a quarter of the original area. At no time should a doodled surface come into contact with the working area.

WASH Before painting a plant it is essential to acquire several simple techniques. One is that of putting down an even wash of colour; this is basic to water-colour painting and is easy on almost any paper that is not over-smooth.

The first step is to draw ten or so rectangles – 8 × 5 cm (3 × 2 in.) is a useful size. The definite boundaries help to teach control of the brush. Label the painted results – 'one layer', 'two layers', 'wet on wet', 'wet on semi-dry' etc. – to provide a reference (fig. 74).

The drawing-board should be sloped at an angle of about thirty degrees to allow the wash to keep moving down under the brush, without being steep enough to permit an uncontrollable run.

Mix a wash of any hue well diluted with water in a paint-box reservoir or palette. The amount of colour used is not critical but it is best to use light tones until the behaviour of the paint and the paper are assessed. Mix more wash than you are likely to need – this is a good habit to acquire, to avoid running out when only part way through an area.

A grade 3 brush is used for small sections such as these – though when you have mastered the technique you might also test it on bigger areas using the largest brush. The 8 × 5 cm rectangles will allow many possibilities to be presented on one sheet. The technique (fig. 75) for laying in a wash is:

1 Load the brush in the wash mix. The hairs should absorb enough to swell the tip without risking drips (*a*).

2 Apply the brush to the top corner of a rectangle and take it in one stroke to the opposite corner, holding it at a shallow angle so that the line of pigment left behind is broad – part of the body of the brush is used rather than the tip alone (*b*). Paint will accumulate along the bottom of the stroke – if this threatens to break and dribble the drawing-board is at too steep an angle.

3 When the first stroke is completed, make a second stroke a fraction lower down to return to the side started from (*c*). If the first stroke yielded ample pigment along its lower edge the second movement may be continued without lifting the brush from the paper. However, if the paint has not formed this reservoir, the brush should be reloaded. Depending partly upon the absorbency of the paper, it will probably be necessary to reload for the third sweep across.

4 Follow this simple process until the bottom of the rectangle is reached – back and forth strokes with a well-loaded brush. Keep enough pigment on the brush to give an accumulation at the bottom of each stroke –

OPPOSITE
Ferdinand Lucas Bauer
(1760–1826) *Flindersia
australis* R. Br.

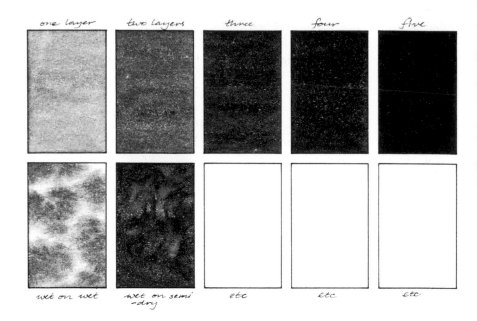

one layer   two layers   three   four   five

wet on wet   wet on semi -dry   etc   etc   etc

74 Layout for wash exercise

though this can be allowed to lessen as the bottom of the rectangle is reached. Ideally the last stroke will finish off so that a slight twirl of the brush-tip will lift all surplus wash as the last corner is reached. Often this does not happen and a runnel may remain at the base. If this is left, the bottom edge will dry darker and perhaps more unevenly than the rest. The remedy is to wash the brush and squeeze it semi-dry on the rag, then take the brush-tip along the accumulation, absorbing it throughout. If a surplus still remains the brush should be washed, squeezed out again, and the action repeated.

Depending upon the quality of the paper, the dilution of the pigment, and your skill, this first rectangle may dry with an even finish as intended, or it may be streaky. A streaky result may be improved on in the next try if the area is painted over initially with a wash of clear water. This is especially helpful if the paper has not been stretched, though even stretched paper can be made more cooperative in this way.

Apply the wash technique to most of the ruled-up panels, keeping a few in reserve for further experiments suggested below. After the first coat has

75 Wash technique

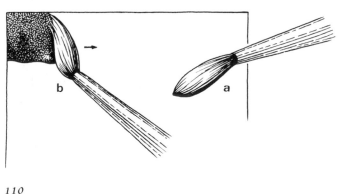

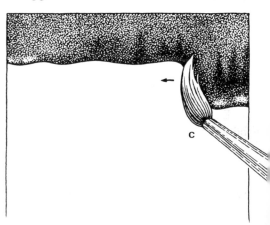

dried thoroughly, try a second layer. One panel should be left with only one coat so that a difference may be seen between this and the rest. Continue to exclude one panel with successive layers so that one rectangle has one coat, the next carries two, the next three and so on, up to five or even six layers of wash as in fig. 74. Depending upon the variables noted earlier, at some point the paper will absorb no more pigment, and no matter how patiently you wait for the wash to dry, an attempt to add another coat will only dislodge earlier layers, with unsightly results. It becomes second nature to be aware that this stage is near and to hold back.

The remaining rectangles are worth using to find out what happens if you cannot wait for a wash to dry before trying to add to it. An attempt to add when the wash is over half dry is usually a mistake – instead of adding pigment the brush picks it up. You will quickly learn that an even wash (as in the underlying colour of a leaf) is best put on speedily and then left until dry. This is not to say that one pigment may never be introduced into another on *wet* paper – one to several colours may be mixed and modified in this way *provided that the surface remains wet*.

a

GRADATED WASH When you have practised putting down an even wash, another necessary basic skill should be attempted – a gradated wash. Though in water-colour it is axiomatic that one works from light to dark (light colours cannot be put over dark without using gouache or other media), with this technique you can start with a pigment which may be at maximum density or any degree of dilution needed, and then by adding water in steps work through a tonal gradation to a predetermined lighter tone or to clean paper (fig. 76a). The technique allows you to move in one coat from dark to light on a leaf or stem etc. Generally such gradations on plants are found over short distances – a petal dark at the outer edge fading to white at the base would be typical – but the ability to establish such a change over larger areas is also worth cultivating. The method is not complicated but the achievement of a perfect gradation is elusive.

Draw a series of columns approximately 8 × 3 cm (3 × 1 in.) on a sheet, stretched or not depending upon how your papers performed when an even wash was put on. You may or may not wish to pre-moisten the area within each column before pigment is added, again depending on previous results. Then proceed as follows:

1 Load the brush as before.

2 Apply the brush as with the wash technique except that when you reach the point where you wish the tone to lighten, dip the brush-tip momentarily into water instead of the wash mixture. This will dilute the pigment already on the brush and on the lower edge of the previous stroke as the next stroke is taken across.

b

76 Tonal gradation

3 Depending upon the degree of gradation aimed for, more water may be added with each alternate stroke or with successive strokes, until the base of the column is reached.

It is possible to speed or slow the transition by adding or withholding water. The most rapid gradation is made by washing the brush after the first stroke, wiping it gently on the rag to take some of the water, and then taking the brush-tip across the lower edge of the paint to absorb and lift off pigment. It may be necessary to wash out the brush once more to add another stroke in water before mopping up surplus in the same way as with the even wash technique.

A second or third coat may be needed to reach the depth of tone aimed at in the darkest section of the column, remembering that the underlying coat must be dry.

For some papers, it helps to add the water-diluted pigment, and later the pure water, *not* to precisely the lower edge of the last stroke, but to a point 3–5 mm (*c*. $\frac{1}{8}$ in.) above. Then complete the stroke in the usual fashion, remembering to use part of the flat of the brush rather than just the tip. All brush movements should be made with a feather touch.

In trying out the technique it is useful to mimic a stem (fig. 76*b*). Turn a column to a horizontal position and grade off the wash to about the centre, allowing it to dry before turning it about to do the same thing on the other side. By varying the depth of tone on one side or the other, different lighting effects may be simulated.

In some situations a reverse of the procedure described above may be needed, starting with clear water and adding the wash mixture by degrees until the brush is loaded with this alone.

DRY-BRUSH Another route to colour gradation is to use the dry-brush technique. The term is slightly misleading: 'moist-brush' would be a more accurate description. Dry-brush allows colour modifications, strengthening or shading, to be added in a considered way without the speed required when applying a wash – and it may also be used where a further wash coat would result in damage.

In the description below it is assumed that areas are to be darkened to suggest portions of a leaf surface turning away from the light as in fig. 77. The leaf is shown enlarged so that the technique may be more readily followed. At the stage at which dry-brush work commences, an area would already have been established carrying an even wash broken by venation and highlights. Before starting this exercise, check the way in which these features are produced (pp. 113–14). Then proceed as follows:

1 Dip a grade 3 brush into the wash mixture and drag it over the rim of the reservoir leaving the hairs with only a small amount of liquid, reducing this further by trial strokes on the practice sheet.

2 Then apply the merely moist brush to those wash areas that require strengthening, using short vertical strokes with a light touch. Move from light towards shade, treating in turn areas bordered by veins. If the upper edges of the strokes starting in the lighter sections dry in hard lines contrasting with the underlying wash, the pigment mixture has not been diluted enough. Each stroke should dry to blend in imperceptibly at the top, where less pigment is deposited.

3 Move from one side to the other of each portion treated, while continuing gradually down the sheet. This is much like applying an even wash,

except that short vertical strokes are used instead of long horizontal ones. There should be no hint of pigment running to collect at the bottom of a stroke – if this happens the brush is too wet and it may cause damage: a few more strokes on the practice sheet will solve this problem.

4 After completing all the areas with the extra coat of pigment added by dry-brush, the sequence may be repeated again and again, starting each time a little further into the shadowed part of each piece. A number of layers can be added without the surface breaking up, until the density needed in the darkest parts is achieved, or until the paper will not absorb more.

Though dry-brush allows details to complement broad washes, its over-use gives a laboured quality which is the antithesis of the freshness typical of fine water-colours. Plan the initial washes so that most of the work is completed before dry-brush is used for finishing touches. An exception to this stricture is inevitable when minute plants are portrayed – when there may not be room to manoeuvre washes. Dry-brush was also used as described for the ivy leaf on p. 120–21.

77 Dry-brush shading

WHITE AREAS In using water-colour it is necessary to plan ahead, seeing the work in stages. One consideration is the areas that are to remain white. If they are fairly large, they may be skirted by a wash, but difficulties arise when small portions are to be left. There are mechanical ways of leaving white areas – wax, rubber solution and other aids are sometimes used – but none has proved satisfactory enough to recommend. I have so far found only three practices worth using (fig. 78): the first (*a*) is the obvious one

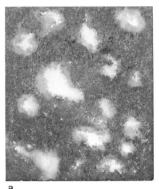

a

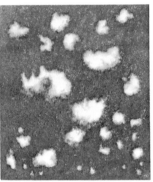
b

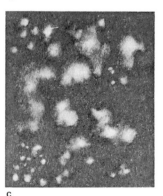
c

78 Effects of three methods of taking out highlights

already noted of painting around the area to be left, allowing the brush just to stray inside the borders; then, if it is possible to pause, the brush is quickly washed out, dried on the rag and used to mop up the excess pigment to create the blurred edge typical of highlights on leaves etc. Speed is essential to ensure that the lower edge of the wash does not dry; the line formed when this happens can't be hidden without adding a further highlight or similar camouflage.

A preferred method (*b*) is to leave small areas, with pigment just inside the boundaries as described above, until the wash is dry. Then, with a clean and slightly moistened brush-tip, the excess pigment can be lifted off at a more comfortable pace by breaking and blurring the hard edges which have been left. The brush should be washed out from time to time to keep the point clean.

The third method (*c*) is best used where a perfectly even surrounding wash is required, or perhaps where there are so many small white spots that it is impractical to paint around them. The wash is taken over the whole area without any attempt to avoid the intended light spots. After the wash has dried, the moist, clean brush-tip is applied to each spot in turn to rub and absorb some of the pigment – which should be washed away in the water-jar. The clean tip can be applied again and again in the same way, until no more pigment lifts off. The process should be stopped well before the paper surface begins to fray. Experiment will show when this point is about to be reached with a particular paper. This method rarely takes out all the colour and so should not be used where clear white highlights are the aim. Small errors may also be erased in this way. For treatment of larger errors see pp. 123–4.

VENATION The venation of leaves may be picked out by an adaptation of the above method. A brush is filled with clean water, squeezed to give a chisel-shaped tip, and drawn along the surface in alignment with the vein. As the sharp tip is drawn back and forth a few times over a short distance – no more than two or three centimetres – pigment is abraded away. The brush should be frequently washed and re-shaped. If the tip is not kept clean, dislodged particles will be deposited along the edges of the vein leaving two dark margins or 'tide-marks'. If the brush-tip is allowed to break from the chisel shape, the cut out line will progressively widen. With a properly shaped-up brush, the lines created may be hair width, and surprisingly few strokes may be needed to indicate fine veins. The effect is illustrated in enlarged detail in fig. 77; it was also used in the plates illustrated in colour on pp. 117 and 118 (bottom).

COLOUR The following exercise will provide a permanent record of the appearance on paper of each of the colours in your paint-box and can be kept to hand as an aid for colour mixing. As the botanical artist is much concerned with accuracy a thorough knowledge of how each colour behaves is invaluable.

It is a help to arrange the colours in your box in the order given on p. 100. At least ensure that all the yellows, reds, blues, greens and earth colours (siennas, umbers etc.) are kept in groups. To avoid confusion, keep the pigments in the same order as they are applied in the exercise. For example, if on your reference sheet you have lemon yellow preceding chrome yellow, and the sequence is reversed in the paint-box, it will be easy to mix one when the other is intended.

Having arranged the colours, rule up on paper enough small panels for all the current pigments and an extra few to allow for later purchases, leaving a space around each for names to be entered (fig. 79). As more hues are acquired they may be integrated into the paint-box sequence; and, if you are methodical enough, painted into the extra panels – with a note indicating their position in the box.

Panels are then filled in with a fairly full-bodied wash from each colour in sequence. Several interesting discoveries are made as the hues are added: most pigments will behave well, drying evenly and with a reasonable density. Some, mixed in the same fashion, will probably turn out darker than expected. Violet lake and Prussian blue have surprising depth of tone, which can be recorded on the chart as a reminder to use them with care. A few pigments are likely to dry in streaks, and are best used cautiously – cobalt violet and alizarin crimson are examples. Sap green also manifests unfortunate tendencies on some papers and should not be trusted – an initial wash may dry with a hint of streaking, and often an attempt to add

79 Water-colour trial layout. Numbers correspond with those in list of colours on p. 100

115

a second coat will even more severely disturb the first. However, on some papers it is compliant, so it is worth keeping as a rich green not easily matched by mixing.

As a refinement, a second layer can be added to part of each rectangle to show two densities of colour.

The subtleties of colour mixing are best self-taught as it is impossible to give more than a few general hints. Most readers will know that if reds and yellows are mixed the result will be orange; blues with reds yield violets and purples; yellows and blues give greens; and reds and greens produce browns. A fuller treatment of colour mixing is reserved for the chapter on acrylics (pp. 132–4), where results may be less familiar. Apart from some slight differences in effects, the information given is equally applicable to water-colour and beginners in this medium may like to do the mixing detailed there.

Even those with some experience of water-colours may not have come across the mixture for black mentioned on p. 100. Equal parts of vermilion and ultramarine with a very little cadmium yellow will produce a black which at its deepest can be distinguished from the commercial product by a marked lively quality and a darker appearance. Other reds, blues and yellows may be used, though this particular mix is recommended for its stability – with some combinations a second or third coat is prone to lift the underlayers.

Manufactured ivory black and lamp black reflect more light, giving a greying effect; the above mixture appears to absorb light to yield a virtually true black. The dullness of the ready-mixes is evident in comparison. The vermilion–ultramarine–yellow combination also gives excellent shadow colours contrasting with the dead greys of diluted ivory and lamp blacks.

The botanical artist will develop a knowledge of all the various greens that can be coaxed from the paint-box. To try out as many greens as possible (in addition to those purchased) use all the yellow/blue combinations and then look at the results of adding minute amounts of other hues as modifiers; for instance, a lemon yellow/ultramarine mix with a hint of vermilion.

MODIFYING Even after a colour has been tried out on the protective sheet, the result may not be exactly as intended. When, for whatever reason, the hue as laid down is inappropriate, a modifying colour may be applied. For this much depends on how much pigment is already present; as noted earlier some papers reach their saturation point quickly and an attempt to add another layer may fail. Experience is the guide here – though to avoid the worst, one can usually find a tiny leaf, or perhaps an unobtrusive portion of a larger one, to make a test on. The methodical worker may already have a part on the try-out sheet carrying the same number of washes as the actual painting and this may then be used. If the area to be changed is close to saturation, much the same effect can be produced – though more slowly – by dry brush. In any event the practice sheet should be used to find out the exact density of pigment and the hue required to correct the original colour, carrying the modifying colour over the area where the original wash was tried out; only a portion of this

Keith West

should be covered at a time, to allow the difference between treated and untreated sections to be gauged.

Trial runs over practice areas are necessary because various factors combine to make it difficult to pre-assess the likely results. It is hard to see in the mind's eye the *exact* effect of, say, dilute pure vermilion over a green which is already a mixture. Water-colours tend to dry lighter in tone than they are when wet; and different kinds of paper will affect responses – some that are extra-absorbent seem to suck an added colour down into those already present, while others keep the pigment on the surface, sometimes giving a stronger effect than intended.

Occasionally the use of an overlying colour is the only way to reach a particular hue, as some pigments when mixed together in the palette are somehow slightly dulled by the process. For instance there is a purplish-blue that is not uncommon in flowers: in analysing its components you might think that either cobalt blue or ultramarine mixed with carmine should get close to the mark, yet when this is tried the result is somewhat leaden. A carmine wash over the top of the blue yields a colour that is subtly more vibrant.

In getting to know how colours interact, a pleasant and useful exercise is to paint a series of horizontal strips followed by overlying vertical strips as shown in fig. 80. Each colour is used, including the shadow-mix described above. The underlying horizontals should be painted in at about half maximum density, in perhaps two thinnish coats, depending upon the characteristics of the working surface. The overlying vertical strips will be most effective if they are thin enough to allow the under-colours to show through clearly. A little experiment will suggest the right density to use.

FIRST PLANT SUBJECT Your first botanical subject in water-colour should be a simple one such as the ivy leaf on p. 118 – a suitable choice, as the species is available from many localities throughout the year, and it will stay in excellent condition for a long time after picking. Also, it is a model which requires the use of washes – even and gradated; lifting off pigment; blending in edges; colour mixing – including shadows; and the addition of an overlying colour by dry-brush.

A scrap of illustration-board was used for the illustration; on this a drawing in HB pencil was made, detailed enough to show the major veins. Smaller venation was not indicated as it would have been hidden by the first layer of paint. The study then moved through the following stages:

1 The paper was dampened as the hard surface needed to be made more absorbent. Water was applied as for a colour wash, inside the drawn outline, with a grade 3 brush.

2 A wash was mixed of sap green plus a little permanent blue. Sap green performs adequately on this surface – though there might have been a problem had an attempt been made later to carry a modifying wash over the darker areas.

3 After being given a good stir around, the wash mixture was added as described on pp. 109–11, treating separately each section defined by the

OPPOSITE ABOVE
Water-colour: *Rhododendron campylogynum*

BELOW
Water-colour: ivy leaf

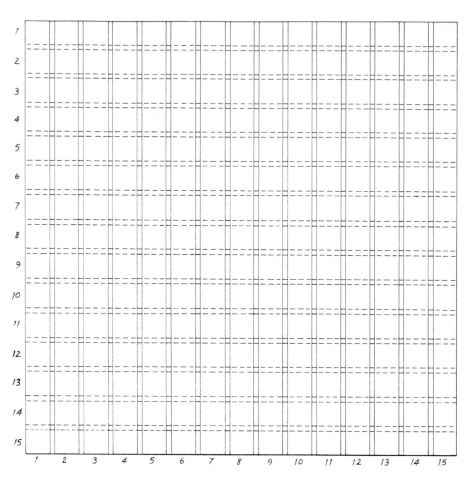

80 Layout for exercise
using overlying colours.
Numbers correspond with
those in list of colours on p.
100, except 15 which may
be used for a shadow mix

main veins running out from the point of insertion of the petiole to the centre of each major lobe. Each of these veins provided a line at which the wash could conveniently be halted before moving on to the next section. As each new piece was started a minute gap was left to define the vein in white. The lower lobe contained several much lighter areas and these were described by a steeply gradated wash with more pigment added again towards the tip of the leaf to give a reverse gradation. At the completion of this phase the leaf appeared as segments divided by five white veins in a green wash grading away to white paper in places.

4 Next the minor veins were shown. As mentioned earlier, the aim with tiny veins is to give an accurate impression without following each nerve to its microscopic conclusion. The method used was that described on p. 114, using a flattened moist brush-tip. The edges of the main veins were also softened by the same process.

5 By the time the venation was completed the wash was thoroughly dry, and another layer was added in places using dry-brush, working away from the light areas towards the dark. This second layer reinforced subtly shaded places such as where the leaf surface dipped in slightly on the right of the midrib and the numerous points where veins caused similar changes. When this addition had dried, it was seen that some portions receiving less

light needed yet more pigment – this was dry-brushed delicately without disturbing the two under-coats. The final use of this colour was to add line (with an eroded grade 1 brush) to the right margin here and there where the thickness of the leaf was exposed.

6   While the last touches of green were drying, the petiole (leaf-stalk) was painted with a lightly loaded brush using carmine with small amounts of other hues. A second layer was then added to the left, shaded side of the stalk.

7   The pale yellow-green of the main veins was then put in; the smaller veins were already the correct colour, since incomplete removal of the wash pigment had left them pale green.

8   Next, well diluted permanent blue was dry-brushed sparingly over the lightest areas, bearing in mind that the more thickly coated adjacent greens would easily be lifted. Many artists leave highlights a stark white; to me this should be reserved for the very brightest shiniest surfaces, whereas any area of slight to medium gloss will, in natural conditions, reflect sky colour. An unobtrusive light blue adds realism.

9   For the final work on the leaf, a shadow colour was mixed of vermilion and French ultramarine in roughly equal amounts, with a brush point of yellow to give the mixture a slightly more neutral tint. This again was just drifted over the darker left lobes.

10   The shadow colour was then added as an even wash behind the leaf. This faintly gimmicky touch is inappropriate for most botanical topics, but it was fun to do in an exercise. After the even wash had dried, dry-brush was used to put more depth into the inner parts of the shadowed area; a hint of violet lake was also introduced. The outer edges of the shadows were faded away, using a moist brush-tip with clean water; and in the same way a small highlight was lifted out of the petiole.

SECOND PLANT SUBJECT On completion of the exercise based on a single leaf, you will have gained enough expertise and confidence to carry out a larger study such as that on p. 117. This painting of the common nasturtium *Tropaeolum majus* was thought of primarily as a water-colour exercise for this book and was kept simple for this reason. An example of a water-colour botanical study carrying a great deal more information about a plant is shown on p. 118 (top).

The nasturtium illustration puts into practice in full scale the exercises and information given earlier and tried out on the ivy leaf, so it is necessary only to note a few special features. Firstly, the flowers themselves bring to mind a factor that every botanical artist must recognize: though some petal hues are easily depicted in paint, others are quite impossible to capture with accuracy. It has to be accepted that neither the ingenuity of the manufacturer nor the skill of the artist can match the glowing colour seen in even quite common blooms. Curiously, when a painting is seen apart from its living model this lack is less evident.

A pigment used at full intensity in order to approach the depth of colour of the plant tissue will often appear far too dark in tone on paper – deep, rich colours produced by the interplay of light and living tissue may appear sadly heavy in a painting, even when the actual hue is within the range of the paint-box. The answer is to key your painting (and this applies to any colour medium used) to the brightness of the paper rather than the unrecordable light of the most vivid part of the flower. The tonal range available to the artist, from black to white, is only a portion of the scale in nature which in many flowers extends to brilliance rivalling sunlight. It is therefore often necessary to sacrifice colour intensity, and hence tone, to capture at least the illusion of brightness; though usually it is still possible, while keeping the overall tone of the flower light, to put in some saturated colour in portions that are less fully lit. An adjustment has also to be made in recording shadowed or darker areas: since brilliance beyond a certain fairly low level cannot be matched, it will be seen that unless shadows are reduced in compensation, the painting will be over-dark. Though this concept seems involved, you will realize the problem immediately you tackle a brightly hued bloom. In the nasturtium painting the shadows have been slightly muted – it is not hard to imagine how dull and heavy the flower would appear if the darker tones present in life were fully represented.

It has been argued that the botanical artist should not show shadows other than by a deepening of local colour, because shadow colour may obscure local colour. In practice only the extraordinarily ham-handed would allow this to happen to a point where the hue of any part of a plant would be in doubt. Shadows reveal form and they should be used with intelligence and restraint. Too much reliance upon shadow colour may have a deadening effect, the work will be greyed and the strength of shadow as a tool lost. In subtle hands, however, the application of shadow, usually at the final stages, will bring a work to life. Except on a light surface, and in the darkest portions, the viewer should not be made aware of shadow as a definite colour. On the lower lobes of the two larger nasturtium leaves, shadows have been used in this unobtrusive way – the green was also intensified, but it is the thin layer of shadow colour that gives the impression of undulation.

A final point about shadows is that they are rarely grey falling away into black. Shadow colours vary greatly in their make-up, depending upon factors such as the colour of the sky, surrounding local colours etc. This is especially important to the artist when handling light objects – white to pale coloured flowers are examples. A basic shadow mix (p. 116) may easily be qualified by an admixture of other hues to reflect correctly any particular situation.

Colour changes due to translucency should also be noted, as they convey extra information about the subject. Some leaves, for instance, will entirely block the passage of light, others vary in the extent to which they allow its transmission. Nasturtium leaves are relatively thick but, as may be seen in parts of the large leaf on the right of the illustration, light does pass through to some extent. Where the lobes are turned so that the light pierces them from behind, the quality of the colour changes from being a matt, fairly glaucous green, towards emerald. Provided that this shows in reproduction, those who 'read' the work as it was intended will recognize these areas as translucence. Though ambiguity is normally to be deplored in botanical illustration, there are inevitably some subtleties which only the perceptive will correctly interpret – just as sometimes delving is required to unravel some plant structures.

The translucent effect is achieved by the method used in adding bluish highlights to the ivy leaf. A gradated wash was applied tailing off in the outer lobes, and allowed to dry before the brighter green of translucence was put in with a lightly loaded brush. The whole leaf was then worked over with a darker green to simulate the rucking of the surface by the minor veins.

You may notice that the larger veins stand just proud of the lamina as they approach the centre – minute shadows indicate this feature. Another small item to observe is the red on the margins of the leaves, which also appears in lighter form on other parts. Coloured leaf edges, unless they are unusually prominent, are often missed even though they are present in innumerable often entirely unrelated species.

ERASURE Minute flaws may be taken off using the technique described for the manufacture of highlights, veins and the like, but bigger mistakes should be handled as follows: a large-sized brush should be used if there is space to do so; this is loaded with water which is transferred to the part for correction and left for a few seconds to allow the grains of paint to loosen while the brush is being squeezed into a semi-dry state. The brush-tip is then lightly taken over the area to soak up the freed pigment – initially little or no rubbing is necessary, since a full load of pigment will be lifted. This is washed out and another brush-load of clean water is applied to the correction with a soft rubbing motion. As the paint comes away, the brush is washed before being used to rub again. The sequence may be repeated until the point is reached where damage to the paper surface seems likely. Unfortunately, paper once coated with water-colour cannot be returned to its untouched state. A residue of pigment always remains – and attempts to take out the last vestiges are likely to spoil the paper surface. If the painting is intended primarily for reproduction, the offending portion may be left untouched provided that it can safely be omitted by the printer without leaving an unsightly gap: simply pencil around it with a request to leave out the encircled piece.

You may prefer to preserve the appearance of the finished painting by one of the following gambits. Sometimes, to return the paper to white, the only feasible method is to remove as much pigment as possible without damaging the paper as described above, and then, after drying, to use several thin coats of white tinted slightly to match the paper. This imperfect solution is rarely used in water-colour, partly because anticipating the difficulty of complete erasure leads one to take extra care; and almost always there is an alternative. Usually extra foliage etc. can be used to mask the error, once the bulk of the pigment has been lifted out and the work is completely dry. Occasionally something may have to be taken from what is otherwise an integral part of the painting – as where a section of leaf has to make room for flowers. This kind of correction is rarely completely successful: the removal of pigment cleanly from the edges of an irregular area requires not only patience and skill but also that the material to be inserted is darker than its surrounds in order to hide deficiencies underneath. If white or pale features are to be added, the use of gouache will almost certainly be required.

WHITE FLOWERS Portraying white flowers on a background that is itself white is a recurrent problem. On a single plate the best solution is to place the flowers against leaves, where this can be done without distortion; but in a series of white or pale-coloured flowers, this becomes boring by repetition. Another tactic is to shade petals so that they stand out some-what, but if the shadow is too dark it may be mistaken for pigmentation, and if it is too light, petals may disappear on printing. Also, this is disappointing to the eye – white flowers may be spectacular and it seems sad to loose them on the page. A strong outline would look out of place in a water-colour otherwise lacking line. In some situations a tinted ground works well, but coloured backings are better used with gouache or acrylics. Sometimes the area behind light flowers may be lightly shaded or coloured with a blurred outline, as in the shadow thrown by the ivy leaf on p. 118. This can look quite good, though when often repeated it seems contrived and also has an archaic air.

Gouache

There are many botanical subjects for which gouache is a sensible choice: these include plants which have a waxy bloom; those with a covering of densely felted hairs; and species with large white or pastel-hued flowers. Though the terms 'gouache' and 'body-colour' both refer to opaque water-colour, 'gouache' is more commonly used of a painting totally, or in the main, in opaque colour; and 'body-colour' is preferred when only portions of the work are opaque – in these instances phrases such as 'with touches of body-colour' are often used in descriptions.

As noted, gouache may be bought ready-mixed or it may be prepared by mixing Chinese white with ordinary transparent water-colours during the course of painting. The latter involves little inconvenience and has the advantage that the degree of opacity may be varied. Transparent water-colours may be dry-brushed over gouache to modify underlying hues.

Even the addition of a small quantity of white causes a radical change in the handling qualities and appearance of water-colour. The modified pigment is used in a more or less creamy consistency and applied in short vertical strokes as described in the section on dry-brush. The dilute wash style of typical transparent water-colour is not appropriate, as experiment will show. Coverage is excellent with gouache, enabling large areas of even colour to be built up with few coats. Depending to some extent upon the absorbency of the paper, it is best to avoid thick layers of paint, as these may be disturbed in adding further colours and may also crack or flake.

Any of the supports suitable for water-colour are appropriate for gouache, but less expensive papers and boards may also be used with success. As subjects which suggest the use of gouache are often light-toned, tinted papers are an advantage: the type known as Ingres is ideal.

In appearance a gouache may resemble a like topic treated in acrylics, and the 'feel' in use is not dissimilar in some respects, yet there is one distinctive characteristic in which they differ, which qualifies the use of each. On drying, acrylic colours become water-proof, and virtually limitless coats of differing colours may be added without disturbing the underlayers; but in adding moist pigment to a dried layer, where a blended effect is wanted, the added colour must be brushed out and/or diluted until it merges evenly. This is fairly difficult to do well. In contrast, gouache remains water-soluble when dry, and edges of added colours may be blended softly into their surrounds by using a moist brush-tip to recombine pigment grains.

Gouache is accommodating – mistakes may be painted over, and second thoughts indulged in a way that the discipline imposed by transparent water-colour would not allow. For all that, method is more effective than a random approach; and, as the handling qualities of gouache resemble those of acrylics, the sequence described in detail for acrylics on pp. 134–8 may be helpful.

The poppies (*Papaver* cultivar) illustrated on p. 135 are typical gouache subjects and would make a suitable choice for a first exercise in the medium. For these large light-toned blooms, a tinted (Ingres) paper seemed appropriate: this was heavy enough not to need stretching. Hues were all from the list of transparent water-colours (p. 100) converted to gouache, as each colour mix was prepared, by the addition of Chinese white. Though the other colours were in pans, white was squeezed from a tube each time it was needed, since a white pan would have been constantly sullied.

Drawing was done with a 2B pencil, as the tinted paper required a blacker mark than would have been possible from an HB without damaging pressure. A grade 3 sable brush was used for all but the hairs which were drawn in with a grade 0 sable.

After the pencil drawing was completed, the sequence was as follows:

1 White was used in several layers to build up the petals, with strokes following the venation – that is, radiating from the centre of each bloom. No attempt was made to achieve an overall even tone; rather, the tinted paper underneath was allowed to show through in places to suggest shadow: opposite in effect, but the same in principle, as allowing the white of the support in transparent water-colour to indicate lighter areas.

2 In contrast with the white petals, the unpainted ovaries, capped by stigmatic tissue, then appeared as disconcerting dark holes, so they were put in next using tiny amounts of various greens, blues and yellows mixed with white.

3 Next came the delicate pink of the petal margins. A mixture of alizarin and a touch of vermilion, with lots of white, was blended in by starting each stroke from the petal edge and merging it gently into the underlying coat.

4 Lightly shadowed parts of the petals were then brushed in using the transparent vermilion-ultramarine-yellow shadow mix noted on p. 116; white was not used here as this would have dulled the effect.

5 Having established shadows on the flowers, it was then feasible to show the filaments of the stamens in white against these darker portions. The filaments were then lightly tinted here and there with a brush moistened with dilute transparent green, before being completed by the addition of bright anthers of cadmium yellow brought to opacity by a small amount of white.

6 A first coat of light-toned bright green was then applied to all vegetative parts, using a mixture of sap green, lemon yellow and white. On the leaves this was kept thin enough to allow the pencilled veins to show through.

7 The same mixture was then darkened with more sap green and a little ultramarine for use on the leaves. It was brushed out thinly and blended in with the bright green underlayer on the lighter areas, and allowed to reach full intensity in the darker portions.

8 This colour was adapted for the shaded side of the stems by the introduction of cadmium yellow. A brush-tip just moistened with clean water softened the edge of the shadow.

9 The mixture used in stage 4 was then prepared for deeper shadows throughout. An especially careful touch was needed about the edges of the petals to ensure definition without either halting the shadow build-up too soon or adding rather too much and so giving the almost filmy structures too much weight.

10 The petals were completed by using the faintest tint of dilute transparent cadmium yellow dry-brushed on to suggest a dusting of pollen and reflected colour from the clustered anthers at the centres.

11 On nearing completion, it was clear that the lighter parts of the stems and bud needed heightening: this was done by adding lots of white to a combination of sap green and cadmium yellow.

12 This same mixture was used with yet more white to establish hairs, showing their characteristic downward inclination on all vegetative parts, using a grade 0 sable brush.

13 The final step was the application of the brightest highlights with white modified by a brush-point of ultramarine.

Though topics consisting mainly of light-toned elements may almost demand the use of gouache, it is of course not restricted to this usage. Some artists work almost exclusively in the medium, though perhaps more prefer to switch between the opaque and transparent forms of watercolour according to which best suits the subject in hand.

10 Acrylics

There are several reasons why the botanical artist who works with traditional materials should consider turning to this comparatively recent medium at least from time to time. These include the manufacturers' claim that acrylic polymer bound pigments are the 'most permanent medium for the artist yet created' – an important factor, even though many water-colours have lasted for hundreds of years without apparent deterioration. For me the great potential of acrylics lies in their flexibility: they may be diluted with water and used in almost the same way as water-colours; or, since the colours are waterproof once dry, they may be built up in transparent layers with as many coats as you wish without fear of the underlayers breaking up. Pigment may also be applied in a thick impasto: and glazes and scumbles may then be carried across this surface. Light colours can be painted over dark with ease, and it is a simple matter to carry out second thoughts – areas may be painted out and re-established at will. When used thinly the pigments dry slightly more slowly than water-colours.

Acrylic colours are ideal for some subjects: plants such as cacti with light spines against a dark ground, species with lots of white hairs – in fact any deeply pigmented object bearing light-coloured details. Some of the more subtle delights of using the medium are not easy to put into words, but will be discovered if you carry out the exercises described below.

A criticism sometimes used of acrylic colours is that they have a 'plastic' feel to them. To a degree this is valid where the paints are used in impasto (though for me this quality is not marked) but not where they are used thinly as in botanical illustration.

Equipment

ACRYLIC PAINTS Though in one maker's catalogue thirty-eight hues are offered, I use only twelve colours, including three that haven't been called on for years. This means that I have been working on and off for a long period with fewer acrylic pigments than were recommended for the *basic* water-colour set. I have painted hundreds of plant species using this small number of hues, without difficulty in mixing required colours other than the rose-purple mentioned in the last chapter. This is probably because the ease with which acrylic pigments may be applied in thin successive transparent layers, until the right effect is obtained, allows more or less primary colours to be used in glazes, each modifying the other so that virtually any colour may be obtained in this way. With experience, these results can be planned, as the method allows hints of the underlying colours to show through in greater or lesser degree, giving a richness to the whole. With water-colours a more direct approach is preferable to preserve the characteristic freshness of the medium and so hues are mixed from the wider range in an attempt to get them right in one or two moves. Whatever the reason, there is no doubt that fewer colours are needed, and the following basic set is also quite sufficient for all botanical uses: 1 lemon yellow; 2 permanent yellow; 3 cadmium red; 4 crimson; 5 red purple; 6 ultramarine; 7 coeruleum; 8 Hooker's green; 9 white; and a 250 ml tin of white primer.

ADDITIVES It is possible to buy a number of items that may be mixed with acrylic paints for different purposes. There are mediums to give gloss and matt finishes; transparent glazes; water tension breakers; and retarders to slow drying. For most botanical illustration they are not vital. The most useful is the water tension breaker; this may be added when one is working on a poorly absorbent surface and is also helpful in assisting washes to flow on evenly.

VARNISHES If acrylic paintings are to be exposed to the air for lengthy periods in exhibitions etc., they should either be framed behind glass or varnished for protection. When acrylics are used more or less in a water-colour mode, varnish will be inappropriate, and a painting will then be matted and glassed; but where layers of paint have been built up so that the general effect is that of a work in oils, the work is treated accordingly and varnish is then an advantage. Gloss varnish in particular gives an added glow to colours. Protective varnishes for acrylics are removable with white spirit or turpentine.

Though the surface of an acrylic painting framed without glass is tough enough to be cleaned periodically with warm water and a little soap, a protective varnish is strongly advised as cleaning may damage the very thinnest paint layers, especially if a glaze medium has not been used. If a work has been allowed to get dirty, such layers may be obliterated quite unconsciously. For example the artist may in places have quietened a brilliant yellow with a film of transparent grey which could all too easily be removed.

BRUSHES There is little doubt that acrylics shorten brush life. Even when washed out thoroughly they still tend to wear faster than when used for water-colours. For this reason it is sensible to keep separate sets for each medium. A fine quality water-colour brush will last for many years in a near-original state, but the same brush will begin to break down quite quickly if in regular use with acrylics. Unfortunately, cheaper brushes are no solution; the demands of botanical subjects are the same when working in either medium and sable brushes remain without peer for the finest work.

For a selection of brushes, the advice given in chapter 9 applies equally here. An addition worth making for acrylics is a grade 8 flat hog-hair; pigments straight from the tube take a certain amount of manipulation before every particle is dissolved into the diluting water, and this accelerates brush wear; hog-hair is preferable to sable for this operation since it is cheaper and the stiff hairs do a quicker job of mixing. A larger brush, about grade 12, of the same kind, is ideal for use in priming.

SUPPORTS Acrylic paints may be used on almost any surface, excepting a few such as glass where smoothness makes adhesion doubtful. For botanical subjects I prefer a sturdy illustration board instead of paper, though the choice is largely subjective. If the best qualities of acrylics are to be exploited, a heavier ground feels more appropriate. As the medium is so undemanding, you may like to experiment – for example, a hardboard panel lightly sanded and primed gives good results. As noted above, an entirely smooth surface may give problems, but otherwise any rag paper or board, wood, hardboard, canvas or other fabric may be found suitable if it possesses a slight tooth or grain. As with water-colour, light-weight papers should be stretched to avoid cockling.

PALETTES Disposable palettes of white tear-off sheets are available, but I favour a white china plate – its shape permits wetter mixes to be made in the recessed base portion, which can afterwards be wiped clean with a paper towel; the rim is ideal for arranging dabs of colour straight from the tubes and for mixing small amounts of dryish pigment. Its white colour allows other hues to be seen without distortion, and it is easily cleaned after use – dried paint peels away freely under hot water.

Once acrylics dry they become waterproof, and when mixed colours are needed for a lengthy task this can be a nuisance. Where for instance a number of leaves are to receive the same undercolour, if the pigment is mixed on the flat surface of the plate it will dry before the coat is completed: at least the edges will almost certainly congeal to be picked up by the brush and deposited on the painting as fragments. There are two solutions: a commercial retarder will slow drying significantly but is tricky to use because if a mistake is made in the amount added – 6 drops to 2.5 cm (1 in.) of pigment is the rule – the reverse effect occurs and drying is hastened. When only 5 mm ($\frac{3}{16}$ in.) of paint is required, it is easy to squeeze out too many drops of retardant. The more acceptable solution is to slow the rate of evaporation by mixing larger amounts of paint into high-sided narrow-mouthed containers; an ideal size is about 6 cm ($2\frac{1}{2}$ in.) in diameter and 3.5 cm ($1\frac{1}{2}$ in.) high. This reduces the area of surface exposed to moving air, and even a shallow layer of pigment at the bottom will last in usable condition for hours rather than the minutes that would have been available otherwise. The life of the mix may be further extended if the jar is covered.

WATER-JAR The same criteria apply as for water-colour.

LIGHT-WEIGHT DRAWING-BOARD This will be needed for the purpose described in the previous chapter, unless stiff heavy-weight supports are used.

MISCELLANEOUS In the main the same items needed for water-colours are also useful here; in addition, if you prefer primed surfaces, a few hard pencils, 3H to 6H, should be included: priming paint creates an abrasive ground which takes the sharp point from softer pencils too quickly – in making outlines a 3H or even harder pencil will behave much as an HB does on a more yielding surface.

Techniques

If you intend to use acrylics more or less as water-colours, you will find that most of the techniques described in chapter 9 may be applied: though as acrylics dry waterproof, the methods for lifting off paint to remove errors and to put in venation or highlights cannot be used.

To get the best from acrylics, you should not use them as substitutes for water-colours, or for oils for that matter. The medium should be enjoyed for its own strengths, explored below. Acrylics may also be used in an impasto with or without the aid of a palette knife, but this technique is generally outside the requirements of botanical topics and is mentioned only in passing as a possible option for special purposes.

PRIMING This is a good point at which to test the difference between working on a primed surface and an unprimed one. Much depends upon the type of support used and personal preference. The colour trial exercise described below may be carried out on both primed and unprimed board so that your own assessment may be made. Once the priming is completed, it takes little time to repeat the exercise on an unprimed surface while waiting for coats to dry. Thick card or illustration board is suitable as this will provide a hard-wearing record.

The object of priming is to create a sealed surface which will bond with colours while not allowing them to be taken into the underlying support. Colours applied thinly on a primed material will dry with a faint semi-gloss, whereas the same mixture used on an unprimed surface may sink in to dry with a matt finish. The difference in effect is slight, and depends a good deal upon variables, but some highly absorbent supports are often clearly improved by priming, as are some hard non-absorbent grounds upon which a first coat of colour may be slow to establish. Though priming before a painting is started may seem tedious, it is quickly done.

White priming paint should be applied with the grade 12 hog-hair brush. Dilute the pigment with water to a thin creamy consistency, thin enough to dry without leaving brush marks yet thick enough not to run too freely down the tilted board; a slope of about 30° is again convenient. Even though acrylics are best used in a slightly less dilute form than water-colour, a slanted surface allows the pigment to move down the sheet which helps in achieving an even coat. Do not go back over any area which is semi-dry as the surface will then be marked with brush strokes – this is a general rule when using acrylics. To avoid moving into partly dry paint when priming a large area, sections should be primed in turn as shown in fig. 81. By the time the moist lower working edge of each section is carried down to the bottom of the sheet, the top edge adjoining the next section should be touch dry. Two or three thin coats usually give a better finish than one thick one. Though no difficulty will be found in seeing the progress of the first layer of white paint against the white ground, due to differences in whiteness and texture, it is sometimes not easy to see where sections of subsequent coats begin and end. This is overcome by putting a pencil mark on the furthest margin of each section. After the first coat, which is absorbed and dried quickly, subsequent layers may remain moist rather longer.

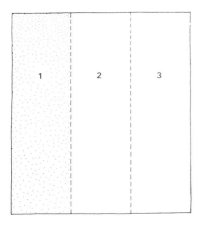

81 Priming in sections (left-handed persons should reverse the sequence)

Enough layers of primer must be used to ensure that there are no missed portions however small, otherwise a blotchy effect will result when paint inside such 'windows' is absorbed more readily and these spots will stand out as being slightly darker than their surrounds. Too many coats of primer create another problem: though the primer film should be smooth and unmarked by brush-strokes, if the layers are too thick they may completely fill the minute depressions that form the tooth or grain of the support. This will create a slick surface on which diluted colours may be dislodged by brush pressure when further coats are added. You will generally be conscious of the possibility of super-smoothness creeping in and stop priming well short of this point, but sometimes paint will 'take' better on some parts than on others, and tooth may disappear from these areas well in advance of the rest. The remedy is to use yet more primer on the offending places, using less dilution so that the stiffer pigment can be 'teased' and worked with the brush to a finely textured finish.

COLOUR RECORD A sensible first step is to provide a permanent record of the appearance of each colour, much as was done with water-colour. Again, a number of panels should be drawn up so that each colour may be represented, plus a few extra to allow for later purchases. However, for acrylics, as white is added on occasion as a means of lightening a colour (rather than to change the mode of use, as in transmuting water-colour to gouache), enough panels should be drawn so that the effect of adding white may be demonstrated on the same sheet as the pure colours.

Hues may be put down in the same order as in the list on p. 128 to give a convenient progression from yellows through reds and blues etc.

When the priming has been completed and the required numbers of panels have been drawn for the first exercise on both the primed and the unprimed boards, painting can begin. As panels will remain moist for some minutes, enough of each colour should be mixed to allow four or five rectangles to be painted at a time. When the last in the sequence receives its first layer, the initial one will be dry and waiting for a second coat. Allow half or so of each area to remain with one or at most two coats while the rest is built up until the hue reaches maximum intensity; you will then have a record of the appearance of each colour in two strengths.

Colours should be fairly well diluted though not quite to the same extent as a water-colour wash. A very slight creaminess should remain. Add the paint with a grade 3 brush using short vertical strokes from top to bottom of each panel, working from side to side. The first coat usually dries with an even finish, but if there happen to be a few small blemishes these will be obscured as additional layers are put down, until each colour at full intensity is represented by an area without flaw.

PASTEL SHADES The next step is to see how colours behave when white is added to lighten them. As in gouache, the pigments become opaque and fewer coats are needed to reach maximum strength. These pastel shades are invaluable in creating *large* even areas of colours at a lessened density. Though lighter versions of colours are achieved, they lose something of their brilliance – and for small areas the direct route of watered down colour is perhaps the best as the quality of the hue is unimpaired. However, when the colour to be matched is itself a pastel shade the addition of white is the most appropriate approach.

As noted above, *large* areas of colours used at less than full intensity are best achieved by the use of pigment admixed with white. But it is difficult to control a big area of diluted colour in acrylics because edges dry in hard lines that are impossible to take out (though see also p. 137). A water-colour wash technique is also unsatisfactory since acrylics used in this way generally do not dry completely evenly, particularly on primed board. Yet in spite of these reservations, problems are not often encountered – the working area for a botanical subject is usually small enough to be tackled directly without a white admixture.

There are several points to make about pastel shades. Where the admixture of white has caused loss of brilliance, it is often possible partly to recover this by adding a thin overlayer of pure colour. Provided small sections are handled at a time this may be very successful. Another feature is that though acrylic colours in general tend to dry marginally darker (in contrast to water-colour) than they are when wet, this is more marked when white is a component. When, for example, a leaf painted in a pastel green is darkened by adding a slightly deeper hue still containing white, it is difficult to assess the amount of pigment needed to reach the correct tone for the new mix: you will find the darker colour hard to apply so that the edges brush out to make a smooth transition into the paler area, because when wet the edges will appear to dissolve into the surround, only to be glaringly visible as they dry. The solution, when working with colours containing a significant proportion of white, is to work from *dark* to *light*, rather than from mid-tones to dark and then back to light as detailed below.

COLOUR MIXING As mentioned in the water-colour chapter, if *pure* primary colours were available to the artist, very few pigments would be required; but as this is not the case, it is as well to be familiar with likely results from elementary mixes, especially the sequence moving from red, yellow and blue (primaries), to orange, purple and green (secondaries). The secondaries are obtained by equal mixtures of the pairs: yellow + red, red + blue, blue + yellow, respectively. Lemon yellow is close to being a primary colour, but the available blues and reds lie on either side of the primaries cyan and magenta – and it is worth exploring all the following combinations to obtain a record of the various results.

1 Lemon yellow + cadmium red, cadmium red + coeruleum, coeruleum + lemon yellow.

2 Lemon yellow + crimson, crimson + ultramarine, ultramarine + lemon yellow.

3 Lemon yellow + crimson, crimson + coeruleum, coeruleum + lemon yellow.

The last example contains some duplications, but the combinations are best carried through in sequence (fig. 82) in order to see the complete

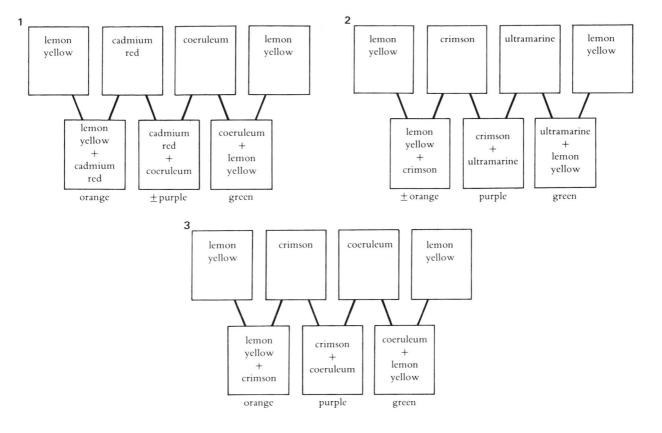

movement from near-primary colours to secondary colours in each instance.

Note the differences in character of the secondary colours, depending upon the reds, blues and yellows chosen. In the first set the orange and green are clear and fresh; but the purple is quite close to brown, because the red and the blue in this instance both have a slightly yellow bias which contaminates what otherwise could have been a pure purple. Similarly, in the second example the orange is unsatisfactory due to the hint of blue in crimson, and the green is dulled because ultramarine contains red. The purple here is rather better than the first example yet still far from the clear colour often required. In the final set the orange and the green have been repeated from the other combinations, the purple is new, and this also has been spoiled, this time through the presence of yellow in coeruleum.

The process can be carried further by mixing combinations of secondary colours, and of secondaries and primaries. Unexpected colours may be produced until the habit of analysis is acquired. For instance, when you recognize that the failure to produce a good purple from the equal mixture of cadmium red and coeruleum is due to the presence of yellow in these colours, and that this contaminant in fact creates a colour close to a chocolate brown, you will see that the familiar 'red and green make brown' may also be expressed as 'red, blue and yellow make brown provided that the correct quantities of each are used'. And, of course, since the amounts required in all colour mixes depend upon the characteristics

82 Colour mixtures

133

of the reds, blues and yellows concerned, it is helpful to think of each of these in terms of their relationship to pure primaries.

Though you will discover many useful colours through the above experiments, they will not include a purple of sufficient purity to be used either on its own or in combinations to paint flowers in the red-purple range. Red-purple is a colour that has to be purchased. My own is satisfactory when used on its own though it tends to become leaden when mixed with other hues, and it is also too opaque: these qualities can be to some degree neutralized by using it as a base colour which may be modified by transparent glazes of other hues – a solution similar to that described for water-colour (p. 119) in obtaining a purplish-blue.

As with water-colour, an excellent black may be achieved by the combination of red and blue with a touch of yellow, and variations of this mixture in dilute form provide basic shadow colours. A preferred recipe for shadow colours is roughly equal parts of cadmium red and ultramarine, though the red may be replaced by crimson where a slightly less grey quality is needed.

To assess the effect obtained by using each colour in turn as an underlayer and as a modifying glaze, try the same exercise in acrylics as was described for water-colours (fig. 80). The aim is to show each colour as it appears underneath and on top of each of the other colours.

The exercises so far, though fairly time-consuming, will provide a useful permanent record; but there will doubtless be some readers who will be content simply to read about trying out their colours without going so far as to carry out the work. Yet the novice in this medium might use even more time getting to know how the paints behave by doodling in an unstructured way than by carrying out the suggested first steps.

PAINTING METHOD Whether or not these trials have been completed, I would urge you to follow the next procedure – the principle of working from light to mid-tone to dark, then from dark to light – as it forms the core of much botanical work in this medium.

The portion of the leaf on p. 136 is a convenient topic to use in acquiring foundation techniques. In this instance it may be better to copy the illustration than to look for a leaf showing all the characteristics included. The steps given below, though also applicable to a host of non-botanical subjects, are ones which I adopt almost invariably in working on plants. From the point when the drawing is completed (in HB pencil on unprimed and 4-6H on primed board) the sequence is as follows:

1 Lightest tones. Assess the lightest *local* colour present: that is, the actual colour of the plant, or portion of the plant, that is lightest in tone, ignoring transitory effects of the light which may produce highlights or bright areas. Frequently the lightest-toned colour will be found on stems, petioles, veins etc. Where this colour covers a significant area, difficult to define here but usually obvious in practice, it is generally sensible to paint it first, using well diluted pigment. Such portions can be put in later, but leaving them white and hence over-bright until the final stages often creates a slight problem in maintaining a correct tonal balance. In the illustration

134

Keith West

the veins were the lightest local colour and were established first with a grade 3 sable (used throughout) in a thin mixture of greenish-yellow.

2 Middle tones. The basic overall colour underlying both shadows and highlights may be thought of as a 'middle tone'. (As used here the term does not describe a tone mid-way between black and white as shown in the scale on fig. 13 – though it may coincidentally be so – but refers to the middle tone of a particular subject. In this context a light-coloured leaf will have a middle tone above the mid-point on the absolute scale, and a dark-coloured leaf will have a middle tone below the mid-point. The ambiguity exists only in writing – the concept presents no problems in the actual work sequence. You may prefer the term 'ground-colour', or perhaps 'underlying colour', yet these also are faintly ambiguous.) The green used as the middle tone in the illustration, a mixture of Hooker's green and a little permanent yellow, was brushed thinly over the whole illustration except the veins. The areas between the veins and the bounds of the illustration formed convenient sections to work in, removing any concern about the moist leading edge of the pigment drying. Almost always an element of planning in this respect is sensible, to avoid having to hide lines of dried pigment. If this seems likely the edge in question should be brushed out so that it fades into the white support surface. A thin paint layer can be blended in later to leave little or no blemish.

More often than not leaves etc. present faintly mottled colours, but if the subject demands a perfectly even middle-tone, a cautious approach using several thin coats is recommended.

3 Darker tones. The middle tone dried almost immediately with such a thin paint film, and the same mix was then used to darken the areas running in to shadow. This procedure is tricky and often calls for the use of a finger-tip as well as the brush. Strokes were applied leading away from the light – from right to left in the illustration. A right-hander might find it easier to turn the board around and reverse the movements. The aim was to start the darkening process from the points on the leaf which appeared gradually to deepen in tone as the surface curved out of the light, and to make the transition so smooth that the beginning of the change was imperceptible. The action of stroking the brush away from the light carries pigment in the same direction, and this helps to blend in the leading edge. Often this is not enough and the merging of the layers has to be assisted by mopping up excess around the point at which each blending stroke begins. This must be done with speed before the pigment begins to settle in, and the only practicable tool that I have found to do the job is the tip of a free finger on the same hand that holds the brush. Three or four blending strokes with the brush are made, moving down the sheet, the finger-tip is then used to dab away a minute amount of moist paint, and because the area is still damp, pigment from the wetter parts of the strokes will ease back partially into the blotted bits to aid in blending. The dabbing action has to be fast to allow the paint to be brushed to its destination before drying: in this case to a vein or the boundary of the leaf. Drying pigment should not be allowed to build up on the finger or crumbs of paint will eventually break away and transfer to the work.

OPPOSITE ABOVE
An example of work in acrylics: dandelion, *Taraxacum officinale*

BELOW
Leaf section (magnified) demonstrating acrylic technique

Each section was completed in this way, moving down the sheet three or four strokes at a time. One darkening coat is seldom enough, and for this illustration three were used, each beginning a fraction further away from the light. Finally, for the deepest shadow, the green hue reached its maximum intensity – additional layers would then have altered only the thickness of the film without other visible effect.

4 Shadows. With the broad areas of light and shade defined, the study still looked rather dull. It is at this stage that the fun really begins. The next move was to deepen the shadows yet further by adding to the dark areas a shadow mixture of more or less equal parts of cadmium red and ultra-marine well diluted. This was brushed on thinly as described for step 3. Though small imperfections in blending were lost in the surrounding deep tone, the use of a finger-tip was still needed here and there. As noted for water-colour, except on very pale surfaces and in the darkest areas, shadow colour should not be evident. In the leaf portion illustrated the deep shadows are not seen as a distinct colour, just a hint of purple in the green, yet their presence makes a major difference in bringing the leaf surface to life.

5 Modifiers. The next phase is the introduction of colours to modify underlayers that have not worked quite as planned, or simply to suggest overlying hues – as in the present exercise where parts are suffused with a hint of warmth. A watered-down cadmium red was used which gave an effect of chestnut brown owing to the green under-colour showing through.

The veins then received another coat; this contained white to render the greenish-yellow more opaque, with the intention of breaking and blurring the hard green edges. The paint was mixed to a fairly thick consistency and put on in tiny dabs which were worked with the brush-point until the required effect was gained. The veins then appeared too chalky because of the added white and so were modified by the thinnest glaze of dilute permanent yellow followed by a little shadow colour. The cadmium red mix was used towards the base of the midrib to give a further lively touch. This time the red acquired an orange tinge through the presence of yellow in the midvein. Note that the cadmium red yielded two colour effects: chestnut over green, and orange over yellow.

6 Highlights. The final step was to define the highlights by blending in a mix of white with a hint of coeruleum. They were slowly brought to full intensity by putting on the pigment in layers using a lightly loaded brush. This was first tested on the protective sheet until each stroke left only a ghost-faint mark. For the brightest part of each highlight extra white was added.

As this sequence is basic to the practice of botanical illustration in acrylics, it will be found helpful for virtually all plant subjects. When you have mastered the above technique you will be equipped for a full-scale topic such as that shown on p. 136.

The subject chosen for this illustration is the widely available dandelion, *Taraxacum officinale*. After the quite complex drawing had been completed, the painting progressed as follows – the sequence being in accord with that described for the last exercise. A grade 3 brush was used throughout, except where a finer tip was needed for minute detail.

1 A pale green mix of dilute ultramarine and permanent yellow established the leaf midribs and the stems of the flowering/fruiting heads.

2 Bright translucent leaf areas were then suggested, using a light-toned lime-green mixed from Hooker's green and permanent yellow.

3 A middle-tone (see p. 137) green mixed from Hooker's green, permanent yellow, ultramarine, and cadmium red formed the basic coat for the leaves. This was blended in to skirt the edges of the translucent portions.

4 Second and third coats of the same mix were applied to darken parts of the leaves to show modelling.

5 Green sections of the flower, the fruiting head and the bud towards the plant base, were put in, modifying the mixture of step 3 with touches of various other colours as required.

6 A satisfactory brown for the clustered fruits of the dandelion 'clock' was also obtained from the step 3 mix by adding crimson and a hint of ultramarine.

7 The feathery *pappus* of the 'clock' had been indicated earlier in very faint pencil in the under-drawing. This was lightly reinforced in paint, using a much diluted shadow mixture of cadmium red and ultramarine modified by permanent yellow – avoiding the already painted fruits and reflexed bracts. Where the pappus passed over these portions it was defined by a network of fine white lines applied with a grade 0 brush.

8 The same shadow mixture was also used on darker portions of the flower head; it was then painted over with a transparent mixture of permanent yellow and lemon yellow, using several coats to build up intensity in parts. To gain the richer hue of the capitulum centre, a minute amount of cadmium red was added to the yellows.

9 Dilute crimson was used for the tips of the *phyllaries*, the lower midribs of the leaves and the peduncles.

10 Shadowed portions throughout were put in with the mix of step 7, with a succession of several layers to approach black in the darkest places.

11 Highlights of white qualified by coeruleum blue (applied as described in the last exercise) added the final lively touches throughout.

11 Photography

As I stressed in chapter 2, I am concerned here with photography as an aid to botanical illustration – as a means of recording information about a subject when, for a variety of reasons, it may not be easily obtainable from live material. Any advice given is therefore relevant only to this aspect of taking photographs and is not intended as a guide to plant photography for its own sake.

Choice of camera brand and general instruction in camera use are beyond the range of this book, but most libraries will have lots of books covering these topics. The best kind of camera for botanical work is a single lens reflex (SLR) with either a macro-lens or a set of close-up lenses. A camera of this type is expensive, and so is a macro-lens. Close-up lenses are relatively cheap and will do a perfectly adequate job, though it is annoying to have continually to put them on and take them off when working on a number of species at a time.

A primary consideration is whether to use colour prints or colour transparencies. Transparencies record colour much more accurately but are too small to work from. This can be overcome with a device consisting of a miniature screen, housed in a cabinet, on to which a slide is back-projected so that you can sit close to it and work directly from the enlarged image. Though convenient, this aid is expensive for limited or infrequent use. My own choice is to use colour prints: they can be handled quite roughly, stored easily, and if sensible field practice has been followed (see below) measurements may be taken off and converted as required. They do, however, deteriorate over the years.

A high-speed film is helpful. Though the larger grain size can minutely affect detail, this is not discernible unless exposures have been made in poor light. ASA/ISO 400 colour print film is sold from most outlets and this allows photography in conditions from brilliant sunlight to deep shade. This flexibility may well be needed in the kinds of circumstances that make photography necessary: in mountains, for example, changes in light during the course of a day may be extreme. Another virtue of fast film is that it will permit photography in the windiest conditions – with an exposure of 1/500 sec. and above, even the most wildly whipping plant will be frozen crisply – if you can keep it in focus. A partner can help to some extent in providing shelter, though if much work is to be done in strong winds, the construction of a screen may be called for. I have not found a tripod essential in photographing plants. The purpose of a tripod is to avoid blurring due to camera-shake – and this problem is largely overcome by using high-speed film. There are occasions when a high f-stop is needed to gain maximum depth of field, and this, depending on lighting, may entail a fairly long exposure – but if one can move into a position in which the camera is firmly braced without the kind of tension that leads to quivering, then excellent results may still be obtained even with exposures of up to 1/8 sec. However, exposures of longer than 1/60 sec. are risky, and if a tripod is available it should certainly then be used. Many SLR cameras have a self-timer, which is worthwhile when exposures of 1/60 sec. or longer are involved as it removes the danger of jarring the camera when pressing the shutter-release button. A flash attachment solves the problem of poor lighting but usually this is not vital.

Many plant photographers find a tripod indispensable because they view flowers more often than not from above. But the botanical artist's camera work is usually done from a position where each section of the plant in question is viewed at eye-level. Unless one is working on taller species, a great deal of time is spent lying down. In this position the body can act as a tripod. The camera, pressed gently against the face, forms the apex of a triangle described by the fore-arms and the distance between the elbows as they rest on the ground; the upper arms and shoulders also give firm support. The height of the camera above the ground may be adjusted by moving the elbows further apart or closer together.

Each exposure should be recorded in a notebook with all relevant details. These will include the species name, the part of the plant photographed – whole habit, upper, mid, lower, inflorescence, detail of flower, detail of calyx, detail of leaf from mid-stem, and so forth. Rapid sketches may be needed here and there to help with details that experience teaches will be obscured on the print – for example, light-coloured stamens and/or stigmas. As colour prints invariably drift towards the blue or the red ends of the spectrum, notes should be taken about critical hues. Probably the most accurate method is to quote from the 800 colour variants shown in the excellent Royal Horticultural Society colour chart; though recording may also be conveniently done by using colour-pencils; or by noting the actual pigment names in the medium to be used for the finished illustration. If film can be processed and printed quickly, it is worthwhile to compare the print with the living plant; colour notes may then be added lightly to the back of the print to indicate the amount of drift that has occurred. In any case, two visits to a locality are often needed, as there will always be one or two exposures that would be better repeated. This problem might be overcome by using one of the newer polaroid-type cameras, but detailed colour notes will be essential.

The light of early morning and evening has a reddish cast which is recorded by sensitive film; yet there are situations where one is obliged to work at these times – prairies and coasts, for instance, may breed vicious winds around mid-day that make photographing flowers, especially those on slender springy stems, all but impossible. On these occasions extra care should be taken to make accurate colour notes.

Plant photographs are best taken when the sun is partly screened by a thinnish layer of cloud – not too thick otherwise shady spots, forest interiors and the like, will become too dark, but just enough to blur hard-edged shadows.

Sometimes there is little choice, and one should be aware of the likely effects of working in direct sunlight. Deep shadows contrast over-strongly with the lighted surrounds, so that if exposure is correct for the lighter portions, the shadows will appear on the print as indecipherable black areas. And, if the shadowed parts are correctly exposed, sun-splashed pieces will be burnt into white splodges. Averaged exposures may be more or less satisfactory; but exposures ranging over several f-stops provide a better hope of success. In bright sunlight even slightly glossy leaves will lose local colour and become pale blue in reflecting the sky, and colours on the whole may seem slightly washed out. A polarizing filter should cut reflected light to an acceptable level.

There are other ways of negating the worst effects of direct sun. A companion can stand so as to throw a shadow over the subject provided that the plant is small enough, but make sure that no splash of sunshine remains visible through the viewfinder, as this could distort the exposure somewhat, or at least ruin what otherwise could have been a pleasing print. A colourless translucent plastic sheet may also be useful on occasion to diffuse the sun's rays; and where shadows are too contrasty, a fill-in light may be introduced by placing a white piece of cardboard on the shadowy side of the subject to serve as a reflector.

A recurrent problem when photographing flowers in close-up is that of capturing the details of white or light-coloured blooms backed by dark foliage; this is related to the difficulty mentioned above of adequately treating subjects involving high contrast through the juxtaposition of sunlight and shadow. The solution is much the same: to make exposures over several f-stops. To ensure that all-important floral details are rendered clearly it is as well to include one or two frames that are distinctly underexposed. This is best done by turning the f-stop ring to a higher number than that indicated by the exposure meter, so reducing the aperture and hence light entry (another way is to increase shutter-speed, but that is slightly more fiddly). The prints will probably show flowers somewhat greyed and surrounded by amorphous gloom, but features such as stamens, stigmas etc. should be well-defined; faint colouring often seen in petal-tips, ovaries and so on (which might vanish with a 'normal' exposure) may then be decipherable if one mentally strips off the shadowy overlying grey, and even such minutiae as petal venation may be captured. The reduced aperture also increases depth of field.

Each exposure should be recorded as it is made; it is almost impossible to remember details later. It is invaluable to have a partner to carry out this work – notes are inclined to be much more complete if they may be dictated while each operation is carried through.

Measurements must be taken for each plant even though voucher specimens are also collected where possible: distortion in dried specimens sometimes makes accurate measurement and the identification of a particular organ photographed next to impossible. Every exposure entered in the notebook should be accompanied by at least one measurement. In each case dimensions taken can be correlated with those present in the photograph – and this gives a key to all dimensions in each print. For example, a flower detail photographed in close-up measures 4.45 cm across on the living plant; the same feature on the print might be perhaps 6.6 cm. By calculation it will be found that any dimension on the print will be restored to its measure in life (in perspective) when multiplied by a factor of 0.67: that is, if 6.6 cm on the photo equals 4.45 cm on the subject, $1 = 4.45/6.6 = 0.67$. (The same principle can, of course, be applied to measurements in inches.) The use of the memory function of a pocket calculator for repeated multiplication by the same factor is recommended. It is preferable to take too many measurements rather than too few, as sometimes dimensions that otherwise appear almost superfluous may be used to check others where an error is suspected.

A convenient instrument for taking measurements is a metal spring-loaded pocket tape marked to millimetres or tenths of an inch.

As noted on p. 30, voucher specimens should always be taken when work is being done for a scientific purpose. Such specimens become doubly helpful when it is necessary to use photographs in making an illustration.

It is wise to protect the camera when working in harsh conditions. An ultra-violet filter kept permanently in place means that scratches and other damage will be sustained by the inexpensive filter rather than the expensive lens. It is good practice in rough country to keep the camera in a small pack on the back to minimize the chances of having it swing against rocks, trees etc., and also to keep it from the heat of the sun's rays which may be damaging in warmer climates.

Photographs in the studio are poor substitutes for living plants; yet good quality prints, backed up by notes, sketches and voucher specimens, may be sufficient for many purposes, as an aid towards illustration, especially when informed by experience and botanical knowledge.

In emphasizing that photographs at best can never be as valuable as live models I do not intend to devalue botanical photography as a mode of illustration in itself; as discussed in the Introduction, there is a place for the botanical artist and for the photographer. It is simply that the artist obliged to rely upon photographs is, even though aided by supplementary material, still largely limited to the information gathered through the lens – which is inevitably of a lower order than that to be taken from living tissue.

12 Preparing for the printer

If your work is to be reproduced, a knowledge of printing processes will be helpful and may be acquired from references such as Steinberg's *Five Hundred Years of Printing*, or the entry under 'Printing' in more recent editions of *The New Encyclopaedia Britannica*.

When illustrations are to appear in a particular journal, note the standard of reproduction shown in previous issues. It is senseless to use the finest detail when the printer is capable only of reproducing the coarsest of lines. Don't modify quality but do use an appropriate medium and technique.

You will be briefed as to whether to work in black and white or colour. Few scientific journals will print in colour unless colour is vital to the author's thesis, and even then this may depend on current economic conditions. Colour is still common in plant books of wide appeal such as those for the amateur botanist and the gardener, and fine prints of plant paintings remain popular.

REDUCTION AND ALIGNMENT Some illustrations will be in demand again and again, and recurrent use may pose difficulties of size and reduction. Diagrammatic rough sketches done at poster scale to illustrate a lecture have later appeared in a journal much reduced but still legible, then further reduced and quite illegible in a bulletin. As far as you can, try to retain control over the degree of reduction that your work receives. This is most important with line-drawings in ink destined for letterpress reproduction. Usually one-third reduction is suitable for drawings with fine lines; one-half reduction may be extreme. Photolithography can handle reductions greater than fifty per cent but the effects are difficult to visualize.

The printer will find it helpful if you put small 'L' shaped register marks in the corners of each plate – these will assist in placing the illustration in an upright position on the page. Dimensions between the marks should bear a relationship to the image area of the printed page. For example if the image area (that is, the area of the page actually covered by print) is 15×11 cm ($6 \times 4\frac{1}{3}$ in.) and your drawing has been done with a one-third reduction in mind for a full-page, then the dimensions between the marks should measure 22.5×16.5 cm ($9 \times 6\frac{1}{2}$ in.). The required printed size of the horizontal dimension may also be written lightly in pencil just below the lower pair of register marks; the printer will not usually need any other instructions on the plate, and the pencil marks are easily removed when the illustrations are returned. The above procedure should be discussed with the editor or printer as there may be 'house-rules' to observe.

A few plant illustrations look almost equally well placed upright, lying down, or even upside-down, and it is wise to indicate 'top' or 'bottom' in pencil on any work that may be misinterpreted.

LETTERING AND SCALE The printer may be asked to add lettering of an appropriate style to a plate; though more often instant transfer is put on by the artist. Lettering should be chosen with the amount of reduction in mind – in general, after printing, it should not appear larger than the type used for the text.

The manner of indicating the scale of an illustration will often leave room for choice. Sometimes a plate will require several different scales: the main portion, a plant habit perhaps, will be drawn at life-size or similar; dissections and like details may be magnified; hair-types etc. may be shown much enlarged – up to ×100 or so. There are two main methods of recording magnification. A series of plates of a single scale placed together in the text may be covered by a single note ('all figures ×2' - or whatever) at a point prior to their insertion, or the scale may be included in the individual captions. Alternatively, scales may appear on the plate itself alongside the subject or grouped in some way.

Magnification signs are open to error. When included in a note in the text, it is not unknown for that note to be omitted. Nor is it unknown for the dimensions of the publication, and so that of the plates, to be changed after preparation of the illustrations and the text: so where accuracy is most critical, it is lost. A neat single-line bar scale expressed in centimetres, millimetres or microns, is the best answer. If several such scales are to appear on one plate it may be convenient to group them in a corner as shown in fig. 65; the degree of magnification then remains on the illustration and will be valid no matter how much the size of the setting is changed.

Scales are often too heavy and obtrusive – they should not be allowed to dominate, though at the same time they should be easy to locate and to read.

PRESENTATION It is sound to present your creations as having some value. If work is grubby and without a protective cover when it is handed to the purchaser, author, editor or printer, it will be treated with the same lack of respect. Plates sent away in a manila folder bearing the request 'Please do not mark originals' are generally returned in good order. Sets of drawings, if small, should be placed in one container cut to size; if, say, full-page then it is best to give each plate its own folder and to provide a container for the set. For mailing, use *rigid* corrugated cardboard sheets to protect both front and back, cut so that the grooves of each sheet run in opposite directions to give extra stiffness and strength. Make sure that the name of the project – book, monograph, paper etc. – is marked lightly in pencil on the back of each illustration and more prominently on the container, which should also carry a return address.

It may be a considerable time after your illustrations have been sent away that they eventually appear in print: usually several months; occasionally longer. Other than for the smallest contributions you should receive a copy or copies. For some works it is sensible for the artist to collaborate with the printer – and then the opportunity may be available to obtain 'pulls'. Such examples of published illustrations should be saved to use in building a portfolio of impressive plant portraits.

Glossary of botanical terms used in the text

Some terms have several meanings: only those applicable to the particular usages in the text are included here.

Abscission The dropping away of plant parts, leaves etc.

Achene A simple dry one-seeded indehiscent fruit (fig. 32*h*). See also *Capsule, Follicle, Nut.*

Actinomorphic Used of a radially symmetrical or regular flower having more than one plane of symmetry (fig. 36 *d, e, f, h*).

Alternate Leaves, buds etc. placed singly along an axis or stem without being opposite or whorled.

Angiosperms Plant group in which seeds are borne within a matured ovary (fruit). See also *Gymnosperms.*

Androecium The male elements collectively, the stamens (fig. 35). See also *Gynoecium.*

Anther The pollen-bearing part of the stamen (fig. 35).

Areole A small pit or raised area, often carrying a tuft of hairs, glochids or spines.

Armature Collectively, barbs, hooks, prickles and spines on a plant.

Axil The upper angle between a branch(let), leaf or leafstalk (petiole), flower-stalk (peduncle or pedicel), and the stem from which it grows.

Axis The main or central line of development of any plant or organ; the main stem.

Basidiocarp A type of fungal 'fruiting' body such as the mushroom (fig. 15*a*).

Basifixed Attached by the base, as anthers may be joined to filaments (fig. 44*a*). See also *Dorsifixed.*

Berry Fleshy fruit which includes one or more carpels and seeds, but no true stone – grapes, tomatoes etc. (fig. 32*b*). See also *Drupe, Pome.*

Bract A modified, usually reduced leaf-like structure on an inflorescence.

Bud An embryonic shoot.

Bulb An underground storage organ comprised of fleshy scale leaves on a short axis (fig. 29*a*). See also *Corm.*

Bullate Blistered or puckered.

Bundle scar Mark on leaf scar left by vascular bundles at the time of leaf abscission (Fig. 26). See also *Leaf scar, Vascular.*

Calyx Sepals collectively. The outside floral whorl (fig. 42*a*).

Capitulum A close inflorescence of aggregated and usually sessile flowers in a compact head, as in a daisy (fig. 37).

Capsule A dehiscent dry fruit developed from two or more carpels (fig. 32*c, d*). See also *Achene, Follicle, Nut.*

Carpel An organ in angiosperms that encloses one or more ovules; a member of the gynoecium (fig. 35).

Carpellate Possessing or composed of carpels.

Column Structure found in orchids formed through union of stamens, styles and stigmas (fig. 43).

Compound leaf A leaf of two or more leaflets (fig. 16*d*).

Corm An erect bulb-like part of the stem as seen in *Crocus* and *Gladiolus*. See also *Bulb.*

Corolla Petals collectively.

Cotyledon Seed leaf. See also *Monocotyledon, Dicotyledon.*

Dehiscence The process of opening in an anther or fruit; hence *dehiscent* and *indehiscent* (not opening).

Dentate With sharp spreading coarse teeth, perpendicular to the margin.

Dicotyledon One of the two classes of angiosperms. Plants in this group have embryos with two cotyledons. See also *Cotyledon, Monocotyledon.*

Digitate Handlike, compound with elements originating from one point.

Disc florets The tubular actinomorphic flowers composing the central portions of flower heads of most Asteraceae (aster family or Compositae, composites) (fig. 37). See also *Ray florets.*

Dioecious Having staminate (male) and pistillate (female) flowers borne separately on different individual plants. See also *Monoecious.*

Dorsifixed Attached by the back, as anthers may be joined to filament (fig. 44*b*). See also *Basifixed.*

Drupe Fleshy fruit, with one seed enclosed by a hard covering; stone fruit (fig. 32*g*). See also *Berry, Pome.*

Entire With a continuous margin lacking teeth or indentations (fig. 19*a*).

Epigynous With sepals, petals and stamens apparently growing from the top of the ovary. See also *Hypogynous, Perigynous.*

Falls Outer whorl of perianth parts in an *Iris* flower (fig. 40).

Family The taxonomic group between order and genus.

Filament The stalk of a stamen (fig. 35).

Floral tube A cup or tube formed by the fusion of the basal parts of sepals, petals and stamens.

Floret Individual flower, especially of composites and grasses (fig. 37).

Follicle A dry, dehiscent fruit opening along one side, derived from a single carpel (fig. 32*i*). See also *Achene, Capsule, Nut*.

Gamopetalous With a corolla of one piece, the petals united, at least at the base. See also *Polypetalous*.

Genotype The genetic constitution of an organism. See also *Phenotype*.

Genus The taxonomic group between family and species. Plural *Genera*.

Gills Plates on the underside of the cap in some species of fungi (fig. 15*a*).

Glabrous Without hairs.

Glands Secreting organs (fig. 24).

Glochid A minute barbed spine or bristle, often in tufts, as seen in many cacti.

Gymnosperms Plant group in which seeds are not enclosed in an ovary (conifers etc.). See also *Angiosperms*.

Gynoecium The female elements collectively, the carpels (fig. 35). See also *Androecium*.

Habit Characteristic growth form of an organism.

Hyaline Thin and translucent (fig. 29).

Hypogynous With sepals, petals, and stamens attached to the receptacle below the ovary. See also *Epigynous, Perigynous*.

Imperfect flower Lacking either stamens or carpels. See also *Perfect flower*.

Indehiscent See *Dehiscence*.

Inferior Beneath or below, as an ovary that appears below the calyx. See also *Superior*.

Inflated Appearing blown up, bladder-like (fig. 42).

Inflorescence A flower cluster with a definite arrangement of flowers.

Irregular flower See *Zygomorphic*.

Keel The two lower united petals of a papilionaceous (pea-type) flower (fig. 41).

Lamina The blade or expanded portion of a leaf.

Leaflet One unit of a compound leaf (fig. 16*d*).

Leaf scar Mark left on site from which a leaf has fallen (fig. 26). See also *Bundle scar*.

Lenticel Small spongy openings in stems and other plant parts in surrounding impermeable tissues, allowing an interchange of gases between internal tissues and the atmosphere (fig. 26).

Linear Long and narrow with margins parallel or nearly so, as in grass leaves.

Monocotyledon One of the two classes of angiosperms. Plants in this group have embryos with one cotyledon. See also *Cotyledon, Dicotyledon*.

Monoecious Having staminate (male) and pistillate (female) flowers borne together on individual plants. See also *Dioecious*.

Mucro A short spur or spiny tip (fig. 19*f*).

Nectary A nectar-secreting gland, often formed as a pit, protuberance or scale (fig. 45).

Node Point on a stem where one or more leaves are attached.

Nut One-celled and one-seeded indehiscent hard-coated fruit (fig. 32*j*). See also *Achene, Capsule, Follicle*.

Ontogeny The life-history of an individual organism.

Opposite Buds or leaves occurring on each side of an axis in pairs at nodes.

Ovary The ovule-bearing part of a carpel or a gynoecium composed of fused carpels (fig. 35). The ovary becomes the fruit after the fertilization and maturation of the ovules.

Ovule The organ, contained in the ovary, which after fertilization becomes the seed (fig. 35).

Palmate Divided in a hand-like fashion (fig. 16*b*)

Papillae Minute pimple-like protuberances (fig. 33*d*).

Pappus Tufts of hairs, bristles or scales, on the fruits (achenes) of composites (Asteraceae or Compositae).

Pedicel The stalk of an individual flower in a cluster.

Peduncle The stalk of an inflorescence.

Perfect flower Having both stamens and carpels. See also *Imperfect flower*.

Perianth The corolla and calyx together.

Perigynous With petals and stamens arising from the margin of a cup-shaped extension of the receptacle. Often apparently attached to the ovary. See also *Epigynous, Hypogynous*.

Petal One of the units of the corolla.

Petaloid Resembling a petal (fig. 40).

Petiole Leaf stalk.

Phenotype The appearance of an organism due to interaction between its genetic constitution (genotype) and the environment. See also *Genotype*.

Phyllary A bract, especially of the inflorescence of the composites.

Pinnate A compound leaf with leaflets placed on each side of the rachis (fig. 16*d*).

Pistil An organ consisting of stigma, style (where

present) and ovary; a pistil may be of one carpel or several fused together (fig. 35).

Pollen Grains carrying the male reproductive element produced in the anthers.

Polypetalous With a corolla of separate petals. See also *Gamopetalous*.

Pome Simple fleshy fruit found only in one subfamily of the Rosaceae (apples, pears, quinces etc.). See also *Drupe, Berry*.

Pubescent Covered with short soft hairs; downy.

Rachis Axis; in compound leaves the extension of the petiole corresponding to the midrib of the entire leaf.

Radially symmetrical See *Actinomorphic*.

Ray florets The zygomorphic flattened flowers surrounding the *Disc florets* in most Asteraceae (aster family or Compositae) (fig. 37).

Receptacle The part of the axis of the flower stalk that bears the floral organs (fig. 35).

Reflexed Abruptly bent downward or backward.

Regular flower See *Actinomorphic*.

Revolute With margin rolled toward the lower side (fig. 19b).

Rosette Leaves radiating from a crown or centre.

Rugose Used of a wrinkled leaf-surface with the venation seemingly impressed (fig. 20c).

Scarious Applied to leaflike parts or bracts lacking green that are thin, dry, and more or less transparent.

Seed The ripened ovule (fig. 33).

Sepal A unit of the calyx (fig. 35).

Serrate Used of a leaf margin with forward-pointing saw teeth (fig. 19f).

Sessile Lacking a stalk.

Sinuate See *Undulate*.

Spathe valves One or more scarious bracts enclosing a developing inflorescence or flower.

Species A taxonomic category below genus. The primary unit of classification for plants and animals.

Stamen The unit of the androecium; comprised of anther and filament, though sometimes the latter is lacking (fig. 35).

Staminate Male; having stamens and no carpels.

Staminode A sterile stamen or a structure resembling a stamen carried in the staminal part of a flower.

Standard The upper petal of a papilionaceous (pea-type) flower (fig. 41c); the usually erect unit of the inner series of the perianth of an iridaceous (iris-type) flower (fig. 40).

Stigma The part of the carpel that receives the pollen (fig. 35).

Stigmatic Of the stigma.

Stipule A basal appendage of a petiole (fig. 18).

Style More or less elongated tissue connecting stigma and ovary (fig. 35). Sometimes absent.

Superior An ovary free and separate from the calyx.

Taxon Any one of the categories such as family, genus, species etc. into which organisms are classified (plural *Taxa*).

Taxonomy The science of the classification of organisms. Hence *Taxonomist*.

Tepal A unit of those perianths that are not clearly differentiated into corolla and calyx.

Trichome An outgrowth of the epidermis such as a hair, scale or water vesicle (fig. 24).

Tuber Short, swollen, underground stem functioning as a storage organ, as in potato (fig. 29d).

Tubercle A rounded protruding body as in some cacti (fig. 25).

Tunic The loose, often fibrous membrane about a corm or bulb.

Undulate A leaf or petal margin waved up and down at right angles to the body of the organ (fig. 19d); contrasting with *Sinuate* where movement is in the same plane as the rest of the leaf, petal etc. – towards and away from a midrib (fig. 19c).

Vascular Used of plant tissue consisting of or giving rise to conducting tissue.

Venation The arrangement of veins.

Versatile Attached near the middle and usually moving freely, as with mode of attachment to filament.

Whorl A circle of leaves or flower parts.

Wings Lateral petals of a papilionaceous (pea-type) flower (fig. 41c).

Zygomorphic A flower divisible into matching halves along one plane only. Used of a bilaterally symmetrical or irregular flower (fig. 36a, b, c, g).

Selected bibliography

ARBER, A. *Herbals: Their Origin and Evolution: a chapter in the history of botany, 1470-1670.* Cambridge University Press, 1938

BLUNT, WILFRID *The Art of Botanical Illustration* New Naturalist series, 4th edn, Collins, London, 1967

BLUNT, WILFRID & RAPHAEL, S. *The Illustrated Herbal* Frances Lincoln, London, and State Mutual Book, New York, 1979

CALMANN, GERTA *Ehret: Flower Painter Extraordinary* Phaidon Press, Oxford, and New York Graphic, New York, 1977

Curtis's Botanical Magazine 1787-; currently published by the Bentham-Moxon Trust, Royal Botanic Gardens, Kew in assoc. with Curwen Books, London

DESMOND, R. *Dictionary of British and Irish Botanists and Horticulturists, including plant collectors and botanical artists* Taylor & Francis, London, and Rowman & Littlefield, Totowa, NJ, 1977

DUNTHORNE, G. *Flower and fruit prints of the 18th and early 19th centuries* Dulau, London, 1938. Facs. edn Da Capo Press, New York, 1975

HUBBARD, C. E. *Grasses* Penguin, London, 1959

HULTON, P. & SMITH, L. *Flowers in Art from East and West* British Museum Publications, London, 1979

Hunt Institute for Botanical Documentation *Catalogue of the ... International Exhibition of Botanical Art and Illustration* Carnegie Mellon University, Pittsburgh, 1964-

Index Londinensis to illustrations of flowering plants, ferns and fern allies ... from botanical and horticultural publications of the XVIIIth and XIXth centuries [to 1920]. Prepared under the auspices of the Royal Horticultural Society at the Royal Botanic Gardens, Kew, by O. Stapf. Clarendon Press, Oxford, 1929-31. Supplement for 1921-35 by W. C. Wordsell, Oxford, 1941. Lubrecht & Cramer, Monticello, NY

ISAACSON, R. T. *Flowering Plant Index of illustration and information.* Sponsored by The Garden Center of Greater Cleveland. G.K. Hall, Boston, Mass. 1979

KING, RONALD *Botanical Illustration* Ash & Grant, London, 1978; Potter, New York, 1979 (dist. by Crown)

LAWRENCE, GEORGE H. M. *Introduction to Plant Taxonomy* Collier-Macmillan, London, 1955

LAWRENCE, GEORGE H. M. *Taxonomy of Vascular Plants* Macmillan, New York, 1955

LOWSON; J. M. *Textbook of Botany* 15th edn E. W. Simon *et al,* University Tutorial Press, Cambridge

NISSEN, C. *Die botanische Buchillustration: ihre Geschichte und Bibliographie* [*Botanical book-illustration: its history and bibliography*] Hiersemann, Stuttgart, 1951-66

'Printing' by Helen Hemingway Benton in *The New Encyclopaedia Britannica* (vol. 14) 1975

RAVEN, PETER with RAY EVERT & HELENA CURTIS *Biology of Plants* 3rd edn Worth Publishers, New York, 1981 (dist. by European Book Service, Weest, Netherlands)

RIX, MARTYN *The Art of the Botanist* Lutterworth, Guildford & London, 1981; Overlook, New York, as *The Art of the Plant World*

SITWELL, SACHEVERELL & BLUNT, WILFRID *Great Flower Books 1700-1900* Collins, London, 1956

STEARN, WILLIAM T. *The Australian Flower Paintings of Ferdinand Bauer* Basilisk Press, London, 1976

STEINBERG, S. H. *Five Hundred Years of Printing* revised edn Penguin, London and New York, 1979

A Vision of Eden: the life and work of Marianne North abridged text by Graham Bateman; Webb & Bower, Exeter, 1980 in collaboration with The Royal Botanic Gardens, Kew; Rhinehart & Winston, New York

In preparation

CARR, D. J. (ed) *Sydney Parkinson, artist of Cook's 'Endeavour' Voyage* Australian National University Press, Canberra

Index

Italic numbers indicate illustrations. Plants are entered under their scientific names, except where common names alone have been used in the text. The *Selected Bibliography* (p. 149) is not indexed.

Accuracy, 26
Acrylics, 127-39; additives, 128, 129; brushes, 128; colour mixing, 132-4, *133*; colour record, 131-2; drawing-board, 129; first trial subject, 134, 137-8, *136*; palettes, 129; pastel shades, 131-2; pencils, 129; pigments, 127-8; plant subject, 138-9, *136*; priming, 130-1, *130*; retardant, 129; supports, 129; techniques, 133-9; varnishing, 128; water-jar, 129
Adams, Lee, 19
Alkyd resin paints, 10, 11
Analysis of subject, 34-6
Angiosperms, 57
Art of Botanical Illustration, The, 20
Ascarina lucida, 74

Basic sketch, 33-6, *35*
Bateman, James, 14
Bauer, Ferdinand L., 13, *108*
Bauer, Franz, 13, 14, *15*, *107*
Bellini, Giovanni, 12
Bewick, Thomas, 17
Bignonia hybrid, 97, *96*
Biology of Plants, 25, 52, 58
Blunt, Wilfrid, 7, 19, 20
Body-colour, *see* Water-colour, opaque (gouache)
Botanical Magazine, 13
Brunfels, Otto, 12
Brushes, 100-1, 128
Buds, 48, *48*
Bulbs, 45, *46*

Cactus structure, 43, *43*
Calculator, 24, 143
Camera, 23-4, 140, 141
Campsis radicans, *105*
Capitulum, 52-5, *53*, *54*
Caspari, Claus, 20
Codex Vindobonensis, 98
Colour mixing, *see* Acrylics; Water-colour
Conservation (plant), 11, 31

Continuous tone, *see* Pencil
Convallaria majalis, *12*
Corms, 45
Craft knife (mat knife), 24, 65
Crayon, 10
Crocus baytopiorum, *18*
Curtis, Helena, 58
Curtis, William, 13

De Materia Medica, Dioscorides, 98
Dissecting needles, 24, 28
Dissection, 28, 87-91
Diverse plant structures, 33
Dividers, 24; proportional, 24
Dowden, Anne Ophelia, 19, *19*
Drake, Miss, 14
Drawing-boards, 22, 102, 129
Drawing-stand, 22, *22*
Dry-bush, 112-13, *113*
Dry point, 10
Duo-tone, 64
Dürer, Albrecht, 9, 12, *10*

Egg tempera, 10
Ehret, Georg Dionysius, 13, *13*
Emery paper, 66
Engraving: copper, 10, 12; lead, 10; steel, 10; wood, 10, 16-17
Epilobium latifolium, 85, *86*
Equipment, basic, 21-4; specialized – under relevant chapter heads
Erasers, 66-7; in use, 67, 77, 82
Etching, 10
Evert, Ray, 58

Fawcett, Priscilla, 19
Feather, 24, 67
Fitch, John Nugent, 16
Fitch, Walter Hood, 16, 40, 58, *16*
Five hundred Years of Printing, 144
Fixatives, 64
Flindersia australis, *108*
Flowers: actinomorphic, 52-5, *53*, *55*; dissection, 87-91, *89*; parts, 52-63,

52, *61*; zygomorphic, 52, 56–9, *53,
  56, 57, 58*
Fruits, 48–50, *49*
Fuchs, Leonard, 12

Gamopetaly, 57
Gardeners' Chronicle, The, 40, 58
Gauci, 14
Goethe, 11
Gouache, *see* Water-colour, opaque
  (body-colour)
Grasses, 63
Grierson, Mary, 19, *18*
Growth-phase, 27
Gummed paper strip, 102
Gymnosperms, 59

Hand-lens, 23, 87
Hatching, *see* Ink, Pencil, Scraper board
Herbarium specimens, 30–2
Herbarum Vivae Eicones, 12
Hubbard, Charles Edward, 63
Hunt Institute for Botanical Documen-
  tation, 10, 20

Iberis semperflorens, 13
Inflation, 57
Ink, 78–91; erasers, 82; errors, 82, 85,
  87, *83*; hatching, 84–5, *85*; line, 83–4,
  80, 81, 84; paper, 81–2; reduction,
  78, 144–5, *84*; stipple, 84–5, *85*;
  studies, 84–7, *80, 86*

Krateuas, 12, 98

Lathyrus latifolius, 14
Lawrence, George H. M., 9
Leaves, 36–42; arrangements, 42; forms,
  37–8, *37*; margins, 38, *39*; modelling,
  39, *39*; outlines, 37–8, *37*; in perspec-
  tive, 40, *40*; posture, 41, *42* venation,
  39–40, *39*; venation in water-
  colour, 114, 117, 118, *113*
Leonardo da Vinci, 12
Les Roses, 13
Lettering, 145
Letterpress, 64
Lighting, 21, 28–9
Line, *see* Ink, Pencil
Line, subjective or implied, 69–70
Linnaeus, 12–13, 26
Lino cuts, 10
Lithography, 10, 14, 16

Magnolia grandiflora, 19

Measurements, 34–5, 36, 142–3
Meyer, Albrecht, 12
Microscope, dissecting, 23, 28
Models, plant, 27–8; handling, 28–9;
  storage, 29–30

Nectaries, 63, *63*
New Encyclopaedia Brittanica, The, 144
North, Marianne, 19

Oils, 10, 98
Orchidaceae of Mexico and Guatemala, 14
Orchids, 57–9, *58*
Ornamentation (of stems and branches),
  43–5, *44, 45*

Paeonia suffruticosa, 106
Palettes: for water-colours, 102; for
  acrylics, 129
Papaver cultivar, poppies, 125–6, *135*
Paper: for acrylics, 129; for ink, 81–2;
  for pencil, 66; stretching, 103–4, *103*;
  for water-colour, 101–2
Parkinson, Sydney, 19, *17*
Pencils: aquarelle, 10; colour, 10; extender for, 65, *65*; for use with ink, 83;
  for use with scraper board, 92–3; for
  use with water-colour, 103; grades,
  64; sharpening, 65–6, *65*
Pencil techniques, 67–77; continuous
  tone, 72–7, *frontispiece, 73, 74, 75, 76*;
  doodling, 67–8, *68*; hatching, 70–2,
  71; line, 67–70, *69*; on textured
  paper, 66, *66*; white line, 77, *75, 76,
  77*
Pens, 78–80; and wash, 10; marks, 80,
  83–5, *80*
Perspective, 25, 35
Phenotypic variation, 27
Photography, 9, 17, 140–3
Pisanello, 12
Plant names (scientific versus vernacu-
  lar), 26
Plant-stand, 23, *23*
Pliny the Elder, 12, 98
Polypetaly, 57
Posture, plant, 41, *41*
Presentation of work, 145
Pricker, 24
Proserpina, 11, 59
Pteris serrulata, 17

Ranunculus bulbosus, 79; *R. repens*,
  creeping buttercup, *frontispiece*
Raven, Peter H., 58

Redouté, Pierre-Joseph, 13, *14, 106*
Reduction, 78, 144, *84*
Register marks, 144
Rhododendron campylogynum, 118
Rieful, Carlos, 20
Roots, 46–8, *47*
Rosa canina, dog rose, *69*
Ross-Craig, Stella, 19, *79*
Ruskin, John, 11

Scale, 34, 89–90, 145
Scalpel, 24, 28
Scanning electron microscope, 50
Scraper board, 92–7; cutting, 95–7; doodling, 93, *93*; hatching, 93–4, 97, *93*; leaf study, 94–7, *95*; priming white board, 94; plant study, 97, *96*; tone, 93–4, *93*, *95*, *96*; tools, 92, *92*; transferring design, 94–5
Seat, 22
Seeds, 50–1, *50*; lighting, 51, *51*
Selenicereus hamatus, 16
Serigraphs, 10
Sexual structures and expression, 59–62, *61*
Solanum macrocarpon, 13
Spaëndonck, Gerard van, 13, *13, 105*
Steinberg, S. H., 144
Stems, 43–5, *44, 45*; shading, 85, *85, 87*
Stereocaulon sp., 73–7, *73*
Stipple, *see* Ink
Stipules, 38, *38*
Stones, Margaret, 19
Storage of plant material, 29–30
Storage organs, 45, *46*
Strelitzia reginae, 107

Tape, invisible mending, 24
Taraxacum officinale, dandelion, 138–9, *136*
Taxonomy of Vascular Plants, 9
Thutmose III, 12
Tone (shading), 44, 45, *45*; acrylics, 132, 134, 137–9, *136*; ink, 47–8, 78, 83, 84–5, 91, *47, 79, 80, 85, 86, 87, 89,*

91; pencil, 67–9, 70–7, *frontispiece, 68, 69, 71, 72, 73, 74, 75, 76, 77*; scraper board, 92, 93, 94, 97, *93, 95, 96*; water-colour, 111–13, 119–23, 125–6, *113, 118, 135*
Tone values, 25, 121–2, *25*
Trichomes, 42–3, *42*
Tropaeolum majus, nasturtium, 121–3, *117*
Tubers, 45

Venation, 39–40, *39*; in water-colour, 114, *113, 117, 118*
Voucher specimens, 30, 143

Water-colour, opaque (gouache or body-colour), 98–9, 124–6, *135*; technique, 124–6
Water-colour, transparent, 98–124; brushes, 100–1; colour layout, 114–16, *115*; colour mixing, 25, 111, 116; dry-brush, 112–13, *113*; erasure, 123–4, first plant subject, 119–21, *118*; gradated wash, 111–12, *111*; modifying colours, 116, 119, *120*; pans, 99; paper, 101–2; pigments, 99–100; second plant subject, 121–3, *118*; shadow colour, 116; stretching paper for, 103–4, *103*; techniques, 103–23, *110, 111, 113, 114*; tone, 111–12, 121–2, *111*; for translucency, 122–3, *117*; tubes, 99; as used for venation, 114, *113*; wash, 109–11, *110*; white areas, 113–14, *114*; white flowers, 124
Water-jar, 102
Weiditz, Hans, 12, *12*
White line, *see* Pencil
Withers, Mrs, 14
Woodcuts, 10, 12, *12*
Working surface, 22
Work space, 21

Zahn, Martin, 20